The Practitioner's
Guide to EDP Auditing

The Practitioner's Guide to EDP Auditing

Jack B. Mullen

New York Institute of Finance

New York   London   Toronto   Sydney   Tokyo   Singapore

Library of Congress Cataloging-in-Publication Data

Mullen, Jack B.
  The practitioner's guide to EDP auditing / Jack B. Mullen.
    p.   cm.
  Includes index.
  ISBN 0-13-691262-1
  1. Business—Data processing—Auditing.   2. Electronic data
processing—Auditing.   3. Electronic data processing departments—
Auditing.   I. Title.
HF5548.35.M85   1990
657'.45'0285—dc20   90-45818
                                                                      CIP

This publication is designed to provide accurate and
authoritative information in regard to the subject matter
covered. It is sold with the understanding that the publisher
is not engaged in rendering legal, accounting, or other
professional service. If legal advice or other expert
assistance is required, the services of a competent professional
person should be sought.

From a Declaration of Principles
Jointly Adopted by
a Committee of the American Bar Association
and a Committee of Publishers and Associations

Printed in the United States of America

10   9   8   7   6   5   4   3   2   1

To Judy,

the love of my life,
whose support and dedication made this book possible.
May everyone be as blessed as I.

Preface

In the past 15 years, practicing audit managers have found it necessary to train the vast majority of entry level EDP auditors. Few college graduates come to the workplace with sufficient skills to complete audits of data processing. Also during these years, the need for EDP auditors has increased dramatically, thereby pressuring audit managers to train people quickly. This all means that a great deal of management time that would be better used explaining the application of concepts as they relate to their specific environment is spent explaining basic concepts.

This book is designed to help entry and intermediate level auditors learn how to complete EDP audits. Basic knowledge of data processing concepts is helpful but not absolutely necessary. This book focuses on how and why specific audit procedures are performed while using basic audit programs as a foundation for the explanations.

This material will increase auditor productivity by aiding self-learning and by relieving audit managers from explaining basic audit concepts and procedures. Furthermore, anyone who wishes to learn basic EDP auditing skills can do so on their own time, at their own pace.

This book is not designed to be a compendium of audit programs for evaluation of every data processing environment. The audit programs can be used as a foundation for customizing an audit approach to fit specific environments.

The Practitioners Guide presents its material in a logical training sequence, starting with basic theory and progressing through basic EDP audits to those on intermediate and advanced levels.

The author greatly acknowledges the assistance of Fred Palmer, L. Michael Ewald, Tracey Hibbs, Susan Barry, Sheck Cho, and Philip Ruppel.

Contents

The EDP Auditing Profession

1.1 THE DATA PROCESSING AUDITING PROFESSION

According to Webster's dictionary, auditing today is the "formal or official examination of an account book" and the "final report of an examination of books of account by auditors."[1] Auditing has existed since the days of the Roman Empire, when businessmen required the reading of accounts aloud in public to prevent fraud. The term "audit" originates from the Latin *audire,* which means "to hear."

Auditing differs from accounting in that auditing involves investigation, verification, and evaluation, whereas accounting is the "system of recording and summarizing business and financial transactions in books. . . ."[1] Auditors, in other words, evaluate and verify the quality of control over financial matters that methods and procedures maintain (accounting control system). Data processing (EDP) auditors are those auditors who evaluate and verify the controls over computer (or "application") programs. EDP auditing has only become possible with the advent of computers and requires that the auditor not only observe generally accepted auditing standards (GAAS), but also maintains and employs a high level of computer expertise.

As the history of computers evolves, from highly centralized mainframes in the 1960s to decentralized microcomputers in the 1990s, EDP auditors' challenges and solutions will also evolve. So to speak, the histories of auditing and computers converge with the development of EDP auditing. A review of both the evolution of computerized data processing and auditing forms the background of this study of EDP auditing standards, methods, and practices and informs the projection of its trends.

Chapter 1 will discuss the evolution of the profession and the purpose of EDP auditing, providing an overview of the foundations and functions of EDP audit and the issues facing the profession.

Computers and their uses have developed rapidly over the past 30 years. Today, businesses use microcomputers with memory size, and peripheral storage greater than mainframe computers had only 15 years ago. In just 40 years, computers have advanced from huge machines that required separate floors in office buildings to small computers that sit on desktops. Business use of computers was developed with the strategic objective of eliminating human handling of transaction processing's massive amounts of paper. The decision to buy computers to automate business functions was based on the potential for labor cost savings. The elimination of salaries provided the savings to pay for the automation that would, in turn, produce reduced processing expenses in the future. Automating manual business functions was aimed at increasing efficiency and productivity, or doing more work in less time for less cost.

1.1.1   Evolution of the Auditing Profession

In today's environment, the auditor is considered the "eyes and ears of management." Auditing, however, was not recognized as a necessary function in modern times until businesses began to grow and require the support of the public, and bankers, to keep their businesses running. In the 1920s, the expanding U.S. economy brought fears of inflated balance sheets and erroneous income statements. The banks began to require independent verification of company financial statements in order to approve loans.

1.1.1.1   LEGISLATIVE INFLUENCES

With every great debacle, there usually comes legislative change—the stock market crash of 1929 produced the Securities Act of 1933 and the Securities and Exchange Act of 1934 (the Acts), both of which are aimed at protecting the public from overeager or fraudulent businessmen. The purpose of this legislation is to regulate the securities and banking industries. The accounting profession was seen as an appropriate group through which to accomplish compliance with these new laws, because accounting necessarily involves rules for the treatment of financial statements. A discipline for verification of these financial statements was, however, also necessary, making the need for auditing manifest. Publicly traded companies needed independent accountants to verify the adequacy of financial statements.

These companies also needed information about their own internal workings, which an independent accountant could not provide because this was beyond the scope of independent verification. Therefore, companies hired internal auditors to assist the independent accountants with their verification of accounting records and also to perform reviews of compliance with company policies and procedures and internal accounting controls.

1.2 THE EVOLUTION OF COMPUTERS: MAINFRAMES TO MICROCOMPUTERS

The development of mainframe application systems brought with it the centralization of transaction processing and operations. In recent years, the centralized mainframe systems and programming (S&P) functions in some businesses have developed a reputation as being unresponsive, unable to adapt to particular lines of business, too slow, and too expensive. But with the development in recent years of microcomputers—"micros"—end users are now beginning to believe that they can beat the S&P function at its own game. During the 1990s, microcomputers will replace some mainframe functions, as businesses trade the cost of maintaining expensive mainframe processing for inexpensive microcomputer processing. The microcomputer revolution, however, with its comparatively cheaper technology, is bringing back the decentralization characteristic of pre-computer auditing. Moreover, microcomputer development has brought a shift in strategic business objectives and justifications for computer systems—the ability to create additional income. Cost reduction has become a secondary consideration.

1.3   PROFESSIONAL RECOGNITION

In 1941, the Institute of Internal Auditors, Inc. (IIA) was formed. Its purpose was to change the image of internal auditors in the eyes of business management and to make them an integral part of a business by helping management to function better.

The internal audit profession has, with the support of the IIA, made steady progress in demonstrating that auditing is more than just verification, it is meaningful productive assistance. Unfortunately, the public's acknowledgment of the real need for the audit profession was only brought on by well-publicized frauds.

1.3.1   Emergence of EDP Auditing

As computers began to take over daily transaction processing, the auditing and accounting fields put them to good use, increasing accuracy and saving time through the use of various application programs. The conventional, tangible audit trails began to disappear. Technicians were needed, not only to audit, but also to understand the computers. The need for the computer-literate auditor began to emerge. But it took more than just the advent of computers to convince the business world that the EDP auditor was needed.

In keeping with the tendency for fraud to highlight the need for auditors, one case, in particular, is credited with advancing their need—the Equity Funding Life Insurance Company (Equity Funding) fraud. The press at the time blamed the fraud on computer use—but the irony is that ordinary accounting methods would have revealed the fraud even though some fictitious policies were computer generated. Mair reports that "only 19 percent of the fictitious assets claimed by Equity Funding had any relation to the use of computers."[2] Hermanson reported that from 1964–72, Equity Funding booked approximately $143,000,000 in completely fraudulent income.[3] Weber reported that the fraud consisted of three major elements: (1) overstating earnings, (2) acquisition of foreign subsidiaries, and (3) the resale of bogus insurance policies to other insurance companies.[4]

Most of the assets of Equity Funding were bogus, but the firm still received certified financial statements for those years during which it remained in business. Not surprisingly, this led to lawsuits against the accounting firms involved and resulted in a $53,000,000 total settlement, of which $39,000,000 was paid by the accounting firms.[3] Despite the fact that in this case, computer use was not fundamental to the fraud, the case caused federal regulators and the American Institute of Certified Public Accountants (AICPA) to reassess the public accounting profession, and it reinforced the need for internal EDP auditors. Major accounting firms, regulators, and businesses began to place more emphasis on the need for EDP auditing.

1.3.2   GAAS: The Foundations of Internal Control

The AICPA's generally accepted auditing standards define objectives of internal control that form the foundation for its evaluation.

They also define standards by which the financial auditor and the EDP auditor must evaluate internal control. The AICPA audit standards, recited in AU Section 150, include "general standards, standards of field work, and standards of reporting."[6] These standards for internal control evaluation relate to the quality of the completion of audit procedures and the audit judgment used in completing the work. They are essentially in agreement with standards defined by the IIA and the EDPAA, and BAI.

To comply with the objectives of internal control, a company must establish an organizational structure, and policies and procedures, to ensure that management maintains internal control over essential aspects of financial transactions. In order to accomplish this, the following conditions must be met:

1. Transactions must be executed in accordance with management's general or specific authorization.
2. Transactions must be recorded as necessary, (i) to permit preparation of financial statements in conformity with generally accepted accounting principles (GAAP) or other criteria applicable to such statements, and (ii) to maintain accountability for assets.
3. Access to assets may be permitted only in accordance with management's authorization.
4. The recorded accountability for assets must be compared with the existing assets at reasonable intervals and appropriate action must be taken with respect to any differences.[6]

1.3.3 EDP Auditors Association

"In 1969, a small group of auditors in Los Angeles, California, formed the first chapter of the Electronic Data Processing Auditors Association (EDPAA). The EDPAA is dedicated to the promotion of research, education, and certification for EDP auditing. The association's prime objectives are to (1) provide to its members a forum that encourages a free exchange of EDP auditing knowledge and skills, and (2) assist individuals in their professional development and growth.[5] These auditors believed that because of the rapid development of computer technology and growing emphasis placed upon it by the business world, the need to develop EDP auditing and EDP capability was pressing. The EDPAA filled this need by sharing experiences and ideas with fellow practitioners and by developing training courses and educational materials to assist others who were assigned similar EDP audit responsibilities. In 20 years, this association has grown to over 43 chapters and 80,000 members. It has become a worldwide organization of EDP audit professionals, including

FIGURE 1-1 EDP Auditors Foundation
General Standards for Information Systems Auditing

Independence

General Standard No. 1: **Attitude and Appearance**—In all matters related to auditing, the information systems auditor is to be independent of the auditee in attitude and appearance.

General Standard No. 2: **Organizational Relationship**—The information systems audit function is to be sufficiently independent of the area being audited to permit objective completion of the audit.

General Standard No. 3: **Code of Professional Ethics**—The information systems auditor is to adhere to the Code of Professional Ethics of the EDP Auditors Foundation.

Technical Competence

General Standard No. 4: **Skills and Knowledge**—The information systems auditor is to be technically competent, possessing the skills and knowledge necessary in the performance of the auditor's work.

General Standard No. 5: **Continuing Professional Education**—The information systems auditor is to maintain technical competence through appropriate continuing education.

Performance of Work

General Standard No. 6: **Planning and Supervision**—Information systems audits are to be planned and supervised to provide assurance that audit objectives are achieved and compliance with these standards is met.

General Standard No. 7: **Evidence Requirement**—During the course of the audit, the information systems auditor is to obtain evidence of a nature and sufficiency to support findings and conclusions reported.

General Standard No. 8: **Due Professional Care**—Due professional care is to be exercised in all aspects of the information systems auditor's work, including observance of applicable auditing standards.

Reporting

General Standard No. 9: **Reporting of Audit Coverage**—In preparing reports, the information systems auditor is to state the objectives of the audit, the period of coverage, and the nature and extent of the audit work performed.

General Standard No. 10: **Reporting of Findings and Conclusions**—In preparing reports, the information systems auditor is to state findings and conclusions concerning the audit work performed, and any reservations or qualifications that the auditor has with respect to the audit.

with an "unbiased viewpoint." In other words, all matters must be met with an open mind. Independence in appearance refers to the impression that the EDP auditor gives to an observer. An outside observer must be able to see that the EDP auditor is independent of the auditee.

General Standard No. 2[5] involves organizational independence. Organizational independence is defined as the audit function's having a direct reporting relationship to the president and/or chief executive officer with a direct reporting relationship to the board of directors via an audit committee. The auditor should report to an individual sufficiently high in the organization that the auditor reportee has nothing to fear from objective reporting by the auditor.

General Standard No. 3[5] deals with compliance with the code of professional ethics that focus on honesty and integrity. This is straightforward and easily understood, so it is not covered more extensively here.

Category No. 2: Technical Competence:[5] The second category deals with "technical competence." It covers "skills and knowledge."

General Standard No. 4[5] demands that the EDP auditor be "technically competent" and that he must "possess the skills and knowledge necessary to perform the auditor's work." The EDP auditor is responsible for obtaining all the skills and knowledge necessary to complete the audit engagement to which he is assigned. Although audit management has a responsibility to train its auditors, that responsibility does not rely solely on its shoulders.

General Standard No. 5[5] requires the EDP auditor to "maintain technical competence" by taking appropriate training courses. This is straightforward—to maintain technical competence requires continuing education. The responsibility for this is shared by management and the EDP auditor. The standard should not be construed to mean continuing education in EDP and auditing alone, but should include a mix of auditing, accounting, business, managerial, and interpersonal skills. Continuing education should also include knowledge about the business aspects of the auditor's company and its field, be it banking, insurance, manufacturing, or another business.

Category No. 3:   Performance of Work:[5]   The third category of standards deals with the performance of audit work.

General Standard No. 6[5] covers "planning and supervision." The EDP audit should be "planned and supervised to provide assurance that audit objectives are achieved and compliance with these audit standards is met." This standard is similar to the AICPA's Standard of Field Work No. 1.

Planning refers to the establishment of objectives, the extent of review necessary, design of testing, staff assignments, time estimates, and projected start and target dates. Audits that are inadequately planned will be inadequately executed and will wander aimlessly, while consuming significant time.

General Standard No. 7[5] states that sufficient evidence is to be obtained during the course of the audit, in order to support the "findings and conclusions reported" to management. Sufficient testing, therefore, should be performed, in order to verify that evidence. This is similar to the AICPA's Standard of Field Work No. 3.

General Standard No. 8[5] involves "Due professional care." This means that the staff auditor must aim for a high degree of accuracy in all audit work. All audit program steps and instructions must be carried out, and all work papers must be completed in accordance with departmental standards. Due professional care is also aimed at supervision and the review of completed audit work papers by audit management. The audit supervisor or manager must gain an understanding of the work being done through a review of the work papers. This ordinarily involves the completion of review notes that the staff auditor must answer. These notes are necessary to maintain the quality of audit work papers.

Category 4: Reporting:[5] The fourth category of standards involves reporting.

General Standard No. 9[5] requires the "stating of audit objectives, the duration of time covered, and the nature and extent of the audit work performed." This information is necessary in order for the report reader to understand the extent of the audit. Most internal audit departments have limited resources and cannot afford to review all of the auditee's activities. The objectives of the audit explain to the auditee exactly what was covered and what was not. Formally reporting this information eliminates confusion.

General Standard No. 10[5] involves the reporting of findings and conclusions. The EDP auditor "is to state findings and conclusions, and any reservations or qualifications that he or she has with respect to the audit." This involves explaining the condition, cause, effect, and recommendation for improvement for each major finding. Comments should explain how conclusions were drawn and the facts upon which these conclusions are based.

1.4 INTERNAL CONTROL

"Internal control" refers to any policy, procedure, or activity that serves to safeguard assets, maintain the accuracy of financial data, improve operational efficiency, and enforce adherence to management's policies.[6] The adequacy of internal control can be measured by comparing the purpose of the intended control to one or all four of the AICPA's objectives (see Section 1.3.2). These goals establish the basis for the development of all policies and procedures within an organization.

The AICPA defines internal control by defining administrative control separately, to include the policies and procedures concerned with management's decision-making process for the authorization of transactions.[6]

1.4.1 Management and the EDP Auditor: Reporting Responsibilities Regarding Internal Control

The adequacy of internal accounting control is the central core around which auditing revolves.

AICPA professional standards distinguish between the responsibilities of the auditor and those of management.[6] Management is responsible for the financial statements themselves, whereas the auditor is responsible for expressing an opinion on those financial statements. "Management is responsible for adopting sound accounting policies and for establishing and maintaining an internal control structure that will, among other things, record, process, summarize, and report financial data that is consistent with management's assertions embodied in the financial statements."[6] Both the internal and external EDP auditor's review of internal control originates from this basic standard.

The auditor is responsible only for the review and the expression of an opinion on the internal control system. He or she can recommend changes and improvements in internal control; it remains management's final decision to implement those changes. Many auditors have a struggle with this responsibility because management will not make the recommended changes. The auditor must always remember that his or her job is completed and his or her objective satisfied when the audit is reported with a workable recommendation for cost-effective change.

Management must adopt an internal control structure that will record, process, summarize and report financial data. This is not accomplished with the general ledger alone, but with all the other reporting systems that support the general ledger. Therefore, all computer programs that feed the general ledger are an integral part of the company's internal control structure. Furthermore, the data processing environment—the operating system, on-line systems, database systems and the like—in which all these applications operate is also an integral part of that internal control structure. It is this internal control structure that supports the financial statements. The EDP auditor must evaluate the adequacy and effectiveness of this internal control structure.

1.5   EDP AUDITING'S PURPOSES AND OBJECTIVES

1.5.1   Purpose of EDP Auditing: The Evaluation of Internal Control, Effectiveness, and Efficiency

The EDP audit is designed to evaluate the adequacy of internal control with regard to both specific computer programs and the data processing environment as a whole. This includes evaluating both the effectiveness and the efficiency of the data processing functions and systems. "Effectiveness" and "efficiency" are often used in the same sentence, but they have distinctly different meanings.

The word "effectiveness" refers to the accomplishment of an objective. An inventory system could be done with either paper and pencil or a computer system and still be effective, although the inventory is usually so big as to make the paper and pencil method too slow. No matter how slow the method, if the objective is accomplished, the word "effectiveness" applies.

The word "efficiency" is applied to the accomplishment of the objective within the least amount of time and/or the least cost. For example, a program could create records on either tape or disk files. As long as the daily creation of these records does not take an extensive amount of time, both approaches would be equally efficient. However, if the records were to begin to consume three or more tape files, then the measurement of efficiency would change. The tape system would no longer be as efficient as the disk system because the tape system would take significantly more processing time to post the records to the tape file than it would to the disk file.

When the auditor evaluates the adequacy of internal control, he or she also touches upon the evaluation of the effectiveness of a system. The system could accomplish management's objectives and, therefore, be effective for management's purpose. If adequate internal control did not exist, however, the system might be effective for management, but would be inadequately controlled.

When faced with limited audit resources, the auditor must decide which tasks are most important. Generally speaking, evaluating the adequacy and effectiveness of internal control is the first priority, and the evaluation of efficiency is second.

1.5.2   Objectives of EDP Auditing

EDP auditing involves the evaluation of systems and procedures to ensure that assets are safeguarded, that the integrity of computer data is maintained, and that the objectives of the organization are achieved. (Many people believe that auditors are only looking for problems and, if none arise, then the audit was not very good. In fact, a clean audit requires almost as much work as any other.) The objective of the EDP audit is to determine that all control procedures for computer systems are in place and to identify any areas where control can be improved. Both of these functions will reduce potential losses.

1.5.2.1   FINDINGS: CONDITIONS, CAUSES AND EFFECTS

Identifying control weaknesses involves assessing conditions and their causes and effects. Much time is spent obtaining reliable evidence to support such assessments. The EDP auditor must obtain sufficient evidence to support the assessment of the nature of the condition reported, its cause, and its effect. These three elements are vital to adequate reporting of control weaknesses. In assessing the condition, the auditor identifies what is wrong; in explaining its cause, the auditor explains why the condition exists, and in predicting its effect, the auditor describes the detrimental effects that have occurred or can occur in the future if the problem is not corrected.

Although identifying condition, cause, and effect are vital elements of reporting control weaknesses, the most important element is the recommendation to management. This describes the "fix," which is a cost-effective change or enhancement to a procedure that will improve the functioning of the organization.

The auditor is a catalyst who constantly pushes to improve the effectiveness and efficiency of the organization. All good managers want their areas to be effective and efficient.

Most managers, unlike auditors, do not have the time to evaluate all the functions within their responsibility. Management may initially resist an audit, but once it sees the positive effects of the auditors' recommendations, it will immediately learn an audit's value.

1.5.3   Conclusions and Opinions—"Clean," "Subject to," and "Except for"

The reporting of findings and conclusions includes the assessment of the overall adequacy of internal control within the computer system environment. The AICPA has established very specific standards for independent audit reports and for the expression of opinions on financial statements. These are all appropriate to the opinions that can be expressed by the EDP auditor. Three opinions are the most appropriate for use by the internal EDP auditor: the unqualified or clean opinion, the "subject-to" or "except-for" opinion, and the negative opinion.

The unqualified opinion states that internal control in the area reviewed as a whole is adequate. This does not mean that there are no control weaknesses, but that the control weaknesses that exist do not significantly impede the adequate functioning or financial reporting of the area.

As control weaknesses become increasingly serious, detrimental, or numerous, however, the auditor is forced to give a subject-to or except-for opinion. This states that internal control is adequate except for the control weaknesses identified in the comments-and-recommendations section of the report. It means that the items identified could have, or already have had, a negative or detrimental impact on the functioning or financial reporting of the area. If allowed to continue, the adequate functioning of the area could be further impaired.

The negative opinion is used for an area that has a significant number of functions with serious internal control weaknesses that have already had, or very soon will have, negative impacts on the area. The issuance of the negative opinion, in written form, is usually accompanied by a phone call by the auditor to the senior management of the area. The negative opinion is a serious warning flag to management that the problems must be corrected immediately.

1.6 ELEMENTS OF EDP AUDITING

EDP auditing is a mixture of skills. Financial auditing, which originates from the independent audit practice, follows the standards issued by the AICPA. These involve the attest function and the expression of opinion on the adequacy of financial statements. This requires the traditional audit skills of tracing, vouching, and comparing records.

The data processing skills, programming, analysis, and design, also form an important basis of EDP auditing. The EDP auditor is much like the systems analyst who identifies the elements of a system that need to be designed and programmed.

All auditing includes effective use of interpersonal skills, for part of the success of the EDP audit depends on the auditor's interview, conversation, and logical thinking skills.

The use of EDP auditors grew from the need to understand the functioning of computer systems in a profession that was already burdened with excessive demands for knowledge of accounting principles and business concepts and principles. For any auditor to evaluate effectively an internal control system, he or she must have at least a basic understanding of the functioning of the business. The internal EDP auditor knows a little about a lot of areas and a lot about internal control and evaluation. The focus of the EDP audit is on the evaluation of computer system control that permits the auditor effectively to meet his or her objectives while maintaining some knowledge of the business that is being reviewed.

1.6.1   Functions of an EDP Audit

Internal EDP audit functions consist of four major areas: 1) supporting the financial audit staff; 2) audits of environmental data-processing areas; 3) audits of computer programs (Application Systems); and 4) system development reviews. The EDP audit staff supports the financial audit staff by preparing software programs that generate independent computer reports for use in the completion of audits. In addition, the EDP audit staff works as a consultant to the financial audit staff by answering questions about the effects of data processing upon the system of internal controls that are being audited. They provide training and information about on-line systems, database systems, and various effects of the EDP environment upon the system of internal controls.

The environmental EDP audits involve areas such as systems software programming, on-line systems, database administration, and the data center, to name a few. These areas are labeled "environmental" because these EDP functions establish the environment in which all computer programs run. Adequate and effective internal controls are vital in the environmental areas because a critical weakness could detrimentally affect all programs, which would affect all processing.

Computer applications are all the programs that perform the processing of daily transactions. These programs accept all the daily transactions, perform the edit routines, and post the transactions to master files and history files. Computer reports, which summarize the processing of the transactions, are generated daily by these programs. The reports are used for control and management information.

The system development review involves participation in the project development teams and includes two functions: 1) on-going review of the controls that are implemented within the computer system as it is being designed; and 2) monitoring and evaluating the administrative project controls over the progress of the project. System development projects are divided into major phases—certain critical activities are completed within each phase. The auditor has specific responsibilities in each phase that vary depending upon what the phase is trying to accomplish, the audit objectives, and the technical expertise of the EDP auditor.

1.6.2   Organizational Structure

The structure of the EDP auditing group depends upon audit philosophy, the size of the company, and the size of the EDP audit staff. The EDP audit group has traditionally been a separate section of the audit department because of the technical specialization it requires. The EDP audit resources, under the supervision of the EDP audit supervisor and manager, are then used by the financial audit staff on a consulting basis. This organizational structure makes the EDP audit function a staff function.

Some companies have organized the EDP audit as a line function that creates audit functions for major business units of their companies. An EDP auditor is assigned, on a functional and administrative reporting basis, to the audit group for specific business functions. This makes EDP auditing a line function, but it is also similar to the combined or integrated audit team approach.

Aligning the EDP staff as a staff function is the most prevalent organizational structure because, traditionally, data processing has been centralized and the technical expertise and training needed for the EDP audit group makes it easier to control and accomplish its training and auditing tasks. In the future, as data processing decentralizes, there will be pressure on this alignment. The financial or business audit groups will need more training and experience in microcomputer concepts and processing controls.

1.6.3   Career Path

The audit function has been viewed, in the past, as a transitory function. People would only work at the job for three to five years and then move somewhere else in the company. Because of the speed of technological change, however, pressure is building to keep auditors in their positions longer. The first viable career path, for the EDP auditor, is within the audit function itself. The entry level EDP auditor can seek out promotion through the ranks of the audit function conceivably all the way to the general auditor position. With the heavy reliance on data processing, this is even more possible today than it was ten years ago.

A second potential career path leads to the data processing area. The EDP auditor's job, especially system development reviews and application audits, is very closely related to the system analyst's job. The EDP auditor, however, must remember that the requirements to become an EDP auditor are different from those for an analyst. In order to follow this career path, the EDP auditor must accumulate the knowledge and experience required by data processing management. This potential problem can be circumvented by taking accredited courses in programming and other subjects required by data processing management.

Another career open to the EDP auditor is operations processing. These operations areas are the most frequent targets of all audits since they process the transactions for the company. The EDP auditor's exposure to the operations areas gives him excellent experience that could enable him to handle supervisory and managerial tasks within operations.

With the decentralization of data processing, more computer knowledge will be needed in the administration and management units of a company. During the next ten years, the EDP auditor should see career paths opening up in the business units. Because of the nature of the EDP auditor's job, his work and report tend to be highly visible and receives much attention from management. This exposure frequently opens doors for career moves that are generally unexpected.

1.7 EXTERNAL AUDIT

Internal auditors will interface with external auditors to some extent, depending upon the organization. Some companies assign internal auditors to work directly for the outside accounting firm while other companies perform audits utilizing the external auditor's objectives but under the supervision of internal audit management. The purpose of either scenario is to reduce the external audit fee. In any event, good coordination of the audit efforts is highly cost effective because the internal audit work can be used by the external auditor in accordance with the AICPA Statement on Auditing Standard (SAS) No. 9[6] and reduces the time needed for the external audit, thereby potentially reducing the fee.

From an EDP auditor's standpoint, the areas for possible coordination with, and assistance to, the external auditor involve confirmation of assets and liabilities performed with an audit software package, the general control evaluation of data processing, testing of critical internal programmed functions, on-line security, program change control, systems software change control, internal control evaluations, and substantive testing of transactions.

AICPA SAS No. 9[6] establishes the standards for use of internal audit work by the external auditor who can use the internal auditor's work for determining the nature, timing, and extent of the external audit procedures. SAS No. 9, however, prohibits substitution of the internal audit work for that of the outside auditor. If the external auditor wishes to use the internal auditor's work, he or she must evaluate the competence and objectivity of the internal auditor. Objectivity is determined by the organizational placement of the audit function within the company. To be objective, the internal auditor must not report to any area that he audits. Furthermore, objectivity can be measured in terms of the auditor's attitude for independence in that all areas are reviewed with an unbiased and objective approach. The external auditor's evaluation of the internal auditor's work involves the review of internal audit work papers and audit programs. The independent auditor must perform tests on samples of internal audit work by essentially re-auditing a sample of the internal audit. This can be accomplished by reperforming the test on a sample of the transactions that the internal auditor selected or by selecting separate transactions that are similar in nature to those tested by the internal auditor.

To achieve the optimum effectiveness, the plans for audit work should be discussed between the external auditor and the internal auditor in advance. The usefulness of the internal audit work is governed by the nature, timing, and extent of the work performed. An internal control review, performed early in the year, may be too old for the external auditor to use for year-end financial statement work simply because its timing is incorrect. If the key controls are not evaluated, then the "nature" of the internal audit work may be incorrect. Likewise, if insufficient samples of transactions are used, then the "extent" may be incorrect. To whatever extent the external auditor decides to use internal audit work, audit decisions about matters that relate to the certification of financial statements must always be the judgment of the external auditor.

The primary objective of using internal audit work is the reduction of the external auditor's fee. To accomplish this task, the internal audit work must be of a nature that does not require significant correction and research of the work by the external auditor. Confirmation of assets and liabilities, which can be obtained by using the audit software package, is a cost-effective reduction of external audit time. The internal audit approach requires sending confirmations each year and, once the audit software programs are written, confirmations are generally easy to maintain, quickly executable, and readily verifiable by the external auditor. The nature, timing, and extent of confirmations involves validating the attributes of the accounts needed by the external auditor, sending the confirmations at an appropriate time during the year so they are usable for year-end financial statement audit procedures, and utilizing the sample sizes suitable to the external auditor. The sample sizes are determined by the historical response rate to achieve a certain number of responses needed by the external auditor.

The general control evaluation involves the collection of evidence that explains all the data-processing functions and that includes the internal control review of certain critical EDP environmental areas—Information Security, Program Change Control, and System Software Programming. These three areas have the most pervasive effect on internal control, since they can affect the processing of all transactions that flow through to the financial statements. The nature of this work involves the testing of key controls within the three environmental areas. The external auditor has specific attributes that he is seeking. The extent of the procedures refers to the sample sizes required by the external auditor. Because this is an internal control evaluation, it can usually be performed at some interim date.

1.8 LOOKING TO THE FUTURE

The late 1980s and early 1990s brought the beginning of a shift from mainframe-developed systems to microcomputer-based systems. In late 1989, mainframe vendors began to see the effect of this shift in their financial statements. In the 1980s, many companies offered high-speed microcomputers with extensive memory capabilities for less than $2,500. The Intel 80386 and 80486 microprocessors[7] bring sufficient power, memory, and speed to the desktop to replace mainframe applications. Microcomputer software programs, with capabilities that rival many mainframe applications, are being developed in commercial package form. The future will see the development of faster and even more powerful microcomputers and more pressure to shift to decentralized computer processing. Networks of microcomputers will abound, and electronic mail, for example, will become standard rather than exceptional.

The decentralization of computer processing will bring problems of control and security that did not exist in the mainframe environment of the 1960s and 1970s. Companies will need physical security and on-line access devices so that they can install passwords and control access to microcomputer-based data and application programs (change control). The biggest problem for EDP auditors will be the number of microcomputers—the mainframe was located in just one place, but microcomputers are located in every office throughout a company, and every microcomputer may need review.

1.8.1   Decentralization and the EDP Auditor

The decentralization of control over computer use inherent in the use of micros creates additional risks in the EDP audit. The ability to develop new systems quickly on the microcomputer reduces the possibility for developing proper accounting controls. Essentially, the EDP auditor in the 1990s will face the possibility that proper controls will not have been integrated into micro-computer processing. This will create a battle over controls, between the end user and the auditor. Such a scenario will be similar to the battles the EDP auditor fought with data processing management during the 1970s.

During the 1970s, the EDP auditor struggled with management to convince it of the need for physical access control of data centers, for programmatic edits in computer programs, and for access control over on-line systems. The EDP auditor's job in the 1990s will be somewhat easier, and much more challenging, because management now understands the need for computer controls. In addition, it stands behind the EDP auditor's request for control over the microcomputer network. During the 1970s, EDP auditors also fought for recognition of their knowledge of controls and computers and for respect for their place in the business environment. That battle has been won. Many EDP auditors have become microcomputer specialists because of their closeness to computer technology. Many, in fact, have much more knowledge than the end users who are trying to automate functions with microcomputers.

1.9   KEY ISSUES FACING THE PROFESSION

In the future, significant pressure will be placed on EDP auditing because of the proliferation of microcomputers. The dispersion, or decentralization, of computer processing will force the EDP audit profession to review more areas within the company. To accomplish this task, the EDP audit group will need to incorporate reviews of microcomputer programs within the financial audit of a business function. The necessity for these reviews will help enable an integrated audit approach—the completion of audits with a team of auditors that can audit both the financial and EDP portions of a business function.

NOTES

1. *Websters New Collegiate Dictionary. Springfield MA, 1981.*

2. *Mair W.C., Wood D.R., Davis K.W., Computer Control & Audit,* Deloitte & Touche, Wilton, CT, 1978, p. xi. Reproduced with permission from Deloitte & Touche.

3. Hermanson R.W., Strawsen J.R., Strawser R.H. *Auditing Theory and Practice,* Irwin, Homewood, IL, 1987, pp. 178–80.

4. Weber, R., *EDP Auditing, Conceptual Foundations and Practice.* New York, McGraw Hill, 1982, pp. 16–17.

5. EDP Auditors Foundation, Inc. *General Standards for Information Systems Auditing.* 1987. Publication available upon request from EDPAF, P. O. Box 88180, Carol Stream, IL 60188-0180.

6. American Institute of Certified Public Accountants, AICPA Professional Standards, New York, 1989.

7. 80386 and 80486 is a trademark of Intel Corporation.

EDP Auditing and Internal Control

2.3.1.4   Data Processing Environment

2.3.1.5   Application Control Techniques

2.3.1.6   System Development

Chapter 2 will discuss the relationship of internal control to EDP auditing, specifically focusing on the theory of audit standards that support and define the elements of internal control and its evaluation. The effects of data processing on internal control are explained, with specific focus on the types of internal control and control techniques.

2.1   FOUNDATIONS OF INTERNAL CONTROL AND EVALUATION

Audit standards issued by the AICPA, the EDPAA, and the Institute of Internal Auditors (IIA) focus on internal controls and how they must be audited and reviewed.

AICPA professional standards state in AU Section 110[1] that the establishment and maintenance of sound internal control procedures is management's responsibility. The external auditor's responsibility is to express an opinion on the financial statements, and the internal auditor's responsibility is to express an opinion on the internal control system. Because computer systems are an integral part of the control system, the EDP auditor must periodically review the systems to determine that the relevant internal controls have not deteriorated.

It is infinitely easier for management to establish internal controls than to maintain them. Internal controls are a product of human effort and, therefore, are prone to error. Internal controls programmed into computer systems have a distinct advantage over manual controls because a computer program will consistently run as programmed until changed. Changing these computer programs, however, introduces the potential for compromising control. Therefore, changing the computer programs becomes a critical event for the EDP auditor to monitor and periodically to review. This makes auditing any change to computer programs—application, change control—essential (see Chapter 10).

Management needs the help of the auditing staff to maintain internal control systems; otherwise management would have periodically to review the procedures themselves to ensure their adequacy. Neither managers nor the people who work for them have the time to accomplish this review; moreover such reviews are not likely to be completely objective.

Computer programs, or application systems, for such categories as accounts payable, accounts receivable, and inventory, among others, process the transactions that are recorded in the financial statements. Such programs replace the traditional subledgers referred to in accounting textbooks and support the general ledger that makes up the financial statements. Therefore, the broad objectives of internal control apply to all such application systems.

The broad objectives of internal control, according to the AICPA Professional Standards, are accomplished by:

- Transaction authorization,
- Transaction recording,
- Access to assets, and
- Accountability and comparison.[1]

Management, however, must delegate these responsibilities without abdicating its own responsibility. Management delegates authority to the supervisory level, which sees that policies and procedures are followed and that people live up to their job descriptions.

Access to assets: This refers to the authorized use or distribution of company assets. It requires preventive controls for safeguarding those assets. This is accomplished through the use of both physical security devices and, for computer resources, on-line security software. Passwords for access to on-line systems and keycard entry devices for the computer center are examples of methods for ensuring authorized access to assets.

Accountability and comparison: This refers to recordkeeping of assets and liabilities. Accountability and comparison can still occur in traditional ways, but the computer program can print a list of assets to check against physical inventory.

In many cases, accountability and comparison has been improved to include real-time verification. A sale or return at many retail stores automatically updates inventory records, not only at the one store but all stores in the chain. Another example is airline computer systems, which maintain a real-time inventory of remaining seats on each flight.

Company resources can still be vulnerable regardless of the quality of control. Such detection and corrective controls as application system balancing reports and exception reports are needed to accomplish this objective.

Monitoring of the internal control system: This refers to management's responsibility to ensure the adequacy of the control system—that it functions properly and is changed as needed. The auditor reviews and evaluates internal control and recommends changes to improve the system. However, management must take the steps to maintain the system by means of supervision and review.

Transaction authorization: This is the means by which companies ensure that resources are used as intended. Transaction authorization is accomplished by supervision, review of subordinates' work, and adherence to documented policies and procedures. In terms of data processing, for example, senior management may authorize the data processing department to begin a computer program development project. Management reviews its progress at various points and authorizes the project to continue. The user reviews the design and testing of the system to ensure that it processes transactions properly.

In a manual system, a manager could authorize the posting of accounts receivable payments by examining source documents and reviewing a journal. In a computer system, once the transactions are input, the posting to the customer's accounts, calculation of interest and new balance, and posting of totals to the general ledger occur sight unseen inside the computer, with the entries represented by electrical impulses. The traditional audit trail of hard copy books and records disappears, in fact, audit trails needed for verification of transactions for the financial statement audit may not be available.

Transaction recording: This assures conformance with generally accepted accounting principles (GAAP). The design of the transaction recording program is the result of the system development life cycle (SDLC). In the manual system the recording of transactions could be accomplished by evaluating invoices, subledgers, and journals. In the computer system, this occurs in the design and programming of the system. Once the computer begins to record transactions a certain way, it continues those instructions until the program is recoded.

The company's accountants can review the program and test its results to ensure that all transaction processing conforms to GAAP. This is accomplished on an ongoing basis by daily review of computer reports. This daily review of computer-generated transaction reports creates an audit trail.

2.1.1 The Basic Premise of Auditing

Compliance audits are performed to determine that policies and procedures are being executed—to provide management with reasonable assurance that the broad objectives of internal control are being accomplished.

People perform their job duties with varying degrees of diligence and make judgment calls on items that fall outside established policy and procedure. The execution of delegated instructions tends to deteriorate over time. Management needs the internal audit function to ensure the maintenance of an adequate internal control system. Management's responsibility and normal human error create the need for auditors. A periodic independent check of the execution of policies and procedures is necessary, if for nothing else, to ensure that changes in business conditions have not made the internal control system inefficient or obsolete. Employees and managers responsible for the daily execution of the policies and procedures do not have the time or the objectivity to review their own work. For this reason, auditors are necessary.

2.1.2 Types of Internal Control: Prevention, Detection, Correction

Internal controls can be classified in three ways: prevention, detection, and correction. Preventive and detection controls catch errors, omissions, unauthorized uses, and fraud, whereas corrective controls serve to correct these problems. Every control has a cost, which must be balanced against the cost of what is being protected. The cost of the potential loss is not always in hard dollars, but in customer goodwill, business reputation, bad publicity, or even moral values the company might choose to support as well.

Preventive controls stop an error, omission, unauthorized use, or fraud from occurring. Generally, preventive controls are more expensive than detection controls. Preventive controls are used for high-dollar-value items or their cash equivalents. With regard to preventive controls, for example, passwords are used for access to on-line computer systems. If a person's password is not on file, then access is prevented. Preventive controls are generally exercised in early stages of transaction processing and act upon specific conditions. Preventive controls do not stop all errors from occurring, however.

Detection controls allow the error, omission, unauthorized use, or fraud to occur and report it for correction later. An on-line control system that detects the unauthorized use of an on-line transaction code is less expensive than a system that prevents unauthorized use because the preventive system must be programmed to know which transactions are authorized for each specific user. The loss from fraud, however, may exceed the cost of the preventive control. Detection controls usually require human intervention—if human intervention fails, there is no control.

Corrective controls are procedures that fix an error or omission. An audible alarm activated by an infrared device is a corrective control, but, again, a human being must intervene to make the control effective. Transaction data that is corrected must be subjected to the same preventive and detective controls as was the original data.

2.1.3 Controls and Loss Potential

All controls cost money, some more than others. The cost of the control must be balanced against the value of the item being protected, whether the item is being protected from fraud or error, and the loss potential. Loss potential is a key factor here— loss potential is the amount of money or other commodity (goodwill, reputation) that will most likely be lost. Often the loss potential is not the total value of the asset for the company's total retained earnings. The auditor must be careful to evaluate and to recommend controls on the basis of the real amount of exposure, rather than just the total value of the asset.

The value of the control is measured by its cost versus the amount that the expected loss is reduced, by either reducing the probability of the loss occurring or reducing the extent of loss if it does occur. Mair cited nine areas of loss potential that all have various causes.

- Erroneous recordkeeping,
- Unacceptable accounting,
- Business interruption,
- Erroneous management decisions,
- Fraud and embezzlement,
- Statutory sanctions,
- Excessive costs,
- Loss or destruction of assets, and
- Competitive disadvantage.[2]

Controls are used to reduce or eliminate these causes of exposure to potential loss. The auditor evaluates the quality of the control, how effectively the control limits causes of loss (detection or preventive control) and how well it reduces loss after it occurs (corrective control).

2.1.4   Risks and Exposures

To conduct an effective and efficient audit of an organization and its individual areas, the auditor must identify the risks and exposures that can threaten the organization. On a general basis, this begins on an organizationwide basis and is refined for each individual area. The exposures are potential problem areas. Because all exposures have causes, the auditor will look for them according to six general categories:

- Errors,
- Omissions,
- Improper authorization,
- Improper accountability,
- Ineffective activity, and
- Inefficient activity.

Errors and omissions can be categorized further—data, procedure, processing, judgment, and comparison make up the errors and omissions categories. Improper authorization, improper accountability, and ineffective activity apply to procedures, processing, judgment, and comparison. Inefficient activities applies only to procedures, processing, and comparison. A detailed explanation of terms follows:

Comparison error: This occurs when two pieces of data are compared either manually or computer programmatically and the comparison yields the incorrect result; the two data items match but the comparison check says a no match or two data items do not match and the comparison check passes them as a match.

Comparison omission: This occurs when two data items should have been compared, but the comparison was not performed.

Data errors: This means that the data in a field is wrong. It can be caused by incorrect transcription on the source document or incorrect key punching.

Data omission: This occurs when data that should be provided on the source document or in the data stream has been omitted.

Ineffective judgment activity: This occurs when a decision is made with insufficient facts—a snap judgment that has no basis for its conclusion, that is, a prudent man, when analyzing the existing facts, would not come to the same conclusion.

Ineffective comparison activity: This occurs when the established comparison procedures do not properly isolate errors, reconciling items, or omissions.

Ineffective procedural activity: This occurs when a procedure has been established that does not achieve the desired objective.

Ineffective processing activity: This occurs when a processing scheme fails to satisfy the processing objective. An example of this is a computer program that may arbitrarily drop records from processing.

In proper authorization of judgment: This occurs when someone makes a decision that they do not have the right to make—management has not authorized the person to make that decision. For example, a manager's authorizing payment of an invoice greater than $500 when he or she is authorized to approve invoices only up to $500.

Improper authorization of processing: This occurs when an account is subjected to a set of program code that has not been authorized by management. This could occur if user management and data processing management did not enforce correct testing procedures for changes to computer programs.

Improperly authorized procedure: This occurs when a person performs an unauthorized activity, for example, a loan officer might approve a loan that is greater than the officer's authorized approval limit.

Improperly authorized comparison: This occurs when a comparison test is delegated to too low a level in the organization; in other words, management abdicated its responsibility.

Omission of judgment: This occurs when a person should have made a decision but neglected to do so.

Procedure error: This occurs when a person executes an activity incorrectly.

Procedural omission: This occurs when a person forgets or intentionally does not execute their assigned activity.

Processing error: This means that a computer program has executed incorrect program code that results in incorrect results.

Processing omission: This occurs when a set of program code that should have been executed was not executed, or an account or transaction that should have been processed was omitted.

Inefficient comparison: This occurs when the activity could be performed faster or with less cost by another method.

Inefficient procedure: This occurs when the cost to complete the procedure exceeds the value of the asset or the income derived from the procedure. An inefficient procedure is also one that could be performed in a more efficient way, such as using a microcomputer for spreadsheet analysis instead of a columnar pad and calculator.

Inefficient processing: This occurs when it costs more money to process the items than either the asset is worth or the amount of income derived.

Improper accountability procedures: These occur when incorrect procedures are designed to perform a task. For example, an invalid reconcilement scheme between a subsystem and general ledger might be designed, or if there was an incorrect count of items in inventory, the specific procedure that accounts for intransit freight may have been eliminated.

Improper accountability comparison: This occurs when an asset is incorrectly compared to the company's records. For example, the inventory listing shows 100 gallons of green paint in inventory, but it was checked off against 100 gallons of white paint.

Improper accountability processing: This occurs when a program generates an incorrect list of accounts, transactions, assets, liabilities, or other items.

Improper accountability judgment: This can occur in cases where an incorrect estimate was made on the value of a company asset or liability.

The audit should be designed to evaluate the control system's ability to detect these causes of exposure. The control system should reduce or eliminate these causes or reduce their impact once they have occurred. General risks and exposures are identified in the planning phase of the audit. More specific risks and exposures and their causes are identified during the preliminary phase of the audit.

A company can be exposed to substantial loss by one cause of exposure, or several causes can combine to cause one exposure. There is no simple relationship between the causes and the exposures, or, for that matter, between the causes and controls. A single control could eliminate multiple causes, or just one cause (obviously the former is more efficient and is preferred). The various causes can result in misstated financial data, increased expenses, or reduced revenue. Each cause of exposure must be examined to determine the resulting effect on the organization. The manual and automated systems must be studied in order to recommend a cost-effective control to reduce or eliminate each and all causes of exposure.

2.1.5   Identification of Control Weaknesses

The quality of an audit is not measured by the number of findings reported, but by the auditor's evaluation of the control system and his or her discovery of any and all weaknesses in it. This sounds contradictory, but the quality of the control system is the first priority—any weaknesses are detrimental to that end.

The evaluation takes two forms: 1) review and documentation of the system, whereby the system's flow, manual and automated, is documented in flow chart or narrative form. Those points at which control can best be effected, whether manual or automated, are identified and described. These control points are evaluated and judged as to their effectiveness by the auditor. Weak controls are documented on a "finding form." 2) Procedures are reviewed or tested as necessary to determine if actual practices are in compliance with prescribed company policy and procedure. Compliance testing is performed on the key controls to determine that the controls actually worked during the audit period. The effective controls are tested during the compliance testing phase.

Figure 2–1 shows a typical finding form used to identify control weaknesses. The auditor must identify the condition, cause, and effect of the internal control weakness.

The condition describes the problem, or, more specifically the company's exposure. Evidence that the condition exists should be documented. Evidence of the number of errors should be recited. The "effect" section is for the description of the extent of loss that has occurred or the possible loss that could occur. The probability of, and potential extent of, the loss should be accurately estimated, if possible.

The "recommendation" section of the form describes the possible solution to the problem—how the cause can be eliminated or the extent of loss can be reduced. This is the positive side of auditing, the culmination of the entire effort. The auditor must research the condition and use imagination and judgment to solve the problem. This is accomplished through direct discussions with the auditees, because they know their function and system best.

The last section on the form describes management's response to the auditor's finding and recommendation. The auditor must discuss the findings with auditee management prior to writing the final audit report. This discussion improves the rapport between the auditee and the auditor and prevents the reporting of comments to senior management without giving subordinates time to explain and correct honest errors.

FIGURE 2–1   Internal Audit Form*

Condition:	The accounts payable online system has 7 on-line update transactions which are not assigned to specific terminals which could permit their use on any company terminal.
Cause:	When the accounts payable on-line update programs were modified to include all update transactions in a menu screen format the old transaction codes were not deleted from the system.
Effect:	The possible use of these update transactions on other company terminals provides the opportunity for entry of unauthorized transactions.
Recommendation:	Remove these transactions from the system or assign them for use on specific terminals within the accounts payable processing area.

MANAGEMENT RESPONSE:	On-line transactions are assigned, by the access control system, only to the individuals who need to use them, regardless of what terminal they use. However, since accounts payable personnel should use the terminals in the accounts payable processing area and these transaction codes have been replaced by a menu function, EDP will be instructed to remove them from the system.

Prepared by:
Reviewed by:
Approved by:

* Adapted from Wilmington Trust Co. Internal Audit Division.

2.1.6   Standards of Internal Control

In section 2.1 the elements of internal control and how they were supported by professional audit standards were discussed. The auditor's evaluation of internal control is governed by audit standards of the AICPA, the Institute of Internal Auditors (IIA), and EDP Auditors Association (EDPAA).

The IIA, EDPAA, and the Bank Administration Institute (BAI, a banking trade organization) standards are more general than those of the AICPA, because they are intended primarily for internal audit. Detailed or highly specific standards could be too restrictive, in some circumstances, and frustrate the accomplishment of internal audit objectives.

Internal audit objectives differ from those of the external auditor: the basic difference is in the audit standards for internal control evaluation. The external auditor's primary objective is to obtain reasonable assurance that the financial statements are correct. The internal control evaluation's objective is to determine if the system can be relied on to generate accurate financial data. The quality of internal control helps the external auditor establish the number of transactions, or sample sizes, that he will need to examine during substantive testing. The results of the substantive test permit the external auditor to determine the fairness of the financial statements.

The internal auditor is also concerned about the fairness of the financial statement presentation, but management looks to the internal auditor for more detailed information about the company. Moreover, if an internal auditor verifies financial statements, the external auditor's work would be duplicated, thus wasting money. The internal auditor's primary objective is to ensure that the internal control system is adequate and operating effectively. It may appear that the internal control evaluation is also performed twice, by the external and internal auditor, but the internal audit evaluation is more detailed and comprehensive. The external auditor needs to evaluate internal control and perform compliance testing to "plan" the audit of the financial statements. But the internal auditor's evaluation and testing goes beyond the elements that affect just financial statement accuracy into managerial, operational, administrative, and organizational controls that have direct and indirect effects on the economic health and well-being of the organization.

2.1.6.1   EDPAA STANDARDS

The EDPAA's internal control evaluation standards are very general. They concern planning and supervision, evidence requirements, and due professional care. The EDPAA directs its efforts toward the definition of specific control objectives, to assist the

EDP auditor by providing standard controls. These "control objectives" are extremely helpful, especially for inexperienced auditors, because they establish a benchmark for measurement and evaluation. However, the EDP auditor must carefully apply standards because control objectives may not fit the auditee situation effectively or efficiently. The EDPAA also prescribes general guidelines for the assignment of responsibility to internal audit:

1. To determine whether the design of general and application controls in data processing comply with management intentions, established standards and procedures, and legal requirements,

2. To determine whether the controls operate effectively, and

3. To ensure that system development and program changes comply with policies, have proper controls and leave audit trails, are cost effective and efficient, and are adequately documented.

These guidelines form the foundation of the EDP auditor's internal control evaluation and are a required element of the EDP auditor's knowledge. The student or new auditor would do well to memorize and totally understand the theory and purpose of these standards.

2.1.6.1.1 Theory and Purpose of EDPAA Standards. The general controls cover the environmental data processing areas, such as the data center, system software, on-line systems, database administration, and microcomputer use. Computer program or application controls govern the activities within the computer programs themselves and ensure that processing is complete and accurate. Remember that management is responsible for implementing and maintaining the internal control system. This standard requires the auditor to perform procedures to obtain reasonable assurance that the controls management has implemented are operating as management intends. The auditor must also obtain reasonable assurance that the controls operate effectively.

Computer systems are subject to change because the business environment is subject to change based on such external influences as customer demand, changes in the economy, and changes in regulations. The computer systems are also subject to change from internal (company) influences such as organizational changes, changes in service levels, changes to increase efficiency, and demands to increase revenue or reduce expenses. Therefore, computer systems must be easy to modify in a controlled environment. Policies establish proper procedures for accomplishing computer changes. Change controls include review and approval of design specifications, and review and verification of the test results. The change process should be documented, to provide an audit trail to permit someone else, not familiar with the system, to figure out how the system works, how the changes were made, and how the changes effected the system. Computer programs must generate audit trails of the functions it performed on the data, the data it received, and the data it generated. The audit trails must be sufficient to allow a "reasonable man" to determine the program's functions.

The EDPAA standards specifically cover data processing audits. Although they appear to ignore non-data-processing audits, they really do not, as there is no sense in duplicating standards that exist from another professional organization.

2.1.6.2   IIA STANDARDS

The IIA has developed both general and specific standards for internal audit practices that deal with independence, professional proficiency, the scope of audit work, performance of audit work, and management of the internal audit function, and which apply to any internal audit evaluation of internal control.

The specific standards relevant to internal control evaluation are 1) the scope of the audit and 2) the performance of the audit.

The word "scope" specifies the elements of the organization that must be included in the internal control evaluation, whereas the word "performance" refers to how the auditor should complete the work.

2.1.6.2.1 Theory and Purpose of Audit Scope. Figure 2–2 states the specific IIA standards for the scope of the audit work—the audit scope is defined as the extent of coverage, the areas to review, and the activities in the areas being reviewed. Management and the board of directors, through an audit committee, provide general direction for the audit department. However, the official reporting structure should have the audit department reporting on an administrative basis to management and on a functional basis to the audit committee. Management can provide a direction as to areas to review, but should never try to prevent the audit department from reviewing an area. Administrative reporting to management encompasses staffing approvals, salary administration, and expense budgets. Functional reporting to the audit committee comprises review of administrative matters handled by management and review of audit progress, staffing, and audit reports.

Reviewing the internal control system ensures that such controls are functioning as management intends, whereas the performance review is concerned with the accomplishment of goals and objectives.

The review of the reliability and integrity of information involves computer processing, because these systems provide information for decision making, control, and compliance with regulations. To satisfy this standard the auditor must determine the "accuracy, reliability, timeliness, completeness, and usefulness of the information."[4] The internal control ensures that these elements are evaluated.

The compliance standard involves management's responsibility for developing and maintaining internal controls that ensure compliance with policies, procedures, plans, and regulations. The IIA requires the auditor to determine the adequacy of the internal control system, just as does the AICPA. The IIA's

FIGURE 2-2   Excerpt from IIA Standards[4]

300   SCOPE OF WORK—The scope of the internal audit should encompass the examination and evaluation of the adequacy and effectiveness of the organization's system of internal control and the quality of performance in carrying out assigned responsibilities.

310   Reliability and Integrity of Information—Internal auditors should review the reliability and integrity of financial and operating information and the means used to identify, measure, classify, and report such information.

320   Compliance with Policies, Plans, Procedures, Laws, and Regulations—Internal auditors should review the systems established to ensure compliance with those policies, plans, procedures, laws, and regulations which could have a significant impact on operations and reports and should determine whether the organization is in compliance.

330   Safeguarding of Assets—Internal auditors should review the means of safeguarding assets and, as appropriate, verify the existence of such assets.

340   Economical and Efficient Use of Resources—Internal auditors should appraise the economy and efficiency with which resources are employed.

350   Accomplishment of Established Objectives and Goals for Operations or Programs—Internal auditors should review operations or programs to ascertain whether results are consistent with established objectives and goals and whether the operations or programs are being carried out as planned.

400   PERFORMANCE OF AUDIT WORK—Audit work should include planning the audit, examining and evaluating information, communicating results, and following up.

410   Planning the Audit—Internal auditors should plan each audit.

420   Examining and Evaluating Information—Internal auditors should collect, analyze, interpret, and document information to support audit results.

430   Communicating Results—Internal auditors should report the results of their audit work.

440   Following Up—Internal auditors should follow up to ascertain that appropriate action is taken on reported audit findings.

safeguarding-of-assets objective is also similar to the AICPA objective.

The phrase "use of resources" deals with management's responsibility for establishing a system to ensure efficient resource usage. The auditor should determine that management has established standards for performance measurement and that performance is indeed measured against these standards. These standards should be clearly communicated to personnel to ensure adequate understanding. Variances between the actual situation and the standard should be identified, analyzed, and timely resolved. These reviews are concerned with excessive expenses, lost revenue opportunities, wasted assets, and unnecessary or inefficient programs and procedures.

The audit of goals and objectives deals with the evaluation of strategic planning by management and with the subordinate, or tactical, plans to accomplish strategic objectives. Management must ensure that the appropriate functions and activities are being worked on to fulfill the strategic objectives. Internal audit can provide valuable assistance by evaluating the accuracy of assumptions used in the plan, and determining if the information used by management is correct and relevant. Internal audit has a unique vantage point from which to determine whether the support functions are sufficient to accomplish the objectives.

2.1.6.2.2   Performance of Audit Work:[4]   This involves planning, examining and evaluating information, communicating results, and follow-up.

The internal auditor should plan the work, examine and evaluate information, report results, and follow up on findings and recommendations. An improperly planned and supervised audit will drift aimlessly, missing its objectives and producing poor results.

Planning: Audit planning includes documentation of scope and objectives. Scope includes the identification of all auditee activities as well as the selection of which areas will be reviewed, based on the risk each area poses to the organization. The higher risk areas should be reviewed first, for limited personnel resources usually prevent reviewing all areas. Audit objectives should specify what should be accomplished, so that the targeted end-product is clear and concise.

During the planning stages, staffing needs are decided. This includes deciding on how many auditors, what skills are required, and who will be assigned. It also includes the communication of work assignments to the assigned people. This provides a structured approach and keeps all audit personnel informed of what must be done.

The auditee must be notified of audit commencement, except in the case of surprise audits, because business conditions may require a delay of the audit. At the same time, the auditee should be given the opportunity to voice its concerns. Knowledgeable auditees will use the auditor to examine functions they are concerned about.

Before the auditor can evaluate an area's internal control system, he must first understand its systems and controls. The auditor does not need to be an expert about the area's functions to perform an effective audit.

To maintain the quality of the audit, the auditor must prepare an audit program that provides detailed instructions for the audit staff to follow to complete their work.

At the end of the planning phase, the work plan that documents the results of all the steps mentioned above, as well as audit programs and questionnaires, will have been generated. These must be approved by an audit supervisor, manager, and the general auditor. This keeps all personnel on the same level of understanding about what is to be accomplished and how it will be accomplished.

Examining and evaluating information: Examination and evaluation includes collecting and analyzing evidence, interpreting the evidence, and documenting this information in structured workpapers that support the audit work completed, and the auditor's judgments and conclusions. Information that demonstrates the completion of all audit procedures should be collected and documented. The analysis and interpretations of this information must be documented as well. All judgments should be explained in writing such that a "reasonable person" can understand the auditor's logic and would arrive at the same conclusion. The "information should be sufficient, relevant, competent, and useful."[4] All audit workpapers should be reviewed 1) to ensure compliance with all standards, 2) to ensure that information obtained meets standards, and 3) to ensure that all conclusions are based on fact and supported by evidence contained in the workpapers.

Communicating results: Reporting audit results is the auditor's primary product and service—the reason they are in business. A written report should be provided to auditee management at the end of the audit. Verbal reports of findings should be communicated to the auditee during the audit. Prior to the issuance of the report, the auditor should discuss the findings, comments and recommendations with appropriate auditee representatives. This keeps all communication channels open with the audited area, preventing the disclosure of shortcomings to management before the subordinates are able to explain and correct good-faith errors. It also prevents reporting of erroneous results, which could embarrass the auditor.

Audit reports disclose objectives, scope, results, and an opinion on the adequacy and effectiveness of internal control in the area. The comments and recommendations can be enhanced by including management's response regarding corrective action they plan to take. The report must be reviewed by all levels of audit management prior to issuance.

Follow-up.   It is not enough to simply report findings, make comments and recommendations to management and let things go at that. Management, the audit committee, and audit standards require a review of the audited area to determine that management's response was indeed implemented and is working. Management can choose not to implement any changes and accept the risk of loss, but even then the auditor must make sure that the actual loss is not any greater than originally anticipated. The internal auditor can only recommend changes and improvements; management and the board of directors must decide whether or not the benefits of recommended controls are worth their cost.

The scope of the audit and performance standards form the foundation for the internal control review, establishing targets for quality and requirements of the review. Compliance with the standards produce a "known quantity." The statement in the audit report, ". . . the audit was conducted in accordance with generally accepted internal auditing standards," implies that certain procedures were completed the same way that all other internal auditors would have completed them. The standards specify the "what" to do in the audit, and this section explains the "why" of the standards. This book is designed to explain "how" and "why" the work is done.

2.1.7   Auditor Judgment and Reasonable Assurance

The audit standards of the three professional organizations use the words "reasonable assurance" and "auditor judgment" with regard to accomplishing audit objectives. These terms sometimes cause difficulty for auditors with regard to understanding and practice.

"Reasonable assurance" means the impression, feeling, level of conviction, or the extent of proof that the auditor has or obtains about the quality of internal control in the area, function or activity being reviewed. A common, facetious synonym for reasonable assurance is "warm and fuzzy"—the idea being to examine enough evidence to get a "warm and fuzzy" feeling for the adequacy of internal control. Although it sounds colloquial and subjective, the words "warm and fuzzy" convey an easy understanding of the reasonable assurance concept.

Control systems are designed to provide reasonable assurance, not absolute assurance, that objectives are met. Trying to obtain absolute assurance is simply too expensive. Moreover, uncontrollable events can affect the control system that prevent absolute assurance. Many inexperienced auditors aim for procedures that provide guaranteed control—this is simply not practical.

Auditor judgment is an extremely troublesome concept to teach, because it is subjective. Judgment is an abstract skill that must be learned through trial and error, although there are basic guidelines. "Judgment" means common sense—it refers to whether a reasonable man, given the same facts, would arrive at the same conclusion. The difficulty comes in knowing when enough evidence has been obtained to convince the audit manager and senior management of the conclusion.

Auditor judgment can be conveyed using an everyday example. For instance, someone wants to buy a used car, one that is in good shape—but in spite of the car owner's claims, close inspection reveals serious maintenance slipups and even deceit on the part of the seller. At this point, the buyer makes a judgment call and cancels the deal.

So it is with the auditor's evaluation of the internal control system. If the auditor catches the auditee in one mistruth, the question arises, is the auditee lying or just misinformed? Furthermore, if the auditee did, what else did he or she lie about? If he is misinformed, is he paying attention? The auditor may find that two or three separate control procedures are malfunctioning because the supervisor is not paying attention. The workers may tell the auditor that they seldom see the area manager, that they requested new equipment three months ago and have not heard anything further. As with car buying, the auditor's judgment tells him or her that there is insufficient reasonable assurance—too many things are wrong—that the internal control system is not functioning. You cannot get a "warm and fuzzy" sense of assurance on the controls.

2.2 EFFECTS OF EDP ON INTERNAL CONTROL

Computers have had a profound effect on the business world—increasing service, improving product quality, reducing expenses, and increasing income. Computers also effect internal control, making traditional control techniques ineffective and even eliminating the need for some. Control techniques and the placement of controls may change with computers, but the control objectives *do not* change, they remain the same.

Accounting students are taught the use of hard copy journals and ledgers to record financial transactions from hard copy source documents. Computers convert these documents to machine-readable form on magnetic tapes or disks. These tapes and disks are assets of the organization just as are buildings and inventory. For example, the customer list on a tape file could be valuable to a competitor. If computer files were to be lost or destroyed, the company could be put out of business.

Traditional controls, such as segregation of duties, dual control, and accuracy verification, are now replaced by application controls within computer programs. But incompatible duties that must be segregated still exist. For example, the duty of designing a computer program must be segregated from that of writing the program. This segregation means that the designer and the writer would have to collude to perpetrate a fraud, which is unlikely. In addition, having two people provides an accuracy check on the design of the program and the writing of the program code. Furthermore, the same person should not make financial entries to both the application system and the general ledger—this mitigates the potential for misstatement of both entries and prevents the embezzlement of funds.

A multitude of examples exist explaining the effects of automation on internal control. Automation can take financial records that were dispersed throughout various departments and centralize the processing and control in a separate department. Automated controls can be better than manual controls simply because computer programs perform consistently until they are changed. Computer programs do not get sick, go on vacation, or need a pay raise each year.

However, the microcomputer explosion is pressuring the mainframe system, competing with processing capabilities that rival the mainframe, at cheaper prices. The auditor in the 1990s and beyond will see the decentralization of recordkeeping, that is, organizational areas keeping their own records, as business goes the cheaper, microcomputer route. Control techniques will then evolve again to meet the demands of business, but the control objectives will still remain the same.

2.3 SOME REFERENCES CONCERNING INTERNAL CONTROL TECHNIQUES

A multitude of material has been written about control types and techniques. In the mid 1970s the IIA, with a grant from IBM, contracted the Stanford Research Institute to study the systems auditability and control practices in use at the time at various corporations throughout the world. Three reports were published: The Executive Summary, Data Processing Control Practices, and Data Processing Audit Practices.[5] These reports were landmark accomplishments—nothing like them had ever been published before. The control practices report separated controls into two categories; general controls and application controls. General controls include computer service center and application system development controls, whereas application processing system controls were segregated into six area: 1) transaction origination, 2) data processing transaction entry, 3) data communications, 4) computer processing, 5) data storage and retrieval, and 6) output processing.

Second, Mair, Wood, and Davis published comprehensive explanations of application and system development controls classifying the application controls into preventive, detection and corrective categories[6] in 1978.

Third, the EDPAA published an exhaustive set of control objectives[3] covering management controls, technical services, application systems, and computer operations in 1980. The control objectives were formatted into four levels: 1) the control area—the area being reviewed, 2) the control objectives—the level of control that is needed, 3) the level of standards—describes the control standards, and 4) the technique level—a verification procedure.

Last, Ron Weber presented the book, *EDP Auditing Conceptual Foundations and Practices*[7] segregating application controls into the various phases of data capture, preparation and entry, access and communication, input, processing, output, audit trail, and backup and recovery in 1982.

The reader may ask which of these is correct, or best; the answer is, all of them. Each presentation offers a different perspective, and the more viewpoints that the auditor can absorb the better, for the more knowledgeable and effective he will be.

This book will discuss control objectives and techniques in each chapter because circumstances can vary among companies, and the inexperienced auditor may not understand the reasoning for applying or eliminating a particular control technique in a given set of circumstances.

2.3.1 Categories of Control Techniques

It is useful to classify internal controls into various categories to illustrate the interaction of various groups in the organization and their effect on computer controls. These categories, which are discussed in depth below, are organization, management, financial, data processing environment, application, and system development.

2.3.1.1 ORGANIZATIONAL CONTROLS

Although management effects the organizational structure and its elements, the owners, shareholders, or board of directors establish that organizational structure. In fact, federal bank regulators and the Securities and Exchange Commission (SEC) mandate various aspects of organizational structure, including the appointment of an audit committee and direct reporting of the auditor to it. In addition, the regulators require or recommend that the audit department be independent of all other departments and report only to senior management. Regulators require that delegation of any responsibility to lower levels of management be documented in the board meeting's minutes.

Organizational controls are concerned with the decision-making processes that lead to management's authorization of transactions. Companies with large data processing facilities separate data processing from business units to provide control over its costly hardware, software, and human resources. Combining data processing into the business units would be too much responsibility for one manager.

Organizational control techniques include documentation of:

- Reporting responsibility and authority of each function,
- Definition of responsibilities and objectives of each function,
- Policies and procedures,
- Job descriptions, and
- Segregation of duties.

Applicability to data processing: The EDP function should be segregated from other users to prevent favoritism in the allocation of EDP resources. Data processing must support all users equally. If a user reports to the EDP manager, however that user may tend to get preferential treatment, a situation to be avoided. Circumstances do occur in which the service to other users may need to be reduced because of special needs of an in-house designer working on a new system that needs to be completed in a short time. This decision must be made by senior management through careful analysis of the advantages and disadvantages of resource allocation.

The data processing department must be given the authority to control the growth of such EDP resources as hardware and software acquisitions. All departments using computers must obtain the appropriate approvals from EDP management and technicians, who review and evaluate new hardware and software. The purchase of these items must be approved by a steering committee, company CEO or president, or the senior management group as a whole.

Responsibilities and objectives: These, with regard to each EDP function, must be clearly defined and documented, including systems software, application programming and system development, database administration, and operations. The senior manager, of all these groups, and managers of the individual groups make up the EDP management team responsible for the effective and efficient utilization of EDP resources. Their responsibilities include:

- Providing information to senior management on the EDP resources, to enable senior management to meet strategic objectives.
- Planning for expansion of EDP resources
- Controlling the use of EDP resources
- Implementing activities and functions that support the accomplishment of the company's strategic plan.

Policies and procedures: These are the standards and instructions that all EDP personnel must follow when completing their assigned duties. Policies establish the rules or boundaries of authority delegated to individuals in the organization. Procedures establish the instructions that individuals must follow to complete their daily assigned tasks. Mandating that all requests for changes to existing programs must be approved by user and EDP management before programmers and analyst can work on them is an example of a policy. Documented instructions for filling out a standard change request form, how to justify the cost of the change, how to specify the changes needed, how to obtain approvals, and who to obtain the approvals from are examples of procedures.

Documented policies should exist in EDP for:

- Use of EDP resources,
- Physical security,
- Data security,
- On-line security,
- Microcomputer use,

- Reviewing, evaluating, and purchasing hardware and software,
- System development methodology, and
- Application program changes.

Documented procedures should exist for all data processing activities. These procedures will be expanded upon in the chapters on individual audit areas.

Job descriptions: These communicate management's specific expectations for job performance. Job procedures establish instructions on how to do the job and policies define the authority of the employee. All jobs must have a current, documented job description readily available to the employee. Job descriptions establish responsibility and the accountability of the employee's actions.

Segregation of duties: This is a traditional, noncomputer control technique aimed at separating conflicting job duties, primarily to discourage fraud, because separating duties makes collusion necessary to commit a fraud. Such separation can also force an accuracy check of one person's work by another, so that employees to some extent police each other. Examples in data processing are segregation of:

- The systems software programming group from the application programming group
- The database administration group from other data processing activities
- The computer hardware operations from the other groups
- The application programming group into various subgroups for individual application systems
- The systems analyst function from the programming function
- The physical, data, and online security group(s) from the other EDP functions.

2.3.1.2 MANAGEMENT CONTROLS

These controls are concerned with long-range planning, legal compliance, and resource usage. Planning includes goals and objectives covering at least the next five years, and short-range goals, objectives, functions, and activities needed to meet those long-range goals.

Legal compliance is concerned with federal, state, and local laws, and, for an international corporation, international laws.

Resource usage refers to the planning and allocation of all assets, including buildings, furniture, computer hardware and software, and personnel. Personnel allocation is a function of, among other things, the corporate labor structure. The number of management levels depends on the company's size and organizational structure, but, generally, there are three such levels: senior, middle, and supervisory. Senior management is responsible for strategic planning and objectives, setting the course for the lines of business that the company will pursue. Middle management develops the tactical plans, activities, and functions that accomplish the strategic objectives. Supervisory management oversees and controls the daily activities and functions of the tactical plan.

Long-range planning: This requires that the company determine what resources it has and what resources it needs. The planning process identifies:

- Opportunities—new products or services, market weaknesses or niches that can be exploited,
- Threats—external activities and events that could jeopardize a line of business or the company as a whole,
- Strengths—the resources and capabilities of the company that can be used to exploit opportunities, and
- Weaknesses—the shortcomings of the company that could or will impede the exploitation of opportunities.

The long-range planning process should be quite exhaustive, covering every department, and it must be updated yearly to adjust the elements delineated above. Good long-range planning includes documenting goals and objectives, explaining how strengths will be used, and how weaknesses will be compensated for or corrected. Time allowances, target dates, revenues, and expenses are estimated and documented for use as standards for progress measurement. The elements of long-range planning incorporate:

- the goals and objectives of the plan—for use in measuring progress,
- revenue and expense estimates,
- time allowance and target dates, and
- strengths and weaknesses.

Long-range planning and the data processing department: The data processing area must inform senior management of its strengths and weaknesses, isolating and describing the support that can be given using existing resources to achieve the stated goals and objectives. Computer system shortcomings, relative to the support of goals and objectives, must be isolated and reported during the planning process. The data processing management must establish a plan for correction of the shortcomings, with times given for completion that are sufficient for having new capabilities ready when the company needs them. Of course, the possibility exists that EDP cannot correct the shortcomings, or that the company cannot afford the system it needs to support the business. With proper long-range planning, these deficiencies should come to light early enough for the company to react and correct the deficiency in time. Improper planning will permit the weaknesses to go unnoticed, and the company will have to try to implement a new business or service without the proper computer resources. Terms and situations inherent in these concerns are presented below in descending order of importance.

Short-range planning, or, tactical planning: This refers to the establishment and documentation of goals, objectives, functions, and activities needed to meet all of the elements of the long-range plan. The functions and activities are performed every day, whereas the tactical goals and objectives define deliverables (final products) that span periods of time as close as tomorrow and as far away as five years. For data processing, the short-range plan defines the daily activities of developing software and obtaining hardware in sufficient time to support business activities.

Legal compliance: This means for many companies, ensuring that all statutes are adhered to, which can be a daily activity. Data processing must be constantly aware of the changing legal environment that effects the department's business. Computer programs may need modification each year to keep processing and reporting in line with regulations. The extent of regulatory compliance varies with the type of business, and whether or not it is a public company.

Resource usage: This refers, on a day-to-day basis, to the securing of physical assets from unauthorized use and to ensuring adequate support capabilities. The layout of the facility must be conducive to efficient and effective operation. Part of long-range planning should address providing adequate physical facilities to satisfy the needs of the long-range plan.

In terms of data processing, the facilities requirements must be part of the strategic and tactical planning to ensure that an adequate environment is prepared to house anticipated equipment needs. The plan must address the amount of space needed and structural and environmental requirements that will be adequate for current and anticipated computer hardware. Security and safety requirements must be satisfied. Adequate physical access control, fire detection equipment, fire extinguishing equipment, and computer control equipment must be provided. The specific control requirements and techniques for the physical data processing facilities are discussed in detail in later chapters.

Data processing personnel resource management: This involves activities and functions to accomplish the administration of individuals, salary, and benefits costs. The control techniques are:

- job descriptions,
- salary and benefits budget,
- recruiting standards and criteria,
- training and development programs,
- job performance evaluation, and
- screening and security standards.

Job descriptions: These are also an organizational control. They also function as a management control from the standpoint that they communicate management requirements to the employee and provide a standard for performance measurement.

Salary and benefit budgets: These help management control these costs and plan for the future. New products and services must be sold and supported by people. These costs must be known when pricing a product or service. The strategic and tactical plans should identify these cost factors since they can make or break the offering of a new service or product.

Recruiting standards and criteria: These are particularly applicable to EDP because of the technical training and experience requirements needed for EDP positions. The pool of available personnel could be thin if the company uses unique or unusual hardware and software that demands specialized training and development programs to obtain the proper staff. Programs that support EDP are EDP management's responsibility, largely because the personnel department may not be able to develop and maintain technical EDP training courses.

Job performance evaluations: These are needed to counsel and motivate employees who are measured against their job descriptions and other performance criteria. In data processing, job performance evaluations should consider the quality of the designed and written programs, the conformance with deadlines and budgeted time, and compliance with data processing standards.

Screening and security checks: These have unique applicability to data processing because program design is a pervasive activity that can have a profound effect on the entire company. Programs that are fraudulent or intentionally erroneous can damage a company, even causing bankruptcy. Thorough screening of the prospective employee, obtained by talking with previous employers and obtaining credit reports, is one preventive control against fraud and sabotage. Applicable labor laws and regulations, however, affect the extent of screening an employer can perform.

2.3.1.3 FINANCIAL CONTROL TECHNIQUES

These controls are generally defined as the procedures exercised by the system user personnel over source, or transaction origination, documents prior to system input. These areas exercise control over transaction processing using reports generated by the computer application to reflect unposted items, nonmonetary changes, item counts and dollar amounts of transactions for settlement of transactions processed and reconciliation of the application (subsystem) to general ledger. The financial control techniques are numerous; some are delineated in the following list.

Authorization: This entails obtaining the authority to perform some act, typically access to such assets as accounting or application entries.

Batch dollar totals and item counts: These are used to control groups of documents, and include the dollar total and a count of items in the batch. A summation of the dollar amount of each item in the batch should equal the batch dollar total. The item count identifies how many documents should be in the batch. They help detect errors and omissions.

Budgets: These are estimates of the amount of time or money expected to be spent during a particular period of time, project, or event. The budget alone is not an effective control—budgets must be compared with the actual performance, including isolating differences and researching them for a cause and possible resolution.

Cancellation of documents: This marks a document in such a way to prevent its reuse. This is a typical control over invoices—marking them with a "paid" or "processed" stamp or punching a hole in the document.

Documentation: This includes written or typed explanations of actions taken on specific transactions. It also refers to written or typed instructions which explain the performance of tasks.

Dual control: This entails having two people simultaneously access an asset. For example, the depositories of banks' 24-hour teller machines should be accessed and emptied with two people present. Many people confuse dual control with dual access, but they are distinct and different. Dual access divides the access function between two people; once access is achieved, only one person handles the asset. With teller-machines, for example, two tellers would open the depository vault door together, but only one would retrieve the deposit envelopes.

Input/output verification: This entails comparing the information provided by a computer system to the input documents. This is an expensive control that tends to be over-recommended by auditors. It is usually aimed at such nonmonetary data as name and address changes, which cannot be reconciled by dollar totals and item counts.

Safekeeping: This entails physically securing assets, such as computer disks, under lock and key, in a desk drawer, file cabinet, storeroom, or vault.

Segregation of duties: This entails assigning similar functions to separate people to provide reasonable assurance against fraud and provide an accuracy check of the other person's work. For example, the responsibilities for making financial entries to the application and to the general ledger should be separated.

Sequentially numbered documents: These are working documents with preprinted sequential numbers, which enables the detection of missing documents.

Supervisory review: This is exactly what its name implies, a review of specific work by a supervisor; but what is not obvious is that this control requires a sign-off on the documents by the supervisor, in order to provide evidence that the supervisor at least handled them. This is an extremely difficult control to test after the fact because the auditor cannot judge the quality of the review unless he or she witnesses it, and, even then, the auditor cannot attest to what the supervisor did when the auditor was not watching.

Transmittal documents: This is a piece of paper describing the contents of the items attached to it or sent separately, a type of cover letter. It provides a double check of the processing accuracy of the documents or items represented by the transmittal document. It typically includes a brief description of the items sent, dollar totals of all items in the group, and an item count. The document tells the receiving area what items should be attached.

2.3.1.4   DATA PROCESSING ENVIRONMENT

These controls are hardware and software related and include procedures exercised in the EDP environmental areas. The environmental areas include system software programming, on-line programming, on-line transaction systems, database administration, media library, application program change control, the data center and the media library. The controls in these areas are discussed in detail in various later chapters.

2.3.1.5   APPLICATION CONTROL TECHNIQUES

These include the programmatic routines within the application program code. The financial controls, discussed earlier, are performed by the user to help ensure the accuracy of application processing. Some authors refer to these only as application controls, whereas others differentiate the definition. Any function or activity that works to ensure the processing accuracy of the application can be considered an application control. This book treats both the programmatic controls and user performed financial controls as application controls (see chapters 11 and 12).

2.3.1.6 SYSTEM DEVELOPMENT

These are functions and activities generally performed manually that control the development of application systems, either through in-house design and programming or package purchase. The first control requirements are system development standards that specify the activities that should occur in each system development life cycle (SDLC) phase. For example, these standards specify the type and quantity of testing that should be conducted. The second element of controls is documented procedures that communicate how the activities in each phase should be accomplished. These procedures establish control functions in each phase. These controls are discussed in detail in later chapters covering the system development audit.

NOTES

1. American Institute of Certified Public Accountants, AICPA Professional Standards, New York, 1989.

2. Mair, W.C., Wood, D.R., Davis, K.W. *Computer Control & Audit.* Deloitte & Touche, Wilton, CT, 1978, p. 11. Reprinted with permission of Deloitte & Touche.

3. EDP Auditors Foundation, Inc. *Control Objectives: Controls in a Computer Environment: Objectives, Guidelines, and Audit Procedures,* 1990. Publication available upon request from EDPAF, P.O. Box 88180, Carol Stream, IL 60188-0180.

4. Institute of Internal Auditors. *Standards for the Professional Practice of Internal Auditing.* Altamonte Springs, Fl, 1978. Reprinted with permission.

5. Systems Auditability and Control Study: Data Processing Audit Practices Report, Data Processing Control Practices Report, Executive Summary. Altamonte Springs, FL, 1977. (Prepared by the Institute of Internal Auditors. Researched by the Stanford Research Institute. Under a grant from International Business Machines Corporation.)

6. Mair, W.C., Wood, D.R., Davis, K.W. *Computer Control & Audit.* Deloitte & Touche, Wilton, CT, 1978. 98–105. Reprinted with permission of Deloitte & Touche.

7. Weber, R. *EDP Auditing Conceptual Foundations and Practices.* McGraw Hill, New York 1982. pp. 24–27.

3

EDP Audit Methodology

3.1   INTRODUCTION

Chapter 3 will focus on the EDP audit methodology. The phases of the EDP audit will be explained in detail, relating theory to practice. The chapter will finish with discussions of audit tools and techniques that have a specific focus on computer-assisted audit techniques. An effective evaluation of, and compliance with, audit standards requires a structured methodology. This structure begins with the preparation of the annual audit time budget and job schedule and continues with the system flow evaluation process.

3.2 ANNUAL AUDIT PLANNING

Most audit departments are faced with limited personnel resources: there are not enough auditors to cover the total number of areas of the company. This makes planning important. An auditing plan begins with a risk assessment and results in a time budget based on the risk assessment's risk rating score.

The planning process begins with the risk analysis. This determines which areas of the company have the highest risk and, therefore, should be audited in the coming year. A priority rating is assigned to each audit area based on its risk level—the higher the risk the higher the priority. By auditing the areas of highest risk first, the auditor can be sure they are covered before all personnel resources are used.

The next step is to assess the amount of time needed for each area, and assign a time limit to each. This indicates the number of auditors needed for each area. Few companies can justify hiring enough auditors to audit all areas of the company each year. In fact, many areas may never pose sufficient risk to warrant audit coverage at all.

3.2.1 Risk Analysis

The audit areas are assigned a one digit priority number of 1, 2, or 3 based on their risk score. The highest risk areas receive the highest priority rating of 1, intermediate risk areas a 2, and lowest risk a 3. Another category, known as "required" audits, is not analyzed because required audits are needed to satisfy government regulation, federal regulator policy, a senior management or audit committee request, or by the external auditor.

Most audit departments perform some type of risk analysis that varies from sophisticated microcomputer models to pure subjective judgments. Whether by more, or by less intuitive methods, the audit management team decides to audit a specific area based on some set of objective facts or subjective information. A risk analysis model (a collection of mathematical formulas that are used to calculate a numerical score based on risk factors and their importance to the organization) should be simple and workable, otherwise it will not be used properly. It is important not to spend unnecessary time shuffling risk ratings that have minimal effect on the results of the risk analysis. The elements or categories of risk analysis models vary depending upon the organization. All models, however, should incorporate such elements as internal controls, changes in procedure, transaction volume, the recency of the last audit, the materiality of each area, and a variety of external factors, which are discussed below.

3.2.1.1 INTERNAL CONTROLS

A numerical rating should be devised to represent categories of poor, fair, or good controls. The higher the number, the poorer the controls. The objective is to assess the quality of internal controls, based on the auditor's knowledge. The more critical the control weaknesses and the more weaknesses that exist, the poorer the score. A poor rating's high numerical score is then reflected in an increased total point scoring that shows on the risk analysis model. To complete the risk analysis, a priority rating of one, two, or three is assigned to a range of risk scores. For example, a score of 25 or greater would receive a priority 1; 19 to 25 would be assigned a priority 2, and so on.

For areas that have not been audited in several years or not at all, absent any other knowledge, the highest rating could be assigned as a conservative approach. This is based on the fact that not knowing the quality of internal control can create almost as much risk as having a poorly controlled environment.

3.2.1.2   CHANGES IN PROCEDURES

Changes in company management, procedures, or computer support systems negate the auditor's knowledge of the internal control environment. The greater the impact of the change, the higher the risk rating that should be assigned. This risk rating should consider completed or anticipated changes.

3.2.1.3   TRANSACTION VOLUME

In some cases, processing error rates fluctuate with transaction volume. In this instance, a rating for transaction volume should be included in the analysis. High volume areas are assigned high risk scores, thereby permitting the model to push areas with high potential error rates into higher risk categories.

3.2.1.4   RECENCY OF LAST AUDIT

AICPA audit standards suggest, and external audit firms consider, internal audit departments to be an internal control. Internal audit departments cannot prevent, detect, or correct errors on an ongoing basis, but periodic internal audits help management locate and correct areas of weak control. The risk rating score for an area to be audited should increase in direct proportion to the number of years since the last, usually internal, audit was conducted.

3.2.1.5   DOLLAR EFFECT AND MATERIALITY

The risk rating score varies with the dollar effect that a given area has on the balance sheet, income statement, or, on fiduciary liability. Monetary loss via error, omission, fraud, or lawsuit has an effect on the company's ability to continue business. The ratings can be based on the dollar value of items processed, but it is important to remember that a loss will very seldom be a total loss of all dollars handled by the area.

3.2.1.6 OTHER RISK FACTORS

The risk analysis models used by external auditing or public accounting firms heavily consider economic or industry factors that are external to the company. The external auditor does not participate in the company's daily activities and may not be immediately aware of the effect of economic or industry trends. Therefore, external auditors' risk models must be more sensitive to external events.

For example, in recent years, the price of oil declined drastically, which significantly reduced the income generated for companies and individuals involved in the oil business. This, in turn, reduced income, which reduced borrowers' ability to repay their debts to banks. In addition, the value of real estate in some areas of the country declined, reducing the value of collateral pledged for loans. Therefore, a risk analysis model, which considers economic and industry sensitivity, would have rated company activities connected to oil and real estate with a higher than usual rating directing the auditor to closely evaluate the effect of these factors.

3.2.1.7 PRIORITY RATINGS

When scores from the above-mentioned risk categories are tallied, a priority rating is assigned. The priority ratings instantly tell audit management where to focus their attention. The minimum objective is to cover all priority one areas during the year. In terms of audit frequency, priority one areas should be audited every year, priority two areas could be covered once every eighteen months, while priority three areas could be covered once every two to three years. Risk analysis models change the risk score of individual areas based on recency of last audit and quality of internal control. As internal control improves, the risk decreases and the priority is reduced, thereby reducing the urgent need for audit resources and permitting their redirection elsewhere.

3.2.2 Time Budget

An estimate of the time to complete each audit based on historical experience must be assigned to each individual audit area. The amount of time will fluctuate with the scope of the audit—the activities or functions, which are called areas of concern or transactions, that will be reviewed and tested. Obviously, the more transactions reviewed and tested, the greater the time estimate must be.

Because this time estimate is based on historical experience, it is advisable to keep track of details concerning time spent processing audits in the past. For example, audit management cannot determine the effect of auditing five more transactions this year than last if the audit time charged for each transaction was not recorded during the course of the last audit. The time tracking system must be devised to suit the needs of the audit department.

When time budgets are assigned to each audit job, audit management can then calculate the total hours needed for "required," and priority one, two, and three audits. The number of auditors needed for the coming year can be calculated depending on the audit coverage desired, such as all required and priority one audits or some other mix. The important point is that personnel resources should be allocated to cover "required" audits first, priority one audits second, priority two audits third, and priority three audits last.

3.2.3 Job Scheduling

The last task in annual audit planning is to schedule the completion of the audits. Many factors affect audit job execution, such as staff availability, management and audit committee requests, and requests from external auditors. Therefore, the basic requirement is to schedule the audits by quarter. Near each month's end then the audits can be rescheduled more finitely with specific start dates for the coming month. Staffing requirements for each audit job and target dates for completion of each phase can only be accurately calculated after the completion of the individual audit planning phase.

3.3 AUDIT WORKPAPER FILES

To comply with audit standards, the auditors' work must be documented and organized in a standardized fashion for easy reference in future audits and reference by other auditors. A minimum of four separate files are needed:

- Test workpapers,
- Permanent workpapers,
- Pending files, and
- Report files.

Each workpaper should contain a page heading that identifies the name of the audit, the area being audited, and a label of what is contained in the workpaper.

3.3.1 Testing Workpapers

The testing workpaper files are those prepared as a result of compliance and substantive testing and are relevant mainly to the current year. They are also relevant for review during the planning phase of a subsequent audit. However, they are temporary in nature, which distinguishes them from permanent workpapers. The compliance test file should contain documentation of:

- The review of existing internal controls,
- The summary of tests conducted,
- Documentation of procedures performed, and
- Supporting documentation of detailed tests.

Substantive test files require the same elements as compliance test files except for the review of existing internal controls.

Existing internal controls: This review and documentation is completed during the preliminary review phase, using the format similar to that shown in Figure 3-1. This document is cross referenced to the documentation of internal control procedures, which is prepared in either flowchart or narrative form. The second column of Figure 3-1 contains two elements; 1) a sequential number as an identifier to link the document to the flowchart or narrative wherein the control point is identified and, 2) the internal control is described in two or three lines of text. The third column identifies the type of internal control. The fourth column should explain the risk or exposure that the control procedure would minimize or eliminate. This document is prepared during the preliminary review phase. Because it is relevant to subsequent audits, a copy of this document should be placed in the permanent workpaper file for the specific audit transaction being completed.

FIGURE 3-1   Identification of Existing and Non-Existing Controls

Identification of Existing Controls				
Source W/P Ref.	Internal Control	Control Type	Risk/Exposure	Tested/ Not Tested
A-1	①Program change request approved by user.	Auth.	Changes could be made to application without user knowledge.	T

Identification of Non-Existing Controls					
Source W/P Ref.	Internal Control	Control Type	Risk/Exposure	Offsetting Control	Finding Form
A-1	Program change approved by user.	Auth.	Changes could be made without user knowledge.	None	FF-1

Adapted from Wilmington Trust Co., Internal Audit Division

Summary of tests conducted: This must be included in the test workpaper file for each compliance or substantive test. The summary identifies:

- The purpose of the test,
- The scope of the test, and
- The results and conclusions.

The purpose of the test can be written as: "to determine whether key internal controls over the auditee's activity are functioning as intended during the test period. . . ." The scope of the test identifies the population of items to be tested and the period of time that the test is covering—for example, all program changes over the last calendar year. The results of each test procedure should be summarized and documented. For example, ". . . of 25 program changes reviewed, five changes were not authorized by management." If statistical sampling is being used, the effect of these errors on the precision and the tolerable error rate must be explained.

The conclusion should explain the number and effect of exceptions found in the tests; whether this is a situation in which no exceptions are noted, exceptions are found for each attribute, or exceptions are found for only some attributes. The conclusion can be worded, for example, ". . . based on the tests performed, key internal controls over program changes were (were *not*) functioning as intended during the test period."

Documentation of procedures performed: This describes the specific procedures performed by the auditors to complete the test.

These procedures are based on the instructions given in the audit program that is usually written by an in-charge or supervisor. They should be written so that the staff auditor can perform them with minimal supervision. The audit program should be understandable, precise, and presented in a logical sequence, including the source where the auditor can obtain the necessary information, what information is to be recorded in the workpapers, the elements or attributes being tested, and explanations of how to perform calculations, if any.

Supporting documentation of detailed tests: This identifies the auditee's documents, accounts, the identification of what is being tested, and the specific elements of the test that these items are being subjected to. This documentation reflects the audit program instructions and can be accomplished in a variety of ways. One suggested format is the matrix format, shown in Figure 3–2. The documentation should identify whether or not the item passed each individual test. This can be accomplished with the use of a few tick marks. For example, a checkmark would indicate that the item passed the test, an "E" would identify that the item failed the test, and an "$\not{E}$" would identify that the exception or the failure of the test was cleared. The meaning of all tick marks should be adequately explained at the bottom of the workpaper or on a separate "legend" page, so that other auditors and reviewers can understand them. The source of the information that tells the auditor that the item passed or failed the test should be noted at the top of the column pertaining to that test. Any exhibits or supporting workpapers for the test should immediately follow the documentation of the detailed testing.

All exceptions should be supported by a copy of the document(s) that prove the item is an exception. This documentation should be included in the workpapers behind the documentation of detailed testing page(s). The detailed test workpapers should be cross referenced, at the specific place where the exception is noted, to the supporting workpaper reference that proves that this item is an exception.

3.3.2   Permanent Files

Permanent files contain the documentation obtained and prepared during completion of the planning and preliminary review phases. They are referred to as permanent because they contain information about the auditee's internal control system, activities

FIGURE 3–2 Application Change Control Detail Testing Workpaper Example

Test of change request approval procedures

User Change Request Number	S&P User Mngmt. Approved Request	S&P Liaison Approved Detail Specs.	User Super. Approved Detail Specs.	S&P Super. Approved Program Code	S&P Liaison Approved Test Results	Super. Approved Test Results	Manager Approved Link to Product
23512	+	+	+	+	+	+	+
25647	E1 FF1	+	+	+	+	+	+
26112	E1 FF1	E2	+	+	E3 C1	+	+

Tickmark Explanation:

+   = Change request form contained proper signature

E1 = User Management signature not present on change request form.

E2 = User Liaison signature not present on change request form.

E3 = User Liaison signature not present on change request form, however, liaison sent programmer separate memo approving of test results, see w/p A-10.1. C1 = Memo accepted as liaison approval, exception cleared.

FF1 = Finding form to document control weakness. See Figure 3–7.

and functions that usually do not change from year to year. The workpaper test files are separated into other binders because they are unique to that particular test for that particular audit, whereas permanent files can be used year after year by updating information as necessary. Permanent files include:

- Documentation of the internal control system,
- Documentation of transaction reviews,
- Internal control questionnaires,
- Review of existing internal controls,
- Identification of existing internal controls, and
- Identification of nonexisting internal controls.

The permanent file should contain a separate summary file, which contains organizational charts of the area, a list of general ledger accounts, financial statement makeup, job descriptions, scope, finding forms, copy of the final audit report, and audit time-tracking reports.

3.3.3   Pending Files

A pending file is a manila or hanging folder held in a file cabinet with the other workpaper files. Its purpose is to accumulate memoranda and other documents obtained at times other than when the audit is in progress. This file is invaluable—it can hold information that explains new procedures in an audited area or any other events that would affect the auditee's area that the auditor should be aware when the audit is performed.

3.3.4   Report Files

All audit reports issued during the year should be retained in a separate binder, or file, for easy reference. Internal audit reports are frequently requested by management, external auditing firms, and regulators. These groups usually need only the report, and this separate binder or file makes these reports easily accessible.

3.4 AUDIT APPROACH AND METHODOLOGY

Audits need a structure for efficiency and effectiveness. This framework is referred to as a methodology.

Audits can be conducted in numerous ways. Two alternatives are 1) a system flow evaluation or 2) prepared ("canned") auditing programs with internal control questionnaires (ICQs).

3.4.1 Prepackaged Auditing Programs and ICQs

Prepackaged auditing programs and internal control questionnaires can be obtained from several sources. These audit programs and ICQs can be used as the main investigative tool, irrespective of the various activities in the auditee's area. The instructions and questions on these documents are to be executed and answered, and the answers are evaluated to identify weaknesses in the internal control system.

The advantage here is that audit planning and preliminary review phases are significantly reduced with this approach, reducing the time needed for audit completion. The disadvantage is that the audit is not customized to the specific environment, resulting in the potential for inaccurate identification of control weaknesses. The canned approach may also miss unique business functions or activities, which can result in inadequate audit coverage.

An ICQ is used to collect information about transaction flow and the control system to help identify control points and locate nonexisting controls. Prepackaged ICQs are developed based on the standard controls that should exist in an area. Prepackaged ICQs, however, may not include coverage of special or unique activities.

Prepackaged audit programs and ICQs should be used as a foundation—as starting points for developing customized audit programs and questionnaires specifically for the particular company. As the audits are performed, the prepackaged material can be enhanced to cover unique areas.

3.4.2 System Flow Evaluation

This method includes seven phases comprising different activities. Each succeeding phase builds upon the information found in previous phases and, therefore, increases the level of detail in the information collected and reviewed.

1. Planning,
2. Preliminary review,
3. Compliance testing,
4. Substantive testing (financial audits),
5. Reporting,
6. Wrap up, and
7. Follow-up.

3.4.2.1 PLANNING PHASE AND SCOPE
SUMMARY PREPARATION

The Planning Phase: The planning phase is usually completed by an intermediate staff level auditor with a minimum of one-and-a-half to two years' auditing experience. This person is usually assigned the title, "in-charge," on the particular audit that the planning phase is being done. To complete the planning phase, the in-charge works with the audit supervisor assigned to the audit to complete all the elements previously described.

The planning phase includes the accumulation of information needed to define the auditing work to be performed. The hours needed to complete the work, the number of staff members and the mix of skills needed, and the start and completion dates for each phase are required by auditing standards. To comply with audit standards, the results of the planning phase must be documented, reviewed, and approved by all members of the audit team and audit management. This documentation can be accomplished by use of a standardized form known as "scope summary." The scope summary is a necessary, deliverable end product for every audit performed. The absence of these standardized activities and their documentation, in some form, indicates failure to comply with standards, allows the audit to wander, and increases the risk of missing vital objectives.

The Scope Summary Preparation: A suggested format for a scope summary is shown in Figures 3–3 and 3–4. While the elements of this document and the activities performed in the

FIGURE 3–3   Scope Summary Cover Page

Job Name:	Job Number:
Audit Budget:	Planned Budget:

General Auditor:	Manager:
Supervisor:	In-Charge:
Staff:	

Target Date Calculation

			AUDIT WORK	REVIEW TIME
Number of Field Work Auditors	=			
Productive Hours Per Day	=	×		
Total Staff Chargeable Hrs./Day	=			
In-Charge FW Chargeable Hrs./Day	=	+		
Supervisor FW Chargeable Hrs./Day	=	+		
Manager FW Chargeable Hrs./Day	=	+		
Total Chargeable Hours Per Day	=			
Field Work Start Date				=
Preliminary Survey Hours	=			
Total Chargeable Hours Per Day	=	+		+
Number of Days to Complete	=			
Preliminary Survey Completion Target Date				=
Compliance Testing Start Date				=
Compliance Testing Hours	=		AUDIT WORK	REVIEW TIME
Total Chargeable Hours Per Day	=	+		+
Number of Days to Complete	=			
Compliance Testing Target Date				=
Closure Phase Hours	=			
Total Chargeable Hours Per Day	=	+		+
Number of Days to Complete	=			
Closure Phase Target Date				=
Report Issue Target Date				=

FIGURE 3–4 Scope Summary

Identification of Transactions/Areas of Concern

Include Activity	Transaction/Area	Exclude	Reason
A	Program Additions/Modifications	I	Critical to Meet Audit Objective 1
B	Program Deletions	I	Critical to Meet Audit Objective 1
C	Program Library Backup/Recovery	I	Critical to Meet Audit Objective 1
D	Program Library Mgmt. Software	E	Not Critical to Control

Risks and Exposures

1. Unauthorized changes
2. Blanket authorization
3. Program logic errors and omissions
4. Inaccurate processing
5. Unnecessary reruns

Control Objectives

1. All program changes are properly authorized
2. Conflicting program change functions are adequately segregated
3. All program changes are adequately tested and the test results are approved by the user
4. Personnel making program changes are adequately supervised
5. Program changes themselves are adequately reviewed

Key Controls

1. Documented policies and procedures
2. Segregation of duties
3. Documented test standards
4. Program documentation standards
5. Supervisory review

Audit Objectives

Ensure that adequate controls exist to:

1. Protect application programs from unauthorized changes
2. Ensure that application programs are error free
3. Protect program libraries from unauthorized access
4. Assure complete data recovery in the event of destruction

Preliminary Review

Activity Code	Transaction/Area	Budget Hours		Actual Hours		Pri	Auditor
		Audit Time	Review Time	Audit Time	Review Time		
A	Program Additions/Modifications	10	2			1	
B	Program Deletions	5	.5			1	
C	Program Library Backup/Recovery	5	.5			1	
	Total of Tasks	20	3				
	Total Preliminary Review Hours	23					

Compliance Testing Hours

Activity Code	Transaction/Area	Budget Hours		Actual Hours		Pri	Auditor
		Audit Time	Review Time	Audit Time	Review Time		
A	Program Additions/Modifications	75	5			1	
B	Program Deletions	10	2			3	
C	Program Library Backup/Recovery	10	2			1	
	Total of Tasks	95	9				
	Total Compliance Testing Hours	104					

planning phase can vary, Figures 3–3 and 3–4 show the minimum elements necessary.

The Cover Page: This item, shown in Figure 3–3 bears some explanation. The job name is the name of the audit, whereas the job number is a unique number used to code this audit into a computerized time tracking system, if one is used. The words "audit budget" refer to the hours estimated as necessary for this type of job based on the past as reflected by the annual plan. The planned budget is the hours estimate derived during the planning phase of this particular audit. These two time estimates may be different; when planning for a particular audit, it may be found that more or less time is needed than is provided for in the annual plan.

The next subdivision—the general auditor, manager, supervisor, and "in-charge"—identifies the management team for the individual audit. The manager, supervisor, and in-charge provide daily management and supervision at various levels during the course of the audit. All staff team members who will be performing the field work are listed.

The target date calculation section gives a step-by-step method for calculating the completion dates for the preliminary survey, compliance testing, closure phase, and report issue date. According to this model, field work auditors, once assigned to an audit, should stay with it until completion. Audit management must take care to avoid switching an auditor back and forth between several jobs because this can severely inhibit the audit's progress.

The productive hours per day should be a realistic estimate of the time the staff auditor will spend. For various reasons, the productive hours per day is seldom the full length of the work day. People get interrupted by phone calls, meetings, questions, and personal situations. Misstating the productive hours per day will cause misstatement of the target dates.

The total staff chargeable hours per day is the daily staff time as calculated by multiplying the number of field work auditors times the number of productive hours in the day. The in-charge and supervisor may enhance audit productivity if they complete some of the transactions that would normally be completed by staff. The supervisory and consulting work performed by the in-charge auditor and the supervisor *are not* considered productive hours for the purpose of the target date calculation, because this formula seeks to account only for hours spent on specific audit tasks. If any members of the audit management team complete audit program or ICQ steps, then this work *would* be considered productive time for the purposes of this target date calculation, as this team usually does not do so. The review time is considered separate from productive hours for audit work largely because it is a distinct and different activity.

The preliminary review hours (the staff time spent completing preliminary review activities) are divided by the total chargeable hours per day to calculate the number of days to complete preliminary survey audit work. The review time spent by an in-charge, supervisor, or manager is calculated in the same way. With the number of days until completion calculated, the preliminary review target date can be extrapolated easily.

A similar calculation is performed for timing compliance testing, substantive testing, closing and wrap-up phases to establish the target dates for audit completion. Figure 3–3 only shows lines for compliance testing hours. If substantive testing is done, then the three steps simply need to be duplicated to calculate substantive testing.

The key target date is the report issuance date because this is the ultimate end product of the audit. There is no specific amount of time after the audit is completed to issue a report; the report, however, must be timely to be useful to management. It is recommended that the report be ready for final issuance within three weeks of the completion of compliance testing.

3.4.2.1.1 Identification of Transactions. The auditor needs to determine the activities and functions for which the auditee is responsible. This can be accomplished by reviewing industry-related textbooks, if available, through discussion with auditee management, and through a review of policy and procedure manuals. If an audit of the area or business has been conducted before, the auditor should review the permanent file, previous audit workpapers, internal audit reports, external auditor's management letter, any reports from regulatory authorities, if they exist, and the pending file.

Figure 3–4 shows a sample of the identification-of-transactions section of the scope summary. The auditor should interview the auditee to determine whether there have been any changes in the organizational structure, job descriptions, policies and procedures, or accounting procedures. Auditee activities are grouped by similarity of function into transactions or areas, and each transaction is assigned an audit activity code. This code can be used as an identifier in the audit time tracking system and is used as the first character of the workpaper reference page number of each workpaper related to that particular transaction. This permits easy access to the workpaper file section in the scope summary by finding the audit activity code. The third and fourth columns of Figure 3–4 indicate whether the transaction will be included or excluded from the audit; column four states the reason the transaction was included or excluded.

3.4.2.1.2   Risks and Exposures.   The auditor must be aware of potential risks and exposures, their relationship with control objectives of the area, and the key controls which serve to minimize or eliminate the risks and exposures. Figure 3–4 shows examples of risks and exposures stated in the scope summary. They can be stated in general terms as are those originally suggested by Mair, Wood, Davis[1] or the risks can be specific, such as lapping (misdirecting a payment intended for one to another, often the perpetrator's, account) of accounts receivable. The auditor must bear in mind, however, that for every risk and exposure, there is a cause, and the more specifically stated the risk and exposure, the closer the auditor gets to defining the cause of the exposure.

On the one hand, sometimes an auditor may define the risk so specifically that the ensuing control objectives, key controls, and defined audit objectives become so narrow that other causes of the same risk or exposure are overlooked by the audit. For example, lapping can cause a general exposure of fraud. But there are often other ways to perpetrate fraud in an accounts receivable system. If the auditor designs the audit to test for lapping only, he or she may miss the other potential fraud possibilities. On the other hand, merely using the general exposures defines risks too broadly for effective use during the audit.

The risks and exposures of an audit area can be determined through review of industry-related textbooks, audit-related textbooks, material from CPA firms, discussions with other auditors or auditee management. These methods are facilitated by the activities sponsored by the IIA, EDPAA, and the BAI.

3.4.2.1.3 Control Objectives. "Control objectives" are a narrative statement of the purpose of the control techniques used. Control objectives describe what the auditee should accomplish with the control system (see Figure 3–4). The audit is designed to determine that the control techniques (key controls) accomplish the control objectives.

3.4.2.1.4 Key Controls. Documented policies and procedures, segregation of duties, documented test standards, and supervisory review are examples of control techniques, or key control procedures, that the area can use to effect the control objectives that minimize or eliminate risks (see Chapter 2). Other key controls will be explained in each chapter as they relate to specific audit areas. These items are documented in the scope summary to provide the audit staff with a reference tool during preliminary review and compliance testing.

Delineations of each of the three previously discussed areas— risks and exposures, control objectives, and key controls—can be enhanced during successive audits, so that as audits progress over the years, a comprehensive list is developed for each area.

3.4.2.1.5 Audit Objectives. "Objectives" refers to the ultimate purpose of the audit, in general or specific terms. The more generally stated the audit objectives are, the broader the audit scope. As the objectives become more specific, the audit programs required for review and testing zero in on increasingly particularized functions. Protecting application programs from unauthorized changes, ensuring that they are error free, protecting data libraries from unauthorized access, and assuring complete data recovery in the event of destruction are examples of various audit objectives. EDP audits tend to use specific audit objectives because such audits are targeted at specific environmental areas or application systems.

3.4.2.1.6 Preliminary Review—Scope Summary. The purpose of the preliminary review phase is to gain an overall understanding of the activities and functions within the audited area and the processing performed by the application. The end product (deliverable) consists of two factors, of which one is the complete documentation of the flows for all transactions in the audited area or, in the case of a computer application, documentation of the elements of application processing. The second deliverable is the identification of existing controls and the identification of nonexisting controls.

Figure 3–4 illustrates the preliminary review page of the scope summary. The activity code and transaction name comes from the list of transactions identified previously in the scope summary. The transactions listed on the preliminary review page will be reviewed, and documentation will be prepared, covering work flow, identification of control points, and identification of existing and nonexisting controls.

The purpose of the planning phase is to identify which auditee transactions are to be focused on in the preliminary review. Figure 3–4 shows that budget hours are estimated for staff work and review work. These are target deadlines for the audit staff and management team to use as benchmarks. Target deadlines should never be "cast in stone" because the preliminary review may uncover significant problems in an area that requires extensive additional review and, therefore, cost more time. However, neither the staff auditor nor the audit management team member should exceed this budget by more than 5 percent without the approval of the audit manager and the general auditor, unless that authority has been delegated to them by the general auditor. These variances and approval procedures are only rules of thumb—different audit departments delegate different levels of authority to their managers and supervisors.

3.4.2.1.7 Compliance Testing—Scope Summary. Figure 3–4 shows a sample of the compliance testing page of the scope summary. During the planning phase, only the transactions that may be subject to testing can be realistically identified. It is impossible and impractical to estimate the budget hours for each transaction that the staff will need to complete the compliance testing. The decision on this estimate can only be made after the results of the preliminary survey for that specific transaction are known.

During the preliminary survey, the auditor finds out whether the defined controls are weak or strong. The transaction review in the preliminary review phase will give preliminary indications whether the control system is working or not. During preliminary review, the identification of existing controls and nonexisting controls will reveal the holes in the control system for the specific transaction. If the controls over a specific transaction are inadequate, then there is obviously no need to subject it to compliance tests because the compliance test will only reiterate to the auditor that the controls are weak.

To finish the scope summary, time estimates are inserted for reporting, wrapup, and follow-up phases.

When the planning phase is concluded and the scope summary is completed and assembled, they are first submitted to the audit supervisor for review and then to the audit manager and general auditor for review and approval. This review and approval constitutes the start of the preliminary review phase.

3.4.2.2 EXECUTION OF THE PRELIMINARY REVIEW PHASE

This documentation for the preliminary review phase can be completed in either flowchart or narrative form, whichever is the standard for the audit department. The flowchart form of documentation includes some narrative description of each step in the flowchart. The flowchart form's advantage over the narrative format is that it provides a pictorial representation, usually on one or two pages, enabling an auditor to obtain a quick understanding of how the processing works. In the narrative format, the auditor must read all of the narrative to obtain an understanding of the transaction flow (or application processing flow), which takes more time than dealing with a flowchart.

As the transaction flow of a manual system or an application is documented, the auditor should note existing controls on the flowchart. In addition, any points in the transaction flow or processing flow at which the auditor believes a control point should exist, but does not, should also be noted. The existing and nonexisting controls should also be documented on a separate workpaper using a form similar to that shown in Figure 3–1. This extra step provides a ready reference for locating existing and nonexisting internal controls—a major point of the audit.

For either the manual system or an EDP environmental area, the accuracy of the transaction flow documentation must be verified. This is accomplished by performing a transaction review, which takes an actual transaction and follows its documentation through the flowchart representation. This ensures that all the auditee's activities and functions were properly included in the documentation. Care must be exercised with transaction documentation to ensure that all "branching" procedures are included in the documentation. There are many situations where a transaction meeting certain criteria are subjected to different verification procedures. For example, invoices under $5,000 may need supervisory review, whereas invoices over that amount must be approved by a manager. When performing the transaction review, the auditor must select a transaction from each group to test all branches of the transaction flow (see Figure 3–5).

3.4.2.2.1   Analytical Review.   An analytical review provides a quick overview of key information. The purpose is to identify areas that require a more in-depth audit review, documentation,

FIGURE 3–5 **Procedural Branching Example**

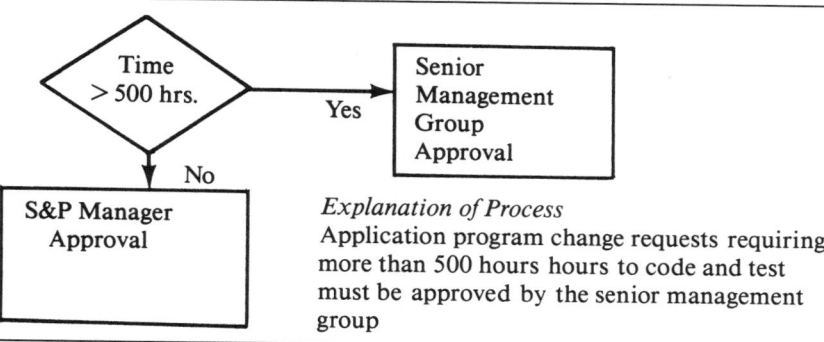

Explanation of Process
Application program change requests requiring more than 500 hours hours to code and test must be approved by the senior management group

or testing. Analytical review procedures are more akin to financial and accounting audit procedures, but they can be used in certain aspects of the EDP audit.

In the financial audit, an analytical review includes ratio analyses, trend analyses, and comparisons of budget versus actual expenses. The auditor is looking for any unusual variances in comparable numbers from one period to the next. Some of the items that can be reviewed analytically on the data processing side are the following:

- The total maintenance expense for an application from year to year: A large increase in maintenance expenses could indicate that significant processing problems occurred during the year, which could lead to processing errors and financial statement errors.

- Comparison of overtime hours or dollars spent: Any variance could be caused by any number of situations: increases in transaction volume, high personnel turnover, an increase in processing errors, or an increase in computer down time.

Other elements that can be analytically reviewed are the number of maintenance changes to the application, the number of updates to application production programs, the number of processing errors, or the number of customer complaints.

3.4.2.2.2   Existing and Nonexisting Controls.   The key elements of review and documentation evaluation are the review of weaknesses and development of testing. The review of internal control weaknesses centers around the identification of nonexisting controls. Because these are controls that do not exist, the auditor must research the condition, cause, and effect of the missing controls and prepare a recommendation for improvement. This is done using a finding form similar to that shown in Figure 3–6.

FIGURE 3–6   Finding Form

Condition:	From a sample of 3 change request forms, 2 change requests were not approved by user management to be designed and coded. This constitutes an unauthorized change to a production application program.
Cause:	With change request #26112, the user liaison was not notified of a change made by the programmer to prevent a program from abnormally terminating. With change request #25647, the user liaison did not obtain his manager's approval, he forgot.
Effect:	Authorization control over application program changes is inadequate. Unauthorized or fraudulent changes could be made to production programs and not be detected.
Recommendation:	Assign a control group to review all change request forms for proper approvals before the program is updated to the production object library. Include in final audit report as a formal comment.

Management Response:	Management agreed that control is weak and agreed to assign the review responsibility to a control group. All exceptions will be reported by the control group to both S&P and User management in writing.

Prepared by: JBM
Reviewed by: SB
Approved by: PR
Page FF-1

Adapted from Wilmington Trust Co. Internal Audit Division

3.4.2.3   COMPLIANCE TESTING

Existing controls that appear adequate must be subjected to compliance testing. The knowledge gained during the preliminary review will permit the auditor to design proper procedures in order to test samples of source documents. These documents are examined so that the adequacy of control points for each of the transactions is verified.

Compliance testing is used to verify the adequacy of internal control points documented in the relevant workpapers. In developing the test procedures, the auditor must consider the key controls and control objectives. The auditor should design the test procedures to evaluate the key controls. The tests involve taking source documents, reports, and other company records and comparing them, in terms of timing and placement, with prescribed policies and procedures.

To execute the test, each item is examined for the specific attributes defined in the test program. As each item tests accurate, the attribute is checked off on the detailed test workpaper, as shown in Figure 3–2. This workpaper provides the evidence supporting the test results. This evidence is mandatory for compliance with audit standards because it provides an audit trail of the work performed.

Then, as always, the results of the test must be summarized and must include a conclusion as to the effectiveness of the internal control being tested. The conclusion should state whether or not the controls are functioning as intended, functioning partially, or not functioning at all.

3.4.2.4   SUBSTANTIVE TESTING

Substantive testing is that which validates the details of financial transactions and balances, whereas compliance testing concentrates on validating the internal control procedures exercised over those financial transactions. Substantive testing validates the amounts of the transactions themselves.

The key differences in the two types of testing are the objectives and the scope of the test. The objective of substantive testing is the validation of the accuracy of the financial transaction, whereas the scope depends on the results of compliance testing. The quality of the control environment reduces or increases the number of financial transactions that must be subjected to substantive testing. The weaker the control environment, the greater the scope—the more transactions—that must be tested. Likewise, the stronger the controls, the fewer the transactions that must be tested. The procedures and documentation for completing substantive test development, test execution, and documentation are the same as those used for compliance testing.

The summary of results differs in that the audit conclusion for substantive testing is related to the accuracy of an account balance as opposed to the adequacy of internal control. The conclusion must state whether or not, in the auditor's judgment, the account balances are correctly stated.

3.4.2.5 REPORTING AUDIT FINDINGS

During the preliminary review and compliance test phases, weaknesses in internal control may have occurred and have been isolated. These weaknesses are documented on a finding form such as that shown in Figure 3–6. These documented weaknesses form the basis for the auditor's report to management. Proper preparation of the report is extremely important. Appropriate members of the management team and audit staff should be assigned to prepare the report.

During the execution of the various audit phases, audit findings are documented on the finding forms. As each transaction in each phase is completed, the auditor who prepared the finding form should write the formal comment and recommendation that will be included in the final audit report. A word processor is an extremely useful tool for this job.

A valuable shortcut can be used to increase the efficiency of audit report preparation. Although the contents of the finding form are seldom worded in a form appropriate to final audit report, the auditor can word process from the finding form, skipping the step of handwriting the formal report.

3.4.2.5.1 Audit Report.   The cover letter of the final audit report contains the opinion, a description of the audit scope, and procedures performed, and comments and recommendations. The scope describes the area covered, period of time covered, and a statement of compliance with audit standards. The opinion summarizes the auditor's conclusion on the quality of internal control and the fairness of financial statement presentation if substantive testing was performed—the unqualified (clean) opinion, the subject-to opinion, the negative opinion. Procedures-performed section of the report describes the audited activities and functions that were reviewed during the audit. The comments-and-recommendations section of the report contains the detailed explanations of the audit findings.

When the four elements of the audit report are completed, a "draft" should be assembled in typed form. This report is reviewed by all members of the audit management team including the necessary staff members from the audit. After the report has passed this first exhaustive review process, a copy of the draft should be given to appropriate members of the audited area, including management (see Chapter 2).

3.4.2.5.2 Post-Audit Conference.   After the audited group has reviewed the draft report, a post-audit conference should be scheduled with the auditee. This is a face-to-face conference with representatives from the audited area and the appropriate members of the audit team. The purpose of this conference is to ensure that both the auditors and auditee understand the points made in the audit report. This conference serves to open communication channels and eliminate comments that are worded improperly or incorrectly state facts. If the auditee wishes to discuss each comment and recommendation, then the auditors should oblige. The ultimate objective is to ensure that the members of the audited area know the contents of the report before senior management sees it. Issuing an audit report without a post-audit conference will blind-side the employees of the audit area and alienate any relationship that may have been established between the auditors and auditee.

After the post-audit conference, any necessary changes can be made to audit report comments as long as the report remains fair and objective. At no time should the contents of the audit report be modified to mislead senior management or other readers of the report. Auditee management may pressure the auditor to change report comments so as to present auditees in a good light, but the auditor must resist the temptation since acquiescence would violate audit standards.

After changes are made, a final copy is typed and reviewed one more time by the audit management team, signed by the appropriate audit department members, and issued to senior management.

At some point, a copy of the audit report should be sent to either the president or chief executive officer of the company. The process by which this happens varies depending on the desires of the company president or CEO. The options are the following:

- Issue the final report to the president or CEO at the same time the report is issued to senior management;
- Wait until management submits their written response to the audit report, then issue the audit report *and* management's response to the president or CEO.

It is more efficient to provide the president or CEO with the report and management's response for review at the same time. But this depends on the wishes of executive management.

3.4.2.5.3 Reporting to the Audit Committee.   Issuing reports to the audit committee depends on their wishes. The options are:

- Send copies of the audit report as they are issued to audit committee members;

- Wait for the auditee's response and send the report and response together to the audit committee;
- Collect the reports and responses issued on a monthly or quarterly basis, and report them to the audit committee; and
- Summarize critical audit findings in a separate report to the audit committee on a frequency dictated by the audit committee.

In any event, it is advisable to meet formally with the audit committee at least once per quarter.

3.4.2.6 WRAP-UP

Three activities occur during this phase even though they do not affect the audit report or completion of audit field work. They are extremely important however, for compliance with audit standards and effect the quality of audit follow-up and procedures for the next audit. The three tasks are listed below:

- Final assembly of all workpaper and permanent files,
- Completion of performance evaluations, and
- Preparation of the budget variance analysis.

Assembly of the workpapers into formal binders in an organized fashion is necessary to comply with audit standards. These files should be placed in file cabinets in an organized fashion for easy retrieval. The more disorganized the assembly and filing of the workpapers, the more time it will take to conduct follow-up procedures on this audit and accomplish the review of the workpapers during the next audit.

In addition, it is vital that audit staff members be given feedback as to the quality of their performance after each audit. These evaluations include ratings on the quality of work, quantity of work, diligence, creativity, and compliance with departmental and auditing standards.

The budget variance analysis is a documented comparison of actual hours charged for each individual audit transaction. Significant variances from preliminary, projected estimates, either favorable or unfavorable, should be explained. The reason for these variances should be evaluated to determine how the variance can be avoided on the next audit. Documentation of this budget variance analysis and communication to audit management provides information to justify additional staff or explain inadequate completion of other audits caused by unfavorable budget variances. Audit committees keep a very close watch on these variances in order to determine that audit staffing is sufficient.

3.4.2.7 FOLLOW-UP

The first step in this process is to ensure that auditee management responds to the audit report. Its response should include the actions it has taken, or plans to take, with respect to audit comments and recommendations. Management's planned action should include a timetable for implementation of any changes. Management's response, once received, must be evaluated for its adequacy and the completeness and accuracy of its intention to comply. Executive management expects the auditor to evaluate the adequacy of management's response and advise it if the response is inadequate.

3.4.2.7.1 Reporting Channels. The auditor should first try to rectify all compliance problems with middle or senior management. If the problems cannot be resolved, then the issue should be taken to the president or CEO. If the problems still cannot be resolved, then the auditor must objectively report all of the facts to the audit committee.

3.4.2.7.2 Effect of Changes. Another key event in follow-up is the ultimate implementation and affect of the implementation in the audited area, six months to one year after the audit. It is important that the auditor ensure that the recommended control was implemented as agreed to by management and that the control is working effectively and efficiently. This can be done during the next audit as long as the audit is performed within a maximum of 15 months from the last audit. If another audit will not be conducted within this period, then a "limited review," of compliance with the audit report recommendations, should be performed.

3.5 AUDITING TOOLS AND TECHNIQUES

3.5.1 Computer-Assisted Audit Techniques (CAATs)

CAATs can provide the means to achieve a high level of efficiency and effectiveness to the audit. Moreover, conditions will arise where CAATs are the only viable audit tool that can accomplish the stated audit objective and evaluate all items in a population with a few minutes of computer time. Manual audit procedures use only samples of transactions because testing of the entire population is cost prohibitive.

CAATs are absolutely necessary when an audit trail has disappeared in the normal course of processing. In some cases, computer application programs make decisions based on pre-established criteria that are not retained on a data file. Therefore, the auditor cannot test this decision-making process because the criteria used to make a previous decision no longer exists. CAATs can be used to duplicate or simulate the decision-making process by recalculating the preestablished criteria used for the decision. Another alternative is to use CAATs for capturing the criteria and decision-making process as it actually occurs. Some widely accepted CAATs are discussed later in this chapter.

3.5.2 Workpaper Techniques and Standards

These techniques and standards relate to the completion of documentation to provide the evidential matter necessary for compliance with evidence standards. Workpaper techniques are instructions and methods for documenting evidential matter discovered during the audit. Workpaper techniques are based on common sense and vary for each company.

3.5.3   Flowcharting and Narrative

Both of these tools are used to document the auditee's manual or automated processing system and the control points. Figure 3–7 shows the flowchart symbols and their meanings.

The narrative form is simply a written description of the system, procedure, or item that the auditor needs to explain. The narrative should be prepared clearly and concisely. It should be organized, with headings to identify each activity or function that the auditor is describing.

FIGURE 3–7   Flowcharting Symbols and Meanings

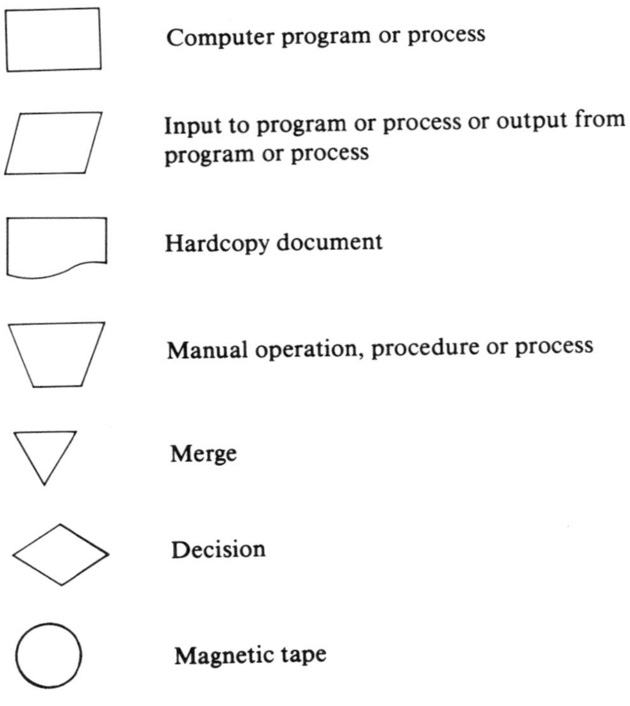

Computer program or process

Input to program or process or output from program or process

Hardcopy document

Manual operation, procedure or process

Merge

Decision

Magnetic tape

FIGURE 3–7 *(Continued)*

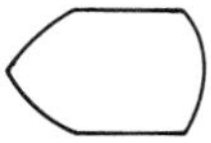

CRT or microcomputer display terminal

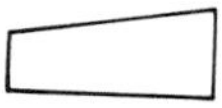

Manual input

Collate

Auxiliary operation

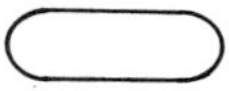

Interrupt, start, or stop program or process

Punched card

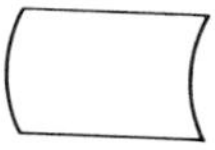

On-line or disk (DASD) file

Transmittal tape

Connector to other item on same page

Connector to a different page

Sorting of items or transactions

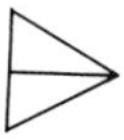

Internal control process

Flowcharts and narratives accomplish the same objective. As a general rule, however, flowcharts are for long or complicated procedures while narratives are for simple and easy-to-explain procedures.

3.5.4   Audit Software[2]

This is a generic term that refers to computer programs used by the audit department to collect data from computer system files to accomplish the audit objective. These computer programs can be written in a high-level language such as COBOL, generalized audit software, or report writer packages.

Generalized audit software is a prepackaged set of programs that accepts user coding instructions in the form of English-language parameters (coding instructions containing reserved words that are interpreted by software package codes to perform specific operations). These parameters are interpreted and translated into an assembly language code, then linked by a compiler or translator and executed against defined input files. Generalized audit software is the most highly utilized computer-assisted audit tool in the industry today. Its success can be attributed to use of English language statements and parameters that are easily learned by people with limited data processing knowledge.

Auditors can independently create programs that access data files and produce reports for audit use. Some specific uses are confirmations of assets and liabilities, exception reports of accounts or conditions that meet specific criteria, and simulations of application system reports or functions.

Audit software use is a very cost beneficial approach because it gives the auditor independent access to computer files without having to rely on the data processing department for programming. Audit software package use is easily learned; a working knowledge can be developed within one month, and a reasonable level of proficiency can be attained in three months. Although the time needed to develop these programs can be more costly than manual audit procedures, the programs can usually be used repeatedly in later audits with little or no modification. The programming logic portion of programs can be duplicated for use against other application files with minor changes.

3.5.4.1 LIMITATIONS

The major limitation to the use of audit software is the cost of development. Manual audit procedures can generally be developed and executed in less time than it takes to develop and execute the computer program. Although the learning curve for prepackaged audit software is shorter than for high-level language programs, audit management must still provide training to the audit staff in order to make audit software effective.

3.5.5 Test Data Method

3.5.5.1 EXPLANATION OF TECHNIQUE

The test data method, or "test deck," is used to test program edits (program-coded instructions that validate input data) and application functions. The objective is to test specific functions of an application or individual programs. This method uses fictitious data created by the auditor and entered into actual application processing.

This method is useful for testing program edits against input transaction data when the edit criteria cannot be ascertained either by reviewing documentation or through computer program listings. Program edits use preestablished criteria to validate entered data. Violations of the criteria cause the transaction to be rejected.

However, the computer program listing, or program documentation, may be out of date and may not reflect the criteria used in the production program. Or, the computer program may be too complicated to follow, or require too much audit time, to isolate all the program edit procedures. Therefore, test deck use is important for determining that the user and the computer programs execute the procedures that ensure processing accuracy and completeness.

3.5.5.2   PROCEDURES FOR TEST DATA DEVELOPMENT AND EXECUTION

The test data method involves the creation of data that complies with the actual application's input format. This input data is created and is "fictitious." The auditor creates this data after determining the exact edit criteria to test. To do so, the auditor must predict the effect of the actual application on the test data. Furthermore, the auditor must determine an effective means to eliminate the effect of the fictitious transactions after their use. These three activities can be quite time consuming, but they produce valuable results that otherwise might not be obtainable.

The auditor must prepare test transactions that contain both valid and invalid data. The use of invalid data is called the "make-it-fail approach"; it permits the auditor to determine exactly what combinations of invalid data can get into the application system.

After the test data is prepared, the auditor must predict the action the application will take on such test data. The purpose of the predicted results is to measure actual activity against a standard. This need not be exceedingly complex. A very short explanation about the predicted result is sufficient.

Any of these fictitious transactions accepted by the live application must then be removed from working, or production computer files, so it is best to use the actual production programs only in a test environment. The auditor must be absolutely certain, however, that the application program that is set up in the test environment is an exact duplicate of the production (working) application program.

The audit documentation of predicted results need not be extensive. If, however, processing logic for master record creation or computational routines is being tested, then the auditor must be meticulous at predicting the results and in documenting that prediction. The reason for this is that there is a possibility of extensive variables occurring. The auditor may not be aware of all program effects that may occur during processing, and in researching actual results the predicted or standard result may become quite confusing absent a documented prediction of results.

The results of the test are evaluated by comparing the predicted to the actual results. The auditor may find it necessary to repeat the test to ensure validation of all program activities. Deviations between standard and actual results should be investigated to determine the cause of the deviation, and to determine whether the condition represents an actual control weakness that threatens data integrity or increases the risk of loss.

3.5.5.3 Cost/Benefit

Because merely basic knowledge of data processing is needed to develop and implement test deck technique properly, lower-level staff can be used, thereby reducing the cost. The greatest time cost involves the preparation of the test data, which varies in direct proportion with audit scope and the number of functions being tested. This technique is designed to look for processing errors and omissions, thus reducing the chance that the test data will be usable in subsequent years. The reason is that it is hoped that changes will be made to correct the program flaws causing the errors and omissions. The only reason for reuse of the test data would be for periodic accuracy checks concerning the original problems. But if the next audit is defined to look at other program functions, then audit's test data would be outdated.

3.5.5.4 Limitations

Because of the amount of time required for creation of the test data, testing should be limited to specific program functions, and the volume of test data should be kept to a minimum. Furthermore, it is advisable to separate different test objectives into separate transaction samples. For example, the test of program edits should be separated from a test of internal calculation routines or master file posting functions. Separate test objectives and samples will permit the auditor to isolate errors attributable to specific program segments.

3.5.5.5 APPLICATION EXAMPLE

Dates that are entered into an application and that are later used for "tickler activities" (conditional dates—events occur or activities are required on such conditional dates) should be extensively edited to prevent erroneous dates. Some examples are the maturity dates for loans, bond payments, or interest payments. Because these are critical events, the application should prevent acceptance of invalid months or days. Furthermore, program editing of dates is very basic and easy to code.

The auditor can easily create test data for month values other than one through twelve and day values greater than thirty or thirty-one in specific months. Input transactions can be created using standard transaction formats, making the test relatively simple. The application should reject any date with a month not equal to one through twelve, and, therefore, only one transaction with an invalid month is needed to test the edit. However, several transactions will be needed to test the handling of invalid days because some months are different lengths.

3.5.6   Base Case System Evaluation[3]

The base case system evaluation (BCSE) is a comprehensive test deck that evaluates all processing aspects of the application system. It is appropriate as an acceptance test method of a purchased system or an in-house developed system. From an auditing standpoint, it is appropriate for systems that require extensive validation of many transactions, files, and reports.

Its biggest drawback, from an auditing standpoint, is that all processing conditions must be validated that require significant preparation time to create and maintain the data. In addition, many of today's computer systems use on-line terminals and have telecommunications capacities. The BCSE must be able to validate all on-line and telecommunication functions. This requirement prevents preparing all input transactions on a machine readable file, which is counter-efficient. Because a separate program would be needed to read the file into the application, the test of on-line and telecommunication interfaces would be precluded.

3.5.6.1 PROCEDURES

BCSE requires the development of test transactions that include all working, or production transactions, including valid and invalid data for all variables in each transaction. Test data must also be prepared for all critical application functions. The output files and reports must also be tested. The effect of processing on all test data must be predicted in order to compare actual results to a standard. Preparation and execution procedures are similar to the test deck method, except that they are on a much larger scale, requiring voluminous data requirements.

3.5.6.2 LIMITATIONS

The sheer volume of required test data and scope of functions to be tested make this a more appropriate technique for application testing. It is cost prohibitive for audit use except in very special circumstances, when complete validation is necessary and other, less complicated means cannot be developed.

3.5.7 Integrated Test Facility

The integrated test facility (ITF) is a means of entering test data into the live production system without affecting live accounts or transactions. It involves the creation of fictitious accounts, companies, or other entities on the production files. The test transactions are entered during production with actual live transactions, hence the term "integrated." Special controls are necessary to prevent the fictitious data from affecting production data and to prevent the data from being included in reports used for control of production work and management information.

A simple example of an ITF that needs no special processing considerations is a bank employee's checking account, savings account, or loan. All transactions to these accounts would be subject to the same activities and functions as are customer accounts. These would tend to validate the accuracy of processing in the complete system of automated and manual functions. These employee accounts, however, are seldom relied upon as valid tests for internal or external audit purposes, because the test environment is not controlled, and specific attributes may not be identifiable. Nonetheless, these employee accounts can be used to detect problems that need further research.

The integrated test facility can be used to verify the accuracy of internal calculations that leave no audit trail—the elements used to perform the calculation are not saved on a data file and, therefore, are not traceable.

3.5.7.1 PROCEDURES FOR ITF DEVELOPMENT AND EXECUTION

The activities to be tested must be selected, and the associated data needed to execute the activity must be prepared. The effect of processing, based on the test data, is precalculated and documented for later comparison to actual results. The data is then entered into the system and posted to the records of the fictitious entity on the transaction and master files. The auditor must reverse the transactions if this is not done programmatically.

To conclude the procedures, the auditor compares actual results to precalculated results and isolates and researches the cause of any variance.

3.5.7.2 COST BENEFIT

The major benefit of the ITF is its repeatable use, and the fact that it can be performed on a surprise basis on the audited area.

After implementation, the ongoing costs are minimal. The ITF can even be used to test changes to the application system.

The front-end cost originates from the creation of a fictitious entity on the production data files and the programming needed to reverse the effect of ITF transactions. The ongoing audit costs originate from the preparation of ITF transactions, comparison of the actual to precalculated results, and the time spent researching variances.

3.5.7.3 LIMITATIONS

The biggest limitations on ITF use are the front-end programming and development costs and the amount of time needed for its development. Because it is an integral part of a computer system, the ITF must be implemented under conventional SDLC procedures by Systems and Programming (S&P), which somewhat reduces audit independence. Implementation by S&P is necessary, therefore, programmers would know how the ITF functioned and could develop ways to circumvent it.

3.5.8 Parallel Simulation[4]

Parallel simulation is the re-creation of an application process or function, using the same input and creating comparable output. For example, if the application program creates a master file, the simulation program should create a master file. Parallel simulation uses special programs to process live data files and simulate application processing. The auditor can simulate the entire application, a single program, a single program function, or a critical report. Parallel simulation is valuable because computer processing has made it difficult for auditors to establish conventional audit trails, forcing reliance on alternative techniques for proving the validity of system processing. Parallel simulation permits the auditor to verify complex application logic in less time than other audit methods, without the need to understand it.

With parallel simulation, the auditor uses duplicate input (and other) files to produce the same results as does the production application program. Because these results can be verified either manually or through the computer, the auditor can be confident that the application processing is valid. Parallel simulation is a thorough approach because the auditor can programmatically test the entire population instead of relying on test samples.

Parallel simulation requires some programming expertise, which can be obtained from the audit staff or the programming department. Using the talents of an audit programmer is best in order to maintain audit independence. Programming with generalized audit software provides the flexibility needed to simulate an application program at a fraction of the cost of using conventional programming. Care should be taken, however, to code the programs as efficiently as possible to minimize computer resource usage and permit easy modification.

Simulating a Posting Program: A simulated master file can be in the form of a printed report instead of a tape or disk file, eliminating the need for a comparison program. A program can be coded to extract the needed elements from the production master file. The simulated master file can then be compared manually to the master report. This shortcut can reduce program coding, testing, debugging time, and tape or disk usage. The manual comparison of the two reports, however, is a laborious task, the difficulty of which varies in relation to the number of records on the master.

Posting programs are suitable for simulation, but a programmatic comparison program is needed to match the simulated file to the production file. The comparison program should also create an exception report, which summarizes factors that match and lists the details of the records that do not match. The simulation of a large posting program however, could be very costly and tedious.

Simulating a Single Program Function: Certain programs within an application can perform many different functions in a single execution. Because it may be too difficult to simulate the entire program, the most significant, such as interest accrual, should be simulated. The simulation program is coded to duplicate the single function using the same input and producing comparable output, which can be analyzed manually or programmatically.

Simulating a Critical Report: Control and exception reports can be simulated to test their validity. Testing their validity is an important aspect of the application audit because management and operations personnel rely on these reports to make decisions and to prove the accuracy of processing.

The simulation technique can be used to detect data manipulation or erroneous coding by testing calculations or codes that are automatically activated.

System Documentation Review: The objective of this review is to obtain sufficient information to prepare the specifications for the parallel simulation program. The system flowchart identifies the 1) location of the program within overall processing, 2) the input files used, and 3) the output files and reports generated. Program narratives provide the specifications of the program to be simulated, the transactions that are automatically generated, and the conditions under which they are generated. Report narratives explain the fields printed on reports, the purpose of the reports, and any special processing results printed. Job control language provides a list of the processing steps in the live job stream in which the chosen program is executed. The auditor should also obtain a copy of the source program listing and discuss the routines that are to be simulated with the application programmer. This source program listing should be used only as a reference and should not be duplicated in the parallel simulation program. It should be coded based on the auditor's understanding of the application's processing logic. If the application program's logic is duplicated, the simulation program will not provide an independent test.

Parallel Simulation Program Development: The auditor must first develop functional specifications, which should be refined until they can be easily translated into source program coding. The specifications should include the fields that will be extracted from the input or master files, the formula to calculate each field, the fields to be printed on reports or files, and the matching scheme of any comparison program.

To illustrate the development of a parallel simulation program, consider a simulation of accrued interest receivable on securities held for investment. The amount of interest due is the result of the bond coupon rate multiplied by the par value of the bonds held. The coupon rate and the par value must be extracted to prove the correct values of these fields. The amount due must be calculated through the use of the par value and the coupon rate.

Interest receivable on the securities can be calculated monthly, quarterly, semi-annually, and at maturity. The simulation program must be designed with the flexibility to handle all interest periods. If these conditions are not provided for in the functional specifications, the simulation program will produce incomplete and inaccurate results. Simulations should be designed to cover all possible conditions, so that the auditor does not have to rely on manual testing to achieve complete audit coverage. After the functional specifications are completed, a flowchart of the simulation program logic should be prepared.

Program Testing: The simulation program must be sufficiently tested to ensure the inclusion of all possible conditions that can occur on the live file. This can be done by preparing a checklist of conditions that may occur during live processing and using a file from a prior period. As the output is reviewed, each condition is checked off to ensure that it is accounted for.

Output Analysis: This involves evaluating the processing results and researching any exceptions. The output of the simulation audit test can be a report comparing the actual field values on the application file to the simulated results. These values can be compared manually or by using a comparison program, which can be coded to flag any unacceptable records.

The choice of output analysis method depends on the simulation alternative selection. The auditor can take any of the following approaches to output analysis:

- Print the simulated results of each record and manually compare it to a similar report generated by the live application. The number of records examined affects the amount of time needed to compare output results. Although this method is the easiest output format to prepare programmatically, the manual analysis can be extremely tedious and time consuming.

- Print the extracted and the simulated information for each record. This approach allows the reviewer to scan the file information and the calculated results together. This method is significantly less tedious than preparing two separate reports, permits quicker isolation of any differences, and increases the auditor's confidence in the results.

- Print extracted information, simulated information, and diagnostic messages. The diagnostic message should only be printed if a difference exists between the extracted and simulated information of certain key fields. This method requires a programmatic comparison of the key fields and internal coding to generate the diagnostic message. The fields can be easily subtracted, with the difference loaded into a work field and printed with the diagnostic line. The output reviewer can examine each record or scan the report for the diagnostic message, and then review only the exceptions.

- Print simulated results to a file so that live and simulated master files can be compared, and an exception report generated. The creation of a simulated file may not be required for every simulation; however, if the purpose of the simulation is to test live file contents, creating a simulated file is absolutely necessary.

In any simulation or other automated audit approach, it is necessary to generate a file foot, which is an accumulated dollar control total of the primary control field within each record, and an item count of the number of records on the file. This dollar control field could be the outstanding balance on an accounts receivable file or the current balance on a checking account file. This field is reconciled to the independent general ledger control total for that day. This reconcilement is performed to prove that all records on the file were processed by the simulation.

Evaluation of Results: The auditor's final task is to research any exceptions to find the cause for the difference. All exceptions should be resolved and documented using normal audit procedures.

3.5.8.1 COST BENEFIT

The greater the coverage of an audit procedure, the greater the benefit derived, making it easier to justify high costs. The cost of the approach increases with the complexity of the coding necessary to simulate a program. If hardware and personnel costs exceed the potential loss, the auditor should consider an alternative technique.

Simulation, however, can provide 100 percent verification of internal program calculations and, therefore, can be the only way to detect some errors or a defalcation. A simulation program can also be used on a surprise basis, which might be the advantage needed to detect a fraudulent program that might not be uncovered by manual testing.

Simulation can also be used to test the effect of certain maintenance changes. A program that contains automatic internal calculations or generated transactions runs a higher risk of loss, because it is just as easy to insert a code that generates a valid transaction as it is to insert a code that generates an invalid transaction. Internally generated transactions occur as a result of certain conditions. All possible conditions were probably not a part of the system test date upon installation. A simulation program may be the only way to test these types of calculations effectively. A simulation program can also effectively test for program alterations of data such as debit/credit switches from one account to another.

Although the initial costs of developing a simulation program can be high, the technique can be used repeatedly with low recurring costs. This characteristic makes parallel simulation extremely valuable for applications that process high dollar volumes of transactions or have a high exposure to loss.

3.5.8.2   LIMITATIONS

The major limitation to parallel simulation is the front-end development cost. However, once the program is coded, it can be used repeatedly in subsequent years. The ongoing costs include maintenance of the simulation program for production file layout logic changes.

3.5.9   Extended Records

The extended record technique gathers all the data elements used during the entire job stream and saves them on a tape or disk file for audit extraction and examination.

3.5.9.1   EXPLANATION OF TECHNIQUE

This technique is used to collect all data used during on-line or batch processing to bring a transaction or account to its finished end product. During transaction processing, various programs will complete various tasks on each transaction record. Work fields may be used to store the results of intermediate calculations, which are used by a program module executed later in the job stream. Although the auditor may have access to the input and the end result of the processing, he or she does not have any substantive evidence to validate the intermediate steps.

The extended record technique can be compared to manual testing of transactions, in which information about the transaction must be gathered from two or three separate areas to validate the accuracy of the final end product. The extended records technique brings all of these data elements together in one place, streamlining the data collection process for the auditor.

3.5.9.2 PROCEDURES FOR EXTENDED RECORD DEVELOPMENT AND EXECUTION

The extended record programming code is prepared by programming personnel based on specifications provided by the auditor. Because these routines are inserted in application programs, the S&P programmer must prepare the code. A triggering mechanism, such as the use of parameter cards or one-byte flags entered via an on-line terminal must be devised. The auditor can insert these triggers at any time to execute the extended record collection program code.

The collected data can then be saved on a tape or disk file, or printed on a hard copy report for physical verification by the auditor. If the data is stored on magnetic media, an audit software package can be used to improve reporting or to perform the analysis.

To insert the program code within the application program, the auditor must follow the SDLC or program change procedures established within the organization. Because of control considerations, the auditor must rely on S&P to insert the extended record program code in the application program. The ideal time to create this program code is during system development, but it can be implemented via program change procedures.

To develop the routines, the auditor must analyze the job stream to determine the appropriate point for the program code. The auditor must then decide what pieces of data are to be collected and how the collection routine should be activated. After the program code is inserted, the auditor must test the routine extensively, making certain that the data collection routine does not interfere with normal production processing. Once the collection routine is found to work properly, the auditor can instruct the programmer to enter the program into production.

During ongoing use of the extended record technique, the auditor must determine the time span for execution. Once the data is obtained, the auditor must analyze it to determine whether the actual results of processing are accurate. The purpose of the collection of this data is to recalculate a critical field (or fields) used for financial statement purposes or for internal control. An example of an extended record's use may be an accounts payable payment system wherein an internal file of vendor names and other codes that control pricing may be used to calculate the payment amount. Although the vendor could be validated through procedures external to the computer system, special codes, flags, or pricing tables may not be readily available or may only be accurate for the period in time in which the payment was calculated.

3.5.9.3 COST BENEFIT AND LIMITATIONS

Like other CAATs previously discussed, the major limitation of the extended record technique is design, programming, and implementation into the application system. Some audit independence is sacrificed by this use of the systems and programming staff, but program validation procedures can be used to compensate for this compromise.

Another potential drawback is that an extensive amount of data could be collected, requiring significant audit time to validate the results. The auditor must be very careful in executing the extended record collector so that excessive data is not collected and excessive computer time is not consumed.

The extended record technique is most beneficial for high dollar applications whose transactions utilize numerous internal codes, flags, and tables to calculate results.

3.5.10 The Snapshot, Buffer Dump, and Core Dump Techniques

The snapshot technique is used daily by systems and application programmers to assist in debugging computer processing problems. The technique is called "snapshot" because a utility program is used to take a picture of memory at a specific point in time. Another type of snapshot is known as the "buffer dump," which prints all data in the input buffer of a program at a particular point in time. The snapshot of the computer memory is known as a "core dump." All major computer vendors can provide utilities that perform the core dump and buffer dump, and most of them have techniques for easy triggering of the utility.

Many operating systems contain a utility that automatically activates a core dump when a program fails or abnormally ends. Most of the audit software packages automatically perform buffer dumps when an error has occurred during processing. These errors may not be fatal in terms of ending the program when the error occurs. One example of a nonfatal error is the performance of a numeric function or calculation on an alpha field. This type of error will force a buffer dump.

The snapshot technique has become largely used for debugging computer program problems.

3.5.10.1 PROCEDURES FOR DEVELOPMENT AND EXECUTION OF SNAPSHOT TECHNIQUES

The conventional output of a core or buffer dump is in hexadecimal on hard copy. To be useful for extensive audit purposes, the snapshot data could be written into a tape or disk file and then read with an audit software program for printing on hard copy in conventional alpha numeric format.

The auditor must: 1) determine how the snapshot will be triggered, 2) code and insert these triggering mechanisms into the application programs, and 3) program an audit software program to read the created files.

The most critical element of this technique is that of determining where and when the snapshot should be executed. A good snapshot point is between programs within a multiple-step job stream. Each program within the job stream performs a different function and creates a different effect. The auditor can activate the snapshot as the data leaves each program, providing a picture of the progress of the data as it progresses through the entire job stream.

The auditor must determine the triggering mechanism while bearing in mind that printing all records would consume a great deal of computer resources. One technique is the use of one-byte flags that can be inserted in the transaction data. The application programs will need to have a program code inserted that triggers and executes the snapshot when the flag is encountered.

A packaged audit software program can be used to read the snapshot files and produce a readable hard copy report. Care should be taken in designing the report, so that the data is presented in the most efficient format for audit use.

3.5.10.2 SNAPSHOT TECHNIQUE COST BENEFIT

The major cost of the snapshot technique is in researching processing to determine the best location for the snapshot triggers. Obviously, the systems and programming staff will be used to integrate the snapshot code into application programs.

On an ongoing basis, the execution costs are minimal. However, modifications to application programs must be reviewed after the snapshots are installed to determine that its usage has not been detrimentally affected. The major benefit of snapshots is the possibility for repeated use of the technique.

3.5.10.3 SNAPSHOT TECHNIQUE LIMITATIONS

This technique requires detailed review of processing. Interpretation of the data requires an auditor with a good understanding of the application processing so that the use of the data elements retrieved can be understood. Because the trigger code is inserted by S&P staff, some independence is sacrificed. To ensure proper operation, maintenance changes to the programs containing the triggers must be reviewed.

3.5.11 Tracing

This is an automated technique borrowed from a traditional audit approach. Most auditors trace financial transactions through various activities and functions to determine that they were performed properly. The purpose of tracing is to print out the program code that was executed during processing. Tracing is normally executed by specifying a parameter in the programming language compilation routine. Tracing permits the auditor to examine program codes executed in sequential order to verify compliance with policies and procedures. Most major hardware vendors provide a tracing utility for use with the high-level languages.

3.5.11.1 PROCEDURES FOR DEVELOPMENT AND EXECUTION OF TRACING

The development of the tracing technique is relatively simple, but it can be expensive. The application program must have the parameter set to execute the trace during processing. This may require that the programs be recompiled with the parameter specified. The auditor will need to interface with the systems or applications programmers to determine how the trace program works.

A typical trace function requires significant computer processing time. Once the program is compiled and linked with the trace option, it will continue to trace until it is recompiled. Therefore, it is advisable to execute these programs only in a test environment, and not in production.

When the hard copy output of the trace is available, the auditor can examine it line by line and determine whether the processing is appropriate. Program documentation and user information can be reviewed to determine how the particular parts of the program should function.

3.5.11.2 COST BENEFITS OF TRACING

The major cost is the recompilation and use of Central Processing Unit (CPU) time to execute the program. Audit review of the tracing output requires a working knowledge of the programming language. The auditor's review of the program code, although not requiring an extensive effort, will take time to understand in terms of the trace and the inner relationships of the program code lines. The more experience that the auditor has with the language, the quicker his review.

3.5.11.3 TRACING'S LIMITATIONS

The major drawback to tracing is the heavy consumption of computer resources. Because, however, tracing is used only for a short time, the cost is easily justified. When the programs are recompiled from the source library, however, there must be a means to prove that the compiled version that the auditor is testing is the same as the compiled version of the production program. If the organization lacks control over the updating or migration of the source program to the production library, then it is difficult or impossible to validate whether the program the auditor is testing is the same as the production version. Because the output is a listing of high-level language code statements, the auditor who reviews it must have sufficient training and experience to understand the components of the language.

3.5.12 Tagging

This technique involves the identification of a transaction or account with a one-byte flag to distinguish it from other accounts. The tagging is similar to selecting transactions for audit testing. Its purpose is to identify a transaction, account, or record for later review by the auditor.

3.5.12.1 PROCEDURES FOR DEVELOPMENT AND EXECUTION OF TAGGING

The technique requires the preparation of program code that turns on the one-byte flag based on some event.

An example best explains tagging's use. For instance, deposit accounts in a bank are defined as dormant when the account has had no activity for an extended period of time, such as five or seven years. The application system flags these accounts as dormant. If the accounts remain dormant for a predetermined length of time, usually specified by state law, the funds in the account must be escheated to the state. However, the accounts can be reactivated by a deposit or withdrawal. Unfortunately, dormant accounts are good targets for an embezzler, because the customer is not there to verify them. It is desirable to be able to examine dormant accounts if they are reactivated, to validate that they were, indeed, reactivated by the customer.

The tagging process takes place when the dormant flag is turned off by reactivation of the account because of a deposit or withdrawal. The tagging program code triggers a one-byte flag that stays on until turned off by the audit department. When this flag in the "on" position as stored on the master file, an audit software confirmation program can extract the accounts and print confirmations, for mailing to the customers. Positive confirmations are used and each confirmation is followed up even if there is no customer response after the sending of a second request. Alternative procedures must be performed to determine that the customer, and not some unauthorized person, is using the account. After the audit testing is completed, the audit flag is turned off.

3.5.12.2   COST BENEFIT OF TAGGING

The implementation costs of tagging consist of the programming time required to write the code that triggers the flag, as well as the code needed to turn off the flag. The ongoing costs consist of the preparation of an audit software confirmation program and staff time to follow up on the confirmations. All of these costs, both implementation and ongoing, are very modest, especially when measured against the benefit of this excellent fraud detection technique. Very few fraud detection techniques are as efficient and inexpensive as, for example, the dormant account tagging technique.

The tagging technique can be utilized in many other scenarios, bounded only by the auditor's imagination. The cost and benefit vary with the complexity of the program code needed to turn on and turn off the flag.

3.5.12.3 LIMITATIONS OF TAGGING

The major drawback of this technique is the need for reliance on S&P programmers to code, and implement the tagging function and the transaction needed to turn the tagging off. If they know how the audit technique works, they could circumvent it.

3.5.13 Job Accounting Utilities

Mainframe vendors provide job accounting utility programs that collect and record data about system and job-related activities. These utilities have components that work within the operating system. The components pass information to the main utility program, creating records on tape or disk for later usage. The typical packages provide exit points for the insertion of user routines that monitor jobs and job steps and create additional accounting data. Each record is generally assigned a number to identify the record as to the type of data collected.

Although the types of records generated vary among vendors, the major types are records for accounting, data set activity, disk and tape volumes, and system data.

3.5.13.1 PROCEDURES FOR DEVELOPMENT AND EXECUTION OF JOB ACCOUNTING UTILITIES

Accounting records pertain to computer resources used by the operating system, including programming terminal sign-on and sign-off, job step and job termination, output writing, and purge or delete operations.

Data set activity records are created when data sets are created, updated, scratched, or renamed. Other records are created for the cataloging, opening, closing, deleting, or renaming of disk files or data sets. Separate records are created for input, output, data set scratching activities, and file renaming activities.

Volume records pertain to direct access storage devices and tapes. System records can indicate when accounting data has been erased, statistics on CPU activity, and information regarding the cold start or initial program load (IPL) of the mainframe. Particular attention should be paid to the cold start information because the accounting utility itself, or the records it will generate, are initialized at mainframe system startup.

The job accounting utilities can provide an excellent audit trail for all mainframe activity, provided the records needed by the auditor are generated. The accounting utility data can be used to evaluate the adequacy of access controls by revealing unauthorized access to data sets and programs. The auditor can determine if files or data sets have been renamed during application processing. This is important, because a volume data file or program file can be substituted during processing for a live production file.

The auditor can use the data to evaluate computer operations and the scheduling of application runs. The accounting data will provide the time of day when an application was processed, which can be compared to the run schedule for compliance. Program failures can indicate potential problems with applications. The accounting records will indicate what programs failed and when they failed. These program failures can be traced to a log report and the follow-up by operations and other data processing personnel can be examined.

Records are also created about errors occurring in the volume table of contents or disk file directories. Using this data, the auditor can inquire as to the research and resolution procedures completed by S&P personnel. Statistics are also recorded about tape read-and-write errors that indicate the possibility of faulty tapes.

The systems statistics pertain to CPU usage. Of particular interest is the CPU wait time that indicates that the CPU is waiting for work. Extended CPU wait time can be caused by faulty programs, poor scheduling, or on-line programming problems. The auditor should first determine if the systems software group is monitoring this data and utilizing it for some useful purpose to improve system usage and productivity.

Accounting utilities can also be used to detect application program problems by examining program failure or abnormal completion codes. The auditor should use this data to determine if S&P personnel followed up to determine the cause of the failure and whether or not it was fixed or just patched to get it running again. Excessive program failures may indicate the need for rewriting or modifying the programs.

The job accounting utilities typically do not include a report writer, forcing the auditor to rely on COBOL programs or audit software to manipulate the job accounting utility data records. The auditor needs only to obtain the record layouts from systems software personnel and code a simple program to print the data in a usable format.

3.5.13.2 COST BENEFITS OF JOB ACCOUNTING UTILITIES

In most installations, the accounting utility runs as part of production, so the auditor's use of the data is not a special use that will increase cost. Only a moderate level of data processing experience is needed to understand the meaning of the created records. Audit experience can be developed over time through usage of the data. The more experienced the auditor becomes with the meaning of the records and audit use of the information, the more effective and less time consuming the audit effort will be.

3.5.13.3 JOB ACCOUNTING UTILITY LIMITATIONS

The job accounting utility and the records it creates are initialized at initial program load. The utility can be turned off, or record generation can be inhibited, any time that a cold start of the system is performed. Because auditors typically deal with past history, the potential exists that the data needed by the auditor for a particular time may not be available because the accounting package was either turned off or needed records were not created.

Therefore, a control is needed to ensure that the accounting utility is running all the time or at least during the periods of time that the auditor is interested in.

3.5.14   Program Code Comparison

Changes to production programs are of particular interest to auditors because they increase the risk of processing errors and omissions and provide an opportunity for fraud. Program code comparison permits the auditor to compare two versions of a program and isolate the different lines of code. This technique tells the auditor that the program has been changed, lists the lines of code that are different, and gives the auditor the opportunity to review all code that was changed.

3.5.14.1   PROCEDURES FOR DEVELOPMENT AND EXECUTION OF PROGRAM CODE COMPARISON

The first step in developing a program code comparison is to save the program or programs on tape that the auditor is concerned with. This version of the program is called the benchmark version. A copy of the program from production, taken at a later date, can be compared to the benchmark version. If there were no program maintenance changes during the time lapse between the benchmark and the current version, then both programs should match identically. If S&P personnel stated that there were no changes and differences are found, then the auditor is confronted with the potential of unauthorized maintenance changes.

If changes have been made during the time between the creation of the benchmark and the current version, the changed code will be highlighted on the output of the program code comparison program. These changed lines of code can be reviewed for propriety and compared to the functional specifications of the change request to determine whether the new program code appropriately accomplishes the functional specifications. If all code that was changed is appropriate and matches the functional specifications, the current copy of the program or programs becomes the new benchmark version.

3.5.14.2 PROGRAM CODE COMPARISON COST BENEFITS

Program code comparison programs are relatively inexpensive and are sometimes provided with the package of other utilities by the operating system vendor. The major cost is the auditor's time spent reviewing the differences in the program code, tracing them to program change authorizations, and comparing them to functional specifications.

3.5.14.3 PROGRAM CODE COMPARISON LIMITATIONS

Proper review of program code requires experience and knowledge of the high-level languages that are used, not a universal attribute. Also, the extent of control over the migration of the source program to the production object library may be limited. The program code comparison utility works only against the source code, but the production object version is in machine language. If the control over the migration from source to object is weak or nonexistent, there is no guarantee that the source programs being compared are the actual source version that was compiled and linked to the production object library. The absence of this control reduces the effectiveness of the source code comparison as an audit test.

NOTES

1. Mair W.C., Wood D.R., Davis K.W., *Computer Control & Audit,* Deloitte & Touche, Wilton, CT, 1978, p. 11. Reprinted with permission of Deloitte & Touche.

2. Mullen, J.B., *Standards for Using Audit Software.* Adapted from *EDP Auditing* (New York: Auerbach Publishers). © 1988, Warren, Gorham & Lamont, Inc. Used with permission.

3. Mullen, J.B., *Defining a Base Case System Evaluation.* Adapted from *EDP Auditing* (New York: Auerbach Publishers). © 1979, Warren, Gorham & Lamont, Inc. Used with permission.

4. Mullen, J.B. *Parallel Simulation.* Adapted from *EDP Auditing* (New York: Auerbach Publishers). © 1980, Warren, Gorham & Lamont, Inc. Used with permission.

The EDP
Audit Group

4.1   INTRODUCTION

This chapter will specifically focus on the EDP audit group whose job it is to execute the theory discussed in previous chapters. Such issues are covered as audit responsibilities, organizational structure, EDP audit staff positions, and their specific duties, and how to develop an EDP auditing plan.

4.2   EDP AUDIT RESPONSIBILITIES

Internal EDP audit groups provide services to, and are responsible for, five areas:

- Audit software support,
- Supporting the financial audit staff,
- Audits of environmental data processing areas,
- Audits of application systems, and
- System development reviews.

4.2.1   Audit Software Support

Audit software support involves providing computer-generated reports for use by the financial and EDP audit groups through the use of generalized audit software, report generator, or other programming language. In addition, the EDP audit group provides technical assistance in use of CAATs, which are executed by the financial audit staff. This would include design and implementation of the CAATs through interface with S&P.

Both the EDP and financial audit staffs require computer-generated information to complete their audits. The auditors who perform the programming and execution tasks of audit software support have typically been EDP auditors. Of course, this depends on audit department philosophy. Some organizations train financial and EDP auditors to use generalized audit software because it is "user-friendly." As microcomputer usage increases, more financial auditors will learn how to use the software functions provided by them. However, programming in high-level languages, such as COBOL, is still left to the EDP auditors because of the extensive training and experience needed to become, and remain, proficient in their use.

EDP audits that need audit software support will have an EDP auditor assigned to the job to perform all programming tasks.

4.2.2 Supporting the Financial Audit Staff

The EDP audit staff can support the financial audit staff by preparing audit software programs and providing technical assistance during audits, like a consultant. Audit software programs generate independent computer reports that the financial staff can use to complete their audits. Audit-software-generated reports are considered independent because they are designed, coded, tested, and executed under the auditor's control. These reports can be as simple as trial balances or transactions journals or as complex as simulation or accumulated data collection programs.

Financial audits use tracing techniques on financial transactions to substantiate the accuracy of processing. If independent computer reports are used, the accuracy of computer processing is also tested, "around the computer." Testing "through the computer" is best, but independent reports are better than nothing. Use of application-generated reports leaves the financial auditor at the mercy of application processing accuracy; the auditor is forced to assume that application processing is accurate.

Some financial transactions are performed within the computer without creating an audit trail that includes all the data elements used by the application to complete the computation, such as interest payable or receivable. Simulation programs are ideal to test these types of internal calculations. In some cases, the financial auditor can test these with a calculator and estimates of key data elements. The audit budget, however, would only permit the testing of a sample of transactions, whereas simulation would permit testing of all transactions.

Accumulated data collection programs bring multiple data elements together in one report that ordinarily are printed on multiple application reports. Financial auditors normally must check multiple reports to verify audit trail existence or execution of internal controls. In some cases, these special purpose reports can significantly reduce audit time by printing all the data in one place. In another example, exceptions or control weaknesses may be discovered that create data errors or omissions on computer files. Management would certainly want to know the number or dollar impact of these errors. The EDP auditor can create programs that scan all file records for specific errors or omissions. This permits the financial auditor to examine all of the items in the population and eliminate costly manual look-up of transactions or accounts.

Consider an automated billing system for 10,000 accounts that generates monthly and quarterly bills of varying amounts based on fields set up in the system by billing managers. Assume that execution of procedures for preparing and entering the billing setups had deteriorated, resulting in accounts that were not being billed for services rendered. To complicate matters, the information needed to calculate the bills is stored in two separate computer files and the paper source documents are located in five different places. Reviewing 10,000 accounts under these circumstances would be a monumental task requiring significant labor. An audit software program could be coded to scan all records on both files to find the accounts missing billing set-ups; all accounts that have not been billed; and with additional input, calculate the lost revenue. The programming time would be dramatically less than the manual research time. An impact assessment could be completed in a matter of weeks with a handful of people instead of several months with an army. The use of audit software is covered in Chapter 5.

The EDP audit staff can also work on a consultant basis to the financial audit staff by answering questions about specific application controls that compensate for weaknesses in the manual system. For example, application programs can be programmed to edit key data fields instead of using manual verification by clerks prior to input. The financial auditor, not knowing about the programmatic edits, would properly cite the absence of clerical verification as a control weakness. Review of the program or documentation by the EDP auditor could provide an independent answer that clears this exception, saving valuable audit research time. Weaknesses in application controls, however, may require implementation of a manual compensating control until the computer program can be modified. Coordination between the financial and EDP auditors can identify and solve these types of problems. In summary, the EDP auditor can provide valuable assistance to the financial auditor as a skilled technician and consultant. The financial auditors should use the EDP audit for training, problem solving, risk identification, application controls, and automated audit techniques.

4.2.3 Audits of Environmental Data Processing Areas

The data processing operating environment includes:

- Systems software programming,
- On-line systems,
- Data base administration,
- Data center,
- Tape and disk library,
- Systems and programming,
- Information security, and
- Application change control.

These areas form the "operating environment" in which all computer applications run. Adequate and effective internal controls are vital in the environmental areas because they affect all application processing. Control weaknesses detrimentally affect all application processing regardless of the quality of application controls. The environmental areas are to the applications what the engine is to a car.

4.2.4   Audits of Application Systems

The computer applications are groups of programs that process the company's daily transactions. They are also referred to as subsystems in this book. These programs accept all the daily transactions, perform edit routines, and post the transactions to master and history and files. The applications produce computer records—audit trails—that summarize all processing. The reports are used for control and management information.

4.2.5   System Development Reviews

The system development reviews involve participation in the project development teams and include two functions: 1) ongoing review of the controls being implemented within the computer system that is being designed, and 2) monitoring and evaluating the administrative project controls over the progress of the project. System development projects are divided into major phases with certain critical activities being completed within each phase. The auditor has specific responsibilities in each phase that vary depending on the objective of the phase and the audit objectives and the technical expertise of the EDP auditor.

4.3   ORGANIZATIONAL STRUCTURE

The structure of the EDP auditing section depends upon audit philosophy, the size of the company, and the size of the EDP audit staff. The EDP audit group has traditionally been a separate section of the audit department because of the technical specialization required. The EDP audit resources are then used by the financial audit staff on a consulting basis under the supervision of the EDP audit supervisor and manager. This organizational structure makes the EDP audit function a staff function.

Some companies have organized EDP audit as a line function[1] creating audit functions for major business units of their companies. An EDP auditor(s) is assigned on a functional and administrative reporting basis to the audit group for a specific business function. This makes EDP auditing a line function, but it is also kin to a combined or integrated audit team approach. This structure forces the audit management team to be proficient in EDP and EDP audit to supervise adequately and approve the EDP audit work.

Organizing EDP audit as a staff function is the most prevalent organizational structure because, traditionally, data processing has been centralized, and the technical expertise and training needed for the EDP audit group makes it easier to control and accomplish training and auditing tasks.

In the future, as data processing decentralizes with growth of the use of microcomputers, there will be pressure on this staff alignment of the EDP audit function. The financial or business audit groups will need more training and experience in micro-computer concepts and processing controls.

The staff organizational structure creates audit reporting problems. The general auditor becomes the focal point of de-tailed audit information, creating additional risk in the detection of control weaknesses.

The line organizational structure places the focal point at the in-charge auditor level. The EDP auditor in the line organization will work on the audits assigned to his audit manager. This may not provide the exposure the EDP auditor desires, contributing to turnover. Audit management could compensate for this by rotating the EDP auditors among the various audit managers to provide exposure to more systems.

4.3.1 The Integrated Audit Approach[2]

The integrated audit approach places the focal point at the staff auditor level where the complete transaction flow, manual and automated, is reviewed. Because technical expertise is required to understand special business activities, audit departments are of-ten designed around an organization's major business units. Both line and staff structures separate the EDP audit and financial audit of the business unit because of the technical expertise required to perform EDP audits. This approach requires the financial auditor and EDP auditor to be aware of the results of both audit efforts. Decentralized processing with microcomputers will place more pressure on the auditor for coordination of audits.

A long-range solution is to train all auditors in both audit disciplines and develop an approach that permits total system review. As financial auditors review the total system, they gain experience in dealing with the interface between the application processing and the manual environments evolving into more experienced systems auditors.

Experience with integrated audits permits EDP auditors to specialize in environment and development audits. Environmental auditors are technical specialists who concentrate on audits of on-line systems, systems software, and data base administration. They are also best suited to audit systems under development. Training costs are minimized because expensive technical training is limited to a small group of people.

There are two ways to accomplish integration. The first is the one-team audit, which merges the audits of EDP and non-data-processing systems into one overall review, eliminating the redundancies in completing the preliminary survey, internal control questionnaire, compliance testing, and administrative duties. The objective of integrated staffing is to produce a balance of EDP and financial audit expertise that matches the system's sophistication and to eliminate redundant management, specifically at the in-charge, supervisory, and managerial levels. The approach requires one manager, one supervisor, and one in-charge, with an appropriate mix of EDP and financial auditors to review a given area.

The second way to accomplish integration is to combine audits through total integration, in which the staff auditors are trained in both disciplines; there is no distinction between EDP and financial auditors, and only one audit program is used. Total integration is the next logical step after the successful use of the one-team approach. The EDP auditors concentrate on the environmental and system development areas and development of CAATs. By either means, the integrated audit approach:

- Produces an opinion of the total control environment;
- Reduces job staffing requirements;
- Reduces the time needed to audit a system;
- Evaluates the manual system flow as it relates to computer processing;
- Reduces scheduling and interface problems of two separate approaches;
- Lowers the recognition and resolution focal point of weaknesses in the total system;
- Simplifies supervision;
- Increases education of the user and programming personnel regarding the total system;
- Improves career path options for auditors.

4.4 EDP AUDIT STAFF POSITIONS

The most difficult task in maintaining an EDP audit staff is recruiting and retaining experienced personnel with acceptable salary requirements. College undergraduates seldom have sufficient education in both auditing and data processing. Therefore, companies must train most new employees in audit concepts, internal controls, and evaluation techniques.

There are two alternatives to developing EDP auditors: train a person with data processing background in auditing or train a person with an accounting background in data processing. Most colleges offer data processing and accounting curricula, but very few prepare graduates sufficiently to permit a person to perform an internal control evaluation. The typical positions of an EDP audit group are described below.

EDP Audit Manager

The EDP audit manager, who reports to the general auditor, is the key to the success of the EDP audit group. He or she helps the general auditor ensure adequate control by developing EDP audit procedures and CAATs to improve audit efficiency. He or she serves as the focal point for training the audit staff in appropriate EDP concepts and controls, and EDP audit techniques. The EDP auditor's job duties, performed under the approval of the general auditor, are listed below.

The EDP Auditor

- Supervises the collection of risk evaluation information and completes the risk analysis model for all EDP areas, interpreting weights and scores to calculate priority of audit jobs;
- Prepares budget estimates for EDP audits and estimates target starting months;
- Supervises preparation of the annual audit program, including control evaluation techniques, audit testing techniques; designs and develops CAATs.
- Manages execution of EDP audits, ensuring adequate audit scope, proper control evaluation, proper execution of test procedures, adequate documentation of work performed, proper presentation of findings, preparation of the audit report, evaluation of the adequacy of auditee response to the audit report—performs general review of audit workpapers as needed;
- Gives specific assignments to staff based on input from the EDP audit supervisor; monitors progress of the staff's completion of assignments and staff compliance with time budget and target dates;
- Recommends changes in control practices; keeps informed of events that have EDP impact and new services and products.
- Reviews complicated audit software programs, and does the complicated programming;
- Performs performance evaluations of EDP audit personnel and assists in preparation and maintenance of the salary administration program.
- Selects, interviews, and evaluates applicants.

Skills Needed for Position

- Advanced knowledge and understanding of EDP concepts.
- High degree of technical expertise in EDP audit concepts and techniques and mastery of audit software package programming.
- Intermediate to advanced level of understanding of industry concepts.
- Intermediate level of technical knowledge of business unit operations.
- Advanced level of technical knowledge and understanding of financial audit concepts.
- High intermediate to advanced level of knowledge and understanding in organizing, planning, and supervising audit functions.
- Intermediate to high level of expertise in interpersonal skills.
- High level of expertise in written and verbal communication.
- Intermediate to advanced level of expertise in time management.

The audit manager should have at least four years of EDP auditing experience, two to three years of audit supervisory experience as an in-charge or supervisor, a degree in accounting or computer science, and appropriate professional certification or an advanced degree.

EDP Audit Supervisor

The EDP audit supervisor works closely with the EDP audit manager, overseeing daily staff activities, participating in post-audit work, and managing the audit programming function. This auditor should have three years of EDP auditing experience and a degree in accounting or computer science. The supervisor should be experienced in application and environmental audits and audit software programming.

Job Duties of the EDP Audit Supervisor

- Collects risk evaluation information and assists in preparation of the risk analysis model for all EDP areas;
- Assists in preparation of budget estimates for EDP audits through evaluation of hours charged for individual audit tasks;
- Prepares the annual audit program, including control evaluation techniques and audit testing techniques and assists in the design and implementation of CAATs.
- Monitors and supports personnel, executing audit tasks that ensure the audit staff satisfies the audit scope, properly evaluates internal control, properly executes test procedures, adequately documents the work performed, and accurately presents findings.
- Assists the manager in preparation of the audit report and evaluation of the adequacy of auditee response to the audit report;
- Performs a detailed or general review of audit workpapers as needed;
- Decides which staff members would be the best for the specific assignment;
- Monitors progress of the staff's completion of assignments;
- Assists in the evaluation of changes in control practices;
- Keeps informed of new services and products and of events with an EDP impact;
- Reviews audit software programs prepared by staff and assists in complicated programming;
- Provides input to the manager for performance evaluations of EDP audit personnel;
- Assists in the selection of, and interviews and evaluates, applicants; and
- Performs on-the-job training of staff auditors, and prepares and conducts formal training sessions for all auditors.

Skills Needed by the EDP Audit Supervisor

- Intermediate knowledge and understanding of EDP concepts;

- Intermediate degree of technical expertise in EDP audit concepts and techniques;

- Mastery of audit software package programming;

- Intermediate level of technical knowledge, and understanding of industry concepts;

- Intermediate level of technical knowledge of business unit operations;

- Intermediate to advanced level of technical knowledge and understanding of financial audit concepts;

- Intermediate to high intermediate level of knowledge and understanding in organizing, planning, and supervising audit functions;

- Intermediate level of expertise in interpersonal skills;

- Intermediate level of expertise in written and verbal communication; and

- Intermediate level of expertise in time management.

Audit Programmer

Some EDP audit staffs need someone for this job when full-time programming is required for implementation and development of an audit software package. EDP audit groups that must rely on a high-level language for audit software support may need several people in this job. Audit programmer positions should be filled by people with computer science or accounting degrees accompanied by technical school training in data processing. Associate arts degrees are also acceptable in this job. Because audit programmers work with the audit software packages, they should be able to review and understand any application program written by the programming department through experience with COBOL or Assembler.

Job Duties:

These include writing program codes to satisfy the design specifications supplied by the EDP audit manager or supervisor. In addition, the programmer should be able to design basic to intermediate level of complexity programs based on ideas provided by other auditors.

Skills:

Those required depend on the programming approach—audit software package or high-level language. The skills for using a high-level language are much greater, including significant college courses in programming languages and program design. An audit software package programmer should be able to function if he or she has 12 credits of EDP courses, including a high-level language.

Senior EDP Auditor

The person in this position conducts the execution of the application, environmental, microcomputer audit, or system development control review as an in-charge. The senior EDP auditor participates in these audits when another auditor is the in-charge.

Job Duties of the Senior EDP Auditor:

As an in-charge auditor:

- Assists the supervisor in development of the audit scope;
- Prepares audit testing tasks for approval by supervisor and manager and monitors and assists staff personnel in completing the audit tasks;
- Reviews staff-prepared workpapers, drafts the audit report cover letter, and reviews and edits report comments;
- Participates in the closing conference with auditee management;
- Provides input to supervisor and manager for staff performance evaluations;
- Designs, codes, and implements audit software programs;

- Performs on-the-job training for staff auditors;
- Assists in preparation of formal training courses;

Skills Needed by the Senior EDP Auditor:

- Basic to intermediate knowledge and understanding of EDP concepts;
- High basic to intermediate degree of technical expertise in EDP audit concepts and techniques, and an intermediate degree of expertise in audit software package programming;
- High basic to intermediate level of technical knowledge and understanding of industry concepts;
- Basic to intermediate level of technical knowledge of business unit operations;
- Intermediate level of technical knowledge and understanding of financial audit concepts;
- High basic to intermediate level of knowledge and understanding in organizing, planning, and supervising audit functions;
- Basic level of expertise in interpersonal skills;
- Basic level of expertise in written and verbal communication; and
- Training in time management.

The senior EDP auditor should have a minimum of two years EDP audit experience or its equivalent.

EDP Auditor II

This job is a transitory position between entry level staff and senior EDP auditor. The person in this position can conduct the execution of the application, environmental, microcomputer audits as an in-charge. The senior EDP auditor, however, would handle more complex assignments. As a participant in EDP audits, the senior EDP auditor would perform the normal audit functions of an EDP auditor II. The EDP auditor II also participates in audits, more so than the senior EDP auditor, when another auditor is the in-charge.

Job Duties of the EDP Auditor II:

As an in-charge auditor, the EDP auditor II will complete the same duties described under the in-charge section of the senior EDP auditor position.

As a participant in EDP audits, the EDP auditor II:

- Documents auditee activities;
- Identifies existing and nonexisting controls;
- Performs compliance testing of key controls and procedures;
- Performs substantive testing of financial transactions;
- Documents audit findings and control weaknesses;
- Writes audit report comments of findings and weaknesses identified;
- Assists in determining the adequacy of management response;
- Performs follow-up review and testing to validate management's corrective action; and
- Designs, codes, and implements audit software programs.

Skills:

- Basic to intermediate knowledge and understanding of EDP concepts;
- Basic to intermediate degree of technical expertise in EDP audit concepts and techniques and an intermediate degree of expertise in audit software package programming;
- High basic level of technical knowledge and understanding of industry concepts;
- Basic level of technical knowledge of business unit operations;

- Basic to intermediate level of technical knowledge and understanding of financial audit concepts;
- Basic level of knowledge and understanding in organizing, planning, and supervising audit functions;
- Basic level of expertise in interpersonal skills;
- Basic level of expertise in written and verbal communication; and
- Training in time management.

EDP Auditor I

This job is the entry level position. The person in this position can perform the application, environmental, and microcomputer audits under the direction of an in-charge.

Job Duties of the EDP Auditor I:

- Documents auditee activities;
- Identifies existing and non-existing controls;
- Performs compliance testing of key controls and procedures;
- Performs substantive testing of financial transactions;
- Documents audit findings and control weaknesses;
- Writes audit report comments of findings and weaknesses identified;
- Assists in determining the adequacy of management response;
- Performs follow-up review and testing to validate management's corrective action; and
- Designs, codes, and implements audit software programs.

Skills Needed by the EDP Auditor I:

- Entry level to basic knowledge and understanding of EDP concepts;

- Entry level to basic degree of technical expertise in EDP audit concepts and techniques and a basic degree of expertise in audit software package programming.
- Entry level to basic technical knowledge and understanding of industry concepts;
- Entry level to basic level of technical knowledge of business unit operations;
- Basic level of technical knowledge and understanding of financial audit concepts; and
- Entry level expertise in written and verbal communication.

4.4.1   Audit Staff Size

No one has developed a scientific formula for estimating the number of EDP auditors needed; there is much debate on this subject. The best available method is to estimate the number of hours required to complete the audit and support work and then compare the estimate to the available net hours of the total EDP audit staff. If the total hours of work exceeds the available net hours, additional staff may be required.

During new development of an EDP audit staff, additional audit programmers may be needed to support the financial audit function. Experience has shown that in the early stages of audit software development, additional programmers are needed to initiate the programming function quickly. Similarly, when major applications are being replaced, a larger audit staff is recommended.

4.4.2   Staff Training

Audit management should provide internal and external training for audit staff members, continuing their education to keep them current and to bring entry level personnel up to speed in order to adequately perform the work. The auditor, however, must not take this training for granted. Study on one's own can dramatically accelerate the learning curve and improve the auditor's chances for promotion. The person who takes it upon himself to study as much as possible will advance more quickly than those who wish to be spoon fed.

4.4.2.1 TRAINING NEEDS ASSESSMENT

The EDP audit training program depends on the EDP environment, the skill of the existing staff, budget dollars available, internal training expertise, external course availability, and the time available to bring people up to speed.

EDP Environment Assessment

The quantity and quality of EDP audit expertise needed depends on the sophistication of the EDP operating environment. The higher the sophistication, the greater the technical skill needed. Moreover, the organization that uses rare or less prevalent hardware and software vendors will have special training needs because of the lack of available training for lesser-used systems.

The microcomputer environment must be included in this assessment, giving consideration to the hardware, operating systems, software packages, telecommunications methods, mainframe connectivity, and network types.

This assessment is completed by examining the elements of the operating environment and determining the technical EDP skills needed to understand the functions of the organization's operating environment.

The environment assessment will isolate the EDP technical skills needed. The next step is to determine the level of EDP audit skill needed. Does the EDP audit group need sophisticated CAATs, or can it accomplish audit objectives with less sophisticated audit techniques?

Existing Skills

Data processing and EDP audit expertise can be purchased through hiring trained and experienced people at high salaries, or developed internally through a combination of internal and external training. The data processing and EDP audit expertise of each EDP auditor should be measured.

Three pieces of information have now been identified: EDP technical skills needed, EDP audit skills needed, and data processing and EDP audit skills existing in the EDP audit group. These three elements can be plotted in a matrix that will reveal the skills needed.

Available Budget Dollars

This is the most difficult piece of the training puzzle, because the audit department training budget has to be high. To the uninformed, it will seem exorbitant. This budget should probably be close to the highest per-person cost in the entire organization. It is not unrealistic to send 85 percent to 90 percent of the audit staff to one external training course or seminar each year. However, the reality of bottom-line profits pressures the budget.

The available dollars should be spent where they will do the most good, preferably on personnel who can teach what they learn. If three or more people need the same training, consultants could be used to provide the training in-house to a large group of auditors. The use of consultants will permit auditors from other companies to attend the course, which spreads the cost over more people, lowering the costs to the sponsoring organization.

Allocation of money depends on the expertise needed, expertise possessed, and the speed at which the EDP audit group needs a particular type or level of expertise. For example, if an organization is heavily dependent on on-line transaction processing, and the audit department loses their two top on-line system audit technicians, then the need to replace these skills becomes very acute. Audit management will either hire two higher-priced people with existing skills, or use the training dollars to bring existing staff up to speed.

Internal Training Expertise

Having personnel with high technical skills does not mean all training can be performed internally, for two reasons: 1) These hi-tech people have audit work to do, and 2) they may be very poor teachers. Internal training is a very cost-effective method, but the courses must be kept to one or two day sessions, unless the department is large enough to justify a full-time instructor. However, it is highly unlikely that this instructor can teach all subjects needed. The amount of information needed is just too large. The assessment must include what can be taught internally, depending on the knowledge of the teacher, teaching skills available, and the time available for teaching.

External Course Availability

EDP audit training is provided by the professional organizations mentioned earlier, the BAI, and independent consultants. Technical EDP training is provided by colleges, independent consultants, and hardware and software vendors. The greatest challenge is finding the course that provides the proper elements needed.

As mentioned earlier, lesser-known hardware and software vendors may not have a great number of external training options available. In these cases, the vendors usually provide technical training on their products. A qualified EDP auditor could attend these and then develop the EDP audit training as needed.

Training Velocity

This boils down simply to how soon the expertise is needed. The sooner the expertise is needed, the more likely the company will have to hire personnel with the existing skill. On the other end of the spectrum, internal training can be used when the need for skill is low. Changes in the operating environment, changes in services and products, significant control problems, and EDP audit staff turnover all contribute to the speed at which training is needed.

4.4.2.2 TRAINING OUTLINE

The following is a curriculum for the EDP auditor assumed to have a B.S. degree in accounting. For people without a degree, this curriculum can be supplemented with accounting and other business subjects considered necessary by audit management. For people with other business degrees, a minimum of 12 college credits in accounting is recommended, as well as a college-level auditing course. For people with a degree in data processing, a minimum of 12 college credits in accounting as well as a college-level auditing course is recommended. The EDP audit curriculum includes technical EDP topics. Obviously, these can be skipped by people with data processing education or experience, as long as they thoroughly understand the subject matter. The time given is an estimate of formal classroom instruction needed, with home-work consisting of reading text material.

1. Audit Concepts and Techniques—two to three days

   Syllabus

   Overview of EDP auditing, external audit objectives, audit standards, use of audit programs and ICQs, risks and exposures, effects of EDP on internal control, inter-nal control techniques, internal control evaluation, identification of control weaknesses, EDP audit methodology, basic audit tools and techniques (analyti-cal review, statistical sampling, flowcharting, narra-tives, workpaper techniques and in-house standards, and confirmations. These elements are covered in Chapters 1–3 of this book).

2. Industry Concepts and Practices Overview—one half day to one day

   This may only be necessary for new hires who know nothing about the company's business or industry.

   Syllabus

   Products and services, markets and how they are ser-viced, accounting practices, computer systems used, telecommunications methods, company organizational structure and management, company financial state-ments, competitors.

3. Computer System Fundamentals—five to seven days

   Syllabus

   Mainframe hardware components and function, oper-ating system components and function, tape storage concepts and functions, disk storage concepts and functions, tape and disk drive functions, overview of access methods, terminology, overview of telecommunications hardware and software and physical security, overview of database systems, utility program usage, application design and functions, on-line programming system and productivity tools, job control language, data center operations, tape and disk library operations, computer and data security, systems and programming policies and procedures; understanding COBOL programs; program change control, microcomputer components and functions.

4. Audit Software Package Programming—five to seven days

This assumes that the audit department is using an audit software package. High-level language training for the person with no programming education or experience would require considerably more time.

Syllabus

Overview of software package documentation; on-line program development system operation (detailed training on functions needed; overview of other functions); job control language function and use; program and data file library package function and use; coding file layouts; file specification and control parameter coding and use; report formatting and specifications; coding and flowcharting the programming logic; use of copied program logic; use of internal work fields; tables, subscripts, and indexes; programming exercises of various complexities.

5. Application Processing and Audit Techniques—three days

Syllabus

Application activities; transaction origination, transaction entry, processing, data storage and retrieval, output processing, telecommunications interface; database management systems; access methods; batch processing; on-line processing; application controls; risk evaluation;

application audit tools and techniques, overview of CAATs; executing the audit; workpaper standards, applicability of audit software use; creative problem solving with the audit software package; microcomputer applications, controls and risks, and reading COBOL programs.

6. Intermediate EDP Concepts—five to seven days

Syllabus

Minicomputer activities, design, control and audit; S&P policies, procedures, and management; system development methodology; data and computer security exposures, techniques for control and evaluation; activities and design of on-line systems; functions of data-base administration, systems software programming, on-line security system, data center and program change control; backup and recovery techniques and purpose; introduction to operating system function; overview of distributed processing and databases, design and use of COBOL programs; microcomputer operating systems and networks.

7. Intermediate EDP Audit Concepts—three days

Syllabus

Review of basic audit concepts; workpaper standards; interviewing techniques; statistical sampling; use and function of CAATs; creative problem-solving techniques and practice with audit software; introduction to audit of on-line systems, database administration, systems software programming, and on-line security system; audit planning, budgeting, scheduling and supervision; system development methodology and audit approach; internal control evaluation case studies; audit of microcomputer applications; time management.

8. Audit Supervisory Skills—two to three days

Syllabus

Communications, effective listening and verbal presentation; performance evaluation; motivating employees;

progress monitoring; delegation of tasks; handling marginal performance; writing job descriptions; audit planning, budgeting, scheduling and management; time management.

9. Advanced EDP Concepts—five to seven days

Syllabus

S&P management; system development methodology; data communications and networks; data security and administration; management of on-line systems; management of database administration; management of systems software programming and performance evaluation; contingency planning; managing the performance of the operating system; distributed processing and database systems; data dictionary software; microcomputer operating systems and network activities and design; evaluating COBOL programs.

10. Advanced EDP Audit Concepts—three days

Syllabus

Interviewing techniques; case studies on the use and function of CAATs; review of creative problem-solving techniques using audit software; audit techniques, controls, and performance evaluation of on-line systems; auditing database administration; audit of systems software programming management; auditing access control and communication systems and networks; auditing the management of systems in development; auditing techniques for the operating system; auditing with the operating system; auditing distributed processing and database systems; using microcomputer operating systems and packages for audit tools.

Summary

These syllabuses are detailed guides to the contents of an EDP auditor training program. They must be customized to fit the needs of the organization as found in the environmental assessment. Integrated audit approach concepts can be covered in each of the audit courses if the audit department is implementing the approach.

4.5   DEVELOPING AN EDP AUDIT PLAN[3]

The plan must include the five areas of the EDP audit group: Audit software support, supporting the financial audit staff, audits of environmental data processing areas, audits of application systems, and system development reviews. Each area should be broken down into specific activities or tasks with assigned priorities and estimated hours to complete. Auditors should be assigned to tasks that are commensurate with their training and expertise.

Developing this plan involves the risk analysis, planning, budgeting, and scheduling discussed in Chapter 3. This section will briefly review other considerations of the annual audit plan.

First-time audits of an area require approximately 50 hours for audit planning, which involves interviewing the personnel responsible for the area (auditees being reviewed) to identify the area's activities and functions.

4.5.1   Audit Software and Financial Audit Staff Support

Financial staff support will consist of training, consulting, and programming. A time budget must be estimated for this activity. The easiest method is to base this estimate on prior years, considering additions and eliminations for projects in the current year. The estimate may not be exact, although this activity can consume a significant amount of time. Not planning for it will invalidate the total audit budget and make the staffing needs estimate incorrect.

The same planning process must occur for audit software support of the EDP audits. Making this budget artificially high is advantageous because projects will pop up that were not anticipated during planning. It should be assumed that the audit software and financial audit support should be scheduled at least into a likely quarter for advanced planning purposes. If the time is not scheduled, chances are the projects will not get started. If other projects get in the way, the support projects can be moved to an earlier or later time.

4.5.2 Environmental Audits

The areas include:

- Tape and disk library,
- Data center operations,
- Systems and programming department,
- On-line system security and data security,
- Application change control,
- Database administration,
- System software programming, and
- Computer service centers.

Environmental audits involve reviewing standards, policies, and procedures. These three elements form the internal control structure to be evaluated and key controls to be identified and validated through compliance testing. Because the environmental areas form the operating environment in which all application processing is performed, they should be reviewed every 12 to 18 months, unless the risk analysis indicates lower-than-normal risk.

Application Change Control

This audit is necessary because computer programs require periodic enhancements and corrections. Changes to production programs provide areas of exposure, so they must be controlled and thoroughly documented.

The audit should review the procedures for processing user requested changes, and coding, testing, and implementing changes. To ensure that unauthorized changes cannot be made, the auditor should determine that:

- All changes comply with user specifications,
- Procedures are documented and controlled,
- Testing is sufficient, and
- Changes are implemented under strict separation of duties.

Depending on the level of organization and control surrounding the maintenance function, this audit consumes between 200 and 500 hours.

Computer Service Centers

This audit may not be possible, because the contract with the service center may not contain a right-to-audit clause, precluding internal or external audit from reviewing EDP controls (the risks and audit concerns of service centers are covered in a later chapter). Some companies use computer service centers for all their data processing, whereas others use them for individual applications or services. These processing centers are under the control of another management team. User company management may have little or no influence over the controls exercised over processing. Furthermore, the user company's external auditors may need an evaluation of the service center's controls to permit sign-off on the financial statements.

Database Administration

This area needs auditing because if the installation uses a database system, a control group is needed. The head of this group is the database administrator, who is responsible for the organization and integrity of the database. He or she also establishes standards and procedures for database design, definition, and organization. This audit should review these standards and procedures for accuracy, completeness, and compliance. Depending on the extent of the database function, this audit usually consumes 300 hours.

On-line Security and Data Security

This area needs auditing because it is integral to the tracking and protection of company assets. Because of the technical nature of the on-line system, the EDP audit staff must adequately plan for on-line system reviews. At least one member of the audit staff should have sufficient technical knowledge to examine the adequacy of program controls over sign-on, program execution, file access, data input, and inquiry. Data security is included because the on-line system accesses the data that is the commodity being protected.

On-line access control systems should contain tables that identify terminals, terminal users, transactions allowed to be entered, user access levels, and programs that can be executed. Regardless of the level of sophistication, each table should be reviewed for accuracy and completeness. A review of on-line security requires between 250 and 400 hours.

Systems and Programming Department

This is the most fundamentally important area the audit will deal with. Because the EDP environment is controlled by the activities of the S&P department, which includes management, and because programmers maintain the systems that process corporate assets, a careful review of this department is essential. The audit must ensure that management establishes adequate programming documentation standards and that programs are designed, coded, and implemented according to those standards.

The audit staff should also review planning and administration functions to determine whether work assignments are properly made and programmers are adequately supervised. This audit can consume between 100 and 300 hours.

Systems Software Department

This audit ensures efficient operations and control of access to critical programs. The primary responsibility of this department is to keep the operating system running as efficiently as possible. Because members of this department have access to the programs and data that process company assets, they are a potential threat to the organization's security. The audit staff should determine that access to critical programs is adequately controlled, documentation standards are followed, and duties are properly separated. This audit can take 250 to 400 hours to complete.

Tape Library and Data Center Operations

This audit requires determining whether access to the tape library and data center is adequately controlled and reporting any security weaknesses to management. Physical security controls and operations procedures are of major audit concern here because they are the first layer of protection for company assets.

Data centers house all mainframes and most peripheral equipment, as well as the tape and disk files that contain the information about company assets. The audit should evaluate the air conditioning, fire detection, and fire extinguishing equipment protecting these assets.

The input/output section of the data center is responsible for accepting input for processing and distributing output to appropriate users. The auditors should review all standards and procedures for the assignment of processing priorities and for the timely distribution of output. The average data center review requires 250 hours to complete. A tape library audit will require only approximately 200 hours.

4.5.3   Application Audits

These involve reviewing the programs and transactions that are processed by particular applications. Audit priorities should be assigned to each application according to a risk analysis evaluation.

The audit hours are estimated based on the complexity of the application's functions. These audits should be performed simultaneously with the financial audit of the particular application's user area. Preferably they should be performed under the integrated audit approach.

4.5.4 Systems Development Reviews

EDP auditors should examine system controls, planning and administrative procedures, progress in accordance with the development plan, and testing and conversion procedures. Identifying and correcting problems during systems development can reduce both audit review and development time. A complete systems development audit can also eliminate the need for extensive application audits. Depending on the length of the development cycle, this review requires between 300 and 600 hours.

4.5.5 Microcomputer Reviews

Microcomputer usage is increasing at a phenomenal rate. Microcomputers are being used for both non financial and financial applications. In either case, company data processed on them must be protected and controlled. Audit reviews can vary from simple security reviews covering protection and backup procedures to comprehensive application reviews.

NOTES

1. Weber, Ron. *EDP Auditing, Conceptual Foundations and Practice.* New York: McGraw Hill, 1982, pp. 48–50.

2. See Jack B. Mullen, "The Integrated Audit Approach." Adapted from *EDP Auditing* (New York: Auerbach Publishers). © 1990, Warren, Gorham & Lamont, Inc. Used with permission. pp. 5–6.

3. See Jack B. Mullen, "Developing an EDP Audit Staff." Adapted from *EDP Auditing* (New York: Auerbach Publishers). © 1983, Warren, Gorham & Lamont, Inc. Used with permission.

5

Audit Software

5.1 INTRODUCTION[1]

This chapter is the first to deal with actual practice of the EDP audit function. It discusses the environment considerations, standards development, programming, and training that must be considered to ensure success. Such issues as the purpose and function of audit software, the audit software package itself, the use of the software package, designing programs, and microcomputers are dealt with in depth.

5.2 PURPOSE AND FUNCTION OF AUDIT SOFTWARE

Generalized audit software is a programming tool that permits the auditor independently to prepare sophisticated computer programs. Report generators are relatively less sophisticated packages that permit easy creation of simple reports, but they do not offer the programming flexibility of sophisticated codes. Audit software packages can accomplish data retrieval and audit testing in seconds that would require days to do manually. The advantages include reduced testing time, flexibility to expand audit testing scope, independent data generation, statistical sampling, and selection.

5.2.1 Audit Support

Both the EDP and financial audit staffs require computer-generated information to complete their audits. Programming and execution of audit software is typically performed by EDP auditors, but this depends on audit department philosophy. High-level language programming is usually performed by EDP auditors because of the extensive training and experience needed for its proficient use.

The EDP audit staff supports the financial audit staff by preparing software programs and providing technical assistance. Audit software programs generate independent computer reports for the financial staff to use to complete their audits. These reports can be simple trial balances or complex simulations.

Financial audits use tracing techniques on financial transactions to substantiate the accuracy of processing. If independent computer reports are used, the accuracy of computer processing is also tested, "around the computer." The use of application-generated reports leaves the financial auditor at the mercy of application processing accuracy, thereby forcing the auditor to assume that application processing is accurate.

Some financial transactions are performed within the computer without creating an audit trail of all the data elements used by the application to complete the computation. Simulation programs are ideal to test types of such internal calculations as interest payable or receivable. In some cases, the financial auditor can test these with a calculator by using estimates of key data elements. However, the audit budget only permits the testing of a sample of transactions, whereas simulation permits testing of all transactions.

Accumulated data collection programs bring multiple data elements together in one report that ordinarily are printed on multiple application reports. Financial auditors normally must check multiple reports to verify audit trail existence or the execution of internal controls. In some cases, these special purpose reports can significantly reduce audit time by printing all the data in one place.

In another example, exceptions or control weaknesses may be discovered that create data errors or omissions on computer files. Management would certainly want to know the number of, or dollar impact of, these errors. The EDP auditor can create programs that scan all file records for specific errors or omissions. This permits the financial auditor to examine all items in the population and eliminates costly manual looking up of transactions or accounts.

For example, consider an automated billing system for 10,000 accounts that generates monthly and quarterly bills of varying amounts, based on fields set up in the system by billing managers. Assume that the execution of procedures for preparing and entering the billing setups had deteriorated, resulting in accounts that were not being billed for services rendered. To complicate matters, the information to calculate the bills is stored in two separate computer files, and the paper source documents are in five different places. Reviewing 10,000 accounts under these circumstances would be a monumental task, requiring significant labor. An audit software program could be coded to scan all records on both files to determine the accounts missing billing setups, all accounts that have not been billed, and, with additional input, calculate the lost revenue. The programming time would be dramatically less than the manual research time. An impact assessment could be completed in a matter of weeks with a handful of people instead of several months with an army.

5.2.2   Specific Uses of Audit Software

Common uses of audit software include confirmations, statistical sampling, trial balances, simulations, and exception items reports.

Confirmation: This commonly requested program provides significant assistance to internal and external auditors. Tested confirmation programs for each major asset and liability are invaluable. Extensive time should be invested in developing good confirmation programs; to reduce preparation and running time as each program is repeatedly requested, these programs should require a minimum of input. Special confirmation forms should be limited to three or four to prevent confusion and the need for multiple programs.

The confirmation selection method is directly dependent on the audit objective. When statistical evaluation of confirmation results is the objective, random selection and statistical sampling routines must be used; otherwise, a sampling is possible.

Statistical Sampling: These are special routines that accompany sophisticated audit software packages; they are also available in structured-language form. Some are absolutely necessary for audit use (*e.g.,* attribute, stop-and-go, discovery, and dollar value sampling).

Trial Balances: This easily prepared report can range from a simple listing of account numbers and balances to a full print line of information for each account. Trial balance reports simulate the standard trial balance produced by the application program and provide an independent information source, eliminating audit reliance on information generated by the application. If an application program is coded to eliminate various accounts, discrepancies are easily found through comparison to the audit software trial balance.

Simulations: These reports can be simple simulations of special application reports or complicated interest or pricing routines. Certain application reports may have been coded years ago and intentionally or accidentally modified since then without the changes being noticed by the user. Audit software simulation of these reports allows a quick check of their accuracy.

Exceptions Items Report: This report is commonly requested by internal and external auditors to eliminate the manual screening of data for exceptions (*e.g.,* all payments to vendors whose discounts were not taken). Exception reports are straightforward, can take many forms, and are limited only by the sophistication of the audit software or language being used.

5.2.3   Alternative Approaches

Audit software packages use an assembler load-and-go technique to create the computer program for execution by the operating system. This means that the package's internal code reads the auditor-specified parameters and translates them into assembly language instructions that are linked in a temporary program library. This linked program is executed by the operating system; when completed the temporary program library is erased leaving the English-type parameters in the permanent program library for further use by the auditor.

A single audit software package may not be suitable for all EDP environments, especially those with hardware and software from different vendors, in-house developed operating systems, certain database management systems, and specialized access methods. Structured languages can be used by trained audit programmers; or, the audit department can rely on the programming department. Structured-language use is costly but absolutely necessary in some environments to fulfill audit requirements.

Use of the programming department reduces audit independence and reduces the speed of completing audits because audit requests compete with all other company users.

Audit software requires less training and programming time than high-level languages, which helps justify the cost of purchase. Audit software is more functional than report generators owing to the availability of sophisticated coding. High-level languages offer the lowest CPU overhead, but they require extensive training. Report generators are fast to prepare but are limited in their coding function.

5.2.4   Audit Software Benefits

Audit software produces numerous benefits. Among them are the following:

- Providing independent access to computer files,
- Increasing audit scope without increasing staff,
- Reducing time for data collection,

- Providing use of the computer by non-EDP professionals, and

- Providing exposure to data processing functions.

Even though time spent learning package use is necessary, a working knowledge can be developed within one month, and a reasonable level of proficiency can be attained in three months. The front-end program development time can be more costly than manual audit procedures, but the programs can usually be used again or modified slightly for other uses. As explained earlier using the fee billing example, the package can be used to quantify exceptions in much less time than manual procedures. Simulations, exception reports, and accumulated data routines, all previously explained, are but a few of the shortcuts that audit software permits.

5.2.4.1 BENEFIT AS A TRAINING AID

The user friendliness of audit software provides personnel, not trained in data processing, with the opportunity to use the computer and learn its functions. Learning audit software use is usually one of the first tasks for the new EDP auditor. The package is to the EDP auditor what the electric saw is to the carpenter.

The training and its use provides exposure to programming techniques and to the frustrations that programmers face in their job. This gives the trainee an appreciation for what the programmer goes through in getting a program ready for production. With this knowledge, the EDP auditor is better able to evaluate programmer and analyst activities during an audit.

In most cases, the package parameters are entered into the system with an on-line programming terminal's providing an exposure to the internal workings of on-line libraries, data sets, and on-line security. This exposure provides insight in circumventing on-line security and authorized libraries.

Audit software programs need a means to communicate with the operating system just as high-level languages do by using job control language (jcl). With this knowledge, the EDP auditor can more competently review the job control language for an application. Training and use of job control language permits the auditor to identify file and program library definitions to determine that only authorized files and libraries are specified.

Audit software programming exposes the auditor to multiple program use in a job stream, providing an appreciation of how application programs are set up in a string to perform specialized functions and feed data to subsequent processing steps.

To satisfy the requests of financial auditors, the EDP auditor may need to review the COBOL program for answers on processing questions. This provides exposure to researching a program written by another person—following the logic of someone else's thoughts and designs.

The auditor will develop interviewing skills as he or she investigates file layouts and program functions, with programmers, for inclusion in the audit software program. The greatest challenge for the new EDP auditor is knowing a "snow job" when he hears it. Technical jargon can easily get the best of any trainee. Any auditor must become a skilled interviewer, knowing what questions to ask and how, and deciphering the legitimacy of the answer.

Finally, the audit software package provides audit management with a staff testing tool. Generally speaking, the auditor who has trouble learning audit software use will have trouble learning EDP audit skills. This provides both management and the trainee with an early warning signal of potential trouble. However, this assessment should never become hard and fast because there are always exceptions.

5.3   THE AUDIT SOFTWARE PACKAGE

This section explains the functions and characteristics, and some elements of evaluating and implementing, an audit software package.

5.3.1   Package Functions

The most sophisticated audit packages use an assembler load-and-go technique to create an executable program. A computer operating system can only execute instructions in machine language form. Because this is highly complicated, compilers and translators convert special "reserved-word" program instructions to machine language.

Audit software takes this technique one step further. The reserved words are English-style parameters that are more easily understood than machine language. Audit software consists of multiple programs that execute in a controlled sequence to edit and translate the parameters, convert them to assembly language statements (reserved-word instructions), compile, and link edit the statements into machine language. The last step is the execution of the auditor-written program against the specified input files to produce the defined reports.

The typical package permits the definition of the input file(s) and its fields; reports on paper or magnetic media with specifically defined fields, processing logic including mathematic calculations, temporary internal fields, tables and subscripts, and special error handling routines. This flexibility provides the auditor with the means to duplicate the vast majority of high-level programming functions.

5.3.2 Audit Software Vendors

Two popular audit software packages are CA-EDP/Auditor[2] from Computer Associates and Panaudit[3] from Pansophic Corporation. Both of these packages have been in use since the mid-1970s, proving their functionality as a valuable audit tool. The cost of these packages varies.

5.3.3 Evaluating a Package for Purchase

Any computer software is justified by cost savings and greater productivity. Audit package benefits have been described throughout this book, but they must be quantified in some form to convince management and the audit committee to commit to their purchase.

The evaluation takes the form of a feasibility study prescribed by system development methodology (see Chapter 17). Compatibility with the EDP environment must be considered. The feasibility study must address all of the following issues.

A package must satisfy numerous criteria; it must be able to satisfy audit needs—generate the reports from the computer files available in the installation. The vendor should offer a trained staff dedicated to product support. The quality of this support can be easily verified by calls to established users. Vendors who do not provide this service should be avoided, because every package needs additional support. Excellent documentation is a must—the best way to assess documentation quality is to check with auditors who have been using the software package for more than one year.

Will the package run on the company's computers? Some packages run only on computers from one vendor. Furthermore, is the package compatible with the operating system? Can it read the files produced by the system? Some installations use specialized access methods. The audit researcher should determine the access methods used and compare them to package capabilities. The mainframe and operating system questions are answered with a few short phone calls.

There are, however, even more operating system questions that require research. Audit packages have specific core (internal memory) and auxiliary storage (disk files) requirements. Package core requirements that exceed installations specifications will severely limit the package's usefulness. System software technicians or the hardware vendor can provide CPU, core, and disk space constraints within which the package must operate. A "core hog" justifiably upsets EDP management and restricts mainframe use by auditors to minimum work load times (usually during the weekend). If excessive CPU time is required, the program continually runs as a low priority, severely prolonging turnaround time and negating the one justification for acquiring the package.

Many package vendors provide a limited trial period before the final payment is collected. The questions arising from this practice assist in the evaluation of the documentation: proper documentation provides answers; poor documentation generates additional questions.

Will the package provide the calculation and logic functions needed? Can it create the reports or files desired? Is the package easy to program and easy to learn? Finally, do the benefits of the package and its environmental fit justify the cost?

With any computer software purchase, talking to other users is indispensable. Potential buyers should try to talk to the users the vendor did not talk about. Their experience may save untold costs and heartaches.

5.3.4 Package Implementation

This is the simplest aspect of using audit software packages because everything needed is supplied by the vendor and the systems software programming group does all the work. Vendor-supplied training should begin promptly for as many auditors as the vendor will allow. When training is completed, package use should begin. Figure 5–1 shows an implementation timetable.

The audit staff that is trained by the vendor should be allotted four to six weeks for programming practice without the interference of other audit duties. Training without practice is useless—trainees will forget the lessons very quickly without the opportunity to apply what they have learned.

5.3.4.1 TRAINING

All EDP auditors should gain extensive knowledge of audit software, be it a package or a structured language. Temporary full-time training assignments give auditors time to learn how to use the tool and provide them with sufficient programming knowledge to complete the job. Thorough programming knowledge permits EDP auditors to complete application audit programming, leaving the full-time or rotating programmer to concentrate on other needs.

Auditors must be trained in the following areas of audit software use:

- Program code input method,
- Package or language syntax,
- Job control language,
- Operations procedures,

Figure 5–1   Implementation Timetable

Year 1

Programming tool analysis
Decision on tool selection
 — Structured language . . . .►
 — Begin Training
 — Audit Package
Package evaluation—four to six weeks
Selection and installation
Training by vendor
Trial period
Standards development ◄ . . . .
Full-time programming:

- Initiate basic confirmations, trials, exception reports

Year 2

Standards evaluation and modification, if necessary
Full-time programming:

- Streamlined confirmation programs
- Intermediate complexity programming
- Basic simulations
- Development of audit programmer training program by audit personnel

Exposure of complete audit staff to basic concepts

Year 3

Standards evaluation
Advanced complexity programming
Intermediate to advanced simulations
Training program final adjustments
Part-time programmers to replace one full-time programmer
Continuation of training of entire staff

Year 4

Standards evaluation
Advanced programming
Advanced development of training program
Intensification of training of entire audit staff

- Standards, and
- On-line programming.

After the initial vendor training, audit management should conduct most, if not all, training; the ultimate goal is self-sufficiency and consistent quality. Audit may need to participate in EDP department training for structured languages.

Upon package implementation, audit management should consider creating full-time programmer positions, the number of which depends on staff size. This permits increased speed of implementation of programs. After the programs have been used for two to three years, a rotating programmer concept can be implemented, which requires more auditors to be trained in audit software or structured-language use.

The rotating programmer concept works as follows: Initially, an auditor is assigned to full-time programming for six to eight weeks; the first three weeks are dedicated to training; subsequent weeks are devoted to practical execution of actual job requests. (Although the rotating-programmer scheme is useful during the initial program development phase, the need for this position decreases after a significant number of useful programs have been developed). Figure 5–2 outlines a suggested approach.

At least six people can be trained in one year using an eight-week one-in/one-out approach. The rotation program initially requires extensive supervision. As programming knowledge increases, the full-time position can be replaced by rotating programmers.

The most important thing to remember during training is to start simply and build gradually toward more complicated programs. A complicated program, multiple reports, and sophisticated logic only confuse trainees and inhibit their learning ability.

The purpose and objectives of programming and documentation standards must be explained during training; otherwise, standards could be meaningless to the trainee. Misunderstood standards are sometimes eliminated to save time, because they seem unimportant.

FIGURE 5–2   Training Schedule

Weeks 1 and 2

1. Hardware/software overview, data representation, data storage, CPU, I/O devices, program design, and a tour of the data center

2. Coding input method (on-line programming requires more time)

3. Introduction to audit software explaining the use of each parameter, including:

   • File structures—how to define a file to the software package or language

   • Work fields—how to store and utilize constant information or intermediate results during processing

   • Report layout—how to print the data on a report; explaining data representation, sort parameters, and totals accumulation

4. Installation and department standards

5. A test-case program with predefined results to expose the student's weaknesses

Week 3

6. Reading and short lecture on operating systems and job control language

Week 4

7. Database interface coding and advanced topics

Weeks 5 through 8

8. Program design and coding of requested jobs

5.4   USING THE SOFTWARE PACKAGE

The purpose of this section is to introduce some technical details concerning typical audit software packages. It is not a substitute for formal training or for studying package documentation, which should be longer than this entire book.

5.4.1   Programming Functions and Standards

Documentation, programming, job control language, retention, and library standards must be developed to promote the smooth operation of an audit programming function, regardless of the programming approach used. Standards give programmers precise qualitative objectives and specific how-to instructions. Standards also provide a means for evaluating employee performance by comparing them with actual results. Adequate standards reduce future training and program research time. In-house standards should be followed when using a structured-language program, as long as such standards meet audit documentation standards. This section will discuss the specific programming functions and related standards, as appropriate and in their logical procedural order, because they are significantly related.

Documentation Standards: These require narrative explanations of program functions. Additional documentation is required because audit software programs may be used only once per year. By the time the next use rolls around, the auditors who designed or wrote the program may have left the audit department.

The following information should be documented within the program using comment cards: the program ID used in the job control language (jcl), the programmer's name, the application system the program runs against, the input file name, the purpose of the audit software program, the scope of the program (data selection method and how many records), date of first execution, status of the program, names of reports or files created, special run considerations, elapsed run time and CPU time core usage, the job name if the program is part of a job stream, and modifications for future use.

The scope defines how the records will be selected; such as random or judgment sampling, all accounts, or transactions that occurred between two dates. The last execution date is important for determining the effect of application file layout changes; if they changed, then the audit software program must be changed. The status of the program tells the next person who looks at it whether it has been tested or still needs further work. Special run considerations and run time are usually discovered as important variables when the program is being tested. Documenting these for the future helps the auditor schedule testing and execution. The absence of this information could cause a program termination, or operations personnel could "bump" it from the run schedule. During use of the audit software reports, auditors typically find improvements that can be made the next time the program is modified.

Input File: This parameter identifies the data file to be read by the program. The auditor can define fixed length, variable length, or undefined records, the file type, such as sequential, index sequential, or other type, a database file, and other options for matching files, using passwords, and so on. The following documentation elements are often embedded in the program code: file definition, file name, data set name, record length, block size, access method, and record type. Files are made up of records that are made up of fields. Fields are like a series of mailboxes that hold information, each with a unique address. A separate parameter card is used to define the field names within the file, including a field name, start position, field size, and data type such as alpha numeric, zoned decimal, signed packed decimal, bit, and others.

Most packages and structured languages require unique coding for these attributes when such nonstandard access methods as index sequential (ISAM) or hierarchical index sequential (HISAM) are being used. Typical file definition syntax requires coding the field name, start position and field size (or start and ending field position), and data type. Each field should have a precise explanation of the field meaning; numerical or financial data should include a specified range of permissible values; coded data should have a list of equivalent meanings (for example, a one-byte character flag that represents the age of each accounts receivable entry could be defined as $0 =$ current, $1 = 30$ days past due, $2 = 60$ days past due).

The file definition documentation should explain how to recognize file header, trailer, and control records as well as the meaning of their contents. These records are normally bypassed; if the objective is to test their validity, however, it is necessary to understand how to extract them, print their contents, and explain their value.

Report Definition: This parameter coding syntax provides most of the necessary documentation. The print file column heading must be sufficiently descriptive. The program name and report number should be placed in the top of each report to ensure easy identification when the report and control listings are separated and placed in workpapers as evidence.

Totals should be explicitly defined and set apart from other report data in a way that highlights their appearance and differentiates them from detail data (for example, TOTAL SALARY YEAR TO DATE . . . $129,512).

Audit software packages permit total control over report creation, including spacing, field names, editing, and special conditions. The auditor defines data sorting, field positions, field titles and editing attributes.

Work Fields: Certain software packages allow the user to define work fields within the program for use during processing. The work fields are used to hold processed data as well as fixed data for comparison purposes. They also permit the creation of tables for use by subscripts and indexes. They also permit the creation of data tables, which are multiple occurrences of data with related characteristics. The data in the table can be retrieved by using subscripts and indexes that specify the locations of specific data occurrences.

Field names should be entered as acronyms or abbreviated versions of the full names to facilitate coding and debugging (e.g., a field containing the number of days since last payment could be named DYSLSPY). The description of the field and its contents should be placed on the same line as the field name.

Processing Logic: This coding permits the auditor to manipulate data records and fields, perform arithmetic calculations, and compare data fields. The sophisticated packages are so flexible, in this regard, that high-level language coding can be duplicated. Each line of processing logic should be fully explained. Field names, the operation, and result fields should be completely documented, for example:

```
027010 M       RESET    YES-NO2  $RESET YES-NO2 TO BLANK
027020 ACT-TYPE N '1'    DROP    $SELECT ALL BUT TYPE 1 ACCOUNTS
027025 STD-IND-CLA E 99 DROP    $SELECT ACCOUNTS NOT LINKED
```

```
027030 ACT-NUMB E FIRST DROP  $BYPASS CONTROL RECORD
027035 OPEN-FLG N '0'   DROP  $SELECT ONLY OPEN ACCOUNTS
027040 CUR-BAL E 0      DROP  $SELECT ACCOUNTS W/ BALANCES
```

Processing logic can be coded to perform simple equality testing or enhanced with if/then statements and boolean logic. Subroutines can be executed with "perform" statements that automatically branch back to their originating point when finished, or executed with "GOTO" statements that continue sequential processing. Some packages offer the flexibility of branching to subroutines that are separate programs.

The narrative descriptions following the dollar sign explain the function of that line of logic. This is invaluable to another auditor attempting to learn the program's function. Narrative descriptions of each program and its reports should be maintained within the program, if possible, and in the permanent workpapers. These narratives should describe the function and objective of each report as well as the contents and purpose of each field.

The printout containing the job control language, the edited source code, and the final report should be filed with the audit workpapers. The scope and objective paragraphs should describe the test use of the reports. During preliminary review, the auditor can determine the feasibility of using the report and modification needs.

5.4.2 Programming Standards

Programming personnel must comply with certain requirements dictated by the constructs of the package or structured language. Programming standards prescribe how certain logic is to be completed and set guidelines for quality. The goal is to reduce the amount of programmer time needed by creating identical procedures for areas that are similar in all programs. Following package installation, a great deal of programming is required; the establishment of programming standards can reduce this effort considerably.

File layouts: Certain application files are frequently used by auditors. The complete file is defined as it is needed, and the definition is stored in a unique on-line library module for future use. Although this requires additional initial programming time, it reduces future costs and avoids multiple definitions of the same fields in separate programs, which consume valuable disk space. The time needed for file modifications should not be significant; most changes are additional fields in filler areas or at the end of the file. For optimal efficiency, the file definitions should be stored in unique modules and then copied into the program during execution, using macro instructions.

Program testing: This is necessary to find errors before final execution, and this phase should be standardized to ensure consistent quality. The standard should require an error-free compilation prior to live program execution. This also applies to audit software packages that generate COBOL source statements.

Assembler load-and-go audit packages permit execution of the program against a data file without a separate compilation phase by forcing a review of the results before executing against a data file. These packages normally have an edit phase before the program is translated into an executable code, but it is all part of the same job stream. In sophisticated packages, fatal errors found in the edit will abnormally end (abend) the compile and execute phases.

The edit phase should never be bypassed before the program is run against the file. In some on-line programming environments, the software package edit phase is separated from the translate and execute phase and is available for on-line execution without accessing data files. This permits repeated exercise of the edit phase until error-free source code is obtained. The reported diagnostics can be returned to an on-line library or printed as hard copy. The edit phase is mandatory before the program can be executed against a live file.

Program testing should be done only against test or copy files to prevent accidental destruction of live data. The CPU-time and print-line limit parameters discussed in the JCL Standards Section 5.4.3 should be used during testing.

Program Names: Established programming standards should require that audit program-naming conventions provide a signif-

TABLE 5–1

```
A U D D 0 3 R A
  |   |   |   | |   |
  |   |   |   | |   |
  |   |   |   | |   |_____ Program version, A = Live, B = Test, etc.
  |   |   |   | |
  |   |   |   | !_____ R = Request, W = Weekly, M = Monthly, etc.
  |   |   |   |
  |   |   |   |_____ Defines output type (programmer defined)
  |   |   |
  |   |   |_____ Application type (programmer defined)
  |   |
  |   |_____ Acronym for audit
```

icant amount of information at a quick glance. These conventions should follow the basics outlined by the installation standards, which provide several characters within the name for flexible design. For example, a standard program name length of eight characters (see Table 5–1). The characters not programmer defined are specified by installation standards.

5.4.3 Job Control Language Standards

All operating systems require a control language to communicate processing instructions. Each vendor has a unique acronym for this language, and although the purpose is very similar, the syntax varies greatly. Besides installation and vendor standards, the following additional audit considerations apply.

Operating system vendors usually provide the standard control language needed to run most audit programs. This should be quickly accessible from a central location. Some unique information is required for each separate program; the majority, however, can be standardized and maintained on multiple copies of punch cards or in an on-line library.

Comment cards: Comments are permitted by control language syntax by special characters preceding the data and should be used to explain the following nonstandard conditions:

- Job stream situations,
- Special output data sets,

- Utility use, and
- Temporary data sets.

File disposition statements: File dispositions (e.g., old, new, share, catalog, delete) must be used cautiously to prevent improper combinations that could delete a file and require program reruns. Audit standards should limit disposition statements to old or share, and supervisory approval should be required for any other type. All control language prepared by new programmers should be reviewed by an experienced audit programmer until a satisfactory level of success is achieved. Verification utilities are available for most on-line programming systems; their use should be a standard requirement.

Processing limit parameters: CPU-time and print-line limiting parameters should be used in testing. Program coding errors often occur in the early stages of training and cause program loops or extract more records than desired. Limitation parameters reduce the risk of printing reams of paper or using unnecessary CPU time.

5.4.4 Retention Standards

Various types of data must be retained to facilitate future program use and satisfy audit standards. The standards should address what to retain, the format, and the retention period. Data that must be retained includes:

- Job summary listings,
- Source program listings,
- Control language,
- Report samples,
- Program narratives, and
- File definitions.

The source code can be readily accessed through an on-line terminal; however, a source program listing or file definition is sometimes needed when the on-line system is unavailable. Source program listings can be maintained in binders, but discretion should be used because such listings can become excessive. Labeled hanging file binders are the easiest storage method, facilitating reference of a specific program listing.

Job summary listings are needed if special control language is used or run-time statistics are retained. Voluminous listings can be eliminated by recording statistics on a form along with a simple listing of the job control language statements. Job control language card decks should be maintained for each program and separated by application. Program narratives and report samples should be maintained with audit workpapers. All programs and package software code maintained on disks should be subject to standard backup procedures.

5.4.5   Library Standards

The overall objectives of library standards are to minimize the number of libraries, provide for specific and defined use, and separate programs and data by similarity of structure. With EDP management's permission, audit can create the separate libraries it needs to accomplish these objectives. The purpose of each library should be strictly defined, documented, and enforced. Library standards decrease redundancy and classify information into specific categories, which reduce disk space and save research time.

Several libraries can be used to store programs, documentation, and package software code. These libraries are accessible by the programmer through the on-line programming system. However, each has separate and distinct access rules defined by management for security reasons.

One system library contains program-source code, subroutines, file definitions, and internal program tables in package software format. The program module name should differentiate between live and test programs. Audit programmers are granted read-and-write access to this library.

A second system library has a unique function. Because of their unique nature, database management system file definitions are maintained in this library under the exclusive control of database administration, which maintains the IBM information management system (IMS)[4] database and file definitions for the entire installation. These standard file definitions are accessed by audit software programs when reading database files. Audit programmers are allowed only read-access of this library. Audit software programs can only "call" individual file definitions through use of installation defined parameters.

A third system library contains subroutines written in structured languages for such purposes as sign conversion, date conversion, system date capture, and special assess-methods interface. The subroutines are accessed by exit routines in the software package, or by copying them into the program. Audit programmers are allowed read-and-write access to this library.

A fourth library is the programmer's on-line library. It contains the source code written by the individual programmer. This code is loaded into one of the system libraries for permanent retention and execution. This is the programmer's personal library, accessible through the on-line programming system with read-and-write access.

5.4.6 Reference Material

Proper completion of programming tasks requires reference manuals that explain the rules of system processing. Vendors provide documentation that explains system operation. Although the needs of the audit programming function must be carefully analyzed to determine exact reference material needs, the following manuals are generally needed.

Audit software package documentation includes the users guide that explains all of the coding parameters and how to use them, a subroutine manual containing their source code and usage instructions, a system manual that explains the technical details of software package operation, and a database interface guide explaining special coding instructions for handling database files.

Mainframe operating system documentation includes system messages and codes to help debug programming errors, a utilities guide that provides utility operating instructions, an overview of operating system functions, and a job control language usage and reference guide.

Documentation of the database system should explain system messages and codes. Other documentation is needed to explain application programming rules, printer usage, and on-line programming. Depending on installation design, other system operation reference material may be needed.

5.4.7   On-Line Programming System (OPS)

Various vendors provide these systems to increase programmer productivity. Some OPSs interact with the operating system to provide use of system resources; these are called interactive programming systems. Others provide access to certain system resources, forcing the programmer to use some computer functions through the batch environment.

Program code and control language can be typed through the terminal keyboard and saved in the programmer's personal on-line library. The OPS provides editing features to copy lines or words, search, insert, and delete text much like a word processor. Syntax-checking programs are available to find errors, and the programs can be submitted for execution to the mainframe for testing. Some systems offer on-line retrieval of the reports produced by the program to reduce programming time. When the programs are debugged, they can be permanently saved in one of the system libraries.

Access to OPS functions is controlled by a security system with an access control mechanism. They typically require the input of a user ID and password, which are stored in an encrypted on-line control file. At sign-on, the access control mechanism checks the entered ID and password against the file—only a match permits access. The on-line control file also contains computer resource access, which controls the on-line functions that the programmer can perform. To use the system, the programmer must be defined to the control system with the permission of EDP management.

Training courses, manuals, and supervisory instruction help the programmer learn OPS use. The new auditor can shorten the learning curve by studying the manuals and practicing.

5.4.8 Time Requirements

Generally, programming requires approximately 20 percent of the total audit budget during the first two to three years of audit software use. This varies according to the extent of EDP audit commitment and how quickly the completion of audit programs is desired. The more advanced the philosophy and desire for speedy completion, the larger the personnel requirements.

5.5 DESIGNING PROGRAMS

Effective and efficient program design consists of five phases: specifications, program design, programming, testing, and execution. Because each of them relies on the previous phase, the program will only be as effective as its weakest phase. Regardless of program sophistication, the development process must include all five steps.

5.5.1 Program Specifications

Program specifications refers to information that is gathered about the objective to be accomplished and what output is required to accomplish it. It is best to consider the output first, then revert to the input and processing requirements.

To define the program specifications, the audit programmer should determine the output of each data element needed, and how it will displayed in special or simple format. Determine if each field can be extracted as is from the input file or whether calculations will be required. Identify the selection criteria for the report, for example, all accounts, specific accounts meeting certain criteria, statistical sampling of accounts. Determine the amount of time the selection should cover. Determine the title of the reports and the heading name for each column. Determine which columns need totaling and the necessary number of full report totals. It is helpful to refer to the record layout while planning the output.

Having achieved a solid picture of the desired output, review the file layout in detail, determining exactly what fields will be needed, how they will be extracted, and what processing and editing should be performed. This review will indicate any special processing needed or whether the information can be obtained at all. If any data cannot be obtained, discuss this with whomever made the request to determine alternatives.

5.5.2 Program Design

The program design phase translates the specifications into computer logic. To increase the prospects of good results, the processing logic can be flowcharted. Prepare a flowchart of the sequential steps the program will follow, including input file message, calculations, subroutines, and table searches. Determine the equality tests needed and how the data selection will be accomplished. Determine any work field (internal memory) that will be needed. Determine the input file name(s) as specified by the installation's file cataloging and library system.

The report or file should be designed by using a special report layout form. The maximum size of each field can be spread across the paper, segregating each column exactly as it will be seen on the final report. This exercise will indicate whether all data elements will fit on each line. The column titles can be written in to determine the abbreviations needed.

Processing logic is designed by defining how each output field will be created. Processing either prints a record as extracted from the input file, calculates the output field value from input values and formulas, or compares input data fields to other fields or predefined criteria.

5.5.3 Programming

This activity involves translating design specifications into computer language. The logic of the first two phases can be followed by coding the report or file next. As the report or file is translated to program code, report-layout problems and the "fit" on the paper or file will become evident. Code all elements of the report; sort parameters, title, field start position, spacing, edits, column title, and others.

Having coded the report, explain in computer language how each input field or record will be selected, how records will be dropped, and how selected fields will be printed on the report. The programming code must be written in the processing sequence, so the flowchart will come in handy here. Simply translate the procedures in the flowchart into computer language.

The most boring task of programming is coding the input file layout. Most companies have these defined for use by other programs, relieving the programmer of the duty. However, if this option is not available, then two alternatives are possible: 1) Code the entire file and save it in a system library for later use. This requires more time than may be necessary for this particular program, but it will save audit time later. 2) Code only the fields needed by the program. This reduces programming time, especially for large files; if cramped for time, this is the best approach.

5.5.4   Program Testing

Program testing is performed to eliminate all functional errors from the program. The three objectives of testing are to determine whether: 1) the syntax of the coding is correct, 2) the program produces the desired results, and 3) the program can process the entire file properly.

The first objective of syntax checking requires two elements, verification as to whether: 1) all parameters are spelled and formatted correctly, and 2) the coding accomplishes the proper effect. The vast majority of the spelling, formatting, and use of reserved words checking is done by the edit program of the audit software. This program produces a report of all coded parameters with flags and error messages that identify incorrect data. The edit program may be executable through an OPS command, which permits the results to be returned to the programmer's on-line library for review through the terminal. The syntax of the code should be completely error free before moving on.

The second requirement of syntax checking blends into the second testing objective. Both are accomplished by running the program against a copy of the intended input file. The program only need process several records for each different condition to test its functionality. If the code will properly handle a condition for one record, it will process all same-condition records the same way. To understand a condition consider this: the program will be designed to process certain program instructions for different account types, transaction types or dates, balance amounts, and so on. The auditor must ensure that each line of the program code has been executed. The program will produce a report containing the processed records. The auditor needs to verify that these records are being reported as prescribed by design specifications. Have the report user review the test results to identify any potential errors. Identify the processing errors and inconsistencies in design, find the cause of the error and correct the program code accordingly. Several reiterations of this test approach may be necessary to ensure all coding errors are detected and fixed. When the second test objective is satisfied, the auditor can begin to test the complete file. A copy of the production file should be used to prevent accidental destruction. If test objectives one and two were fulfilled properly, complete file testing may require only two or three iterations. The purpose is to examine the full report and test the accuracy of totals processing by reconciling them with general ledger or other independent controls. Have the report user examine each report iteration to identify any potential errors.

5.5.5   Execution

The main concern of execution is control of the processing—ensuring that all records on the file were processed. The auditor may want to observe the execution of the program in the data center. If processing propriety can be assured by inspecting the control language listing, then observation of execution is not necessary.

Another control technique is item counting and file totaling. A file-totaling routine should be used to permit reconciliation of file-control totals with general ledger control totals (for example, the total dollars of outstanding accounts receivable). This is necessary to prove that each record on the file was processed.

In some installations, record counts (for example, the total number of accounts) are reconciled daily. As new accounts are opened and others are closed, the total number of accounts is monitored to prevent accidental or intentional dropping of an account. The record count total can also be reconciled to ensure processing accuracy.

To finish the project, perform a "post-mortem" review to isolate any errors and/or inefficiencies that can be corrected in the program. These can be corrected at the end of the audit, if time permits. More often though, the corrections will be documented in narrative form and placed in the workpaper file as the lead page before the program listing and report. The next auditor will find it during audit planning and provide time to implement the changes. If this review is postponed until "later," chances are the changes will never be made and the errors and inefficiencies will occur again.

5.5.6   Design Considerations

Because each person's programming method is unique, some standard rules are needed to facilitate program research and decrease design time. Programming techniques are simply standardized methods of performing various actions within each program.

Separating major program functions into unique modules minimizes debugging time; an error can be traced to one particular module without a search through all in-line logic. This technique can be accomplished by "go-to" or subroutine procedures. Modular programming facilitates program modification, permitting additional modules to be easily inserted in unused coding areas.

Report and program identification should be standardized. The system date, file as of date, descriptive report name, report

TABLE 5–2

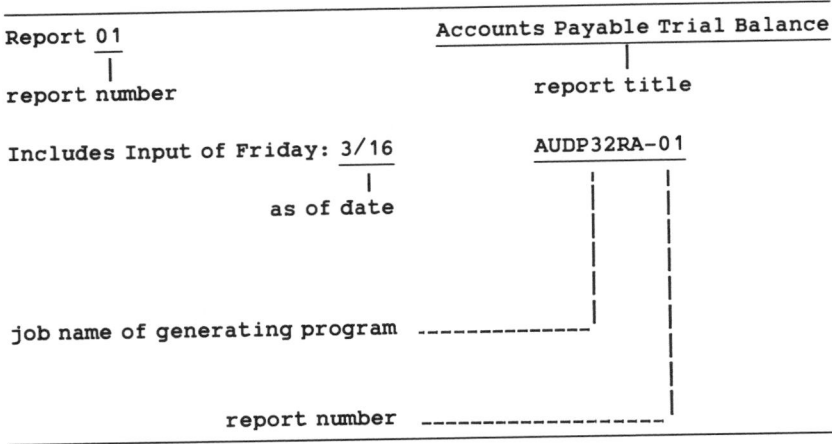

number, and program name should be placed in the report heading for identification. This facilitates workpaper reference and subsequent research when that program is needed again. The program name in the report header provides quick identification of the generating program and eliminates extensive searches through documentation to determine the program. An example of a report header is shown above (see Table 5–2).

5.6 MICROCOMPUTERS

The use of microcomputers and micro-to-mainframe connections is flourishing. Data on the mainframe can still be accessed by audit software. Stand-alone and distributed or decentralized processing cannot be accessed with mainframe-based audit software, unless the data is uploaded to the mainframe. Several packages have been developed for use on micros, but file structures vary for each machine, requiring numerous packages for installations using multiple-vendor hardware and software.

Computer audit programs can be developed using BASIC or other high-level language. All are easier to learn than mainframe high-level languages. Numerous software packages exist that perform specific functions which can be adapted to various audit situations. The major drawback is that all packages have different operating rules, each with a different learning curve.

When microcomputer software packages or programming languages are used, the same rules apply. The previous section on program design can be used just as easily for these microcomputer solutions. Techniques must be developed to ensure that the auditor's programs read the entire file. Any programs or software packages used should follow specific guidelines. These programs essentially fall into the category of structured-language programming on the mainframe. Abandoning these standards for the micro environment may create inefficiencies and render the audit program ineffective.

5.7 CONCLUSION

The success of audit software depends on commitment from audit management and staff. As audit experience increases, new possibilities for productivity improvements through software use become apparent, as do needs for standards and organizational structure changes. The important point is that this is an evolutionary process in which old rules are exchanged for new, more efficient ones.

NOTES

1. See Mullen, Jack B. "Standards for Using Audit Software." Reprinted from *EDP Auditing* (New York: Auerbach Publishers). © 1988, Warren, Gorham & Lamont, Inc. Used with permission.

2. 2 CA-EDP/Auditor is a registered trademark of Computer Associates, Inc., city state

3. PanAudit is a registered trademark of Pansophic, Inc., city state.

4. IBM-IMS is a registered trademark of International Business Machines, Inc.

6

Systems and Programming

6.1   INTRODUCTION

"Systems and programming" is an umbrella term under which all the data processing activities and functions are managed. In addition, the S&P department houses the application analysts and programmers. The organization chart in illustration 6-1 depicts the typical organization structure and the manner in which all of the areas covered in this book fit within the S&P department.

An administrative audit is a review of the administrative procedures and standards required by management. S&P management sets the course for all other areas of EDP. The EDP auditor focuses on the activities and functions that management uses to control all data processing activities, vis-à-vis these management standards. The audit of S&P will set the tone for all EDP audit coverage and provide a "sense" of the quality of internal control throughout the data processing area.

ILLUSTRATION 6-1 Systems and Programming Organization Structure

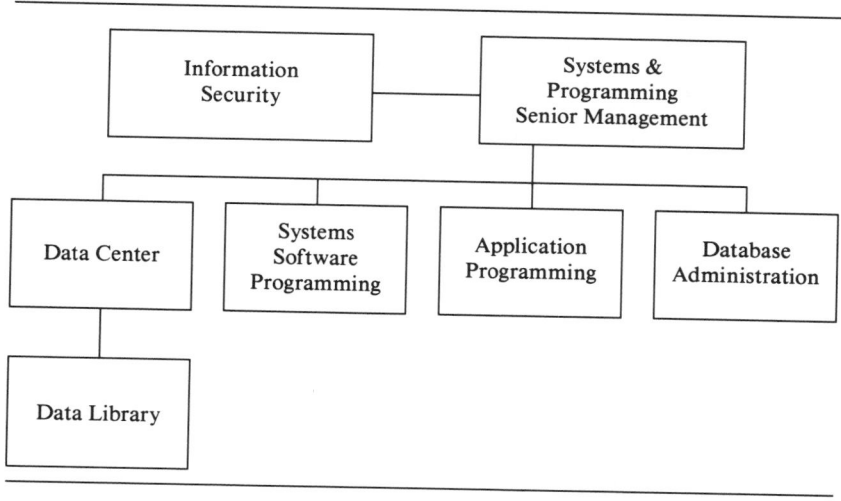

Because this audit reviews administrative elements, it tends to be complicated, usually requiring an EDP auditor with at least two years of experience.

6.2 PLANNING and PREPARATION

A systems and programming audit is largely a review of all elements of EDP that are not covered in other audits, even though there may be some overlap with other audit transactions (see Figure 6-1). This overlap occurs because each of the EDP areas has varying responsibilities for such activities and functions. S&P management, however, establishes the policies and guidelines for all EDP areas.

6.2.1 Risks and Exposures

Such risks and exposures as improperly trained personnel, poor communication, inadequate supervision, insufficient resources,

FIGURE 6–1   Identification of Audit Transactions

Audit Activity Code	Transaction/Area	Include Exclude	Reason
A	Administration	I	Satisfies Audit Objective 1
B	Staff Development	I	Satisfies Audit Objective 2
C	Planning	I	Satisfies Audit Objective 3
D	System Performance Evaluation	I	Satisfies Audit Objective 4
E	Project Management	I	Satisfies Audit Objective 5
F	Costing	I	Satisfies Audit Objective 6
G	Standards	I	Satisfies Audit Objective 7

inadequate performance, project slippage, inaccurate costs, and inadequate instructions are the specific risks and exposures that cause broad exposures, as, for example, erroneous recordkeeping, competitive disadvantage,[2] loss or destruction of assets, or fraud and embezzlement, to name but a few (see Chapter 2, Section 2.1.3). Their specificity helps to provide the focus for the EDP audit. Because the EDP area manages all EDP activities, these risks and exposures could occur in any area.

6.2.2   Control Objectives

The S&P control objectives—ensuring that there are sufficient EDP resources available to satisfy company needs, that such resources are effectively and efficiently used, and that the processing itself is effective and efficient—(see Figure 6–2) are very general; they apply to all areas of data processing. Management must control the use of data processing resources, including programmers, analysts, and clerical personnel in all EDP areas. Company needs for EDP resources evolve rapidly, and require cost and evaluation of resource adequacy and potential future needs.

The quality of management and the quality of internal control, as directed by guidelines and policies, indirectly affect processing accuracy. Weak guidelines and sloppy controls create a

FIGURE 6–2 Scope Summary

Risks/Exposures
1. Improperly trained personnel
2. Poor communication
3. Inadequate supervision
4. Insufficient resources
5. Inadequate performance
6. Project slippage
7. Inaccurate costs
8. Inadequate instructions

Control Objectives
1. To ensure that sufficient data processing resources are available to satisfy company needs
2. To ensure efficient and effective use of data processing resources
3. To ensure effective, efficient and accurate processing

Key Controls
1. Formal organizational structure, job descriptions, effective communication
2. Personnel skill development
3. Effective planning
4. Adequate system performance measurement
5. Adequate project management
6. Accurate chargeback of costs
7. Documented guidelines and procedures

Audit Objectives—Specific
Determine that adequate controls exist to ensure:
1. Adequate staff and salary administration
2. Qualified personnel
3. Effective resource planning
4. Adequate evaluation of hardware and software performance
5. Effective supervision of tasks and activities
6. Accurate costing of services
7. Adequate instructions are provided to personnel

Preliminary Review

Activity Code	Transaction/Area	Budget Hours	
		Audit Time	Review Time
A	Administration	15	1
B	Staff Development	10	1
C	Planning	20	2
D	System Performance Evaluation	15	1
E	Project Management	20	2
F	Costing	10	1
G	Standards	10	2

weak environment that will eventually be manifested in the quality of computer systems.

6.2.3   Key Controls

Key controls are general, and do not need reiteration in terms of S&P. Area-specific key controls are used. These are developed in the relevant sections throughout the chapter.

6.2.4   Audit Objectives

The specific audit objectives—adequate salary and staff administration, qualified personnel, effective resource planning, adequate evaluation of hardware and software performance, effective supervision of tasks and activities, accurate costing of services, and adequate personnel instruction—(see Figure 6–2) have a one-to-one relationship to each audit transaction. The systems and programming audit operates with a more general objective, that of determining that the management philosophy and style promotes an efficient and effective EDP environment.

6.2.5   Completing the Planning Phase

The audit areas/transactions for preliminary review comprise administration, staff development, planning, system performance evaluation, project management, cost, and standards (see Figure 6–2). The audit budget estimates are for first-time review of the individual transactions and are based on a data processing staff consisting of approximately 200 people.

Scope Summary of Compliance Testing: Scope summary of compliance testing is not an issue here; in actual practice, all the transactions included in the preliminary review of the systems and programming audit probably would not be subjected to compliance testing. Typically, all audit transactions covered in preliminary review are not subject to compliance tests for the following reasons: 1) it is useless to test weak or non-existent controls,

2) testing may not provide any additional insight into the quality of the controls, or 3) the audit scope may not require compliance testing.

6.3 EXECUTION OF THE PRELIMINARY REVIEW

The preliminary review of systems and programming is a detailed, fact-finding mission that includes determining the extent of control that the area's standards, guidelines, management philosophy and style provide over the entire data processing environment. That environment comprises administration, staff development, planning, system performance evaluation, project management, costing, and standards, which are discussed below.

6.3.1 Administration

Preliminary review procedure No. 1—documenting organizational structure—(see Figure 6–3) requires that the auditor achieve a graphic picture of how each EDP area fits within the organization. This will help the auditor identify combinations of conflicting functions that should be segregated for control purposes. Organizational controls address decisions that lead to management's means for authorization of transactions. Companies with large data processing facilities separate EDP from business units to provide control over hardware, software, and human resources expenses. Preliminary review procedure 2—determining that all positions have a job description with specific requirements—examine the organizational control techniques. This means documenting the following:

- The reporting responsibility and authority of each job,
- The definition of responsibilities and objectives of each job,
- Policies and procedures,

FIGURE 6-3 Administration

Audit Test Objective

To determine the adequacy of organizational structure and controls

Key Controls

1. Formal organizational and reporting structure
2. Documented and accurate job descriptions
3. Effective communication

Scope

All administrative procedures in effect during the audit period

Audit Procedures:

Preliminary Review   Document the organizational structure

Determine:

1. That all jobs have been defined via job description
2. That each position has specific requirements
3. That analyst and programming positions and other conflicting positions are segregated
4. That all employees report to a supervisor
5. That the frequency of staff meetings communicates information from senior management to the lowest level staff position
6. That a written policy exists for preparing individual performance evaluations
7. Whether there are any preemployment screening practices for sensitive analyst and programmer positions

Compliance Testing

Verify:

1. That actual duties performed match the job descriptions
2. That job duties are segregated
3. That salary levels are competitive in the appropriate market place

---

- Job descriptions, and
- Segregation of duties.

The responsibilities and objectives of each EDP job position must be clearly defined and documented. The senior manager of all these groups, and managers of the individual areas, make up the EDP management team responsible for the effective and efficient utilization of EDP resources. Their responsibilities include:

- Providing information to senior management on the EDP resources that will enable senior management to meet their strategic objectives,
- Planning for expansion of EDP resources,
- Controlling the use of EDP resources, and
- Implementing activities and functions that support the accomplishment of the company's strategic plan.

Procedures 1 and 2 in Figure 6–3 reveal to the auditor the quality of management instructions to S&P personnel. Management must communicate specific instructions and provide a structure for supervision and management. Job descriptions communicate management's specific instructions for job performance. Procedures establish how to do the job; policies define the authority of the employee. All jobs must have a current, documented job description readily available to the employee. This establishes responsibility and the accountability of the employee's actions.

Preliminary review procedure No. 5—the frequency of staff meetings—determines whether relevant information is communicated to all S&P personnel. The auditor can only make sure that staff meetings are held; he or she cannot determine the quality of communication without attending one. If such attendance is possible, the auditor can gain additional insights into the quality of communication.

Preliminary review procedure No. 6—determining that a written policy exists for preparing individual performance evaluations—examines the presence of feedback to employees on the quality of their performance. Because this is performed by a number of different managers, however, it is impossible for the auditor to determine the quality of this feedback. Low morale and productivity levels may be indicators that the quality of this communication is inadequate.

Owing to their high level of technical knowledge and system access, systems programmers, application programmers, and systems analysts, have the greatest opportunity to commit fraud. Management must ensure that the programmer is honest enough to be made responsible for the programs in their purview. The hiring risk for entry level systems programmers can be reduced by transferring an application programmer who has a proven work record and is a known quantity from a security standpoint.

Preliminary S&P review procedure No. 7 reviews pre-employment screening practices. For employees hired from outside, written permission could be obtained from the prospective employee to call prior employers, obtain a criminal record check, and a credit bureau record check. These background checks must comply with federal and local laws.

6.3.2 Staff Development

The review procedure No. 1 relates to S&P staff and begins with the review of management's assessment of needed skills (see Figure 6-4). The quality of systems and programs directly relates to the quality of personnel. Management must determine what skills are needed to maintain all systems. The auditor can accomplish these procedures by interviewing management.

S&P staff review procedure No. 2 examines management's intentions for rewarding personnel for their achievements. Promotions provide motivation that can increase the quality and quantity of work performed. The auditor assesses motivational factors by reviewing documented evaluations. Because numerous managers and supervisors perform evaluations of the staff, the policies and procedures for promotion should be documented to ensure consistency of their application.

S&P staff review procedure No. 3—determining the adequacy of technical training programs for personnel—is also accomplished by interviewing management. This is important, because EDP technology is evolving and changing at a rapid rate, thereby requiring ongoing training merely to maintain adequate skill levels.

FIGURE 6–4 **Staff Development**

Audit Test Objective

To determine that S&P personnel are adequately trained to execute their responsibilities

Key Controls

1. Skill assessment
2. Performance evaluations
3. Adequate training program

Scope

All S&P staff

Audit Procedures:

Preliminary Review

Determine:

1. The procedures for assessing skills needed
2. The policies and procedures for promotion
3. The adequacy of technical training programs provided for personnel

Compliance Testing

Verify:

1. That an adequate skill assessment is performed
2. That employee qualifications match stated job descriptions
3. That promotions comply with guidelines and policies
4. Programmer and analyst experience is adequate
5. The technical training programs adequately meet division needs
6. That individual performance evaluations are conducted in accordance with policy

6.3.3 S&P Planning

The data processing department is responsible for managing the growth of such EDP resources as hardware and software. All user departments must obtain the appropriate approvals from EDP management to review and evaluate such new hardware and software. The purchase of these items must be approved by a steering committee, company CEO or president, or the senior management group as a whole.

S&P planning procedure No. 1 (see Figure 6–5) addresses the development and documentation of long-range planning that is necessary to establish the lines of business the company will pursue over the next five years or more. Along with this, the company must determine what resources they have vis-à-vis what is needed to succeed at these lines of business.

The long-range planning process should be quite exhaustive, covering every department, and it must be updated yearly to adjust to change. Long-range planning is concluded by documenting

FIGURE 6–5 Planning

Audit Test Objective

To determine the adequacy of the planning methodology and compliance with the plans

Key Controls

1. Documented plan
2. Identification and delegation of activities and tasks
3. Progress reporting and monitoring

Scope

Data processing planning methodology

Audit Procedures:

Preliminary Review

Determine:

1. Whether there is a developed and documented long-range (5-year) plan for facilities, hardware, systems software, and application systems
2. Whether a short-range plan (1 to 2 years) has been prepared that outlines specific projects
3. Whether specific tasks and activities are delegated to section managers that support the completion of the short range plan
4. Whether methodology for progress reporting and monitoring in terms of completing the long-range and short-range plan is adequate

Compliance Testing

Verify:

1. The methodologies for planning, and implementation of the plan are being followed
2. Determine that the monitoring and reporting is adequate

goals and objectives and explaining how strengths will be used and weaknesses compensated for or corrected. Time frames, target dates, revenues, and expenses are estimated and documented for use as standards for progress measurement. The control techniques involved are the following:

- The goals and objectives of the plan (used for measurement of progress),
- Revenue and expense estimates,
- Time frames and target dates, and
- Strengths and weaknesses.

S&P planning procedure No. 2 examines short-range, or tactical, planning, because it is this that establishes and documents goals, objectives, functions, and activities needed to meet all of the elements of the long-range plan. These functions and activities are performed every day, whereas the tactical goals and objectives define deliverables (final products) that span periods of time ending as close as tomorrow and as far away as five years. For data processing, the short-range plan defines such daily activities as developing software and obtaining hardware in sufficient time to support day-to-day business activities.

S&P planning procedure No. 3, the verification of short-range task assignments, should be documented by EDP personnel; the supervising auditor can then review this documentation.

S&P preliminary review procedure No. 4, determining the adequacy of progress reporting and monitoring, is accomplished through interviews of management.

S&P planning procedure No. 4 is necessary because EDP management must inform senior management of data processing strengths and weaknesses, identifying the support that can be given, with existing resources, toward achieving goals and objectives. Computer system shortcomings, as they relate to such support must be isolated and reported during the planning process. The data processing department must establish a plan for correction of the shortcomings with deadlines that enable new system capabilities to be ready when the company needs them. Of course, the possibility exists that EDP cannot correct the shortcomings. The company may not be able to afford the system it needs to support the business. But with proper long-range planning, these deficiencies should come to light early enough for the company to react and correct them in time. Improper planning will permit the weaknesses to go unnoticed, and the company may have to try to start a new business or service without the proper computer resource support.

6.3.4   System Performance Evaluation

Performance evaluation is necessary to ensure that there are adequate resources to meet organizational needs. The absence of performance evaluation will eventually catch up with a growing organization, manifesting as a resource crisis and, possibly, resulting in competitive disadvantage or business interruption.[2] A thorough audit performance evaluation can prevent future crisis. The review procedures concern at a minimum, performance levels should be measured for CPU usage and capacity, disk usage and capacity, online terminal volumes and capacity, on-line terminal response time, job and report turnaround and delivery time, and system availability (see Figure 6–6).

For example, the replacement criteria can forecast potential system and application processing problems for the user and EDP management (see procedure 2, Figure 6–6). The auditor should ask, what would trigger the execution of a feasibility study to replace hardware, system software application or communication network component?

Determining who monitors the performance evaluation statistics ensures that the person responsible for monitoring the statistics is sufficiently competent to understand how they are collected and what they mean.

The question as to whether or not the statistics are reported to senior management in terms they can understand in order to make intelligent business decisions is also crucial. Most company managers do not understand EDP well enough to derive any

FIGURE 6–6   System Performance Evaluation

Audit Test Objective

To determine that computer resources are efficient and effective

Key Controls

1.   Establishing adequate performance measurement
2.   Establishing monitoring and reporting of performance
3.   Establishing benchmark criteria for evaluation and replacement

Scope

All hardware, systems software and application programs

Audit Procedures:

Preliminary Review

Determine:

1.   The techniques used to evaluate the performance of hardware, systems software, applications, communications networks, and support of the computer user
2.   The criteria for performance evaluation and replacement of hardware and software
3.   Who monitors the performance evaluation statistics
4.   If the performance evaluation statistics are effectively reported to senior management on a routine basis
5.   The programming productivity tools provided for systems and application analysts and programmers

Compliance Testing

Verify:

1.   That the evaluation methodology and the criteria for replacement is documented
2.   That criteria for replacement of applications and communication networks have been approved by the user
3.   That the performance evaluation criteria is adequate
4.   That personnel are adequately trained in the use of productivity tools

---

meaningful information from technical evaluation statistics. Therefore, EDP management must translate these statistics into useful business terms.

Finally, there should be a focus on productivity tools that increase the amount of work that personnel can do. There are numerous tools in the market today. Such tools as prototyping, computer-aided system engineering, program code generators, and many more are now available. If productivity tools are not used, the auditor should diplomatically ask management to justify why not.

6.3.5   Project Management

Project management focuses on the techniques used to monitor work performance in all areas of EDP. Such work is project oriented; each project has a finite objective, beginning, and an end. Numerous project monitoring packages are available for both microcomputers and mainframe systems. EDP management should require the use and accurate maintenance of one of these systems.

Moreover it is necessary to deal with the estimated quantity of work needed to complete a given project (see procedure 1, Figure 6–7). This is later used to measure how much of the originally estimated work was completed. The estimate usually originates from a proposal or feasibility study that was approved by management. Changes in objectives will increase the time to complete the project and should generally be separated from the time spent on original objectives before being measured and reported. These estimates are usually expressed in total hours needed and should reflect the need for hiring additional programmers, in order to obtain approval by senior management.

The definition of events (an event is an objective) are important because different managers may define things differently. An event can be the delivery of equipment, a systems development life cycle phase, a computer program, a module within a program, a task, or an activity. To properly manage a project, a manager must define events in sequence.

A benchmark—a basis for measurement—must be established for each event to provide something against which actual performance can be measured. The benchmark is usually expressed in terms of hours needed to accomplish the event, including a start date and a target date for completion.

FIGURE 6–7   Project Management

Audit Test Objective

To determine that work is adequately managed and progress reporting is efficient and effective

Key Controls

1. Breakdown of projects into manageable tasks
2. Accurate planning and estimation
3. Progress monitoring

Scope

All projects in progress during the period being examined

Audit Procedures:

Preliminary Review

1. Quantify the work or project originally defined, as a basis for measurement
2. Determine how events are defined
3. Determine how the project progress is monitored
    a. Determine the system used to monitor project progress and completion of activities and tasks
    b. Determine the reports created for monitoring progress, who reviews the reports, and the elements reviewed
4. Determine the extent of project progress reporting to senior management and the frequency on which it is reported

Compliance Testing

1. Verify that the guidelines and requirements found in the preliminary review are complied with

---

Actual performance is monitored by recording actual hours spent, the actual start date, and the actual completion date, or revised target date. The actual performance is compared to the benchmark to determine the adequacy of progress.

The time estimates for accomplishment of the remaining events are added to the actual completion dates to determine the new target date. This new date is compared to the original target date to measure the quality of the progress made. This also reveals whether the original target date is still realistic.

Determining how the project is monitored examines the reporting system used by EDP management. Monitoring techniques only tracks the progress of actual work versus the benchmark.

Resource productivity is difficult to measure because accurate measurement requires an objective benchmark, which can be difficult to obtain. One possible benchmark is the standard amount of time required to write 100 lines of program code. Productivity measurement is accomplished by comparing the actual number of hours spent versus the standard. Difficulty arises in the definition of "standard amount of time." The definition needs two elements: actual number of hours and elapsed time (start to target date). Measuring actual number of hours to a standard can reveal the quality of programmer knowledge, experience, and level of understanding. Measuring actual elapsed time against a standard can reveal the time spent on breaks, interruptions, or other projects.

Another element of project management includes personnel resource planning and the assignment of tasks or activities which include:

1. How much time should be spent per day or week on an activity (the standard), and

2. How much time is actually spent per day or week on an activity (actual performance).

Item 1 above can be derived by spreading the total budget hours for an activity over the elapsed time (start to target date). For example, a budget of 100 hours of work to be done in five days results in an average daily budget of 20 hours. Assuming the budget is correct, if two people are assigned for 7-hour days, then the target completion date will be missed, because only 14 hours of work is being done per day, not 20 hours. The activity will require seven days to complete, not five; either enough people are not assigned to the activity or the target date was incorrectly calculated.

The last element of project management is controlling and estimating completion of the remaining work. This is estimated by calculating the hours per day needed to finish the remaining work by the target date. This estimate is calculated by dividing the total estimated hours needed to finish by the number of remaining work days until the target date.

The estimate of the hours per day needed is compared to the number of work hours per day that are available based on existing staff assignments. This is calculated by multiplying the number of programmers assigned to the project by the number of productive hours in the workday, and multiplying this result by the number of workdays remaining until the target date.

If the available hours remaining equal or exceed the needed hours, then the project is on schedule. Conversely, if available hours remaining are less than the needed hours, the addition of staff is required to finish by the target date.

There are numerous ways to calculate and monitor remaining work; the point is whether EDP management is doing it at all, and if so, is their system effective.

6.3.6 Costing

Review procedures (see Figure 6–8) help the auditor identify the components of the costing mechanism. Data processing costs are usually charged back to the user either in hard dollars or soft dollars to provide a means of accountability for user requests of EDP services. Without this accountability, users would continually request EDP services which may not be justified by the income generated by the business activity.

Costing is generally based on system performance statistics generated by accounting software that is also used for system performance evaluation. The company's accounting department should be directly involved with the allocation of these costs, because they affect the financial statements.

6.3.7 Documentation of Guidelines, Standards, and Procedures

Data processing guidelines and standards are management's instructions to, or requirements of, S&P personnel. Guidelines

FIGURE 6–8   Costing

Audit Test Objective

To determine that the costing methodology is adequate and costs are accurately calculated and allocated

Key Controls

1. Costing methodology
2. Verification procedures

Scope

All data processing costs and chargeback methods

Audit Procedures:

Preliminary Review

Determine the methodology for:

1. Tracking hardware, software, and programming costs
2. Charging back these costs to the user
3. Validating the accuracy of the cost figures

Compliance Testing

Verify:

1. The accuracy of the method(s) used for tracking, allocating, and charging back DP costs.
2. The adequacy of verification techniques.

---

specify how activities and tasks should be accomplished. Standards specify the quality that should be achieved or rules that should be followed, because computers usually function properly only with specific instructions that adhere to specific rules.

Review procedures (see Figure 6–9) simply direct the auditor to focus on management's standards and guidelines for work performed. The auditor's second task is to make sure these standards and guidelines are documented. The absence of documented guidelines and standards creates a critical control weakness that justifies the issuance of a negative opinion on internal control. Without this documentation each person within EDP would be left to his or her own imagination for completing the required

FIGURE 6–9   Standards

Audit Test Objective

To determine that management requirements are adequately documented and communicated

Key Controls

1. Formal documentation
2. Distribution to all S&P personnel
3. Reviews to ensure compliance

Scope

All S&P guidelines and procedures

Audit Procedures:

Preliminary Review

Determine the documented standards that exist for:

1. Systems development, application maintenance, application controls, programming, testing
2. Data including files, reports and library standards
3. Documentation

Compliance Testing

1. If a manual does exist, review the dates of insertion for recency. Determine if stale-dated items reflect current conditions. This can be accomplished along with the test in the next procedure.

    Note: Every page does not need the current year's date.
2. Test the most critical procedures for accuracy to existing environmental conditions, which will also reveal the recency of update. A procedure that doesn't match the processing environment is either outdated or incorrect.
3. Determine that all necessary procedures are included.

---

work and necessary documentation. The result would be complete chaos.

Additionally documented procedures are vital to the consistent operation of S&P. Because of the technical data involved with computer systems operation, each programmer and analyst must be given specific guidelines to follow for the completion of their work. Moreover, these guidelines are a valuable training tool for new personnel, reducing the learning curve and reducing the amount of personal instruction of new personnel, which increases S&P productivity. Inadequate documentation forces S&P management to spend more personal time instructing new hires on details that could be easily documented.

The extent of documentation is installation dependent and is affected by the system's complexity. Significant on-line and database management systems obviously require more in-depth documentation. The auditor, after studying S&P procedures, should be able to assess the quality of the documentation and make appropriate recommendations for improvement, if necessary.

Policies and procedures are the standards and instructions that all EDP personnel must follow to complete their assigned duties. Policies establish the rules, or boundaries of authority, delegated to individuals in the organization. Procedures establish the instructions that individuals must follow to complete their daily assigned tasks. For example, a requirement that all requests for changes to existing programs must be approved by user and EDP management before programmers and analysts can work on them is a matter of policy. Documented instructions for filling out a standard change request form, the manner in which to cost justify the change, how to specify the changes needed, how to obtain approvals, and who to obtain the approvals from are examples of procedures.

Documented policies and procedures should exist in EDP for:

- Use of EDP resources,
- Physical security,
- Data security,
- On-line security,
- Microcomputer use,
- Reviewing, evaluating, and purchasing hardware and software,
- System development methodology, and
- Application program changes.

6.4 COMPLIANCE TESTING

Compliance testing for a systems and programming audit validates the existence of administrative procedures, the actual performance of the procedures, and compliance with standards and guidelines. Because these administrative procedures apply to the entire EDP group, the compliance testing procedures could consume 200 hours for an EDP staff of approximately 200 people.

6.4.1 Tests of Administration Adequacy

Segregation of duties is a traditional control technique aimed at separating overlapping job duties, primarily to discourage fraud, because collusion would then be required to commit the fraud. Such job segregation can also force an accuracy check of one person's work by another. Examples in EDP are segregation of:

- The systems software programming group from the application programming group,
- The database administration group from other EDP activities,
- The computer hardware operations group from the other groups,
- The application programming group into various subgroups for individual application systems,
- The systems analyst function from the programming function, and
- The physical, data, and on-line security group(s) from the other EDP functions.

One test (see Figure 6–3) is accomplished by interviewing a sample of programmers and analysts to determine their actual job duties for comparison against documented job descriptions. Any significant difference between the work actually done versus what is documented should be reported to management and the human resources department manager.

A second test requires the auditor to verify actual segregation of job duties. It is important for the auditor to determine that the duties are segregated in practice, because actual performance may not follow the documented requirements.

A third test, making sure salary levels are competitive, is important, because the company must be able to attract qualified personnel. Salary information is typically confidential in most companies, precluding the staff auditor from analyzing the competitiveness of salary levels. Therefore, the auditor should suggest that the human resources department and EDP management evaluate the salary levels on, at least, an annual basis.

6.4.2 Staff Development Tests

The staff development test procedures (see Figure 6–4) validate that management does assess the skills needed versus the available skills among staff. Making sure that employees' qualifications match job descriptions determines whether EDP management is hiring qualified people, or just anyone, to fill vacancies. The auditor must bear in mind that qualifications may change from time to time and that job descriptions may need updating.

It is also important that the auditor determine, that promotions are based on performance, not favoritism, which destroys morale and reduces the quantity and quality of work. The reasons for promotion should be documented in performance evaluations. The auditor, however, will find it difficult to objectively determine the evaluation's accuracy. Here the auditor must work through informal discussions with employees, being mindful of the disgruntled, and then gauge the quality of work after promotions.

Moreover, the auditor must evaluate the adequacy of programmer and analyst experience, which can be very difficult.

The auditor is looking for gross mismatches of people to specific job duties. For example, the assignment of a programmer with only batch-processing programming experience to a major database programming project is a gross mismatch.

Making sure that technical training programs meet company needs is also crucial. These training programs are generally needed for new programming products and systems. The auditor can do this by examining management provisions for training when new systems or products are purchased.

Lastly, making sure individual performance activities are conducted in accordance with policy is also part of the auditor's purview. This can be accomplished by examining files in the human resources department. These files may be confidential, precluding the staff auditor from conducting the test. Therefore, the auditor should determine that human resources department employees follow procedures for verifying that performance evaluations are completed.

6.4.3   Planning

Planning test procedures (see Figure 6–5) require the auditor to validate the planning elements found during preliminary review. Generally speaking, the planning is either performed or it is not. If the planning is completed, but necessary elements (see Section 6.3.3) are not documented, the planning phase will have little effect and provide little benefit for the company. To quote a common audit axiom: if it is not documented, it is not done.

6.4.4   System Performance Evaluation

S&P performance evaluation tests (see Figure 6–6) focus on determining that all things are monitored that need to be. An absence of criteria provides no basis for comparison and permits systems to deteriorate without management knowledge, which can result in a resource crisis.

Performance evaluation procedures should follow management-established criteria for monitoring the performance of hardware and software to evaluate power, capability, and timeliness. The evaluation should include the following elements described below.

6.4.4.1 PERFORMANCE CRITERIA TO ESTABLISH A BENCHMARK FOR MEASUREMENT[1]

Such criteria as throughput, capability, turnaround time, and response time make up the performance criteria with which to establish a benchmark for measurement.

Capability: This is the measure of the maximum ability of the system, that is, system capacity: the point at which the system can no longer accept any more data. The capabilities of tape and disk drives, CPU, printers and on-line networks should be measured. One means is to monitor the percentage of unused capability, that is, to see how much more the system can take. This factor can be used to predict when a more powerful system or component may be needed. This percentage will decline as applications grow or as more terminals are added. Systems software management should have a benchmark number, for example 90 to 95 percent, that signals the need to consider a more powerful system.

Response time: This measures the elapsed time from entry of an on-line transaction to delivery of the correct response on the screen. Response time can be measured for any output device that queries the system for information.

Throughput: This is the measurement of the total data processing work successfully completed during an hour, a shift, a day or any other predetermined period. Throughput can be measured in various ways: transactions, programs or applications completed per hour, depending on the installation's needs. Throughput can be used to measure workloads of CPU core (main memory), tape drives, disk drives, and printers. Average throughput rates—benchmarks—should be developed for all major equipment and used to measure daily production.

Turnaround time: This measures the elapsed time from the start of input to delivery of final output. Benchmarks should be developed for each application, since processing characteristics will vary. An average turnaround time can be established to measure daily production.

Generally, the systems software unit should closely monitor system effectiveness and efficiency.

6.4.4.2 QUANTIFICATION OF INITIAL AND RECURRING COSTS TO INSTALL AND MAINTAIN THE SYSTEM

This is the responsibility of S&P management, but tracking the units of measurement upon which costs are based for all hardware and systems software is usually the responsibility of the systems software group. Hardware and systems software is used by all users and, ideally, should be charged back to the users on a pro rata basis. This is a simple exercise done in conjunction with the accounting department, but it is the auditor's job to determine that the adequacy of the accounting mechanisms is maintained.

6.4.4.3 ASSESSMENT OF PROJECTED VENDOR SUPPORT, THE FUTURE BENEFIT OF THIS SUPPORT, AND THE EXTENT OF IN-HOUSE SUPPORT THAT WILL BE NEEDED

Any system purchased from a vendor will probably need to be customized to fit the organization, and systems programmers may not understand the new system sufficiently to make the changes. So the organization has either to live with the system as is or to pay the vendor to modify it. These costs must be identified and quantified before the decision is made to purchase the system. Most software needs modification to keep pace with the changing business environment. Reputable vendors typically update the company's system once a year. An annual maintenance fee is charged to cover these updates and to pay for such ongoing support as answering questions and updating documentation.

Before a system is purchased, the quality and cost of vendor support, the benefit of the support, and the extent of in-house support must be quantified and made part of the decision criteria.

6.4.4.4 QUANTIFICATION OF WORKLOAD HANDLING AND SYSTEM CAPACITY NEEDED TO ACCOMPLISH THE WORK

These attributes must be considered with regard to the purchase of new systems. The company can measure these factors against the benchmarks of existing systems to determine whether the new system is indeed an improvement and meets the needs of the organization.

6.4.5 Project Management

The auditor is required to validate the information found during the preliminary review (see Figure 6–7). This involves determining that a time tracking system does exist and adequately reports project progress. The absence of a tracking system constitutes a critical internal control weakness that precludes the necessity for any testing. If a system exists, it should track, at a minimum, actual performance versus the budget for each defined event in terms of hours and elapsed time (see Section 6.3.5).

6.4.6 Costing

Ascertaining the accuracy of the method(s) used for tracking, allocating, and charging back EDP costs defines how these elements are accomplished. The auditor's primary objective is to determine that all costs are accounted for by the method being used.

Ascertaining the adequacy of verification techniques involves validating that EDP management requires, and a person or group actually does, verify the accuracy of the tracking, allocation, and charge-back of EDP costs to various users. This is accomplished by selecting statistical samples of cost categories for users, and tracing the samples through the various aspects of the costing system to determine that the auditee did execute appropriate verification procedures.

6.4.7 Standards

The auditor must determine that adequate guidelines exist to instruct S&P personnel in the completion of their duties (see Figure 6–9). Additionally, the guidelines must be accurately maintained.

The terms "guidelines," "standards," "policies," and "procedures" are, to some extent, used interchangeably, because the definitions of these terms vary from company to company. The EDP auditor must, therefore, first determine the definitions used in his company. The following suggested definitions are provided for clarification:

Guidelines: These are suggested rules, with latitude for individual judgment. Omission or deviation from the guidelines should be justifiable to the extent that another person would have made the same decision.

Standards: These are required rules. Omission or deviation requires pre-approval by a manager or supervisor.

Policies: These are very similar to standards. The key distinction is that policies generally are reviewed and approved specifically by a senior management committee or board of directors. Deviation or omission is usually forbidden.

Procedures: These are step-by-step instructions for the completion of a task or activity. Deviation or omission must be justified and pre-approved by a manager or supervisor.

The age and currency of the documented guidelines and standards must be documented, and the documentation compared to actual conditions. Failure to compare favorably is the primary criteria for the standards and guidelines being outdated.

Making sure that all necessary procedures are included is basic, and may require consulting EDP-related texts, external auditors, the IIA, the EDPAA, or the BAI.

The administrative procedures that must be accomplished in each phase of the system development life cycle must be documented (see Chapter 17).

It is impossible to cover all guidelines, standards, and procedures that would be necessary for every environment. The following is a list of usual items.

6.4.7.1   GENERAL INFORMATION

This includes a general policy statement that governs the company's EDP activities; time logging procedures, explanations of various forms, and a description of the general framework in which data processing operate. The most critical information is the standard numerical or alphabetic code identifiers of departments, divisions, companies, or branches which are used in programs. It should also include a current list of user liaisons, coordinators in the user areas that the programmer or analyst should contact regarding each system.

6.4.7.2   PROGRAMMING STANDARDS

Programming standards are necessary for writing programs. Deviations from these standards requires prior S&P management approval. The installation's supported languages should be identified, with details included on the use of critical instructions or reserve-words of the language. This should provide guidelines for how to define files, how to use database files, the arrangement or procedure statements, and the definition of reports.

6.4.7.3   SYSTEM STANDARDS

System standards are established to cover files, programs, execution, and operations functions in order to permit effective processing of both test and production jobs. Such standards are usually established by the systems software programming group.

Naming Conventions: These are necessary for data files, program libraries, individual program names, application identifiers, and reports. Each character in the name has a specific identification meaning.

An application identifier may be a three-character acronym, such as AUD (for all audit applications). They can be further refined to specify a specific range of numbers for the type of application program. For example, input programs use the 100 series, posting uses 200, and reports use 300, and so on.

Standard names could be required for defining field names in file definitions. For example, the name and address field should be named NAMADDR. This may be important to central file retrieval systems. A single program can query the name and address on any installation file by calling up NAMADDR.

Data set characteristics refer to the specifications for files and include block size, record size, expansion constraints, and labels. Labeling standards are necessary so that all S&P personnel and programs can readily identify files by their label. Block and record size and expansion constraints are necessary to manage disk and tape file resources. Excessively large files waste space.

6.4.7.4 PROGRAM DOCUMENTATION STANDARDS

Program documentation standards specify what should be documented regarding the programs and changes to the programs. The absence of this documentation will increase the complexity of a programmer's job when deciphering the functions of program codes written by someone else. Most documentation manuals list these items in their logical order, as follows:

Documentation revision record: This is a log of who last revised the documentation and when. This gives the programmer a trail to a previous author if there is a need to ask questions.

Systems and program narrative and flowcharts: These explain the overall functions of the system and of the individual programs. The list of programs identifies all of the programs within the application.

Transaction code list and explanations: These describe all of the batch or on-line code identifiers that specify processing for a given transaction.

Output distribution: This specifies the reports generated, the program that generates them, their frequency, and the identity of the user who gets them (see Chapter 8).

Operator procedures: These explain the execution and support instructions for data center computer operators to follow. These are vital to consistent and accurate execution of the programs (see in Chapter 8).

File retention schedules: These are vital to data library operations. They specify the files generated, when, and by what programs. They are necessary to provide file backup.

Restart/recovery procedures: These explain how to recover partially processed files to avoid complete reruns, and how to restart the programs.

Data set definitions: These are the file specifications (see Section 6.4.7.3).

File layouts: These are the descriptions and name of each field in a file, its start position, size, and data type. These are necessary to write program codes to access the fields on a file.

Job control language listing: This lists all of the jcl instructions necessary to run the programs.

Output layouts: This describes the fields and their positions on computer printed reports or terminal screens.

User/application operating procedures: These are detailed explanations for properly operating the application. They include input transaction codes and how to use them, and the reports generated by the application.

6.4.7.5   PROGRAMMING FUNCTIONAL PROCEDURES

Programming functions are step-by-step procedures that S&P personnel must follow. Program change authorization includes how to obtain approval to make changes to a computer program (see Chapter 10).

The defined libraries, their authorized use, and how they are updated should be explained. This defines the rules for programmer access, including the utilities the programmer is authorized to use.

The procedures for desk checking of the program explain how to identify program-coding errors before testing is performed. This leaves fewer errors to identify during programmatic testing. Testing standards should specify the quality of the test that should be conducted and the quantity of data the program should be subjected to. It also includes user review and authorization of test results. The test standards should cover batch and on-line programs.

Compiling and linking procedures are necessary to translate the English version of the program into machine-readable form for execution. Specific utilities perform this function, and the resulting program is written into an object program library. The procedure specifies how to use the utility and how to access the proper library.

Job control language procedures explain the syntax rules for avoiding program failures. These procedures are usually provided by the operating system vendor. S&P procedures should explain the use of cost-center charging codes and the use of passwords or other security information.

Job execution categories specify the processing priority assigned to a specific program by the operating system supervisor. The programmer can specify the category, but the use of too high level a code could cause degraded system performance. Production programs receive a higher priority than test programs.

Output categories specify whether the report is printed to a CRT on-line programming screen, hardcopy report, or both. The rules are very specific; the wrong category can cause the report to be purged from the system or not printed at all.

Abnormal job ending constraints specify the debugging aid reports that the programmer can request if the program fails. These include core dumps, (see Chapter 3), and system messages that provide error codes. The syntax rules used to request these special reports are very specific; the wrong specifications can result in failure and require a rerun.

Sensitive utilities are those which can perform system functions with single commands and without producing any audit trail. Sensitive utilities can modify data files, program libraries, or operating system program codes. Such use should be controlled through a pre-authorization procedure and password to access the appropriate library. S&P procedures should specifically outline the rules for sensitive utility use, and the authorization procedures to use them (see Chapter 14).

NOTES

1. See Mullen, Jack B. "Audit and Control of Program Changes." Reprinted from *EDP Auditing* (New York: Auerbach Publishers). © 1990, Warren, Gorham & Lamont, Inc. Used with permission.

2. Mair, W.C., Wood, D.R., and Davis, K.W. *Computer Control and Audit*, Deloitte & Touche, Wilton, CT, 1976. Reprinted with permission of Deloitte & Touche.

7

Tape and
Disk Library[1]

7.1 INTRODUCTION

The tape and disk (data) library and the data center house
the assets for which S&P management is responsible, that is,

7-1

mainframes, minicomputers, tape and disk drives, multiplexors, front-end processors and printers. Management must develop techniques to ensure that these assets are used as intended, for company activities. Management must also ensure that the company has sufficient resources to meet its data-processing needs. Failure to prepare and follow both long- and short-range plans can cause competitive disadvantage.

The tape and disk library is the custodian and controller of all the magnetic media that contain all of the company's records. Any misapplication of these files can cause business interruption. The data library is often physically located within the data center and under the control of its manager. Because of its unique function and the sensitivity of the magnetic media, however, the duty of tracking these files is segregated from all other data center functions. Access to the library should be restricted to library employees. Management must provide employees with rules by which these files can be used for testing and production that does not jeopardize their security and integrity.

The tape and disk library is one of the simpler audits in the EDP environment because it includes a few easily understood functions. This simplicity allows it to be used as a training ground for new EDP auditors. Control weaknesses in this area threaten the entire control environment, for if the company's files are subject to destruction, loss, or alteration, the company's business may be interrupted.

Natural disasters, including fire, sabotage, theft, and normal wear and tear, are risks that tape and disk library personnel have to control. This chapter identifies library controls, their purposes and discusses audit objectives and procedures for auditor use to evaluate the internal control environment.

7.2 PLANNING AND PREPARATION

According to EDP audit methodology, the auditor should complete the scope summary during the planning and preparation phase. The auditor's work begins by researching previous workpapers for the results of the last audit. The auditor should determine the extent of audit documentation on the transactions to be audited this year, areas of major concern in prior years, and comparison of report and response for potential unresolved items. All unresolved items from last year's report should be discussed with management.

The auditor should interview the data center manager and the tape and disk library manager. The library manager reports to the data center manager. Data centers for most large companies will run the data center for at least two shifts per day, and so the data library will have a supervisor and a staff for each shift, as required by company size. Small data centers may only have one staff person per shift. If this one person works the night shift, he or she may report to a supervisor that works the day shift. The auditor needs to observe operations on all shifts, especially if there is no direct supervision of the night-shift staff.

The auditor should ask the data center manager and the data library supervisor, in separate meetings, to identify the activities and functions that the data library is responsible for. Separate meetings provide the opportunity to compare the answers of manager and subordinate. The auditor should never assume that subordinates perform all the activities that a manager expects. Comparing answers from several different people is the first step in evaluating internal control. The results reveal information about the quality of staff, management, and communication. This is particularly critical when several different groups of people are working in shifts, and even more critical if the evening and midnight shifts operate without supervision.

The standard activity groups for which the data library is responsible include physical security, administrative and functional procedures, and file back-up procedures.

Library Physical Security

Deals with the custodian function (see Figure 7–1, audit transaction A). The data library is usually located in the data center—both areas are concerned with the same security issues. To access the data library, a person must satisfy data center

FIGURE 7–1   Identification of Audit Transactions

Audit Activity Code	Transaction/Area	Include Exclude	Reason
A	Physical Security	I	Satisfies Audit Objective 1
B	Admin./Functional Procedures	I	Satisfies Audit Objective 2
C	File Backup	I	Satisfies Audit Objective 3

security. In cases wherein the library is separate from the data center, however, the auditor must evaluate library security. In addition, library security must prevent access by employees authorized to enter the data center but not authorized to use the library. During the interview of management, the auditor should determine:

- What security is required by management,
- How it is accomplished, and
- What specific equipment is used to accomplish security.

Library administrative and functional procedures

These include the daily activities that the data library staff must perform. The primary manager probably works the day shift and seldom sees the evening or midnight staff. This makes documentation of procedures and the quality of communication with shift managers increasingly important. During the interview of management the auditor should determine:

- To what extent of procedures are documented,
- What activities must be completed daily by each shift,
- What the organizational structure and staffing are, and
- Who is responsible for what activities.

File backup

These procedures are the primary defense against file destruction and natural disasters. The backup files are created by application systems personnel, under control of the mainframe operators. The data librarian should not need to order any significant copying of files for backup. This should be set up as part of application processing. Any other arrangement is inefficient. During the interview of management the auditor should determine:

- The extent of standards documentation and any changes in these since the last audit,
- The extent of the procedures documentation and any changes since the last audit, and
- The extent of testing, as required by management, of the condition of the backup files.

To finalize the interview with management the auditor should determine:

- The major risks perceived by management in each area,
- The procedures that management considers to be key controls,
- The follow-up on previous report comments,
- The frequency with which the data center manager meets with his supervisor,
- The concerns that the manager has, and
- The most important issue to management for each audit transaction.

7.2.1 Risks / Exposures

"Exposures" are too broad to guide the auditor properly in control evaluation. The causes of exposure give the auditor more focus (see Figure 7–2; see also Sections 2.1.3, 2.1.4).

Management must protect the organization from such potential risks and exposures as natural disasters, malicious mischief, sabotage, corporate espionage, and errors, and omissions. Management may try to dismiss these risks as improbable, but many a

FIGURE 7–2   Scope Summary

Risks/Exposures

1. Natural disasters
2. Malicious damage
3. Faulty fire detection or extinguishing system
4. Poor physical handling of files
5. Theft of files
6. Faulty access control system
7. Inadequate documentation update procedures
8. Inaccurate setup sheets and retention schedules
9. Inadequate job descriptions
10. Inadequate assignment of accountability
11. Hardware and software failure
12. Backup files not moved off site
13. Inadequate file inventory
14. Inadequate recovery plan

Control Objectives

1. Protect files from unauthorized access, destruction, or unintentional errors
2. Ensure that administrative and functional procedures are effective, efficient, and consistently executed
3. Ensure that all data and program files can be recreated

Key Controls

1. Restricted access
2. Construction with proper materials
3. Proper physical design
4. Fire prevention, detection, and extinguishing devices
5. Temperature control and air conditioning
6. Air purification
7. Protection and cleaning of tapes and disks
8. Adequate procedures manuals
9. Application run setup sheets
10. File retention schedules
11. Separation of duties
12. Established accountability
13. Disaster recovery plan
14. Off-site storage of backup files
15. File inventory controls

FIGURE 7–2 *(Continued)*

Specific Audit Objectives

Determine that adequate controls exist to ensure:

1. That there is adequate data library physical security
2. That there are adequate, accurate, efficient, and effective procedures and documentation
3. That sufficient file backup exists at any point in time

Preliminary Review Hours

Activity Code	Transaction/Area	Budget Hours	
		Audit Time	Review Time
A	Physical Security	25	1
B	Functional Procedures	35	2
C	Backup and Recovery Procedures	25	1

company was not prepared for that first fire because it had not happened in 40 years of doing business.

The auditor must give adequate consideration to the probability of any of the various causes of exposure occurring. For example, the probability of an earthquake's damaging a California data center is high. Tornados are real threats for Nebraska businesses, whereas floods are common occurrences along the Mississippi River.

7.2.2 Control Objectives

Data library risk exposure control comprises the protection of files from unauthorized access, destruction, or unintentional errors, ensuring effective, efficient, and consistently executed administrative and functional procedures, and the certainty that all data and programs can be recreated. Each audit should enhance the definitions of the control objectives until they optimally match the unique company environment. Increasingly specific control objectives are isolated during the preliminary review, by identifying existing and nonexisting controls. These objectives delineate the threats that management wants the control system to reduce or eliminate. Each risk or exposure can be categorized under these broad control objectives.

7.2.3   Key Controls

Such controls as restricted access, fire prevention, detection, and extinguishing devices, temperature control and air conditioning, disaster recovery plans, and off-site storage of backup files, to name a few, are among specific key controls used by management to accomplish control objectives (see Figure 7–2). This extensive list is the type appropriate after several years of auditing an area. It can be easily developed from the prior year's control identification sheets. The auditor should have the data center manager and data library supervisor review these controls during the planning interview to determine whether they are still in effect.

7.2.4   Audit Objectives

The adequacy of data library physical security, the adequacy, accuracy, effectiveness, and efficiency of procedures and documentation, and the sufficiency of file backups make up the data library audit objectives. The auditor can design this audit, during planning, to achieve very specific results without limiting the audit scope and risking an increase in the level of detection risk. Analyzing the extent of compliance with these three objectives will provide adequate information to determine the risk that the data library imposes upon the data-processing environment (see Figure 7–2).

7.2.5   Planning Phase Completion

To wrap up the planning phase, the auditor completes the scope summary schedule for preliminary review, identifying the transactions to be reviewed and documented and estimating audit time for each transaction. The scope summary is then submitted to the audit supervisor for review. The general auditor should meet with the audit team to review and approve the scope summary (see Figure 7-2).

7.3 EXECUTION OF PRELIMINARY REVIEW

The EDP auditor will review all available documentation to gain an understanding of data library activities and functions. The end products are documentation of the procedures, identification of existing and nonexisting controls, and identification of the functions that should be tested.

The data library is responsible for:

- Secure storage of tape and disk files not in use by computer operators,
- Correct and timely setup of files to be used in processing,
- Adequate retention of files according to preestablished standards, and
- Rotation and backup of critical files.

To ensure secure storage, the duties of file handling must be separated from those of computer operation, thus limiting file access to a few people.

The audit programs delineated by Figure 7-3 through Figure 7-5 can be used as a foundation for creating customized audit programs applicable to the auditors' organization. They are provided as a basis for training in the creation and use of audit programs and techniques, and as an exposure to EDP audit topics.

7.3.1 Physical Security

First, the auditor must examine the access control system. Library access should be controlled with a card access system or, at least, locks. The card access system should be programmed to permit only library and key supervisory personnel to enter the

FIGURE 7-3   Physical Security

Audit Test Objective

To determine the adequacy of data library physical security

Key Controls

1. Restricted access
2. Construction with proper materials
3. Proper physical design
4. Fire prevention, detection, and extinguishing devices
5. Temperature control and air conditioning
6. Air purification
7. Protection and cleaning of tapes and disks

Scope

The data library area

Audit Procedures:

Preliminary Review

1. Document the functions and components of the physical access control system
2. Ensure that library walls, ceilings and floors are constructed of fire resistant material
3. Ensure that walls extend from the concrete floor to concrete ceiling, not from the raised floor to a suspended ceiling
4. Determine that holes in the concrete ceiling are sealed to prevent the spread of water from an upper floor, in the event of fire or other water source
5. Determine that the data library is not located near a fire-prone area such as a cafeteria
6. Document the fire detection devices used in the library
7. Determine if tape/disk files are transported in protective containers
8. Document the procedures for specific management authorization to transport files to other processing centers

Compliance Testing

Verify that:

1. Access to the library is restricted to specific employees by keylocks or a card access system
2. Adequate fire extinguishing equipment protects the library itself separate from the data center or other areas
3. Tape/disk files are transported in protective containers
4. Tape/disk files are periodically cleaned
5. Specific management authorization is given for transport of files to other processing centers

FIGURE 7–4 Administrative and Functional Procedures

Audit Test Objective

Determine the adequacy and accuracy of the procedures and the documentation

Key Controls

1. Adequate procedures manuals
2. Use of setup sheets
3. Effective retention schedules
4. Adequate separation of duties
5. Established accountability

Scope

All activities and functions performed during the period being examined

Audit Procedures:

Preliminary Review

1. Document the procedures for job scheduling and preparing setup instructions
2. Document the procedures to obtain or prepare external file labels
3. Determine that file retention schedules are included in the procedures manual for each system
4. Document the procedures for off-site storage and file rotation
5. Document the procedures for saving files beyond their normal retention period
6. Document the procedures for off-site transport of files, logging of the files, and authorization to transport them
7. Document the procedures for performing a periodic inventory of the tapes and disk files
8. Document the procedures and frequency for cleaning and recertification of tapes, and disk packs

Compliance Testing

Verify that:

1. Job scheduling and setup instructions should match the requirements of the corresponding job run
2. Files are moved to an off-site location according to a preestablished schedule as soon after they are created as possible
3. Indefinite saving of files is generally avoided
4. Files leaving the library for purposes other than job setup are logged, and the transport is authorized
5. An accurate periodic inventory of the tapes and disk files is performed
6. The tapes and disk packs are periodically cleaned and recertified for quality according to a preestablished schedule
7. The documentation of procedures properly explains all activities and functions of the library

FIGURE 7–5   Backup and Recovery Procedures

Audit Test Objective

To determine that the data library can recover all data and program files

Key Controls

1. Disaster recovery plan
2. Off-site storage of backup files
3. Effective retention schedules
4. File inventory controls

Scope

All backup and recovery procedures executed during the period being examined

Audit Procedures:

Preliminary Review

1. Review the disaster contingency plan—determine that it adequately explains the librarian procedures for a disaster

Compliance Testing

Verify that:

1. The length of time that the critical (most current) files remain in the library or data center. For a sample of applications locate the most current master and transaction files
2. Operating system and program libraries are copied and moved to the off-site location at least daily
3. The accuracy of the off-site storage inventory record by comparing it to the actual inventory
4. The adequacy of the off-site storage location—it should be protected to the same degree as the data library for access, fire protection, water damage, and environmental control
5. The extent of disaster plan testing which has been performed

data file library. If a lock is used, key distribution should be limited to appropriate personnel and a log of the keys should be maintained. Cards and keys should be collected from employees on termination, and management should consider changing any important locks accessed by terminated employees.

The physical design and construction materials should help prevent or at least reduce the spread of fire or water from adjacent areas. For example holes are often drilled through concrete ceilings and floors for cabling conduits. If the unused holes are not sealed, water used to fight a fire on an upper floor could leak through to the data library.

The auditor should inspect the ceiling and beneath any raised floors to make sure of the presence of fire and smoke detectors capable of detecting heat, smoke, and toxic fumes.

Tape and disk files should be transported to off-site locations for storage or processing in containers that prevent damage from external blows; however, this requirement must be reasonable. Files leaving the processing center for off-site processing should be specifically authorized for removal by stringent screening and checkout procedures and should only be turned over to authorized carriers (see Figure 7–3).

7.3.2 Administrative and Functional Procedures

Documenting the procedures for job scheduling and preparing setup instructions relates to the librarian's duties for daily application processing. A setup sheet tells the librarian which files should be prepared for processing and the files that will be created. The setup sheet should contain appropriate job-processing information, processing time, run frequency, program names, input files used by the program, output files created by the program, file IDs, and volume serial number. The external file ID number should be recorded on the setup sheet by the operator. The setup instructions should specify on which work shifts each of the files are to be set up for execution.

The application programs usually create an internal file label that is used by a file library management system. However, since they are in machine-readable form, the files need external labels that are in English. A sample of file labels should be compared with setup sheets for accuracy, while a separate sample of setup sheets should be compared to the file labels. This test will identify missing labels and files without set-up instructions.

Determine that file retention schedules are included in the procedures manual for each section. These schedules can be compared with the data-center's manual and application documentation for accuracy.

The procedures for off-site storage and file rotation provide the librarian with a schedule for files transfer to the off-site vault and a list of the files to be moved. The auditor can review these items for accuracy by comparing them with the actual events. The assessment of their adequacy requires judgment on whether all necessary files are included and whether the schedule provides for adequate backup at all times.

Data and program files are routinely saved beyond their specified retention period. Procedures for saving a file past its usual retention time must be documented. A special log sheet should be maintained containing the file name, file ID, volume serial number, retention time, purpose for saving, and the name of the person requesting the save. The auditor can assess the accuracy of this information by comparing the file identification data with the file and by verifying the purpose, reason, and name with the person requesting the save. The librarian should be able to contact the person requesting the save to determine when the file can actually be erased. Indefinite saves should generally be avoided.

Review step 6 examines procedures for logging files that leave the library for purposes other than off-site storage. The log should contain file identification, date, the time the file is removed, the name of the person taking the file, and the time the file is due for return. Files should not be allowed out of the data center unless authorized for transport to another processing site under normal operating procedures or for special testing situations.

The librarian should perform a periodic inventory of files to ensure none are missing. Obviously this pertains to files other than those needed for daily processing.

7.3.3   Backup and Recovery Procedures

Backup copies of computer files are the primary defense against file destruction and file processing errors. If the files are in the data center at the time of the disaster they will most likely be destroyed, therefore, they must be moved to an off-site storage location as soon as possible, after creation. The creation of primary files and backup files are embedded in the application processing procedures. The librarian role in this activity is embedded in the job scheduling and file set-up and the moving of strategic files to off-site locations.

The librarian will have specific procedures to follow in the event of a disaster which should be explained in detail in a disaster contingency plan. Preliminary review step 1 in Figure 7–5 instructs the auditor to determine if this plan exists and review it for adequacy. The auditor can trust the librarian knowledge of the disaster contingency plan by interviewing the librarian. Obviously a copy of the disaster contingency librarian procedures should also be stored in an off-site location.

7.4 COMPLIANCE TESTING

Compliance testing confirms that required control procedures were performed and consists of the two following elements:

1. *Evaluation* of the testing results, review of the entire function, and assessment of the adequacy of existing controls to determine whether these controls ensured organization control objectives.

2. *Testing* of previously completed activities or transactions to determine whether they were performed accurately, consistently, and in compliance with existing policies and procedures.

The first step indicates whether the individual controls provided a satisfactory level of reliance within the organizational environment at a given time, whereas the second step ensures that the controls were functioning throughout the entire period being examined. Performing only the first step allows the auditor to assess the adequacy of controls but does not prove that they were consistently used. This can result in an audit opinion that may not be valid for the entire period in question.

Audit Scope and Test Objective:

The audit test objective defines the end product of each test, whereas the audit scope specifies the amount of testing and review that must be done to accomplish the audit objective. In an EDP environment, the audit scope should include user interfaces, because processing accuracy is a user responsibility even though application programs are run on computers not under user control. The data center is a service department whose primary purpose is to process user input, with adequate controls. Users, however, know better than anyone how the output data should be presented, and, therefore should control the processing of the data belonging to them.

Computers are machines that perform as instructed. Therefore, once they are adequately tested, computer applications perform consistently, barring hardware failure or program maintenance errors. Manual controls, on the other hand, are prone to error; most incorrect processing is caused by their misapplication.

7.4.1   Physical Security

Physical security refers to the protection of the files containing data and programs from unauthorized access, destruction, or unintentional errors.

Restricting access to specific employees is a fundamental element of physical security. The auditor should obtain a list of library employees from the personnel department and compare it to either the log of personnel issued keys for locks, or the printout of library employees from the card access system. The card access system can be further checked for time-of-day access by comparing the card access system information to the work shift schedule. Another possible test is to have a library employee(s) try his or her card during an unauthorized period.

Fire extinguishing equipment is difficult to test because the only effective test is to discharge either the CO_2 or Halon gas that is typically used. The auditor should inspect the system to determine that it can be automatically triggered and that this triggering can be manually delayed to give personnel time to evaluate the situation. It may be better simply to verify that extinguishing equipment is regularly inspected by trained personnel.

Testing for transport of files in protective containers means that the auditor should watch the transport to off-site storage or to customers. Obviously, if there are not protective containers available then a control weakness exists.

Tape and disk files can be cleaned with special equipment that will extend the life of such magnetic media. The auditor should determine that this cleaning is done on a regular schedule and is, indeed, actually performed. The cleaning activities may be deferred to evening and midnight shifts, but with this reduced supervision, the cleaning may not be performed, so verification is important.

All files transported to customers or other processing centers should be recorded in a log specially designed for this purpose. The auditor should verify that all files are accurately logged and that no files leave the library or data center without being logged (see Figure 7–3).

7.4.2 Administrative and Functional Procedures

The auditor should verify that the administrative and functional library procedures are effective, efficient, and consistently executed. All of the compliance tests should be performed on samples of activities or events occurring during the audit period.

First, the auditor should determine the impact of the application on job scheduling. This requires researching application documentation to verify that sufficient CPU time and elapsed time are allocated in the job schedule. The application documentation should also explain the set-up instructions that are used by the tape librarian to provide appropriate input files and scratch files for output file creation.

The second step requires verification of files moved to off-site storage. The auditor can review these items for accuracy by comparing them with the actual events. The assessment of their adequacy, however, requires a judgment call based on whether all necessary files are included and whether the schedule provides for adequate backup at all times. Inventory a sample of files in the data center at any point in time. Any files present would be destroyed if a fire actually occurred.

The third step is that of ensuring that files are not saved indefinitely. The fourth test is that of examining the logging of transported files by comparing the files transported to the log. The fifth test, verifying that accurate periodic inventory of the tapes and disk files is performed, does not mean the auditor should perform an inventory unless the inventory controls are so weak as to indicate that tapes and disk files are missing. The focus should be on what the auditee does to maintain adequate inventory records. The sixth test, making sure magnetic media are clean and quality controlled, can be performed by inspecting external tape labels for recorded cleaning and inspection dates. The seventh test, making sure that procedure documentation properly explains all activities and functions of the library is accomplished by observing library personnel performing their duties and by interviewing library personnel to determine if they think the documented procedures are adequate.

7.4.3   Backup and Recovery Procedures

The objective of these procedures is to permit recreation of data and program files if they are damaged. Most installations use the grandfather-father-son method of generation data set creation.

Simply explained, on day one the application processes the transaction files and updates the master file. On day two, the application reads the current transaction file and day one's master file to create a new master. With the creation of this new master, the day one master files becomes the "father" and the current day master becomes "son." On day three, processing continues in the same way and the new master becomes the son, with day two being the "father" and day one being the "grandfather" file. This processing scheme is continued day after day.

An effective backup strategy is to move the son file and current day transaction file to off-site storage as soon as possible. If the data center is destroyed by fire, the "son" master can be retrieved from off-site storage, allowing computer processing to continue at another installation. When the son file is delivered to off-site storage, the grandfather file is brought to the data library. The father and son generations and the corresponding days (transaction files) are then in the off-site location. Obviously, to perform daily processing, the father file must be brought back to the data center at some time before the execution of daily processing. The time of highest risk is when this father file is in the data center, because the father file and current day's transaction file, used to create the new son, are all in the data center at the same time. If a disaster occurs and the father file and current transaction file are destroyed, then the father file would have to be re-created from the grandfather and prior day's transaction file. It is to be hoped that the source data of the current day's transaction file transactions will still be available to re-create the current day's master. The auditor should determine that the current day's transactions can be re-created from source documents or other means.

Systems and program libraries that contain all of the operating system, utilities, and application programs do not adhere to the grandfather-father-son principal because there is no transaction file. However, during a day's work, changes are made to the production libraries that at some point during the day should be copied and the copy moved to the off-site location. Installation management can determine whether this copying and moving off-site should be done more than once a day.

Examining the inventory records of the files that should be maintained and updated daily in off-site storage is also necessary. This is necessary to help the librarian find needed files. The auditor should test the accuracy of the inventory record by comparing it to the inventory of files in the off-site location. Computer installations frequently keep weekly, monthly, quarterly, and year-end application files. Depending on the importance of these files, copies should be considered for storage in the off-site location.

Disaster contingency plans are only good if they work. A disaster is not the time to find out that the plan is missing essential elements. Therefore, the disaster plan should be tested at least annually, possibly twice a year, to help identify any inadequacies.

Compliance testing in this area requires the auditor to locate the current master and transaction files in the data center, which serves to validate the adequacy of the procedure to move files off-site as soon as possible. The longer the critical (most current) files remain in the library or data center, the greater the risk of destruction. The auditor can simulate a disaster by selecting any time of day and taking inventory. The files found in the data center or library during such an inventory will need to be re-created if a disaster actually occurs (see Figure 7-5).

NOTES

1. See Mullen, Jack B. "Auditing the Data Center: Setting Audit Test Objectives." Adapted from *EDP Auditing* (New York: Auerbach Publishers). © 1989, Warren, Gorham & Lamont, Inc. Used with permission.

8

The Data Center[1]

8.1 INTRODUCTION

The data center shares the risks and exposures of the data library, with which it shares its location organizationally and physically. Each has distinct duties that are incompatible and, therefore,

8-1

must be segregated for control purposes. Physical security of the data center is critical to overall EDP environmental control. The audit should concentrate on the procedures that provide security, as well as effective and efficient operation. Data center functions are similar to assembly-line manufacturing, for such functions have specific production goals to meet each day. Data center personnel must follow security procedures to protect hardware, software, and data from unauthorized access, change, or destruction.

The data center audit is simpler than most, and provides a good training ground for the entry level EDP auditor. The physical security audit procedures for the data library and the data center are essentially the same, which provides an opportunity for increased efficiency.

8.2 PLANNING AND PREPARATION

Even though the data library and data center share risks and exposures, their activities and functions are distinctly different. The EDP auditor must execute the audit planning procedures to identify data center activities and functions.

The major concerns from previous years will most likely be physical security weaknesses or breakdowns in functional procedures. For example, development of a disaster recovery plan has been an industrywide concern in recent years. Preparation of the plan is costly and time-consuming. This may be an unresolved item from the prior audit.

The pre-audit conference should include the data center manager and his or her superior. This conference permits the auditor to interview management to determine:

- Management's perception of data center risks,
- Key controls relied upon by the data center manager,
- Open items from the previous data center audit report,
- Communication quality between the data center manager and his manager, and

- Management's most important issue for each audit transaction.

Data center activities include loading and executing application programs, mounting and dismounting tape and disk files for use on the application programs, preparing the printer with appropriate forms, responding to requests from the operating system and application programs, maintaining equipment, and correcting hardware and software malfunctions. These activities appear simple and limited, but data center employees and management have other responsibilities as well. These generally fall into the six categories (see Figure 8–1).

Physical Security

This addresses the same issues as concern the data library, except that physical security involves the entire data center. The data center adds to the library's list a few physical security concerns, such as air conditioning, power supply, and access control over the data center. Data center access control is a primary defense and includes some additional considerations not found with the data library.

Functional Procedures

These include the activities performed by the computer operators, job schedulers, and shift supervisors. Data center personnel typically work in three shifts around the clock and are responsible for accepting input data in tape, disk, or punch card form. Input may also be received through an on-line posting

FIGURE 8–1   Identification of Audit Transactions

Audit Activity Code	Transaction/Area	Include Exclude	Reason
A	Physical Security	I	Satisfies Audit Objective 1
B	Functional Procedures	I	Satisfies Audit Objective 2, 3
C	Operating Efficiency	I	Satisfies Audit Objective 4
D	Insurance	I	Satisfies Audit Objective 5
E	Documentation	I	Satisfies Audit Objective 6
F	Contingency Planning	I	Satisfies Audit Objective 7

system. If the application systems update files are in realtime mode, the computer operator must keep the application running. On the other hand, input transactions could be posted to an on-line tape or disk file for use in batch processing. Personnel are responsible for input acceptance and control, system support, output generation and distribution to the approved user.

Operating Efficiency

This involves monitoring system performance for capacity constraints and service levels. The monitoring programs create reports for evaluation by system software technicians. However, a computer operator may receive diagnostic messages from the operating system, utilities, or applications, which may indicate capacity or performance problems. A procedure should exist for the operator to record and report these messages to the appropriate group.

Insurance Policies

These should be purchased to protect the company against errors and omissions, business interruptions, and fraud, because the data center is the custodian of a significant company investment. Although this insurance may not be the responsibility of data center management, it is not inconvenient to audit the list of assets covered by casualty insurance.

Documentation

This is an essential element in maintaining production. Numerous application programs require different operator actions for routine production and problem correction. It is virtually impossible for operators to memorize all of the requirements from all of the applications. Inadequate documentation will contribute to processing errors, thereby reducing the efficiency and effectiveness of data center operations.

Contingency Planning

This involves the recovery from a destructive event's occurring in the data center, or another area of the building that could affect the data center. Such an event can be as simple as a program malfunction that requires application reexecution or as complex as a fire that destroys the entire data center. Data center management and personnel will be key figures in execution of the disaster recovery plan.

Scope Summary

Specific audit objectives are defined that focus on data center control objectives. This is, essentially, the data center environment.

8.3 EXECUTION OF PRELIMINARY REVIEW

Time budget estimates are listed in Figure 8–2 for each transaction included in preliminary review. The preliminary review involves estimates of the time needed to assess documentation, reviewing the control system, and identifying existing and non-existing controls. Such risks and exposures as vandalism, fire, theft, inadequate recovery planning, and inadequate insurance, to name a few, can be used as guidelines for any installation. The auditor should determine that these risks and exposures are actually present in this organization. Such key controls as restricted access, fire detection, documented recovery plan, and adequate insurance can be used as a basis for comparison when identifying existing and nonexisting internal controls. If a key control is not present in the data center being reviewed, the auditor must first determine that the standard key controls are necessary to reduce or eliminate risk.

Preliminary review steps can be used as a foundation for preparing a customized review. The depth of the review depends on the quality of the internal controls found in the data center (see Figure 8–2).

8.3.1 Physical Security

The physical security review and testing procedures in Figure 8–3 are similar to those of the data library, except that they encompass the entire data center. The data library restricts

FIGURE 8–2   Scope Summary

Risks/Exposures

1. Natural disasters
2. Malicious damage
3. Faulty fire detection or extinguishing system
4. Poor physical handling of files
5. Theft of files
6. Faulty access control system
7. Inadequate documentation update procedures
8. Inadequate job descriptions
9. Inadequate assignment of accountability
10. Hardware or software failure
11. Backup files not moved off site
12. Inadequate recovery plan
13. Excess or insufficient capacity
14. Inadequate monitoring of system service levels
15. Inadequate insurance

Control Objectives

1. Protect hardware and software from unauthorized access and damage
2. Ensure that the administrative and functional data center procedures are effective, efficient, and consistently executed
3. Maintain processing adequacy and efficiency at a level sufficient to service the organization
4. Ensure that the insurance coverage for data center facilities is adequate
5. Ensure run manuals contain appropriate data about the execution of all application programs in the data center
6. Data center operation can be resumed within a reasonable time after a disaster

Key Controls

1. Restricted access
2. Construction with proper materials
3. Proper physical design
4. Fire prevention, detection, and extinguishing devices
5. Temperature control and air conditioning
6. Air purification
7. Adequate run manuals
8. Adequate procedures manuals
9. Monitoring of system service levels
10. Routine evaluation of insurance coverage

FIGURE 8-2 *(Continued)*

11. Separation of duties
12. Established accountability
13. Documented disaster recovery plan
14. Off-site storage of backup files
15. Backup processing site

Specific Audit Objectives

Determine that adequate controls exist to ensure:

1. The adequacy of data center physical security
2. The adequacy, accuracy, efficiency, and effectiveness of the procedures and documentation
3. Fair and legal treatment of employees while providing qualified people for the job, adequate security, and control of job functions
4. Data center management effectively measures the performance of hardware and software
5. Insurance coverage is adequate and routinely evaluated
6. The adequacy of the run manual and procedures documentation in the data center
7. The adequacy of the disaster recovery plan

Time Budget

Preliminary Review Hours

Activity Code	Transaction/Area	Budget Hours	
		Audit Time	Review Time
A	Physical Security	25	1
B	Functional Procedures	35	2
C	Operating Efficiency	20	1
D	Insurance	5	.5
E	Documentation	10	1
F	Contingency Planning	10	1

computer operators from entering the library. The data center restricts application analysts and programmers from entering the data center. Entry into the main data center area should be allowed only to the employees who work there, except when programmers or analysts need access to correct a program or systems malfunction. Entrance to the data center should be allowed through only one door; fire regulations, however, require emergency exits. To prevent unauthorized access through fire doors, one-way, alarmed crash doors can be used. To increase security, data center access can be monitored by a closed-circuit video recording system. Data center personnel should be instructed as to how to handle unauthorized personnel's requesting access or entering the data center.

Data centers generally require power interruption protection—uninterruptable power supply (UPS)—to maintain the system's operation. Power interruption control switches should be strategically located, permitting easy access but preventing accidental activation. Fire extinguishing systems may be automatically activated by detection devices, providing a two-minute delay to allow reaction time. The delay allows deactivation in the event of a false alarm. Deactivation switches should also be adequately located, again, permitting easy access but preventing accidental activation.

8.3.2 Administrative and Functional Duties

The preliminary steps vis-à-vis auditing the data center focus on organizational structure and the control of personnel. The organizational structure establishes the reporting relationship for each employee, enabling him or her to know to whom to report. The job descriptions should describe the job qualifications and responsibilities, at least in a broad sense. The documented job descriptions establish senior management's delegation of authority and provide instructions of what it expects.

Data center employees have access to very costly assets, especially the files that contain all company records. For this reason, it is crucial that employees be trustworthy. When allowed by state law and Equal Employment Opportunity Commission (EEOC) requirements, prospective employees' should be screened for criminal records and job histories should be verified. Credit bureau reports are also used by some organizations as an additional screening technique. The rotating of job duties periodically helps cross-train data center employees and reduces the concentration

FIGURE 8–3 Physical Security

Audit Test Objective

To determine the adequacy of data center physical security

Key Controls

1. Restricted access
2. Construction with proper materials
3. Proper physical design
4. Fire prevention, detection, and extinguishing devices
5. Temperature control and air conditioning
6. Air purification

Scope

The data center area

Audit Procedures:

Preliminary Review

1. Document the functions and components of the physical access control system
2. Determine that data center walls, ceilings and floors are constructed of fire resistant material
3. Determine that walls extend from the concrete floor to concrete ceiling, not from the raised floor to a suspended ceiling
4. Determine that holes in the concrete ceiling are sealed to prevent the spread of water from an upper floor, in the event of fire or other water source
5. Determine that the data center is not located near a fire-prone area such as a cafeteria
6. Document the fire detection devices used in the data center
7. Document electrical power control and backup devices

Compliance Testing

Verify that:

1. Access to the data center is restricted to specific employees by keylocks or a card access system
2. Adequate fire extinguishing equipment protects the data center
3. Data center personnel are aware of fire emergency procedures
4. The fire extinguishing and detection equipment is tested periodically by competent personnel
5. The fire detection system detects fire, smoke, excessive heat, and combustible fumes
6. Emergency backup lighting should be provided and tested at periodic intervals
7. The data center fire alarm notifies a central monitoring station
8. Adequate water drainage is provided under the raised floor
9. Verify that backup power supply is adequate to support the computer system and necessary air conditioning
10. The air conditioning system adequately maintains required temperature and humidity levels

of knowledge in one single person. It also prevents perpetuation of fraud, improper acts, or inadequate completion of job duties.

Determining termination procedures—making sure ID badges and access cards are collected, changing passwords and locks, and reconciling accounts controlled by the employee—could also be placed in physical security review procedures, because physical security is a vital element in environmental control. Essentially, taking these steps ensures that former employees cannot easily gain access to the data center. In addition, payroll and other checks and cash items are usually stored in the data center for printing. Reconciling used and unused check stock after each printing is a vital control. These supplies should be reconciled before an employee who was responsible for this activity leaves the company.

Conflicting duties are those which performed together provide a person with the opportunity to divert resources to personal use. One example is the separation of the tape library from computer operator responsibility. The extent of conflicting duties depends upon how activities and functions are designed and assigned to various individuals. Auditor judgment is required in making these decisions.

Documenting such procedures as control of input data, system support of on-line systems by computer operators, and output distribution can be accomplished by flowchart, narrative, or copies of excerpts from procedures manuals. By any method the auditor's responsibility is to identify the control points and weaknesses in procedures. Any method of documentation can be used as long as the evidence standard is satisfied.

The control over input data received by the data center must be reviewed. Many current computer systems use on-line data capture for daily transaction processing. The transactions are posted in a real-time mode—as they happen—or in memo-posting mode to a file for later batch posting. With these methods, the tape or disk input file is already in the data center under computer operator control. However, applications still exist that accept key-to-tape, key-to-disk, or punch card input. They are usually prepared in another area of the company. This input

FIGURE 8-4 **Administrative and Functional Procedures**

Audit Test Objective

Determine the adequacy and accuracy of the procedures

Key Controls

1. Adequate procedures
2. Adequate separation of duties
3. Established accountability

Scope

All activities and functions performed during the period being examined

Audit Procedures:

Preliminary Review

1. Determine the organization structure and job descriptions for each position
2. Determine preemployment screening practices used to avoid undue security risks
3. Determine how job duties are rotated periodically for cross-training and to limit perpetuation of questionable practices
4. Determine the employee termination procedures
   a. ID badges and access cards are collected
   b. Passwords known by the terminated employee are changed
   c. Keys are collected or locks changed
   d. Accounts or resources that the employee controlled are reconciled
5. Determine if all conflicting duties are segregated
6. Document the procedures for control of input data received in tape, disk or card form
7. Document the procedures for system support of on-line systems by computer operators
8. Document the procedures for output distribution

Compliance Testing

Verify that:

1. Job descriptions accurately match the duties of all positions
2. All prospective data center employees are screened for possible security risks
3. Employee termination procedures are followed
4. Verify that input files are logged and identified
5. Verify that output distribution procedures ensure:
   a. Creation of all required reports
   b. Distribution to only the authorized user and
   c. Distribution meets the deadline

media must be physically transported to the data center for daily processing. Data center personnel must maintain an identification log of the input data received to prove they received it and ensure they have all required input prior to starting application processing.

On-line systems use terminals to communicate with applications on the mainframe while updating tape and disk files, as the work day progresses. The major files usually created by an on-line system include a master file, transaction file, and log files. Log files are used to capture before-and-after images of master record updates and logging of transactions entered. This technique maintains the transactions in two places, one on the transaction file and another on the log file. The log file is used for backup of the transaction file and for automatic restart recovery of on-line master files should the on-line system fail or its files become corrupted. The operator's job is to monitor the tape and disk drives to ensure continuation of on-line activities. The application programs should provide messages to the operator to change tape or disk files when they are full.

Output distribution has two major requirements: 1) to ensure that all required output is generated, and 2) to ensure that only the authorized user receives the output. Hundreds of computer reports may be generated in a 24-hour day. Report control listings that identify the reports generated and the authorized user are the only effective means to ensure proper output distribution. Timeliness of output distribution is also a key factor. When reports are delayed, other employees who use those reports sit around with nothing to do.

8.3.3 Operating Efficiency

System performance and capacity levels must be monitored to ensure effective and efficient use of hardware and software. The systems software group and management is largely responsible for performance monitoring. However, the software programs or utilities that accumulate necessary statistics must be kept running by computer operators (see Chapters 6 and 14). The performance statistics that are generated can vary based on management methodology and philosophy.

Determining the methods used to measure system adequacy and performance is a crucial step in data center preliminary review procedures. These can be as simple as measuring the percent of usage and capacity to measuring instructions per second, disk access time, and memory paging rates. When the methods and statistics become too complicated, the EDP auditor should seek technical help from audit management or EDP technicians as needed (see Figure 8–5).

Performance benchmarks are standards that the system should or can achieve. The benchmarks are compared to actual

---

FIGURE 8–5   Operating Efficiency

Audit Test Objective

To determine whether data center management effectively measures the performance of hardware and software

Key Controls

1.   Monitoring of system service levels

Scope

The data library area

Audit Procedures:

Preliminary Review

1.   Determine the methods used to measure system adequacy and performance
2.   Determine the performance benchmarks approved by EDP management
3.   Determine how the performance statistics are reported at intervals useful to company management
4.   Determine the responsibilities of data center personnel for collecting and reporting statistics

Compliance Testing

Verify that:

1.   Performance benchmarks were approved by user and EDP management
2.   The reporting of performance is useful to management
3.   Performance limits are sufficient to indicate the need for additional CPU, disk capacity, on-line terminals or job rescheduling

---

performance, providing a basis for measurement. Generating performance statistics is really meaningless without some basis for comparison. Furthermore, the performance statistics and benchmarks are effective only when used properly. They should be used to help management make system capacity and performance decisions with sufficient lead time to prevent system failure or processing problems.

When the above-mentioned steps are completed, the EDP auditor is better equipped to determine the responsibilities of data center personnel for collecting and reporting statistics. Computer operators may only be responsible for supporting the data collection utilities. Conversely, the data center manager may be responsible for collecting and reporting the statistics in a usable form and meeting a specific deadline.

8.3.4 Insurance

Many types of insurance coverage are available that satisfy business needs. Someone in the company should be responsible for insurance and risk management. This person determines the types of insurance needed, the cost, and extent of protection. The preliminary review should focus on insurance to cover computer hardware and software loss, and related failures. It is not the auditor's responsibility to perform the risk manager's job, but insurance for data-center-related problems can be easily overlooked. An effective audit review could save the company countless sums of money (see Figure 8–6).

All data center equipment should be covered for loss from all types of disasters. Business interruption can cover a portion of income lost due to data center destruction. Business expense insurance covers the cost of using outside facilities for computer processing when the data center is unusable. Media insurance coverage covers replacement costs of physical disks and tape files, plus the cost of reproducing the data recorded on them. Media-in-transit insurance covers theft losses of tape and disk files being transported. A computer crime policy can cover a loss from computer frauds committed by persons outside the company.

FIGURE 8–6 Insurance

Audit Test Objective

To determine whether the insurance coverage is adequate and routinely evaluated

Key Controls

1. Routine evaluation of insurance coverage
2. Established accountability

Scope

All insurance coverage on data processing resources

Audit Procedures:

Preliminary Review

1. Determine the types of insurance needed, their cost and extent of protection
2. Determine that all data center equipment is covered against loss or damage

Compliance Testing

Verify that:

1. Insurance coverage is reviewed at least annually for coverage of new equipment and reductions for retired or obsolete equipment

---

The auditor's preliminary review of insurance should determine; 1) whether adequate insurance is maintained to cover EDP-related issues, and 2) whether someone in the company is evaluating insurance needs.

8.3.5 Documentation

Audit review and testing of documentation will be included within the functional procedures transaction. It is treated separately here because of its importance to the success of data center operations. The preliminary review of documentation is quiet simple. The auditor must find: 1) the documentation prepared by the auditee, and 2) management's requirements for documentation (see Figure 8–7).

Numerous computer programs are executed, using many files that create output files and reports. It would be virtually impossible for operators to memorize all program requirements.

FIGURE 8–7   Documentation

Audit Test Objective

To determine the adequacy of documented instructions used by data center personnel

Key Controls

1.   Adequate run manuals
2.   Adequate procedures manuals

Scope

Documentation existing as of the audit date

Audit Procedures:

Preliminary Review

1.   Determine the policy requirements for data center documentation
2.   Determine the documentation available
3.   Determine that a documented application run schedule exists

Compliance Testing

1.   Verify the application run manuals include detailed explanations of:
     a.   Flow of job steps
     b.   Files to be loaded and created
     c.   Cpu and run time requirements
     d.   Diagnostic messages displayed by the applications or utilities during execution
     e.   Operator action and response to diagnostic messages and other application generated messages
     f.   Restart/recovery procedures in step-by-step format
     g.   Special security procedures for sensitive utilities or other protected programs
2.   A sample of run manual pages should be compared to actual events
3.   Verify the accuracy of the application run schedule

Detailed and accurate documentation is the only effective means to ensure processing accuracy.

8.3.6   Contingency Planning

EDP management is responsible for establishing a disaster recovery plan to provide data processing resources in case of catastrophe. A company can build its own backup computer processing facility, it can contract with companies whose only business is to provide backup data processing sites, or it can us reciprocal agreements with companies that have similar data processing systems.

The sophistication of many computer systems makes it difficult to find two identical computer configurations, thereby reducing the potential for using reciprocal backup agreements. It is impractical to expect that another company would have sufficient excess capacity to handle both companys' processing requirements.

Creating a backup data center is an excellent strategy, but it is extremely expensive unless it is routinely used for other processing. Backup processing companies are another expensive alternative. In fact, any effective backup processing strategy is expensive, but management must weigh the costs and the risks. If a catastrophe destroys the data center, it is likely that all resident documentation will be destroyed. Therefore, a copy of the recovery plan should be stored in the off-site vault with tapes and disks.

The preliminary review steps in Figure 8–8 focus on some of the required elements of a disaster recovery plan; this, however, is a thumbnail sketch of the requirements. Books have been written on contingency planning, which precludes detailed coverage here. The EDP auditor's responsibility is to convince management to focus on preparation and ongoing maintenance of an effective disaster recovery plan, not to prepare it. Then the auditor's job is to ensure that recovery of all activities and functions is provided for, and that the plan is tested at least annually (see Figure 8–8).

8.4 COMPLIANCE TESTING

Some suggested testing procedures are shown in Figures 8–3 through 8–8. They should be used as a foundation to build detailed testing programs of controls found during preliminary review. The following discussion focuses on how and why these tests are necessary, although they are not a substitute for an auditor's judgment in isolating controls that are not covered here.

FIGURE 8–8   Contingency Planning

Audit Test Objective

To determine the adequacy of the disaster recovery plan

Key Controls

1.   Established accountability
2.   Documented disaster recovery plan
3.   Off-site storage of backup files
4.   Backup processing site

Scope

The current disaster recovery plan

Audit Procedures:

Preliminary Review

1.   Determine if the disaster recovery plan includes:
   a.   Provisions for alternate sites, hardware, software, power and air conditioning equipment
   b.   Alternate provisions for each hardware component
   c.   Confirmation of backup hardware arrangements
   d.   Definitions of various disaster scenarios with recovery plans for each
   e.   Temporary plans for manual completion of work performed by computer applications
   f.   Ranking of all applications in priority order of importance to establish their recovery order
   g.   Assignment of accountability and responsibility for critical recovery plan tasks to primary and secondary individuals
   h.   Names, addresses and emergency phone numbers of personnel, vendors, and key customer contacts that should be notified

Compliance Testing

Verify that:

1.   EDP management has performed an adequacy review of the backup site
2.   Copies of the documented recovery plan are stored in the off-site vault
3.   The plan is tested at least once per year
4.   Individuals assigned specific disaster recovery duties have been informed of their accountability and responsibility

The preliminary review isolates auditee activities and functions, many of which may be unique to a particular company. The auditor must design testing procedures to verify the adequacy and effectiveness of the key controls discovered during preliminary review.

8.4.1   Physical Security

Management's objective is to protect hardware and software from unauthorized access and damage. The best method is to forbid access to anyone who does not need to be in the data center. Testing utilizes the same techniques and procedures prescribed for access control and fire extinguishing equipment (see Chapter 7).

Data center employees should be familiar with fire emergency procedures. These procedures should be clearly and concisely documented in an organized fashion for ready access. Many data centers automatically shut down air conditioning and ventilation systems to prevent the fire from spreading. Computer hardware and power supplies may need to be shutdown manually. Each data center employee must have specific duties in a fire emergency. These are best learned by practice. The auditor should verify that fire drills are conducted and that each employee's responsibility is reviewed by a data center manager or supervisor.

Making sure that fire detection and extinguishing equipment is tested periodically by competent personnel is best accomplished by verifying the existence of inspection and testing tags placed on the equipment. To further validate this testing, the auditor could interview the equipment inspector or participate in an inspection.

Making sure such devices detect fire, smoke, excessive heat, and combustible fumes can be verified through the fire department or local fire marshal by providing them with the model number and type of the detection device. Another alternative is to interview the system vendor or review documented specifications from the vendor. Emergency backup lighting is needed because data center power is usually shut down during a fire emergency. Backup lighting can usually be activated by manual testing switches. This lighting should also be inspected by authorized service representatives, whose visits should be recorded in an inspection log.

In a fire emergency, data center personnel will not have time to call the fire department. Notifying a central monitoring station can be accomplished by organizing a test with the manager of the central monitoring system. During the test, the fire department should be informed to prevent response to a false alarm.

All electric wiring and other cabling runs under the data center's raised floor. Accumulated water could cause serious equipment damage and even electrical shock to people in the data center. The presence of drains can be tested by visual inspection.

Making sure that there is enough electricity to support the system and air conditioning requires another coordinated test with trained technicians. More importantly, has personnel tested the backup power supply and was the test adequate? Many data centers have lost main power to find that the backup power supply is not adequate because management relied on the calculated specifications instead of an actual test.

Current mainframe equipment is not as sensitive to temperature and humidity levels as were prior generations; temperature and humidity control is, however, still necessary. To ensure adequate air conditioning, the temperature and humidity requirements should be obtained from equipment vendors. Recording thermometers and humidity indicators should be located in strategic places throughout the data center to allow easy access. These instruments should be monitored routinely by trained technicians. These devices usually record temperature and humidity on a paper disk. The auditor can verify the adequacy of the system by inspecting the paper disks from previous periods of time. Computer hardware requires routine periodic maintenance, cleaning, and inspection by trained technicians. Mainframes, minicomputers, tape drives, and disk drives frequently contain air filtration systems that prevent dust and other contaminants from entering the equipment. These systems are only as effective as their maintenance and cleaning permits them to be.

8.4.2   Functional Duties

Management needs qualified people who consistently execute administrative and functional procedures. Quality employees help ensure effective and efficient operations; for this reason employees deserve fair and legal treatment.

Management communicates its requirements to employees through written job descriptions and procedures. This authorizes employees to make decisions. Verifying that job descriptions match job duties can be accomplished by observing the operators and interviewing the employees to determine their understanding of what is expected of them. Job descriptions can become outdated because of reorganizations or when people leave the company. Therefore the auditor should make sure that data center management keeps the job descriptions current.

By documenting procedures for control of input data, the auditor can identify files that were sent from the data preparation area for a sample of days during the audit period. The names of these files can then be traced to the logs maintained for receipt of input files. The auditor should determine that all files being delivered are identified on the log.

Application documentation should identify all reports generated. The auditor should compare this to the report distribution sheets used by the data center to verify that the data center is aware of all reports created by the application. To ensure that only authorized users obtain the reports, a log should be maintained for the user to sign. In small companies, the report distribution clerk may distribute reports just by knowing the people who arrive to pick them up. In this case, distribution to authorized users can be tested by observation of report pick-up. However, the auditor must bear in mind that proof of authorized user pick-up can only be obtained by documented sign-off.

Testing delivery deadlines can be accomplished by reviewing system logs to identify when the report generation programs were executed, or checking the times logged on report distribution sheets. Meeting report delivery deadlines is important for maintaining user productivity.

8.4.3   Operating Efficiency

Each company requires different data processing service levels to maintain productivity. System performance must be monitored daily to maintain processing effectiveness and efficiency. At a minimum, performance levels should be measured for: CPU usage and capacity, disk usage and capacity, on-line transaction volume and capacity, on-line terminal response time, computer program and report completion and delivery time, and system availability.

Standards for performance levels must be developed effectively to measure actual usage. Capacity levels tell management how much work the system and its components can handle. When capacity is reached, management must take steps to increase it by fine tuning the existing system, adding a component, or obtaining a new system. These capacity levels form criteria for replacement—early warning signals that indicate needed change.

Making sure that insurance covers new equipment, that performance reports are useful to management, and that performance limits indicate the need for additional CPU, disk capacity on-line terminals or job rescheduling can be accomplished by interviewing management and EDP technicians. User management can be interviewed to determine if the performance measurement reports are meaningful and helpful. The adequacy of the criteria can be determined by talking with technicians from the hardware and software vendors. The auditor should verify his conclusions with technicians to ensure their accuracy.

8.4.4   Insurance

Insurance coverage is frequently overlooked from the standpoints of having the wrong kind, the wrong amount, the wrong price. Management must ensure that the insurance coverage for data center equipment is adequate with a systematic and periodic review of assets, coverage, and costs. The auditor's basic mission is to determine whether all data center equipment is covered for loss from all types of probable disasters. Costs and occurrence probability must be considered in insurance decisions. Self-insurance may better benefit the company in cases of high-cost and low-incidence probability. The auditor should compare hardware inventory to asset listings in insurance policies. Insurance evaluation should be performed by someone in the company with appropriate experience. The absence of this review can dramatically increase insurance costs, or increase risks if the policies lapse.

8.4.5 Documentation

Application run manuals provide computer operators with execution instructions. Adequate documentation is the only effective means to maintain application productivity. Management must ensure that run manuals are kept current and accurate. The application programmer should be required to update this documentation when production programs are changed.

The auditor should determine the information needed by computer operators, observe actual events, and compare run manual information to the application system manual maintained in S&P. The run manual documentation execution proceeds sequentially as follows:

Flow of Job Steps

These document the individual programs within a jobstream. The operating system prints the program names on the console screen as each program is started and completed.

Input and Output Files

These identify the internal and external label of input files to be mounted, and when the file is mounted. The operator is also instructed as to when to mount a scratch file for the application to write the output file. Mounting time is usually signalled by the program or jobstep name (see Figure 8–7).

CPU and Run-Time Requirements

These inform the operator of core requirements and processing time. With this information the operator can determine what programs can be executed simultaneously for optimum processing efficiency. Simultaneously executing programs with conflicting resource requirements can degrade system performance and delay processing completion.

Run Manual

This should tell the operator what messages to expect from the programs, and what response or action is needed. Applications are scheduled for processing at basically the same time each day and must stay on schedule to meet report delivery deadlines. Diagnostic or instruction messages without adequate explanation can delay or abort processing.

Restart-and-Recovery Procedures

These are necessary because application processing can fail for any number of reasons. Complex applications may take several hours to complete processing. Management wants to avoid complete reruns because of cost and time considerations. Restart/recovery procedures can be built into the application so that the application can be restarted close to the failure point. These procedures should be documented so the operator can properly execute them without the aid of a programmer. However, the error that caused the failure may require a programmer's attention. To restart, the recovery programs must read the transaction file to determine where to resume processing. The operator needs step-by-step instructions effectively to accomplish recovery.

Computer installations use special utilities to fix file and processing problems by purging faulty information from a file. These utilities could also be used to make fraudulent changes without creating an audit trail. This use of these sensitive utilities, covered in Chapter 14, must be preauthorized by management for the operator to have the authority to run them. The auditor could use job accounting utility records to identify when these utilities were executed. Documented authorization forms should be filed for at least six months to maintain a satisfactory audit trail. If so, the auditor can compare the accounting utility information to the authorization forms to prove that preauthorization was achieved.

Verifying the accuracy of run schedules can be accomplished by taking inventory of the applications through research of documentation and interviews of programmers. Any jobs on the schedule that cannot be found by research should be investigated, to ensure that they are authorized programs. This helps the auditor ensure that data center personnel have not gone into business for themselves by processing other companys' programs.

8.4.6 Activating the Contingency Plan

A backup/recovery plan should be designed to help resume data center operations within a reasonable time after a disaster. The plan should provide for recreating all production processing in a logical sequence, based upon each application's importance to the company. The basic first step is that of obtaining facilities and equipment. Backup copies of all software should have been stored off-site and, therefore, be intact. The auditor's focus is on the practicality and completeness of recovery arrangements.

NOTES

1. See Mullen, Jack B. "Auditing Data Center: Setting Audit Test Objectives." Adapted from *EDP Auditing* (New York: Auerbach Publishers). © 1989, Warren, Gorham & Lamont, Inc. Used with permission.

Information Security[1]

9.1   INTRODUCTION

Information security is a very critical environmental area. Computer information can be accessed by batch computer programs, on-line transaction terminals, microcomputers, and on-line programming systems. There are special security and control considerations for microcomputers that are not relevant to "dumb" on-line terminals. Dumb on-line terminals are referred to as such because they do not contain a microprocessor; they do not have ROM (Read Only Memory) and RAM (Random Access Memory). Some of the material in this chapter is relevant to micro-to-mainframe links, although full coverage of the special microcomputer concerns are covered in Chapter 19.

On-line terminal systems can take several forms: inquiry terminals for data retrieval, transaction capture for batch processing update, on-line memo-posting (on-line capture with accumulation of key fields to provide ongoing status) on-line realtime update of the master file, and on-line programming systems.

Most current corporate systems have some kind of on-line interface, increasing the risk of loss and the complexity of audit issues. Today's growing threats are the "hackers" attempting unauthorized access with a microcomputer, the internal, unauthorized transaction that goes undetected, and the unauthorized program change.

Physical security controls over terminal networks are still important, but insufficient by themselves. Programmatic, or system security has become increasingly important because physical security measures can be circumvented too easily. A company's terminal network, operating 24 hours a day, can spread information across the entire world, requiring internal system security (logical, on-line access control) to ensure adequate protection.

Auditing on-line transaction systems encompasses the evaluation of external physical security and internal system security, the environmental area, and the application interface.

The environmental audit deals with the control system within the telecommunications (tcom) software and on-line programs that interface with the on-line application programs.

9.2 PLANNING AND PREPARATION

Technical training and experience can be a limitation when auditing a complex on-line system. The most complicated step is that of verifying the system security generation programs. The terminal, transaction, and user security is printed on easily read reports, simplifying verification. Tcom control verification requires training in line protocol, modem operation, and data stream verification techniques.

The most severe limitation is the time required to complete the audit because all audit objectives cover areas of high risk. Reducing audit scope is impractical, for all areas must be covered in each audit. Time becomes a big factor when an on-line security package exists, for its functions are performed by customized coding procedures. Even though the on-line system may have been audited, the implementation of an access security package will increase research time tremendously, for the new procedures must be learned.

Audit duration depends on on-line system complexity; the first-time audit of a system containing 150 terminals may require approximately 600 hours in order to satisfy all audit objectives. This assumes that at least one EDP auditor is familiar with the system and with on-line audit requirements. The next audit, assuming that knowledgeable auditors are retained, would decrease to between 300 and 400 hours.

Some on-line communication systems have inherent technical security limitations that expose the environment to excessive risk. However, response time may be too expensive or multiple passwords are needed. Therefore, menu transactions are needed in order to avoid significant keystroke increases with multiple passwords. A special command is then needed to exit the transaction code. Keystroke increases are an important consideration, for errors vary proportionately with their number. Passwords for each transaction would increase the keystrokes required and, therefore, increase the number of errors.

In addition, multiple passwords are frequently written down degrading effectiveness. The audit may prove the existence of good control in every respect, but such technical limitation creates a pervasive internal control weakness that increases the application audit scope and the external auditor's financial audit scope.

EDP auditors must have technical on-line expertise in order to isolate inherent system security limitations and determine their effect on the data processing environment.

9.2.1   Identification of Transactions

Key areas of concern are access control, authorization control and isolation of inherent system security limitations (see Figure 9-1). Limited audit resources may dictate a reduction in scope, but, nevertheless, these three elements must be reviewed. Sufficient time must be spent learning system operation and technical vendor literature in order to isolate inherent weaknesses. Failure to spend this learning time could produce an incorrect evaluation of the quality of on-line system controls, thus exposing the organization to significant risk.

Because significant time will be needed from system software personnel, who are busy, advance notice and careful audit planning are required in order to avoid time wasted waiting for answers.

9.2.1.1   TIME FACTORS

Internal auditors usually measure performance by time spent rather than in hard dollars, but the auditors' time and computer time can be assigned hourly rates. Time, however, is a more relevant factor to the internal audit because of target dates. The

FIGURE 9–1 Identification of Audit Transactions

Audit Activity Code	Transaction/Area	Include Exclude	Reason
A	Administration	I	Satisfies Audit Objective 1, 2
B	Physical Access Control	I	Satisfies Audit Objective 2
C	Logical Access Control	I	Satisfies Audit Objective 1, 2
D	On-Line System Change Control	I	Satisfies Audit Objective 1, 2
E	On-Line Message Control System	I	Satisfies Audit Objective 3
F	Backup and Recovery	I	Satisfies Audit Objective 4
G	Network Control	I	Satisfies Audit Objective 1, 2
H	Environmental Protection	I	Satisfies Audit Objective 2

phases of the audit are shown below, giving approximate time percentages of the total audit time budget relative to the first-time audit (see Table 9–1).

Reviewing on-line access controls is the most time-consuming audit task, followed by access to production data files, controls over changes to on-line software, backup recovery, system and user documentation, verification of processing accuracy, physical access security, and, finally, terminal operator training.

TABLE 9–1
On-Line Transaction Systems Time Allocation

Category	% of Total
Planning	5–15
Preliminary Review	45–50
Compliance Testing	15–20
Workpaper Review	2– 5
Report and Other	5–10

9.2.2 Risks/Exposures

Such risks and exposures as unauthorized transactions, hardware damage, unauthorized changes to software, inaccurate processing, erroneous output, hardware or software failures, and/or computer abuse and fraud confront management using on-line systems (see Figure 9–2). Management must establish a control system to reduce such effects, while balancing the costs versus the benefits. Unauthorized transactions can occur through an existing terminal or by someone tapping into the network. Hardware damage can occur by accident or be caused by deliberate sabotage of a terminal, communication line, or data center equipment.

On-line access can be controlled by a security software system. To keep the on-line network secure, the security software programs must themselves be secure, so management must protect the security software system from unauthorized access. Inaccurate processing and erroneous output can be caused by operator data entry errors or via program errors. Hardware and software failures can also be deliberate, but more often they are caused by program errors. In any event, all data entered up to that time could be lost without appropriate journaling of transactions. Computer abuse can occur from within the organization or from outside. The key is on-line access control, particularly with a dial-up network.

9.2.3 Control Objectives

Key controls must be designed to accomplish such control objectives as effective data security administration, restricted access to the terminal area, restricted logical access to on-line system information, programs, and transactions, monitored and reported terminal activity, post-disaster system recovery capabilities, and current and complete system and user documentation. Management should have the control system designed to maintain an efficient, risk-free environment, but controls can deteriorate for numerous reasons. The auditor must evaluate the system and report to management that control objectives are

FIGURE 9–2 Scope Summary

Risks/Exposures

1. Unauthorized transactions
2. Hardware damage
3. Unauthorized changes to on-line system software
4. Inaccurate processing
5. Erroneous output
6. Hardware/software failures
7. Computer abuse/fraud

Control Objectives

1. Effective data security administration
2. Restricted access to the terminal area
3. Restricted logical access to on-line system information, programs, and transactions
4. Reported and monitored terminal activity
5. Post-failure or -disaster system recovery capabilities
6. Current and complete system and user documentation

Key Controls

1. Monitored physical access
2. Monitored logical access
3. Checkpoint restart, transaction logging, and backup files
4. Operator training and documentation

General Audit Objectives

Determine that adequate controls exist to ensure the control objectives:

1. Protect company records from unauthorized modification
2. Protect computer hardware from unauthorized access and damage
3. All transactions are accurately processed
4. Provide for backup and recovery

Preliminary Review Hours

Activity Code	Transaction/Area	Budget Hours	
		Audit Time	Review Time
A	Administration	10	2
B	Physical Access Control	10	2
C	Logical (on-line) Access Control	15	.5
D	On-Line System Change Control	5	.5
E	On-Line Message Control System	10	2
F	Backup and Recovery	7	1
G	Network Control	3	1
H	Environmental Protection	3	1

being accomplished or else recommend areas for improvement. Management may not always know when a control ceases to function. This is the area in which the auditor can be of greatest service (see Figure 9–2).

9.2.4   Key Controls

The key controls that ensure control objectives are monitored physical access, monitored logical access, checkpoint restart, transaction logging, and backup files, and operator training and documentation. These broadly defined key controls can be used by management to accomplish the control objectives. These are further refined in terms of compliance testing to permit an in-depth audit of each area of concern (see Figure 9–2).

9.2.5   Audit Objectives

The mainframe hardware (and peripherals) supporting the on-line terminal system are usually located within a data center whose physical security falls within the scope of the data center audit. However, the communications lines, CRT, and modems fall within the audit scope of on-line system physical security. This equipment must be accessed only by authorized personnel. All must be located in areas not prone to environmental hazards, even though today's terminal system equipment can operate within fairly relaxed environments.

The general term "modification" (change) includes addition, deletion, and alteration, which can occur via unauthorized personnel access, input errors and omissions, and line tapping inside the company's building, outside the building, or by dial-up connection.

Processing accuracy must be verified on at least a daily basis by reconciling processed data results with an independent control source. The key concern is the transaction effect on the master file. Although on-line capture and batch processing can be verified daily after the batch run, the on-line realtime transaction effect must be verified before master file posting acceptance or periodically throughout the day. On-line realtime transactions provide the greatest audit challenge because of the transaction authorization and reconcilement difficulty.

More specific audit test objectives are needed to satisfy the general audit objectives. These are covered in the compliance testing section.

9.3 EXECUTION OF PRELIMINARY SURVEY

The time budget areas, in terms of actual auditing and later review, include administration, physical access control, logical access control, change control, on-line message control system, backup and recovery, network control, and environmental protection. These must be documented and the controls within them evaluated.

9.3.1 Data Security Administration

The preliminary review steps focus on the structure and duties of, and control provided by, the data security administration function. The auditor's task is to identify data security administration activities and their independence from computer programming and analysis work. The number of people in this function, and its location in the organization, depend on company size and on-line network complexity. Regardless of these attributes, someone in the company must perform these duties if an on-line network exists. The data security administrator is the computer security policeman, utilizing a security software package or other logical access control mechanism to enforce data security policies and procedures (see Figure 9–3).

9.3.2 Physical Access Control

Physical access control includes evaluation of company policies and procedures for physically securing the areas where on-line terminals are located. Key controls to achieve physical access

FIGURE 9–3   Data Security Administration

Audit Test Objective

To determine the adequacy and effectiveness of administration procedures

Key Controls

1. Adequate procedures
2. Adequate separation of duties
3. Established accountability

Scope

All activities and functions performed during the period being examined

Audit Procedures:

Preliminary Review

1. Determine the organization structure and job descriptions for each position
2. Determine preemployment screening practices used to avoid undue security risks
3. Determine how job duties are rotated periodically for cross-training and to limit perpetuation of questionable practices
4. Determine the elements of on-line system performance monitoring
5. Determine the training provided, guidelines, and documentation available

Compliance Testing

Verify that:

1. Job descriptions accurately match the duties of all positions
2. All prospective employees are screened for possible security risks
3. All conflicting duties are segregated
4. Performance monitoring includes this criteria:
   a. Transaction response time
   b. Network uptime (availability)
   c. Thruput capacity and handling
   d. Network downtime, time of day, duration, and cause
5. All security violations are investigated
6. The adequacy of training, guidelines, and documentation

FIGURE 9–4 Physical Access Control

Audit Test Objective

Ensure that access to the terminal area is controlled

Key Controls

1. Door keylocks or magnetic card access
2. Supervisory review
3. Keyboard keylocks

Scope

All terminals within the installation

Audit Procedures:

Preliminary Review

Determine:

1. The population and location of terminals

Compliance Testing

Verify that:

1. The terminals are in an area of controlled access
2. Terminals are watched by a supervisor in the area
3. Keyboards can be disabled or microcomputer uses password control
4. Log of keyholders is maintained
5. Keys collected from employee upon termination
6. Prospective employees are screened to a level relevant to the work performed
7. Personnel should be alert to any unauthorized personnel in the area

control will be identified and its strength evaluated. The control techniques to accomplish physical access control include doorlocks, keycard access, and camera surveillance (see Figure 9–4).

9.3.3 Logical Access Control

Logical access control involves the use of such on-line security software systems as that of the IBM-RACF[2] and the CA-TOP SECRET[3] to establish access profiles for each terminal user. These define the computer resources that can be used by each user, the terminals they can use, and even the time of day that the resources can be used. Some on-line communication systems have inherent technical security limitations that expose the environment to excessive risk. The system may be able to perform the necessary security procedures, but response time may be degraded and/or CPU usage may be beyond practical limits. One on-line monitor system allows password control for each transaction, in addition to initial access, but the password must be reentered each time the transaction code is entered. Another system permits transaction assignment to terminals only, permitting on-line system users to sign on any terminal and perform its transactions. This is a system limitation that cannot be cost effectively corrected without a security software package. The audit may prove the existence of good control in every respect, but this technical limitation creates a pervasive internal control weakness that increases the application audit scope and the external auditor's financial audit scope (see Figure 9–5).

9.3.4   On-Line System Change Control

On-line system change control evaluates the controls over maintenance of the programs that make up the on-line network system. The controls over maintenance to these programs would normally be reviewed in the application program maintenance audit (see Chapter 10). However, they are included here to stress the importance of the control over the programs. The review of these programs (see Figure 9–6) should be included in the on-line system audit if 1) the controls over the program maintenance environment are weak, or 2) the program maintenance audit was not performed within the last eighteen months.

9.3.5   On-Line Message Control System

Verifying that all commands to and from the master console are logged focuses on the on-line message control system. The transaction data transmitted between terminals and mainframes is

FIGURE 9–5 Logical Access Control

Audit Test Objective

To determine that programmatic controls will prevent unauthorized transactions

Key Controls

1. Access control mechanism
2. Correlation of user to EDP resources

Scope

All data processing resources that can be accessed by the on-line terminals

Audit Procedures:

Preliminary Review

1. Determine the functions of the access control system

Compliance Testing

Verify that:

1. By observing on-line system operation that a sign on scheme is used to identify the user, and that the password does not print on the screen
2. By interviewing the data security administrator and systems software programmers:
   a. That the on-line system maintains tables or files that correlate the users' sign on keys to transactions that they can perform, files that they can access, and programs that they can execute
   b. That the on-line system logs all terminal activity and creates a daily terminal activity report
   c. That access to the password table or file is prevented
   d. That the on-line software automatically signs off a terminal after several minutes of inactivity
   e. That the number of master security terminals is limited to two or three and that they are subject to strict physical access control
   f. That repeated sign on attempts automatically disable terminal
   g. That the security administrator is warned, on his terminal, of attempts at unauthorized activity
   h. That unauthorized activity is rejected and reported
   i. That the system requires security administrator response to on-line security violation messages

FIGURE 9–6   On-Line System Change Control

Audit Test Objective

To determine that unauthorized changes cannot be made to on-line access control and on-line processing programs

Key Controls

1. Program change control system
2. Separate test environment
3. Linking of transaction codes to programs and files

Scope

All on-line programs used in the installation

Audit Procedures:

Preliminary Review

1. Determine that the linking of on-line programs to application programs via calls, subroutines, and job control statements are protected from unauthorized changes
2. Determine that an on-line testing environment exists separately from the production environment and is used to test changes to the on-line processing programs
3. Determine that on-line transaction codes call specific programs that access specific files

Compliance Testing

1. Determine that programmer access to the on-line system programs is prevented except to make authorized changes
2. Determine that a procedure exists to control additions or deletions of:
   a. Transaction codes from the system
   b. Users from the system
   c. Terminals from the system

---

enveloped in a digital carrier of necessary system information to permit location of the destination and identify the sender. This is like the mailing and return address on a letter. The tcom system must keep track of all messages sent and received. Messages must be logged, and the system must validate key data in each message for the system to determine its legitimacy and destination (see Figure 9–7).

FIGURE 9–7   Message Control System

Audit Test Objective

To determine that the on-line tcom system can prevent, detect, and correct message loss or change

Key Controls

1. Sequence numbering of messages
2. Message logging and tracing
3. Message verification
4. Acknowledge message receipt
5. Encryption of sensitive data
6. Terminal polling
7. Terminal address verification
8. Identification of messages in transit
9. Retrieval of previous messages
10. Log all master console commands

Scope

All on-line transactions

Audit Procedures:

Preliminary Review

Determine:

1. The system accounts for all messages
2. Messages are logged to permit tracing of on-line system functions and transactions
3. System validates critical information in each message

Compliance Testing

1. Observe system reaction to unauthorized terminal connected to network
2. Verify that:
   a. The system and terminals acknowledge message receipt
   b. The system polls the terminals
   c. Sensitive data is encrypted
   d. System can recover messages in transit
   e. All commands to and from the master console are logged
   f. Network hardware and software verify data accuracy

9.3.6   Backup and Recovery

"Backup and recovery" (see Figure 9–8) means that the auditor must identify the elements needed to recover the on-line system should it fail. During preliminary review, the auditor should identify the elements of backup and recovery and how these are accomplished. This is similar to contingency planning (see Chapter 8).

9.3.7   Network Control

Network control focuses on terminal and microcomputer links to the mainframe through hardwiring, leased lines, or dial-up methods. These review steps are necessary to identify the protection against "tapping" into the network with an unauthorized terminal or microcomputer (see Figure 9–9). Compliance testing procedures are combined in the audit program because the preliminary review isolates the vast majority of information needed for auditor attention (see Section 9.4.7).

9.3.8   Environmental Protection

The environmental protection procedures in Figure 9–10 review the temperature, humidity, and power constraints of the network equipment that are not covered in review of terminal or micro locations, or the data center. Most of this equipment is usually located in the data center and included in that review, but some companies have special facilities or rooms for this equipment. These must be reviewed.

9.4   COMPLIANCE TESTING

The on-line network is an environmental concern within the external auditor's general control evaluation (GCE), performed annually to determine the adequacy of the company's internal control structure. The external auditors will want to review the

FIGURE 9–8   Backup and Recovery

Audit Test Objective

To determine that the on-line system can be recovered after a failure or disaster

Key Controls

1. Transaction and message logging
2. Checkpoint/restart programs
3. Off-site storage of backup files
4. Diagnostic messages of system problems
5. Disaster contingency plan

Scope

All on-line system programs and data files

Audit Procedures:

Preliminary Review

Determine:

1. Transaction and master file data needed to recover on-line processing up to the point of failure
2. Checkpoint/restart programs function properly
3. Copies of programs and files are stored in a secure off-site location
4. Diagnostic messages are produced by the on-line and operating systems to help diagnose the cause of failure
5. Restart recovery procedures are documented for use by computer operators and terminal operators

Compliance Testing

1. Observe test execution of recovery programs
2. Verify that:
    a. Logged data is sufficient to accomplish recovery
    b. The data files can be recovered to the time of failure
    c. Diagnostic and information messages provided to the system and terminal operators are adequate
    d. On-line system support and recovery procedures are adequately documented

FIGURE 9–9   Network Control

Audit Test Objective

To determine that the tcom equipment is protected from unauthorized use

Key Controls

1. Network shutdown
2. Network polling
3. Secure terminal address and verification
4. On-line access control

Scope

The complete tcom network

Audit Procedures:

Preliminary Review and Compliance Testing

1. For tcom equipment that uses leased lines or that is hardwired to the mainframe observe system operation, examine program code and program documentation to determine that:

    a. The network is inoperable during nonbusiness hours
    b. The tcom monitor polls all of the terminals in the network
    c. The logical terminal address is hardcoded with a terminal identification chip or micro circuit
    d. The tcom monitor verifies the terminal address before sending a message
    e. The on-line access control files properly correlate resources to users and to other resources

2. Determine by physical inspection of any appropriate storage areas that all line test equipment is protected from authorized use

3. For dial-up systems observe system operation, examine programs and documentation, and perform tests to determine:

    a. CPU phone number is coded into terminal
    b. System uses dial-back software in appropriate situations
    c. Central phone system accepts calls only from specific phone numbers
    d. Test controls by using a microcomputer outside the installation to attempt dial-up access

results of the on-line terminal security audit. External audit time is dependent upon the quality of the internal control system. Reduced audit time is needed with good internal control. Conversely, poor control requires more audit time, especially in a pervasive area like the on-line terminal network.

Control weaknesses increase audit costs and could threaten the possibility of clean opinion on internal control. Control problems can usually be compensated for in financial statement opinions, but an installation that requires a third-party letter increases the importance of taking extra care to ensure its adequacy.

AICPA Statement on Auditing Standard No. 55 became effective January 1, 1990. It broadens the external auditor's responsibility for internal control review, and requires such auditors to:

- Understand the control structure,
- Test the controls, and
- Assess the level of control risk.

The quality of terminal network control, documentation, and the security audit will reduce the auditor's work and increase the likelihood of a problem-free audit.

9.4.1 Data Security Administration

The testing steps (see Figure 9–3) show the means by which to evaluate the responsibilities of the data security administrator (DSA), whose primary function is security over access to computer data by physical, batch program, on-line transaction systems, microcomputer links, or on-line programming systems. Logical access control is most effectively and efficiently accomplished by a security software system. The activation and deactivation of the security software system should be controlled.

- Startup and deactivation of the security software system should be limited to the data security administrator and, at most, one or two other people.

- Systems programmers should be prevented from activating or deactivating the operating system by themselves. The data security administrator should be present to activate or deactivate the security software system.

Some commercial security software packages permit security definition only to the library level which prohibits individual module security. This can be due to functional limitations of the package or as a way to avoid significant overhead. The review should determine the extent of security provided and the cost benefit of levels of module security (see Figure 9–3).

Emergency Access

This refers to the fact that systems and application programmers sometimes need emergency access in order to fix a problem. This can be provided by security software emergency access profiles. The auditor should determine:

- The existence of emergency access profiles, the extent of their usage, and the rules for their use;
- The defined emergency access levels have been approved by systems and application programming management;
- The defined access levels do, in fact, access only the program libraries and functions that management intends;
- All uses of emergency access levels are reviewed and approved, in writing, by management within two days of the actual usage;
- The emergency access profiles have a tracking or audit attribute coded on them to provide a log of all accesses performed.

Access prevention of all resources may be impractical or too costly, forcing the installation to rely on detective control over some resources. Security software packages provide log, warn, or caution modes for this purpose.

Some software packages cannot start logging access attempts until the operator ID and password have been accepted by the system. In this case, the security system would be incapable of logging invalid sign-on attempts. Therefore, it is important that the system disable the terminal or line after a predetermined number of invalid attempts. The need for the data security administrator to interface with the situation to reactivate the line or terminal will direct attention to this critical event.

The DSA should monitor the performance of the on-line system. Management should establish a program for monitoring the performance of hardware and software that evaluates power, capability, and timeliness. The evaluation should include:

- Performance criteria to establish a benchmark for measurement;
- Quantification of initial and recurring costs for installation and maintenance of the system;
- Assessment of projected vendor support, the future benefit of this support, and the extent of in-house support that will be needed;
- Assessment of projected in-house support;
- Quantification of workload handling and system capacity needed to accomplish the work; and
- Quantification of system response and job turnaround time.

Performance evaluation is necessary to ensure the existence of adequate resources to meet organizational needs. A thorough audit evaluation of this activity could prevent a future crisis.

The on-line security review should evaluate the adequacy of the performance monitoring program of the on-line network. The criteria that should be monitored are:

- Transaction response time;
- Network capacity—the maximum capability of the system;
- Thruput capacity—the transaction load that the network can handle at specific time intervals;

- Thruput handling—the speed at which the network processes the transaction load at specific time intervals; and
- Network downtime—time of day, duration and, cause.

9.4.2 Physical Access Control

Limitation of physical access to a terminal is primarily a fraud control. Errors, omissions, and fraud can occur even with the tightest security. Unauthorized transactions can be accomplished by using an existing terminal or tapping into the network with another terminal. Physical security controls prevent the first method of accessing the network. Physical security can control a hardwired tap into the cable, but a tap by such other means as a dial-up terminal requires on-line access control.

The supervisor of the terminal area should be assigned the responsibility for physical security of the area—this should be included in his or her job description. Equipment sabotage is prevented by good physical security; a key ingredient for effective physical security is to instill a proper attitude among the employees toward the need for, and presence of, such security. The test procedures can be easily completed by the financial auditors in their visits to the functional areas.

9.4.3 Logical Access Control

Evaluating the preventive and detection controls within the on-line system ensures that only authorized users access the proper terminals and that they only execute authorized transactions. It is crucial that employees are identified and verified by an access control mechanism. The on-line software must have sufficient sophistication to detect unauthorized users and prevent their use of the system. (see Figure 9–5).

The audit procedures use the term "transaction" to identify the on-line activity, but the auditor's evaluation must also include any file access or program execution that can be performed on on-line programming terminals.

The auditor may want to consider recommending automatic generation of new passwords if the need for data security justifies it. The most sophisticated on-line security system can be compromised if users do not protect their passwords. Employees may forget to change them on a regular basis if not reminded.

The on-line access control system must be able to monitor and log activity from the moment of the first key stroke. Many security software packages do not begin logging until a valid password and sign on key are recognized. This approach will not detect the password guesser. The making of multiple-guess entry attempts electronically known to the data security administrator may provide clues as to who is attempting unauthorized access. The system should notify the master security terminal upon detection of this guessing activity and, additionally, require a response by data security personnel to ensure acknowledgment.

Controlled sign-on sequences do not alone provide adequate security. The access control system must authorize use of all EDP resources. Transaction authorization can only be accomplished by correlation of the user key to the resource usage matrix or file. These files tell the on-line access control system which transactions an employee can use and permits the system to identify any unauthorized activity.

Controlling on-line transaction code usage by employees eliminates the need for transaction assignment to terminals because employees are then only able to initiate specific transactions, regardless of the terminal they are working on. However, the assignment of transaction codes to terminals provides additional access control.

All EDP environments do not have a packaged security software system—some use the security features provided with the tcom monitor product. The auditor must take extra care in evaluating these environments. The procedures will need some modification to provide a thorough audit, simply because most tcom monitor products do not provide the extent of control that a security software package does. One tcom monitor only provides assignment of transactions to terminals and password control for each transaction. However, the password that must be entered is different for each transaction code, forcing the employee to write down the various passwords. This can compromise security. Although there is password control for sign-on to the system, it provides global access to the entire system, which permits the employee to use any of the transaction codes assigned to the terminal he or she is working on. Furthermore, once the employee is accepted by the control system, he can use any terminal in the installation.

The access control system must log who, what, where, and when. The sign on key identifies who, the transaction identifies what, the terminal ID identifies where, and the date and time identify when. The absence of this information prevents proper evaluation of on-line system activity.

Preventing access to password files or tables appears drastic and creates the question of what to do about forgotten passwords. The simple measure, however, is to forget the existing password and issue a new one. This way there is no need to access the password files. Only a master security transaction to create a new password is necessary. The need for employee identification on password issuance is obvious.

Terminal users busy in their work frequently walk away from their active terminal, opening the door for the quick opportunist to enter a transaction traceable to the distracted employee. Automatic terminal sign off after a predetermined duration of inactivity prevents this. The shorter the time, the better, but this decision is affected by productivity requirements.

9.4.4   On-Line System Change Control

The audit procedures for evaluating the control over changes to on-line programs fall within the scope of responsibility of the systems or applications programmers responsible for the on-line system programs. These programs provide the telecommunications links to application programs, which in turn access the data files. These audit procedures would also fall within the scope of the program change control audit (see Chapter 10). However, if the control over changes to the on-line programs has not been recently reviewed or if the change control system is weak, the auditor should perform these procedures in the on-line transaction system audit (see Figure 9–6).

On-line access to files is controlled by program coding and job control language statements. If an adequately controlled program maintenance environment exists, then risk is significantly diminished. If change control is weak, however, the opposite situation forces the auditor to increase scope in order to review change control adequately in this audit. Adequate review and testing of changes to the on-line programs is vital, because review of the changes promotes accuracy, and testing proves it. Once the system is properly coded, it will function the same way every time until it is changed. Review of the program that was changed is the only effective way to detect fraudulent program code.

A separate testing environment is necessary to prevent unauthorized access of production files. Testing in a live environment can create a multitude of functional problems.

Programmer access to the on-line system programs must be controlled to protect system integrity. This critically relates to on-line security but falls within the program maintenance audit scope. That is, this adequacy question must be answered, if not in the program maintenance audit, then in an expanded on-line security audit.

Transaction codes drive the system and can be entered on any terminal by any operator, unless the on-line system is programmed to control use. The control procedure and, therefore, transaction authorization start with adding or deleting the transactions to and from the system. The control is the assignment of transactions to terminals and to specific operators. Transaction assignment to terminals limits the area in which the transaction can be performed. When researching problems, this area limitation provides a reduced scope of possibilities. This is also true with transaction assignment to operators; a problem is more easily solved when only a few operators could have performed specific transactions.

In order for transaction input to be authorized, the placement of the transaction in the system, the operators, and the terminals to which they are assigned must be authorized. This is the purpose of a standardized request form and for authorization signatures.

Changing transactions on the system must also be subject to accuracy verification, justifying the need for reports of change effect and requiring comparison to a source document. These same considerations apply to adding users to the network. Deleting users' codes or names usually is caused by personnel turnover. Such deletion requires management authorization and results verification. The largest problem is that former employees access IDs may not be removed from the system on a timely basis, which can provide an opportunity for exploitation.

The addition of terminals must be authorized, and the effect of system regeneration verified. The key is to close any "holes" that would permit unauthorized addition of terminals. The key factor in deleting terminals is user awareness that it will occur and that known personnel will remove the terminal from its location. Deletion of terminals from the system must occur to prevent the unauthorized use of logical and physical terminal definitions.

9.4.5   Message Control System

The on-line system monitor programs must prevent, detect, and correct message loss or change. Most tcom monitors properly control message transmission, but the auditor should review the system to be sure it is using suggested procedures (see Figure 9–7). All data transmitted between terminals and mainframes is carried by control information that includes the elements and steps described below.

Each message should contain a sequence number to permit tracking of all messages that are outbound from the system to the terminal and inbound from the operator to the system. This sequence number aids recovery to determine the last message processed.

Messages should be logged to permit tracing of on-line system functions. They are logged on a direct action storage device (dasd) for programmatic tracing, on hard copy for manual tracing, and for assistance in diagnosis of system problems. The tracing permits the system to determine where and when the system failed and also to feed checkpoint restart routines for system recovery.

The system should validate the critical information in each message, such as the terminal address, by comparing it to authorized internal tables that verify the terminal's validity. This permits the system to abort communication with an invalid terminal. It also permits validation of operator ID and password, transaction codes, and supervisors' approval codes for sensitive transactions.

Such critical information as the message sequence number, terminal address, operator key, transcode, approval codes, and negative system action to operator input should be logged by the system.

The system and terminal should be able to acknowledge message receipt, as communicated by the terminal's status lights. The system "polls" the terminals—the system asks the terminals if they have messages to send, and verifies that a positive connection to a legitimate terminal has been made. When the system detects a disconnect, it should disable the line and terminal. Only the DSA should be able to restart the terminal and line.

Sensitive data, such as the password file, should be encrypted. This can be tested by printing the contents on hard copy to verify encryption, disabling the translation key on the receiving end, or using audit software with an embedded translator.

To accomplish system recovery after a failure, the system must be able to identify messages in transit at the time of failure. This is done by identifying the last message processed, because the message in transit is usually lost. The system should send the last message processed to the operator upon restart so the operator knows where to start. The system should permit the operator to backtrack over previous messages to check errors. This eliminates reprocessing the same transaction, reduces calls to the database, and helps the operator recover processing after a system failure.

All commands to and from the master console should be logged to permit tracking of changes to security profiles.

9.4.6 Backup and Recovery

The on-line system must be recoverable from system failures, disasters, and other disruptions. Logging of transactions and master file before and after images on tape or disk permit the use of checkpoint restart techniques to recreate the master and history files.

In order for the computer operators to support the on-line system, the system must provide diagnostic and informations messages to help identify the cause of the failure. Restart and recovery programs and procedures should be able to recover the files back to the time of the failure by using automatic recovery programs that read the transaction log, the checkpoint master, and checkpoint history files (see Section 9.4.5 and Figure 9–8).

9.4.7 Network Control

The security over the tcom equipment and software is essentially the same as the on-line access control audit procedures. Some terminals, however, use leased lines or are hardwired. Microcomputers can use these types of lines, but they are typically connected by dial-up lines, which expose a different set of risks.

On-line networks that remain active after business hours are favored targets of "hackers," and, therefore, it is prudent to shut down the system when it is not in use. A tcom monitor is a set of programs that drives the on-line terminal communication with the mainframe. Examples of these are CICS[4] and IMS DB/DC.[5] These tcom monitor programs must poll the terminals in the network, because the monitor knows which terminals are defined to the network. This polling is like the question, "are you there?": if the connection is made, then the monitor program knows the terminal is still active in the network.

Each terminal has a logical and physical address that identifies the terminal to the monitor. The physical address is the one the human user sees, whereas the logical address is internally coded into a terminal identification chip or micro-circuit within the terminal. This address should be verified by the monitor before any information is transmitted to the terminal. This logical terminal address would need to be duplicated by a bogus terminal to succeed at fraudulently tapping into the network; unfortunately, this is not the only way that a network can be tapped.

To further frustrate the would-be hacker, the access control system correlates tcom lines to terminals, correlates tcom lines to CPUs or to operator sign-on keys, and correlates operators to transactions and terminals. If a terminal were moved from another location and connected to an incorrect line, then the access control system would prevent access when it failed to correlate the line to the terminal. Correlating lines to CPUs permits only certain tcom lines to access the CPU. With these controls the hacker would need to know, or guess, an operator's sign on key and password, the specific terminal that the operator is assigned to, the transactions assigned to the operator, and the correct line and CPU.

The auditor must check the adequacy of the physical access security over line test equipment. This mobile hardware can be connected to telecommunication lines to read the bits and bytes of data traveling in the line. The terminal address, sign on key, password, and other relevant data can be deciphered with this equipment as it is transmitted between the mainframe and terminal. Most of the readouts, however, are in binary or hexadecimal characters, but with the fast-paced technology increases it is best to keep this equipment under secure control.

The use of microcomputers for dial-up mainframe access has exploded in the past five years. File transfer from and to the mainframe was cumbersome in the past; file transfer software, however, has improved dramatically. The security of all mainframe installations has not kept pace as well as it should, but the mainframes must have dial-up and file transfer capability for this event to be a threat.

Another exposure could exist in the form of an asynchronous port accessible by a phone line. Some installations have terminal network controllers with dial-up synchronous ports that cannot be accessed by a microcomputer without a protocol converter, for microcomputers use asynchronous protocols. Network controllers can have one port coded to accept asynchronous protocols; if connected to a dial-up link, a microcomputer user can gain mainframe access via terminal emulation software. The security review should look for this type of inadvertent trap.

To enhance control over the micro-mainframe link the auditor should:

- Determine that the interface or protocol converter is protected by a sign-on or dial-back scheme,
- Determine that hardwired lines are protected by physical security,
- Determine that dial-up lines are protected: by screening phone numbers of incoming calls with the phone computer, the CPU accepts calls from internal or authorized numbers only,
- Determine that receiver software, such as TSO[6], or other Tcomm monitor software that can process micro input is under control of the access security system—that the receiver software is shut down during nonbusiness hours,
- Determine that dial-up terminals can only access installation-designated files.

File Transfer

The function of this firmware and software is to emulate a terminal, perform protocol conversion, and upline or downline load files. The file transfer software must be resident on the mainframe for file transfer to be accomplished. The suggested additional precautions are such that:

- All files should be under security software protection.
- Transfer program should be placed under security so that only authorized users can use it.
- Dial-back modems for file transfer usage are used.

To secure dial-up systems, the CPU phone number should be coded into the terminal, so that dialing the mainframe can be performed by a function key. The phone number should not be displayed on the screen; it should be inaccessible. The phone numbers should be periodically changed, and management should ensure that they are not published in public phone directories.

Micro systems can use dial-back modems in appropriate situations, such as remote branches or for corporate customers. These modems correlate the users' password with a preauthorized phone number held in an internal table. The modem disconnects the user after password entry, and dials back the user on the phone number from the internal table.

Many installations use sophisticated phone computers for voice routing and switching. The central system should route computer connected calls only from specific phone numbers.

9.4.8 Environmental Protection

The on-line network components should be protected from physical threats (see Figure 9-10). These procedures focus on equipment not reviewed in physical access control or in the data center audit. These steps can be accomplished by inspection of the facility. Compliance testing is not really necessary because the objectives are accomplished by simple review. The audit concerns are identical to data center physical security review procedures.

9.4.9 Documentation

Management must ensure that the system and user documentation is adequate. Documentation is the most neglected element of any system simply because of the extra time and energy needed to create it. The pressure is on implementing a workable system and maintaining it. Many companies don't realize the time savings afforded by good documentation because it is difficult to quantify. The documentation must be sufficiently adequate to permit diagnosis and correction of system problems.

FIGURE 9–10   Environmental Protection

Audit Test Objective

To determine that the on-line network components are protected from physical threats

Key Controls

1. Physical access control

Scope

All network components not covered by physical access control review or data center security review

Audit Procedures:

Preliminary Review and Compliance Testing

1. Inspect the environment containing the network components to determine:
   a. Physical access security is adequate
   b. Environmental conditioning is adequate
   c. Smoke and fire detectors and fire extinguishing equipment is adequate
   d. Electrical circuit protectors
   e. Adequate power backup is provided
   f. Communication lines are shielded in areas of heavy interference

The user saves tremendous time with good system operating procedures, especially when new personnel are learning the system. Poor documentation will require an experienced employee to babysit the trainee at the cost of productivity.

NOTES

1. Mullen, Jack B. "Auditing Online Terminal Security." Reprinted from *EDP Auditing* (New York: Auerbach Publishers). © 1989, Warren, Gorham & Lamont, Inc. Used with permission.

2. IBM-RACF is a registered trademark of International Business Machines, Inc.

3. CA/Top Secret is a registered trademark of Computer Associates, Inc.

4. CICS is a registered trademark of International Business Machines, Inc.

5. IMS DB/DC (Information Management System - Data Base/Data Communications) is a registered trademark of International Business Machines, Inc.

6. TSO (Time Sharing Option) is a registered trademark of International Business Machines, Inc.

7. RACF is a registered trademark of International Business Machines, Inc.

Application Program Maintenance[1]

10.1 INTRODUCTION

This chapter will discuss auditing the controls over the application change process. These are the changes made to application programs that process the data entered through the on-line terminal system. Application program maintenance has a pervasive effect on the data processing environment because weak controls may jeopardize the processing of all data including the on-line transaction system.

The control process can vary greatly, and there is no wrong way to control it, excepting no control, or controls that cost too much. For that reason, various control scenarios and program library structures are illustrated to show the auditor different possibilities. The audit programs must be customized to fit individual environments because they supply the audit steps to complete an effective audit of a particular control structure. Documents, reports, and controls are referred to in general terms with explanations of their function to give the auditor assistance in finding these specific items that accomplish the same functions in various companies.

This critical environmental area maintains the computer application programs that process all of the company's daily transactions. The applications consist of computer programs that run on daily, weekly, monthly, quarterly, and yearly cycles. Coding errors in these programs can effect numerous days if undetected by such user controls as reconcilements, settlements, and input/output verifications. Even though the user controls can detect these errors, it is more efficient to prevent program errors from occurring. Flawed data can elude human controls, reach the customer, and subsequently cause lost revenue and poor customer relations—imagine the effect if an airline's computer reservation system printed the wrong destination city on computer screens or customer tickets. Moreover, misguided management decisions can result from erroneous computer output—an inventory control system that moves a decimal two places the wrong way could create havoc with inventory ordering.

A poorly controlled application maintenance environment can detrimentally affect all phases of a business, for all applications may be prone to coding errors. The previous examples explain in what ways the application change environment is pervasive. Control weaknesses in the application maintenance environment can result in the entire company's control environment's being considered weak. Because computer application programs are error prone, their output data, which are eventually passed to the financial statements, are considered also error prone. This error-proneness forces internal auditors and CPA firms to conduct further testing in every company area to obtain reasonable assurance regarding the financial statements. Obviously, this increases internal and external audit costs, but error correction costs and computer program reruns can be even more expensive, for they may be needed on a daily or weekly basis.

Adequate administrative controls must be enforced to ensure controlled maintenance, adequate documentation, and efficient programming. Changing production programs is an extremely sensitive undertaking because it is difficult to verify that the changed programs do not contain unauthorized program code.

10.2 PLANNING AND PREPARATION

During the preliminary survey phase, the auditor reviews various audit workpaper files and S&P documentation. The auditor's objective is to determine the functions that S&P personnel perform to complete program changes.

The key S&P documentation is the application maintenance guidelines. These provide specific instructions on each activity to be performed by the programmer or analyst in order properly to complete program changes. The absence of this documentation is a critical control weakness, because it means personnel have no instructions from management.

During this review of the documentation, the auditor can begin an assessment of its quality, thus killing two birds with one stone. The program change activities performed by S&P personnel are grouped by type. This classification is based on functional similarities that then become the areas of audit concern. These groupings vary for different installations.

10.2.1 Identification of Transactions

Vis-à-vis the audit transactions, program additions and modifications are grouped together because they involve changes to the existing code. Program deletion involves purging programs from libraries and is considered a different activity. This activity could be deleted from the audit as a time-saving mechanism if the programs can be recovered from a backup copy of the library (see Figure 10–1).

FIGURE 10-1   Identification of Transactions

Audit Activity Code	Transaction/Area	Include Exclude	Reason
A	Program Additions/ Modifications	I	Satisfies Audit Objective 1
B	Program Deletions	I	Satisfies Audit Objective 1
C	Program Library Backup/Recovery	I	Satisfies Audit Objective 4
D	Program Library Mgmt. Software	E	Stable Function
E	On-Line Programming Software	E	Stable Function
F	Change Control System	I	Satisfies Audit Objective 1
G	Security Software Control	I	Satisfies Audit Objective 3
H	Program Documentation	I	Satisfies Audit Objective 2
I	Program Testing	I	Satisfies Audit Objective 2
J	Authorized Libraries	I	Satisfies Audit Objective 1

Program library management software is usually a purchased package such as CA-Librarian[2] or PanValet.[3] These systems systematically keep track of changed codes, the various versions of programs, and archiving of various versions of programs.

Programmers use on-line programming software tools to write program code, to access program libraries, and to execute system utilities to do their jobs. The functions of these systems, such as IBM TSO[4] and CA-ROSCOE[5], are usually well controlled and do not require auditing. However, the on-line access the programmers have to systems resources must be audited. The change control system can be manual or automated and provides S&P administrative personnel with the information necessary to control the various programmer functions in the application change process. Security software systems control access to all system resources—terminals, data files, program libraries, utility programs, on-line transactions codes and the like. Two examples of these security packages are CA-Top Secret[6] and RACF.[7]

Documentation refers to the explanations and procedures written by programmers and analysts to explain how an application works. Specifically, the program maintenance audit focuses on the explanations of the program changes and the functions that they change. Guidelines, procedures, and standards make up the documentation that explains programmer activities in the application change process. These are referred to as the application maintenance guidelines.

10.2.2 Risks and Exposures

After the auditee's activities have been identified, the auditor should identify the risks and exposures of the program maintenance function (see Figure 10–2). Several terms, explained below, are worthy of explanation.

Blanket authorization: This refers to a "blank check" type of approval for the programmer to make any changes he or she wishes rather than changes specified by the user, designed by the analyst, and approved by EDP management. Authorization should exist for specific changes that are needed to fix specific problems or enhance program functions.

FIGURE 10–2 Scope Summary

Risks and Exposures

1. Unauthorized changes
2. Blanket authorization
3. Program logic errors and omissions
4. Inaccurate processing
5. Unnecessary reruns
6. Erroneous output
7. Excessive error correction
8. Hardware/software failures
9. Computer abuse/fraud

Control Objectives

1. All program changes are properly authorized
2. Conflicting program change functions are adequately segregated

FIGURE 10–2   *(Continued)*

3. All program changes are adequately tested and the test results are approved by the user
4. Personnel making program changes are adequately supervised
5. Program changes are adequately reviewed
6. Policies, procedures, and guidelines are adequately documented and available to the systems and programming staff
7. All changes to production programs are documented
8. Access to program libraries and data files is restricted
9. Only authorized libraries are used for programs

Key Controls

1. Documented policies and procedures
2. Segregation of duties
3. Documented testing standards
4. Program documentation standards
5. Supervisory review
6. Program change reporting system
7. Restricted library access

Audit Objectives

Ensure that adequate controls exist to:

1. Protect application programs from unauthorized changes
2. Ensure that application programs are error free
3. Protect program libraries from unauthorized access
4. Provide complete recovery in the event of destruction

Preliminary Review

Activity Code	Transaction/Area	Budget Hours	
		Audit Time	Review Time
A	Program Additions/Modifications	10	2
B	Program Deletions	5	.5
C	Program Library Backup/Recovery	5	.5
F	Change Control System	10	2
G	Security Software Control	7	1
H	Program Documentation	3	1
I	Program Testing	3	1
J	Authorized Libraries	3	1

Computer fraud: This begins with erroneous program code placed in the program for the benefit of the programmer. Inadequate library access controls permit any programmer to place code in any program that could make it difficult for an auditor to find the perpetrator. Independent review of the program code is the key control against this exposure.

Errors and omissions: These are simply incorrect or forgotten program code. Fraud is a much-talked about subject with regard to program changes, but errors and omissions are usually more costly. Inaccurate processing, unnecessary reruns, erroneous output, and excessive error corrections: These can all be effects of errors and omissions. They can also be separate risks brought about by inadequate design, testing, and user review of test results.

Software failures: These are abnormal endings (abends)— programs that fail to complete processing—which is usually caused by a program error, or an unanticipated transaction condition such as high transaction volume or data in a field that the program cannot handle. The cause of the failure must be identified and repaired and the program rerun.

Unauthorized changes: These are defined as additions or modifications to program code that are not approved by EDP management or the user. The application system is the user's responsibility and it is he or she who must request and approve changes.

10.2.3 Control Objectives

Certain control objectives are aimed at the exposures—unauthorized changes and blanket authorization. The application user and EDP management authorize all changes, whereas an independent control group follows specific procedures to ensure that all authorizations were obtained.

Most other control objectives are aimed at reducing or eliminating risks. Some are the key defense against computer fraud. Some help reduce the risk of computer fraud, but cannot be relied on alone, without supervision and code review. The use of authorized libraries serves to reduce processing errors because the library names are standardized and the programs are entered into the libraries using standardized procedures. All program updates and library references are standardized thereby eliminating inconsistencies of multiple libraries (see Figure 10–2).

10.2.4 Key Controls

Standard key controls pertaining to the program maintenance function are among the techniques used by the auditee to accomplish the control objectives. Documented policies and procedures include instructions on what authorizations should be obtained. Segregation of duties entails separating conflicting functions, in this case, design of program changes is performed by an analyst and the programming is completed by the programmer. Theoretically, collusion between the analyst and programmer would be necessary to insert fraudulent program code into the program.

Documented testing standards helps control the quality of testing by providing specific instructions for all programmers to follow, thereby making all testing techniques consistent throughout all applications. Program documentation serves as a valuable training tool and as a roadmap for the next programmer who needs to make a change or simply find an answer about program functions. Documentation standards provide quality control over the documentation to provide consistency throughout all applications.

Supervisory review provides an accuracy check of program code, increasing the probability of compliance with the users' specifications for change. Supervisory review of program code is the only effective means of detecting fraudulent program code.

A program change reporting system provides the means for an independent control group to keep track of changes updated to the computer system. Finally, restricted library access confines the programmer and analyst to authorized libraries, reducing the risk of placing programs in the improper libraries. These restrictions also prevent copying of sensitive or extraneous programs to libraries where they do not belong.

10.3   EXECUTION OF PRELIMINARY REVIEW

Once the basic information has been gathered, the auditor can proceed to the preliminary review phase (see Figure 10–2). The auditee activities reviewed during preliminary survey are noted as "include" on the identification of transactions (see Figure 10–1). Note that the activity codes remain the same on both figures. Documentation, in both narrative and flowchart forms, of the functions performed by the auditee and the transaction review should be completed within the budget time. These budgets are first-time audit estimates and should decrease in subsequent years if the procedures remain the same.

10.3.1   Reviewing Program Additions, Modifications, and Deletions

Program changes present a high risk of exposure to loss from errors, omissions, and fraud. Failed production programs cause reruns that disrupt normal data center and programming workflow. This in turn erodes data processing credibility and increases data processing costs. Fraud is costly, but its prevention and detection are inherent problems not easily solved.

Change authorization procedures and requirements vary in every organization. The auditor must determine the procedures in the organization he is auditing. An audit of normal scope will not detect fraud, but it will isolate control weaknesses that could permit errors and fraud to occur. Programs can be modified via batch update or on-line programming. If the data center is geared to batch updates, procedures must exist to screen incoming jobs and segregate the test runs from program library updates. A special form is needed to authorize the updating of a production program library. Unfortunately, these screening and authorization controls are dependent on individuals and, therefore, error prone. The on-line programming environment is riskier if changes can be made without any supervision or an independent review—there is no independent person to add the changed program to the production program library based on an authorization form.

FIGURE 10–3   Program Additions/Modifications

Audit Test Objective

To determine that additions and modifications to production application programs are authorized

Control Objectives

1. Authorized work orders
2. Review of all production updates
3. Independent comparison of changes to specifications

Scope

All program and jcl changes that occurred during the period being examined

Audit Procedures

Preliminary Review

Determine change authorization procedures and requirements

Compliance Testing

1. Verify that program changes were authorized by tracing a sample of program and jcl changes to a signed maintenance form
   a. The change specifications were adequately described, a cost was developed, a target date was established
   b. The change specifications were developed by an experienced analyst and approved by the user
   c. The change form was reviewed and approved by S&P management
   d. The work was reviewed by an analyst and a S&P supervisor
   e. The update to production was approved by an appropriate person
   f. Match the date on the form to the date of production update for agreement
   g. The work order control number is deleted from use
2. Select a sample of update exceptions
   a. Trace them to explanation memoranda justifying the exception
   b. Examine for signature of programming supervisor and S&P management
3. Compare code changes to specifications to determine that the program was changed according to specifications and the update modules are filed appropriately

The program change can be made sight unseen except for library update reports that may not be reviewed as well as they should be (see Figures 10–3 and 10–4).

The delete function presents great risk to the program libraries. The delete procedure should not be provided to programmers, analysts, or the control group for production libraries. This procedure permits any embezzler to cover his tracks easily. In addition, the program libraries are the lifeblood of the organization, and indiscriminate program deleting can cause disaster. The deleting of programs should be performed by a limited group and should be subject to stringent review before the deletion

FIGURE 10–4   Program Deletions

Audit Test Objective

To determine that deletions of production application programs are authorized and that copies are made

Control Objectives

1. Authorized work order
2. Review of programs
3. Copies are made for backup

Scope

All programs that were deleted during the period being examined

Audit Procedures

Preliminary Review

Determine authorization procedures and requirements for deleting programs

Compliance Testing

1. Select a sample of deleted programs made during the audit period and trace to the authorization form to prove the deletions were authorized
   a. The reason for deletion was adequately described
   b. The work order was reviewed and approved by both application analyst and S&P management
   c. The program was reviewed by an analyst and an S&P supervisor
   d. Match the date on the work order to the date of deletion for agreement
   e. Determine that the work order control number is deleted from use
   f. Determine that a copy of the program was made prior to deletion

takes place. Backup files should be available in case programs are improperly deleted.

10.3.2   Reviewing the Program Library Backup and Recovery

The review of program library backup and recovery is done to determine which procedures need to be followed in order to make backup files. The procedures for file recovery should also be reviewed at this time. Testing to determine the effectiveness of, and compliance with, the procedures is done in the compliance testing phase. The review steps concerning backup and recovery focus on whether or not backup procedures are performed. If not, a critical weakness exists that can be documented, and the audit of this transaction needs go no further (see Figure 10–5).

FIGURE 10–5   **Backup/Recovery**

Audit Test Objective

To determine that program libraries can be completely recovered in the event of destruction

Control Objectives

1.   File copying procedure
2.   Off-site storage
3.   All programs are on backup file

Scope

All program libraries at time of audit

Audit Procedures

Preliminary Review

1.   Determine that all program libraries are routinely copied at necessary intervals during the day
2.   Determine that the copies are moved to a secure off-site location at necessary intervals during the day

Compliance Testing

1.   Examine a sample, or all, of the programs on the backup file to determine if all application programs are present

10.3.3   Reviewing the Change Control System

Review of the change control system enables the auditor to determine what procedures are necessary in order to accomplish authorization of changes. This system can be manual or automated, depending on the size and complexity of the EDP environment. The review step concerning change control focuses on the procedure in the authorization system that detects exceptions—changes without authorization (see Figure 10–6).

Unauthorized changes to libraries can be detected by independent programmatic procedures, but such procedures cannot prevent "extra maintenance" (fraudulent code) to individual programs while the authorized changes are being coded. The primary preventive control is review of the changed code by another qualified person. This is easier said than done because most programs are quite long, and it is impractical to review an entire program for coding statements that should not have been

FIGURE 10–6   Program Change Control System

Audit Test Objective

To determine that the change control system properly identifies all update exceptions

Control Objectives

1.   Defined exceptions
2.   Exception identification and reporting mechanism

Scope

All exceptions that occurred during the period being examined

Audit Procedures

Preliminary Review

Determine the conditions that cause reporting exceptions

Compliance Testing

1.   In a test environment, link modules that should be detected by the system as exceptions
2.   Review exception reports to determine that the exceptions were properly reported

entered. Program library management software that tracks changes to programs and can flag all of the code changed in the last update do exist. These make code review considerably easier. This type of program, however, can be circumvented by updating the program twice. In such a case, the first update would contain the erroneous code, and the second update would be submitted for review. The erroneous code would not be flagged because it was entered in the first update. Instituting controlled updates to production libraries could prevent this multiple updating and so maintain the integrity of the flagging function.

A source-code-compare program that compares two versions of the same program and prints out the differences is another means of code review. The effectiveness of this approach is limited by the extent of control over the program update from source to object libraries. If controls ensure that the production source and object versions are identical, then the source-code-compare program is a viable test or review. If the controls, however, do not ensure a match, then the source-code-compare program is ineffective because additional updates that invalidate the usefulness of the code comparison could have occurred.

10.3.4   Reviewing the Security Software Control

Restriction of on-line (logical) access by programmers is an integral part of the change control system. Therefore, review of the security access control system includes identifying the method that EDP management uses to determine what access restrictions should be placed on each programmer (see Figure 10–7).

Evaluating the policies and procedures for assigning on-line access levels to S&P personnel and reviewing the on-line programming access rules to see how they function helps familiarize the auditor with management's intentions and with the defined access rules (see Section 10.5.5). After completion of these preliminary steps the auditor will know the extent of the programmer's and analyst's access.

The on-line access capabilities and system knowledge of a company's programmer become a key issue in application

FIGURE 10–7   Security Software Control

Audit Test Objective

To determine that on-line access cannot be gained to the program files without authorization

Control Objectives

1. Authorized work order
2. Review of all production updates
3. Independent comparison of changes to specifications

Scope

All S&P personnel

Audit Procedures

Preliminary Review

1. Determine via observation that programmers must have authorization to enter the computer room
2. Evaluate the policies and procedures for assigning on-line access levels to S&P personnel
3. Review the on-line programming access rules to see how they function

Compliance Testing

1. Determine the extent of programmers' and analysts' on-line access to test and production program libraries
    a. Select a sample of programmers and analysts; review their access rules to determine that they can only access the libraries for which they are responsible
    b. Determine that they can only use the specific access procedures to which they are entitled (See Control Procedures Scenario Discussion, Section 10.4.2)
    c. Design and perform tests that should violate access rules
    d. Review access profile definitions to determine that programmers do not have access to production facilities or transactions

---

program maintenance. Critical control questions used to determine a programmers' level of access include:

- What programs can the programmer examine (READ)?
- What programs can the programmer change (UPDATE, REPLACE, DELETE)?

- When can the programmer change the programs?
- Which terminals can the programmer use?
- Can the system determine if on-line program updates are authorized?
- Can the programmer execute a data file update program from the terminal to change data for personal advantage and then change the program back to its original condition without detection?

10.3.5 Reviewing the Program Documentation

Determining the extent of documentation required by management examines what program documentation should be prepared

FIGURE 10-8   Program Documentation

Audit Test Objective

To determine that program changes are adequately documented

Control Objectives

1. Documentation standards
2. Quality control review of documentation

Scope

All program and jcl changes that occurred during the period being examined

Audit Procedures

Preliminary Review

Determine the extent of documentation required by management

Compliance Testing

1. Select a sample of program and jcl changes made during the audit period:
   a. Examine the application manual, data center run manual and the users manual to determine that any changed procedures as a result of the change have been documented in compliance with S&P standards (see Section 10.7, Elements of Documentation)
   b. Determine that the update listing that reflects the changed program code has been filed in the program file in the central programming library
2. Verify that the changes in the documentation accurately reflect the effect of the change

by the programmer, how it is prepared, and under what conditions it must be updated. If procedures and documentation requirements are not specified, then the review cannot be completed and testing cannot be performed. This is a major control weakness and can be reported without further audit work. The absence of the documentation guidelines makes it impossible to

---

FIGURE 10–9   Program Testing

Audit Test Objective

1. To determine that program additions and modifications are adequately tested and reviewed before being placed into production
2. To determine that users are aware of changes made to their systems initiated by others

Control Objectives

1. Personnel are adequately supervised
2. Testing standards
3. User review of test results before implementation

Scope

All program changes that occurred during the period being examined

Audit Procedures

Preliminary Review

Determine the standards and procedures for program testing

Compliance Testing

1. Select a sample of program changes made during the audit period:
   a. Verify that the programmer was given adequate specifications on the change requirements
   b. Verify that an analyst or manager reviewed the changed and added program code
2. Evaluate the testing performed on the changed program:
   a. Verify that the testing complies with the testing standards set by systems and programming management
   b. Verify that the user reviewed and approved the test results. Discuss the change with the user to determine that he did review the test results prior to implementation. A documented approval should exist

---

audit actual events for compliance to management requirements because these requirements are absent (see Figure 10–8).

10.3.6 Reviewing the Program Testing

Determining the standards and procedures for program testing can be accomplished by interviewing management and reviewing documented policies and procedures manuals. Management must establish these requirements in writing to control the quality of programs created by analysts and programmers. The absence of these documented requirements justifies a negative audit opinion on the internal control quality of program maintenance (see Figure 10–9).

10.3.7 Reviewing the Authorized Libraries

Determining the specific standard libraries that are used can be accomplished by interviewing systems software programmers and reviewing the table of contents or directory listings for all disk files, even though the review is very time consuming (see Figure 10–10).

Using audit software to write a program to list all libraries used by the system will only be useful if the auditor can verify that the software includes all executed programs; otherwise, independence is compromised.

10.3.8 Summary

The auditor's technical knowledge is important, because the auditor must determine whether the system can be compromised. Programmers' answers should be verified independently through research of on-line programs that perform program update functions. Designing compliance tests to isolate compromising situations challenges the auditors' technical limits and imagination.

The auditor needs to gain hands-on experience with the on-line programming system, program library software, and job

FIGURE 10–10   Authorized Libraries

Audit Test Objective

To determine that unauthorized program libraries do not exist

Control Objectives

1. Specific standard libraries exist
2. All test and production jobs are executed from the standard libraries

Scope

All production and test programs

Audit Procedures

Preliminary Review

1. Determine the specific standard libraries that are used
2. Utilizing audit software, or installation utility, write a program to list all libraries used by the system

Compliance Testing

1. Verify a sample of programs from program job streams to determine that they exist on the appropriate library
2. Trace a different sample of programs from the standard libraries to documentation that proves that they should be present on that specific library
3. Another method is to analyze a sample of program job streams looking for jcl that would direct the program to a different library to find a program for execution
    a. Determine that the specified library is an authorized library
4. Verify that temporary program libraries cannot be created and accessed during execution, then deleted after job completion

control language so he or she can improve his or her performance on the audit. The presentation of the audit findings to S&P personnel often calls for the auditor's communications and human relations skills for many of the controls required for program maintenance will directly reduce S&P productivity. The current business environment requires maximum productivity, but some of the controls over the program maintenance environment can reduce productivity. When faced with this paradox, the auditor may be forced to accept reduced control because of its high cost. Control, however, is management's responsibility. The auditor reviews controls, determines their adequacy, and reports the condition to management and the audit committee. Management, therefore, bears the responsibility for loss from fraud, errors, or omissions that are caused by a poorly controlled programming environment. Nevertheless, the auditor should continually push for realistic changes that can provide adequate control over program maintenance.

10.4 FUNCTIONAL ISSUES AND CONTROL CONSIDERATIONS

Program change environments vary depending on hardware, software, and data processing management philosophy. To properly explain various change control environments, certain standard procedures must be defined. To do so, the auditor must see that:

- A standardized program change form exists with appropriate sign-off procedures and reviews,
- Program changes are completed via on-line terminals,
- All program libraries are retained on direct access storage devices,
- A program test environment with test standards and files exists, and
- An independent control group monitors program changes.

The definitions of the various program libraries are the following:

1. Test Source—the English version of the program code on a file utilized for test purposes only,
2. Test Object—the machine-readable version of the source program for test purposes only,
3. Production Source—the English version of the program code on a file utilized for production only, and

4.   Production Object—the machine-readable version of the source program for production only.

10.4.1   Program Libraries

Various library structures have certain inherent risks that are explained on the following pages.

10.4.1.1   LIBRARY STRUCTURE ONE

One-source program library and one-object program library: This means that test and production programs are maintained on one-source and one-object libraries (see above, Section 10.4, items 1–4). Program changes are made to the source, compiled and linked to the object, and then tested, which creates multiple versions of the test and production programs on both libraries. Because programmers need access to the object library to run such testing, the object library cannot be restricted. Restricted access can only be accomplished by programmatically restricting access to certain program modules, which can be cumbersome and inefficient. Some security software packages require significant overhead to restrict access at the module level, whereas other packages do not even have that capability. Effective change authorization can only be accomplished by an independent control group that has sole access to source and object libraries, that is, programmer access to source and object libraries is prevented, which drastically reduces productivity.

10.4.1.1.1   Procedures Required to Accomplish Control. Adequate control of library structure one can only be accomplished and maintained by using the following procedures:

- Prevent programmer access to source and object libraries,
- Prevent batch program updating,

- Make sure that only one control group releases copies of the source programs and places them in the programmers' library,
- Make sure that the control group updates the object library with the test version of the program,
- Make sure that upon test completion, the control group updates the object library with the production version,
- Make sure that "read-only" access of source can be permitted,
- Require that program-naming conventions have a unique identifier to distinguish test from production versions, and
- Require screening controls of jcl to prevent production execution of a test program when the wrong program name is used.

10.4.1.1.2 Risks and Exposures. Risks and exposures inherent to this structure include the following:

- Multiple program versions,
- Absence of review of changed code for "extra maintenance,"
- Absence of segregation of production and test source code,
- Accidental modification of the live production version,
- Restricted access to the object library can only be accomplished by restricting specific program modules.
- Accidental execution of test version.

10.4.1.2 LIBRARY STRUCTURE TWO

One source library—Test object and production object library: Source changes are made to a copy of the source in the programmer's on-line library and are then compiled and linked to the test object library. After testing, the final program is compiled and linked to the production object library by a control group. The new source program replaces the previous version on the single-source library. Programmer access to the production object library can be prevented. Because programmers have a separate object library for testing, they do not need access to the production object library. In addition, with today's sophisticated on-line programming software, the programmer can use his or her own on-line library to store and change the source. The test object library can be updated directly from the programmer's library. Only the control group is authorized to update the tested program to production object.

10.4.1.2.1   Procedures Required to Accomplish Control. Adequate control of this environment can only be accomplished and maintained by using the following procedures:

- Programmer access to source and production object libraries is prohibited.
- Batch program updating is prohibited.
- The control group releases source programs and places them in the programmers' library.
- The programmer compiles and links the test source version in the programmer's library to the test object library.
- The control group updates all libraries with production versions upon test completion.
- Program-naming conventions require a unique identifier to distinguish test from production versions.

10.4.1.2.2   Risks and Exposures.   Risks and exposures inherent to this structure include the following:

- Absence of clear-cut segregation of test and production source programs.
- Multiple versions of the same program on the source library.

- Absence of review of changed codes for unauthorized changes.

10.4.1.3 LIBRARY STRUCTURE THREE

Test source library—Test object library and Production source library—Production object library: Test and production environments are segregated so access to production source and object libraries can be prevented.

10.4.1.3.1 Procedures Required to Accomplish Control. Adequate control of this library structure can only be accomplished and maintained by using the following procedures:

- Programmer access to production source and object libraries is prohibited,
- Batch program updating is prohibited,
- The control group releases test source and object programs to the programmers' library, and
- After test completion, the control group updates production source and object libraries with the production version.

10.4.1.3.2 Risks and Exposures. Risks and exposures inherent to this structure are the following:

- The presence of nonmatching programs between test and production libraries, and
- The absence of review for unauthorized changes.

10.4.2 Control Procedures Scenarios

The major objective of a control procedure is to ensure that all program changes to both test and production environments are authorized. However, such control over both environments increases cost. Authorization of the changes to the production library is the minimum control necessary. This requires an authorization procedure for the update from test to production libraries. Test and production libraries should be subject to an authorization control because a test version could contain erroneous or fraudulent code. These could be used on the next change to production program code. Upon linkage to the production object, the fraudulent code would be placed into production.

Authorization control of the test environment requires an authorization procedure between the change request process and programmer access to test source and object libraries. This level of control, however, is more expensive because of the repetition of changes during testing. Three control and procedure scenarios are discussed in the following section. Procedures and controls vary among particular environments, but the necessary basic control procedures are presented here.

10.4.2.1 SCENARIO ONE

Unrestricted Programmer Access: When programmers have access to all libraries only detection control is possible. The typical schedule for this type of control follows:

1. A change request is submitted by the user;
2. S&P management reviews the request and assigns an analyst;
3. The analyst develops change specifications with the user;
   a. The analyst develops cost data and target dates,
   b. The user approves cost, targets, and specifications,
4. S&P management reviews and approves data and assigns a programmer;
   a. The control group enters the change request in an on-line disk file,
5. The analyst gives the programmer detailed specifications;

6. The assigned programmer retrieves the program from the source program library;

   a.   The changes are made,

   b.   The program is compiled and linked to object,

   c.   The program is tested according to standards,

   d.   The user reviews the test results and approves them,

7. The programmer adds the program to the production library;

   a.   The programmer enters the change request number in the on-line compile-and-link procedure,

   b.   The change request number is verified to the stored change request number,

   c.   A match or nonmatch permits update to production,

   d.   A nonmatch appears on an exception report for review by the control group and S&P management and returns it to the programmer for explanation,

   e.   A matched change request appears on a change request close report (a listing of change request numbers that are finished),

8. The control group closes the change request and determines if the request was authorized.

10.4.2.1.1 Risks and Exposures. The following list includes the risks and exposures inherent to this scenario:

- There is no control over input of the change request to the control file, so the request can be input on any terminal;

- Procedures do not specify daily verification of change request input;

- Programmers have access to all libraries, including the compile-and-link procedure to production;

- The analyst or S&P manager does not review the changed code for accuracy and propriety;

- The change request authorization program does not abort nonmatches and, therefore, it permits updates of unauthorized changes;
- Change authorization is subject only to an after-the-fact human detection control achieved by reviewing a report;
- The closing of a change request is dependent on individuals and, therefore, subject to failure. This could leave a work order open for use in another update.

10.4.2.2 SCENARIO TWO

Prevent Programmer Access to Production Libraries: This method eliminates some of the risks mentioned before and increases the degree of control. The typical schedule is the following:

1. The change request is submitted by user,
2. S&P management reviews the request and assigns an analyst,
3. The analyst develops change specifications with the user by developing cost data and target dates, then the user approves the cost, targets, and specifications;
4. S&P management reviews and approves analyst data and assigns a programmer;
5. The analyst provides the programmer with detailed specifications;
6. The programmer retrieves the program from the source program library and makes the changes, then the program is compiled and linked to the test object library and is tested according to established standards—the user then reviews the test results and approves the changes;
7. The programmer notifies the analyst that the program is ready for production update and:
   a. the S&P manager approves the change request for update,
   b. the change request is passed to the control group,

c. the control group reviews the change request for the presence of authorized signatures,

d. the control group replaces the previous production source program with the new program (if this separate library exists), and, finally,

e. the control group compiles and links the new source program to production object.

10.4.2.2.1 Risks and Exposures.   Even if these control procedures are followed, there are still risks and exposures inherent to such a scenario. These include:

- The programmer's having access to source libraries and being able to insert unauthorized changes at any time (these could then be included in the next authorized update);
- The analyst or S&P management may not review the changed code for accuracy or propriety;
- Program errors to the production source or object may occur if the control group uses the incorrect source program; and
- The source and object test libraries could grow too large unless old programs are routinely purged.

10.4.2.3 SCENARIO THREE

Prevent Programmer Access to All Program Libraries: Total prevention of programmer access is the most extreme method of control. It removes the chance for programmer-induced errors by following these steps:

1. The change request is submitted by the user;
2. S&P management reviews and assigns the analyst;
3. The analyst develops the change specifications with the user in the same manner as scenarios one and two (analyst develops cost data, target dates—the user approves cost, targets, and specifications);

4. S&P management reviews and approves the changes and then assigns the programmer;
5. The analyst gives the programmer detailed specifications;
6. The analyst notifies the control group of the need for change with a copy of the change request;
    a. The control group copies the program from the source and adds it to the programmer's library;
7. The programmer reviews the program that has now been placed in his or her on-line library;
    a. He or she then makes the changes;
    b. The programmer notifies the control group and the analyst that the program is ready for testing;
    c. The analyst reviews the changed code and authorizes the control group to update the source test and compile and link it to the object test;
    d. The program is then tested according to established standards;
    e. The user reviews the test results and approves them;
8. The programmer notifies the analyst that the program is ready for production update;
    a. The S&P manager approves the change request for update;
    b. The change request is passed to the control group;
    c. The control group reviews the change request for the necessary presence of authorized signatures;
    d. The control group replaces the previous production source program with the new program (if this separate library exists); and
    e. The control group compiles and links the new source program to the production object.

10.4.2.3.1 Risks and Exposures.   The risks and exposures inherent to this scenario are the following:

- The analyst or S&P manager may not review changed code for accuracy or propriety;

- Program errors may occur to all program libraries if the control group uses any incorrect programs;
- The source and object test libraries could grow too large unless old programs are routinely purged.

10.5   COMPLIANCE TESTING

10.5.1   Program Additions and Modifications

Figure 10–3 describes the audit testing steps for ensuring that all program changes are authorized. An unauthorized change can occur for several reasons: 1) the user who is responsible for its application may not be aware of the change, that is, there is no user sign-off on the maintenance change request approving the start of the work, 2) a change request form may not have been formally established, 3) the appropriate S&P manager may not have signed the change form approving work commencement, 4) the user may not have signed the change form that signifies acceptance before the change was updated, 5) the changed program code may not have been properly reviewed by the appropriate analyst, 6) the S&P manager may not have signed the change form that approves the program for update to production, or 7) the programmer may have written in an extra code so he could commit a fraud.

The auditor's detailed analysis should locate any weaknesses in the procedure that would inadvertently permit the occurrence of one of these conditions. If the auditor finds the appropriate procedures in place, then the compliance tests should be designed to find evidence that the identified controls did, in fact, function properly during the period being examined. This detailed analysis should also help the auditor to determine how the control procedures could be intentionally circumvented, allowing unauthorized change to go undetected.

Selecting a sample of update exceptions verifies the control of program updates by the programmer's supervisor or a control group. A system should exist to examine all production updates and to match them to an authorized work order. Updates without a valid work order are exceptions and should be reported to the supervisor, who should then receive an explanation from the programmer. The exception and the explanation should be reviewed and initialed by S&P management.

Comparing code changes to specifications examines the accuracy and propriety of program code. The most effective control over erroneous program codes is the independent review of the program prior to the production update. Unfortunately, it is very difficult to test the quality of the review after the fact. The auditor cannot determine whether the reviewer scanned the code or performed an in-depth review. However, an alternative is to compare the changed code to the specifications. Changes that do not match the specifications strongly indicate inadequate review prior to the production update. The more changes found by the auditor that do not match the specifications, the more suspect the reliability of this control becomes. If a level of unacceptable risk is exceeded the auditor must conclude that the control cannot be relied upon. Determining that hard copy reports of update modules are properly filed partially tells the auditor the quality of the documentation for the production program.

10.5.2   Program Deletions

These can be accomplished by programmers (decentralized) or by a centralized group (see Figure 10–4). Centralized control is best, for there are fewer people deleting modules. If a decentralized system is used, then deletions must follow the same control procedures as additions (previously shown) do; if centralized, the order must still be in writing and reviewed prior to deletion.

A backup copy of the program is necessary in case the program is needed later. In fact, with centralized control of deletions, backup is the primary control. If the auditor is comfortable that the copies are always made, then auditing program deletions can be omitted without posing undue risk. However, in a decentralized environment, the authorization procedure must be audited to determine that deletions are controlled. The programmer could forget to copy the program. A dishonest employee could delete programs to cover his tracks. Or, a disgruntled employee could delete programs to cause trouble.

The auditor should insist that program deletions be performed by a select centralized group, preferably the system software programming group.

10.5.3   Program Library Backup and Recovery

This is an extremely critical element of the audit because destruction of the program files without adequate backup would require manual reentry of the programs from source code listings. Although this means of recovery is possible, the time required for recovery is considerably extended. Rapid recovery from a disaster can mean the continuation of the business.

In addition to previously discussed steps necessary for evaluation (see Figure 10–5) of backup and recovery, the auditor can load a sample of application programs from the backup file to the production system and execute them with live data to see whether they are functionally the same as the production programs. Two alternatives to this are 1) to execute a source-code-compare program between the production version and the backup version to determine that they match, or 2) to execute the "freeze" option of CA-EXAMINE[8] against both the backup version and the production version to see whether identical freeze numbers are produced.

CA-EXAMINE is a software package with numerous functions to validate the integrity and performance of an operating system. It contains a freeze option that can be used to determine whether two versions, either source or object, are identical. It is similar to a source-code-compare program except that the freeze option calculates a version or "freeze" number by adding the binary values of each character in the object version of the program. If two programs are identical then their freeze number should be the same.

10.5.4   Program Change Control System

The maintenance request form provides the means for authorization control, but only when combined with other procedures. If installation management wishes to rely on a detection control system, a control technique must exist to identify all changes to production libraries because a programmer may innocently forget to, or intentionally not, report a production update.

The control procedures performed by an independent control group include:

1.   Daily execution of a utility program that scans production libraries and reports program modules that have been updated;

2.   Daily maintenance of a change request file, closing out completed jobs and adding new ones; and

3.   Matching of updated modules to an open change request.

The programmer should forward the completed change request form to the control group with all necessary authorization signatures. The control group reviews the form for all necessary signatures, ensures that the proper program module was updated, and pulls the copy from the change request file and closes it as an authorized change.

Program updates without the change request form are unauthorized, and the control group should report this to the assigned programmer's supervisor to seek an explanation for the exception. When resolved, the control group is notified and can then provide the authorized change request. Although this procedure is not as effective as preventive control, it nonetheless is sufficient to satisfy external audit and regulatory control requirements. Because the procedure is dependent on individuals, management must ensure that they are functioning consistently.

This detection control mechanism can be automated or manual, depending on the needs of the organization. The following items describe the steps needed to automate the control mechanism:

- The unique change request number must be entered on a disk file;
- The program module update program requires input of the change request number to execute the update utility;
- This program module update program compares the entered request number to the numbers on the disk file; and
- All updates without a matching request number are reported on a hard copy exception report.

The automation eliminates the control group review of all program module updates and manual matching to change request forms. The function of adding change request numbers to the disk file must be limited to the control group. Otherwise anyone could input a change request number and circumvent the detection control. (Cancellation of the program module update utility because of a nonmatching change request number would make this mechanism a preventive control.)

Control structures vary from company to company, and so would the definition of an exception in program changes. One element of compliance testing uses a simulation technique to verify the functions of the exception reporting system. The auditor should review update changes that he knows are exceptions that should be reported by the system.

10.5.5 Security Software Control

On-line access must be reviewed to determine that actual access conforms with installation standards. Testing should also be designed to break these access rules to determine if unauthorized access can be gained. S&P management may not be aware of the potential to break access rules, but a dishonest programmer or analyst will have discovered it.

Senior- and middle-level management need access controls that will prevent and detect fraudulent access. However, in the daily business routine, these managers seldom have the opportunity to ensure that all access profiles were defined properly. Audit review of the access profiles is a vital service to management.

10.5.5.1 ACCESS PROCEDURES

Because on-line access rules vary with each scenario, the audit procedures must be modified accordingly in order to assess installation standards. Generic examples of access procedures are the following:

- Add—the ability to add a unique program module to a library as a separate entry;
- Replace—the ability to replace an existing module with another of the same name;
- Update—the ability to selectively add new lines of codes or replace existing lines; and
- Delete—the ability to erase a program module.

These access procedures are combined with the particular program libraries to form the access rules. The first scenario, explained in Section 10.4.2, permitted carte blanche access; therefore all four access procedures would be permitted against all four libraries. The second scenario allowed programmer access only to test libraries. Therefore, all four access procedures would be permitted for source test and object only—the control group would have all four access procedures for production source and object. The third scenario prevented all access. Therefore only the control group would have use of all four access procedures to the four libraries.

Determining the extent of programmers' and analysts' on-line access to test and production libraries tests the defined access to determine if any compromising situations exist. The auditor, however, must understand that the extent of access actually defined to the system may not agree with management's intentions. For this reason, it is crucial to ensure that programmers and analysts can only use the specific access procedures to which they are entitled.

10.5.6 Program Documentation

Documentation of program changes is vital to the efficient operation of S&P and permits efficient maintenance of programs. Such documentation is an invaluable information source for new personnel that increases S&P productivity by reducing the instruction needed by them. Inadequate documentation causes the need for additional research time: another programmer has to determine the effect of previous changes.

In addition to the previously discussed steps necessary to determine that the program change was documented is the evaluation of the quality of the documentation: For example, 1) does it adequately describe the changes that were made, and 2) are the changed functions adequately explained? Answering these questions requires good audit judgment, developed through experience and understanding of the programming environment.

The application manual contains explanations of system attributes and processing needed by programmers to understand the functions of the application. The data center run manual contains the execution instructions that computer operators need to process various job streams. The user manual contains explanations of system attributes and processing so the user can understand how to prepare and submit input and utilize reports generated by the application.

A hard copy of each program's source code should be maintained in a central location, accessible by authorized employees. Each time a program is changed, a new listing of the source code should be printed and placed in the centralized file. This listing provides a reference for research, as well as a backup should the computer file backup be destroyed or become unusable.

10.5.6.1 ELEMENTS OF PROGRAM DOCUMENTATION

Documented procedures are vital to the consistent operation of S&P. Because of the technical data involved with computer systems operation, each programmer and analyst must be given specific guidelines to follow in the completion of their work. Without these guidelines, individual styles will be manifested, causing inconsistency and disorganization. In addition, guidelines are a valuable training tool for new personnel, reducing the learning curve and increasing S&P productivity by reducing the need for individual instruction. Inadequate documentation forces S&P management to spend time instructing new hires personally on details that could easily have been documented.

The extent of documentation is installation dependent and is affected by the system's complexity. Obviously, complex on-line and database management systems require in-depth documentation. The auditor, after studying S&P procedures, should be able to assess the quality of the documentation and make appropriate recommendations for improvement.

Program standards cover the writing of programs. Deviations from these standards require S&P management approval. The installation's supported languages should be identified with details on critical segments of the language. The elements of documentation are presented below in their usual logical sequence:

Documentation revision record: This logs all changes to documentation in chronological order, giving S&P personnel an encapsulated trail of changes.

System narrative: This is a thumbnail sketch of the application's functions, describing input methods and files, processing techniques that include internally generated transactions, the form of the output produced, and the purpose of the application.

Program narratives: These are detailed explanations of each program's functions, describing input, processing, and output functions. These narratives bring the programmer up to speed quickly and dramatically increase the efficiency of program maintenance, because before the programmer can change a program he must understand its function.

Program flowcharts: These can enhance the value of the narratives, for they can provide a more structured overview of application and individual program function.

List of programs: This is simply an inventory log of all of the programs in an application, providing a quick reference for the programmer.

Transaction code list and explanations: This is the most critical piece of documentation; it provides the programmer and the user with a vital roadmap to input and output functions. The transaction code format should list and explain the purpose of each data field required for input. The output screen response to transaction input should explain each field and its meaning. Possible error codes and messages resulting from wrong input should be explained, including the operator's response and corrective action.

Operator procedures: These are instructions for the mainframe operator in executing the program. Error messages and the operator's intended response should be explained. In addition, the input files used and output files or reports created should be defined.

File retention schedules: These explain the saving and deleting of created files, the length of time they are saved, and on what media they are to be saved. This sets up the file rotation to an off-site storage area to retain backup of files critical to recovery.

Restart and recovery procedures: These describe to the computer operator exactly how to recover the application or program from an abnormal ending, including the procedures to follow, the programs to execute, and the files to use.

File layouts: These explain the file layout field by field, including the field name, data type or format, character size, and its starting and ending displacement position in the file. Included are field redefinitions that assign aliases or nicknames to a group of fields for use in a special program function.

Dataset definitions: These specify the characteristics of files, including the standard name, file size, block size, record size, and expansion constraints. A standard internal file label is also specified for use by the system for identification.

Job control language listing (jcl): This shows all of the jcl's executed during program execution. The listing's retention is necessary to determine the job stream names, files and datasets used, run time, and cpu usage.

Output layouts: These depict the printer setup instructions for each report, examples of reports, and terminal screen output formats. This information gives the programmer an easy reference for identifying what data the application already produces. Users face a common problem, that of not knowing every function and report produced by a system. They frequently request that new reports be created which contain data that already exists on another report or series of reports. These output layouts help the programmer quickly identify what data is printed, thereby eliminating a program change.

The application user must have an organized set of instructions that explain how to operate the system, request various special reports, prepare input, and show how data is processed. These instructions are necessary to produce an informed user who can operate independently.

10.5.7 Program Testing

Written specifications prepared by an analyst are the detailed instructions for the programmer and the authorization for the changes. Any additional changes are unauthorized. The analyst's or supervisor's review is the only defense against using an unauthorized code.

User participation in testing is necessary to determine that the program was modified to produce desired results. Without this review, the user is at risk in accepting what the programmer decides. The documentation of the user's approval protects the programmer if the program should fail later.

Evaluating the quality of program testing after the fact is difficult at best. Approval signatures can be easily discerned, but the manager and user must be interviewed to determine the quality of the reviews, and this is subjective at best. The analyst's or manager's signature or initials should appear on the specifications form and the program code source listing, signifying approval of the specifications and the changed code. Documentation of the user's approval should be necessary to authorize the program compile-and-link to the production library.

The audit period will usually encompass events during the past year. The auditor should discuss the program changes from the sample with the user representative that signed off on the change. They should be able to remember the purpose of the change, their review of the test results, and any problems that may have occurred in testing. A user who cannot remember some information about the change may be trying to fool the auditor. If several users cannot remember reviewing the test results, this review should become suspect. Then the auditor should consider enlarging the sample of program changes in order to talk with more users to increase the level of reasonable assurance that the key control of user review is in fact functioning and can be relied upon.

10.5.8 Authorized Libraries

The audit procedures can be time-consuming, but they are necessary to determine that extraneous program libraries do not exist. The most difficult situation is that in which temporary libraries can be created during execution and be deleted upon job completion. The only traces are the steps in the jcl summary, system logs, or job accounting/monitoring reports. If tape or disk job logs exist, audit software could possibly be developed programmatically to analyze the logs for the presence of such temporary libraries.

To accomplish the audit procedures, the auditor will need to research jcl reference manuals to determine how program libraries are specified.

NOTES

1. See Mullen, Jack B. "Audit and Control of Program Changes." Reprinted from *EDP Auditing* (New York: Auerbach Publishers). © 1990, Warren, Gorham & Lamont, Inc. Used with permission.

2. CA-Librarian is a registered trademark of Computer Associates, Inc.

3. PanValet is a registered trademark of Pansophic Systems, Inc.

4. IBM TSO (Time Sharing Option) is a registered trademark of International Business Machines, Inc.

5. CA-ROSCOE is a registered trademark of Computer Associates, Inc.

6. CA-Top Secret is a registered trademark of Computer Associates, Inc.

7. IBM-RACF is a registered trademark of International Business Machines, Inc.

8. CA-EXAMINE is a registered trademark of Computer Associates, Inc.

An Overview of Application Processing

11.1   INTRODUCTION

Application systems differ from systems software in that software serves *all* application programs. The operating system is the environment in which the application programs function; the operating system executes the application program code while using the mainframe hardware components for storage, computation, and logic. It is easy to see how a control weakness in the system software is more pervasive than a control weakness in an application system. The system software affects all applications. Two different groups of programmers service systems software and applications, which properly segregates these critical, incompatible duties.

An application program is an individual, separately identified set of program code written in a high-level language such as COBOL. An application system is a collection or group of individual programs that relate to a common function, such as accounts payable, accounts receivable, or inventory. These three application system examples are used because they are the most common to all businesses and the most familiar to business students. It is important for the reader to understand that a company could have numerous applications, perhaps 50, 75, or over 100 different ones.

A computer application is also a collection of computer programs designed to process data and update master files on a periodic basis. The period could be a day, a week, or a month, but because businesses accept transactions daily, most applications are executed daily. Because most applications process transactions on a daily basis this discussion will focus on daily processing.

The computer applications are all the programs that perform the processing of daily transactions. These programs accept all the daily transactions, perform the edit routines, and post the transactions to master files and history files. Computer reports are generated daily that summarize the processing of the transactions. The reports are used for control and management information.

The results of application processing are tied to individual line items or balances on the company's financial statements. For every balance sheet and income statement line item or balance, an application system will process transactions that change the balance. Application systems such as accounts payable, accounts receivable, and inventory process the transactions that flow to the financial statements. Application systems replace the traditional subledgers referred to in accounting textbooks, and, therefore, support the general ledger that makes up the financial statements.

Application systems can exist for nonfinancial functions— those that do not directly effect the general ledger and the financial statements. For example, an airline may have an application system that monitors maintenance and repairs for all aircraft. The cost of parts and labor has a direct effect on an expense line item in the income statements, but the major objective of this application is to ensure that all aircraft maintenance is performed.

11.1.1   Application Phases

All applications are divided into three major phases: input, processing, and output, each with specific attributes. Each of the three phases can be subdivided into more definitive sub-phases. These will be explained later in the chapter.

11.1.2   Batch Processing Versus On-line Processing

Figure 11–1 demonstrates a simple example, a batch application system. The transactions enter the process in the user department, so called because it "uses" the application system. Transaction source data is prepared and sent to the data preparation area, where the data is transcribed into machine-readable media. This can be either punch cards, key-to-tape, or key-to-disk methods of data conversion. Very few companies use punch cards for large volumes of transactions. In the past 10 years these have given way to key-to-tape, key-to-disk, or on-line terminal input.

FIGURE 11-1 Batch Application System

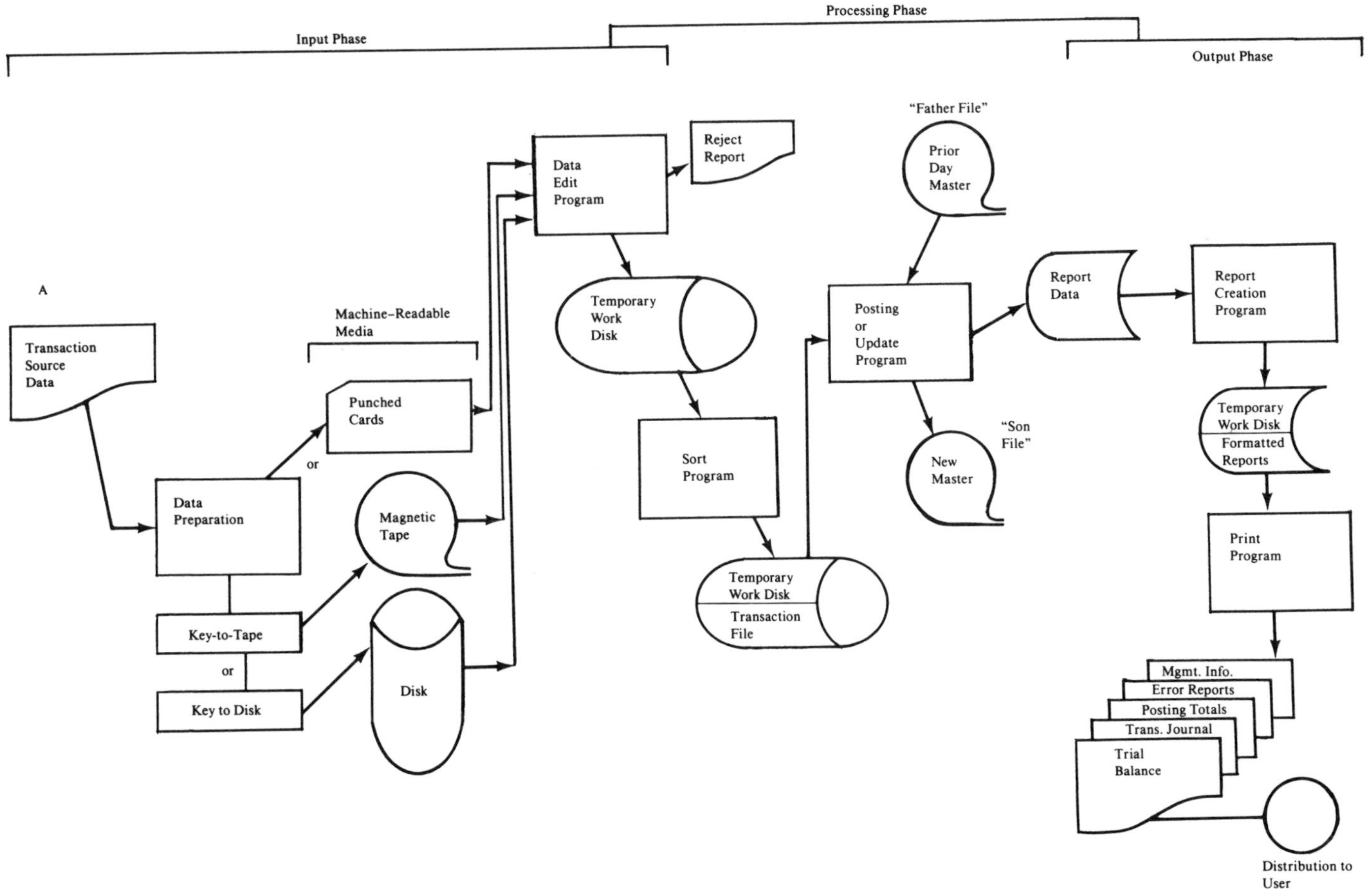

Key-to-tape or disk systems are usually minicomputers that can be programmed to perform edits of input data. Any errors can be immediately reported on the operator's screen for correction, or rejected and sent back to the user department. The method of handling the errors depends upon established procedures that vary for each company. When corrected, the machine-readable media is transported to the data center. A computer operator executes the batch application, the data edit program sends a message to the operator's console instructing him or her to load the tape or disk, or input the punch cards.

The data edit program checks the data based on its programmed functions, sending the output to a temporary work disk and printing any rejects on a hard-copy report.

A sort program reads the edited data and creates a sorted transaction file. The reason for sorting is to arrange the data in an efficient order to make the update program operate at peak efficiency. The posting or update program reads the father file and the son file. Then all transactions are posted to the appropriate accounts and recorded on the new master.

Either the update program or another program in the job stream will create the disk file containing the report data. This disk is read by a report-creation program that formats the reports and prints them to a temporary disk file. This file is read by a print program that sends all reports to a high-speed printer.

Management information, error reports, posting totals, the transaction journal, and the trial balance reports are identified as output from the print program in Figure 11–1. In actuality many more reports will be generated by the typical application. These five are mentioned as the minimum requirements of a good audit trail. In actuality, there could be 10, 15, or even more programs in the daily application processing. All of these programs are referred to as a "jobstream." Their function and use will be explained later in the chapter.

Figure 11–2 shows a simple example of on-line application processing. The differences are obvious, as the input and output phase are labeled as one group.

An on-line realtime system accepts transactions from a) terminal or microcomputer, performs edit checks on the data, and

FIGURE 11-2 On-Line Application Processing

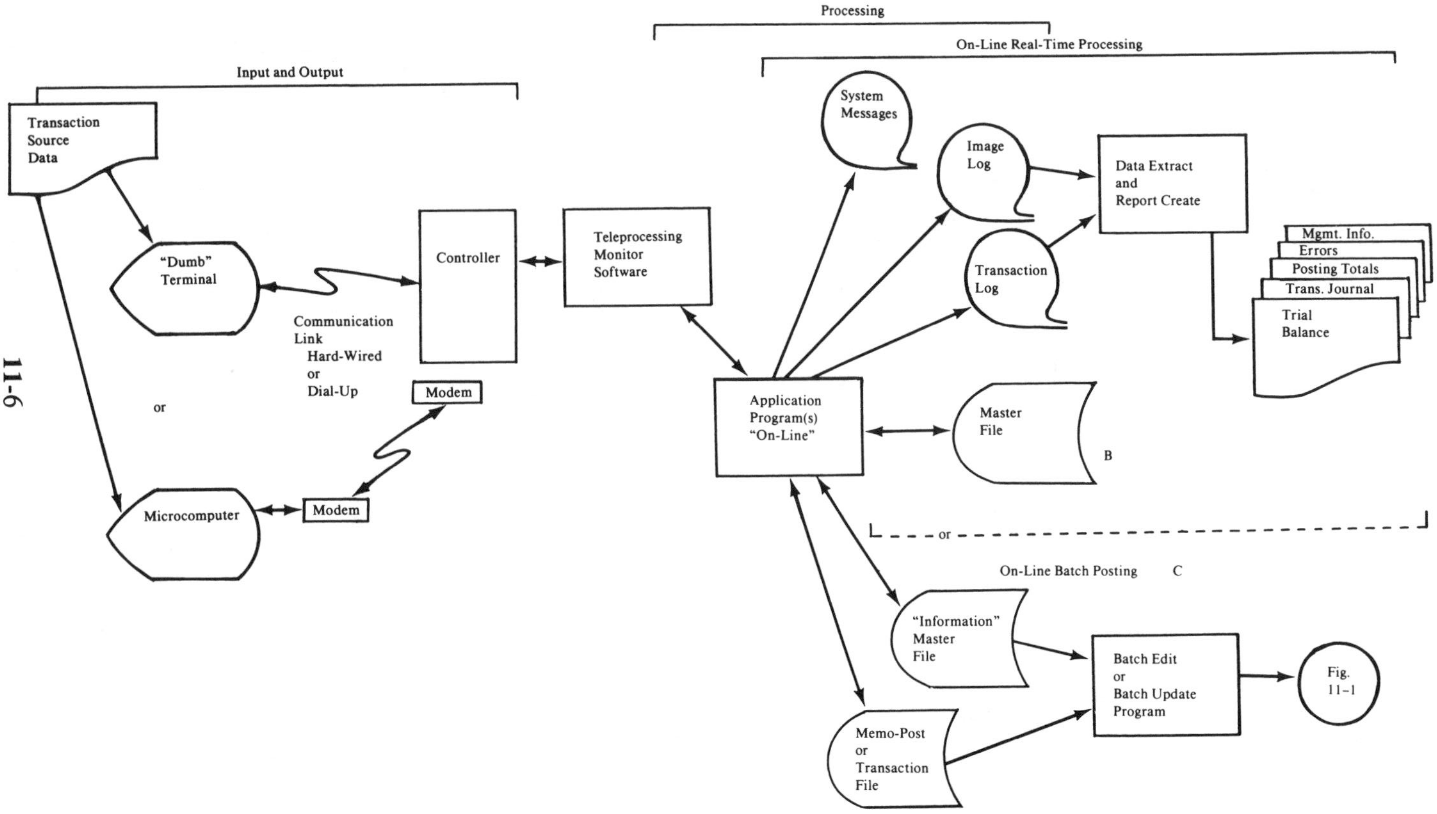

posts the transaction to the master file, at b), changing the master record. Output is returned to the terminal operator to let him or her know that the transaction was accepted or rejected. If rejected, the system will display an error message and give the operator an opportunity to correct the data and resubmit it. There is also an output phase from the on-line realtime processing system showing the five minimum reports for control of accuracy and completeness of processing.

An on-line batch posting application, shown at c, uses an information master file to report status data to the terminal operator. When the operator enters a transaction for update it is recorded on a memo-post or transaction file. Depending on system design, the transaction file and information master file may be read into batch edit or batch update program. The batch posting would continue as shown in Figure 11–1. Typically, the transaction file is passed to the batch program, which reads the father file from tape, instead of using the information master, to avoid any problems with possible corruption of the information master file during daily on-line access. When the on-line information system is started the next day, the new master is loaded to a disk file and becomes the new information master file.

There is a slight difference between a memo post file and a transaction file. A transaction file is simply a list of all the transactions that were entered during the day. A memo-post file, however, holds transactions, but does not have a direct effect immediately on the master during batch update. An example of this would be a credit card system. When a product or service is charged, the merchant typically obtains an authorization for the amount of the charge and records an authorization number on the charge ticket. The presence of this authorization number guarantees payment by the bank to the merchant for the charge. The charge that is memo posted is like a notation. When the authorization is obtained, the available credit line is reduced for the amount of the authorization. This authorization amount is memo-posted to keep down the available credit limit until the real transaction arrives and is posted to the credit card account.

Upon posting of the real transactions the memo post is dropped and disappears from the files.

Examples of teleprocessing monitor software are CICS, IMS DB/DC, and VM/CMS (see Chapter 9). Although these three examples are IBM products, there are many teleprocessing monitor products from various vendors on the market today. The teleprocessing monitor software and the application on-line programs function within the mainframe CPU under the control of the operating system. The controller is independent of the mainframe and can be just hardware or firmware—a combination of hardware and a software program.

Notice the difference between the dumb terminal connection and the microcomputer connection to the controller. This is because the dumb terminal uses synchronous communication protocol, which is the mainframe's language. Microcomputers use asynchronous protocol and, therefore, must be converted to synchronous protocol in order for the mainframe to understand the micro. The modem connected to the controller may or may not convert the protocols to synchronous. If this is not the case, then another software product, a protocol converter, is needed between the modem and the main frame.

11.1.3 Control Objective

The application system belongs to the user, even though system and programming personnel maintain the system. The user's control objective is simple: to execute procedures that ensure the accuracy and completeness of processing. Accuracy means the application system posted transactions correctly. Completeness means that the application system processed all the transactions it received.

11.1.4 Control Techniques

Application controls include the programmatic routines within the application program code, acting during processing, to prevent, detect, and correct errors. Financial controls are generally defined as the manual procedures executed by operations area personnel—the application system uses—over source or transaction origination documents prior to system input. These areas also exercise control over transaction processing by using reports generated by the application. Both the manual and automated controls are needed to accomplish the control objective, which clouds the distinction between financial controls and application controls.

Some authors refer to only the automated controls as application controls, whereas others differentiate the definition. Any function or activity that works to ensure processing accuracy and completeness of the application can be considered an application control. This book treats both the programmatic controls and user-performed financial controls as application controls.

11.2 APPLICATION PROCESSING PHASES[2]

Four phases will be discussed in the following sections: input, processing, output, and data storage and retrieval.

11.2.1 Input Phase

The purpose of the input phase is to get data from its generation source into the application programs. The two major activities in this phase are transaction generation and data entry.

11.2.1.1 ACTIVITIES

11.2.1.1.1 Transaction Generation. The activities completed during transaction generation are:

- Source document generation—preparation of the input form;
- Authorization—approval that the transaction is legitimate;

- Input preparation—assembling data for transcription;
- Source document retention—storage of documents for backup and research; and
- Error handling—correcting identified errors.

11.2.1.1.2 Data Entry.   The basic data entry activities are:

- Data conversion—translating data to machine-readable form;
- Online terminal input—online realtime or on-line batch update;
- Batch input—punch card, key-to-tape, or key-to-disk transcription;
- Data validation—editing the data; and
- Error handling—error detection, correction, and resubmission.

11.2.1.2   CONTROLS OVER INPUT

At this point, for ease of reference, we will repeat sections of Chapter 2.

Dual control: This entails having two people simultaneously access an asset. For example, the depositories of bank 24-hour teller machines should be accessed and emptied simultaneously by two people. Many people confuse dual control with dual access, but they are distinctly different. Dual access separates the access function among two people. Once access is achieved, only one person handles the asset. In the teller-machine example, the tellers would open the depository vault door together (under dual control), but only one person would retrieve the deposit envelopes.

Segregation of duties: This entails assigning incompatible functions to separate people to provide reasonable assurance against fraud and provide an accuracy check of the other person's work. For example, the responsibilities for making financial entries to the application and to the general ledger should be separated.

Sequentially numbered documents: These are working documents with preprinted sequential numbers to provide a means of detecting missing items.

Transmittal documents: These are pieces of paper describing the contents of the items attached or sent separately. Such a document provides a double check of the processing accuracy of the documents or items represented by the transmittal document. The document typically includes a brief description of the items sent, dollar totals of all items in the group, and an item count.

Batch dollar totals and item counts: These are used to control groups of documents and include the dollar total and a count of items in the batch.

Supervisory review: This is exactly what its name implies, review of specific work by a supervisor; but what is not obvious is that this control requires sign-off by the supervisor on the documents to provide evidence that the supervisor was there. This is an extremely difficult control to test after the fact because the auditor cannot judge the quality of the review unless he witnesses it and even then the auditor cannot attest to what the supervisor did when the auditor was not watching.

Authorization: This entails obtaining the authority to perform some act, typically access to assets, such as accounting or application entries.

Safekeeping: This entails securing assets under lock and key, in a desk drawer, file cabinet, storeroom, or vault.

Documentation: This includes written or typed explanations of actions taken on specific transactions. It also refers to written or typed instructions which explain the performance of tasks.

Cancellation of documents: This requires marking a document in such a way to prevent its reuse. This is a typical control over invoices—marking them with a "paid" or "processed" stamp, or punching a hole in the document.

Data edits: These are programmatic procedures that can be installed within the key-to-disk and key-to-tape programs. The only edit device for punch cards is key verification which requires another operator to repunch the cards from the original source documents. If the original card was in error the punch card will be ruined.

Error handling: This requires procedures to prevent, detect, and correct errors during the input phase. This is accomplished through supervisor review and review of the source documents by an independent person. To control errors, each error should be recorded on a log, control totals of dollar amounts and item counts should be calculated. The error should be corrected preferably preparing a new document, cancelling the old document, then submitted to data entry for reentry.

11.2.2   Processing

The purpose of the processing phase is to assimilate all transactions and update the master file.

11.2.2.1   ACTIVITIES

At this point, for ease of reference, sections of Chapter 2 will be repeated. The activities that make up processing are:

- Transaction identification—determining the program logic that should be executed for the particular transaction;
- Processing logic—the application control techniques;
- Computer operator interface—support procedures executed by the computer operator;
- Internally generated transactions—transactions created by the processing logic based on some preset criteria;
- Restart/recovery—recovery of files processed to the point of failure and restarting the application processing; and
- Error handling prevention, detection, and reporting.

11.2.2.2 Control over Processing

As explained, the controls described here can be either automated or manual to verify processing accuracy and completeness. Controls that are strictly automated will be so noted.

Sequence checks: These are the programmatic accounting of numerical sequence number on each input item. Even though sequential numbers are not input to the system, the data edit program shown in Figure 11-1 could assign a sequence number to each transaction as it edits the data. Then as the update program reads each transaction it can account for the sequence numbers to make sure that all items are processed.

Batch dollar totals and item counts: These can be used together or separately to control groups of transactions and to include the dollar total and a count of the items in each batch. Each batch is assigned a unique serial number that the update program can account for. The update program could programmatically total the dollar amounts of each transaction and count the items in a batch, and programmatically check the calculated total to the supplied input totals. This, of course, depends upon system design.

Run-to-Run Control totals: These are dollar totals of transaction amounts calculated by the program and saved in a trailer record on a tape file or a control record of the disk file. In Figure 11-1, a control record containing a dollar total could be written to the temporary work disk between each program. As the subsequent program finishes processing, it can validate that all records were processed by comparing the totals it processed to the total on the control record from the input file.

Data edits: These include field and record checks to validate that the information makes up all the data relating to one specific transaction—in other words, an individual source document. A transaction record is composed of multiple fields. If the transaction fails one field or record check, it should be rejected, but the rest of the fields should be edited. Ron Weber[1] identified field checks and record checks. The titles of the field and records checks are generic categories. In practice, specific names may be used. For example, a date check can be a range check, a reasonableness, or a limit check.

Field checks: These operate independently on individual fields; they do not depend on data in other fields:

- missing data: a field is blank that should contain data—file information would be erroneous;

- alphabetic/numeric: wrong data type in the field, programmatic mathematical calculations would fail if alpha characters are in a numeric field.

- range: field data falls within acceptable range, for example, month greater than 12, day of the month greater than 31, year field is current year.

- set membership: value belongs to a permissible group, for example, account types are only 1, 4, or 7; transaction code must exactly match that defined in the update program.

- check digit: valid account number, each individual number in the account number is summed with a special algorithm and verified to a calculated check digit. Standard examples in the banking industry are referred to as Mod-10 and Mod-11 check digits. Each of these use a slightly different algorithm. This test only determines that the account number may be among the account numbers on the file, but it does not prove that the account is an opened, "live" account.

- master reference: matching a key filed on the transaction file to the master file. This could be used to verify that an account number is an open, "live" account.

- size: Number of characters in the input transaction fit within the defined field size. Exceeding the field size will cause a data overflow condition. If a program is not designed to handle data overflow, this could cause the application program to abort (abend) the entire program.

Record checks: These are dependent on data in other fields, and used as bases for comparison. This is similar to a set membership check.

- reasonableness: one field compared to another, for example, maximum salary for a level 16 job is $35,000. The job level number "16" and the salary are both fields in the record.
- limit: a field value cannot exceed a certain value for a particular account type. For example, the maturity date for a specific series of municipal bonds cannot have a year value greater than 2010.
- valid sign/numerics: numeric fields have proper positive or negative sign. A debit to an account needs a positive sign, while a credit needs a negative sign, this depends on system design.
- size: record size depends on record type when variable length records are used.

Matching: This can be performed when both transaction file data and master file data are available to the program. This involves comparison of key fields between two files for equality. A mismatch would cause a transaction to be rejected.

Internally generated transactions: These can have a financial effect on the monetary value of a given record. They are generated by the program based on some preestablished criteria. Programmatic control procedures include a hardcopy list of each transaction, each account or record, and dollar totals, and item counts for all transactions.

Rejects: These are transactions that are kicked out by an application program (usually the update program), because data in the fields failed an edit check or matching check; the program could not figure out what to do with the data. To control rejects, the application system should generate a hard-copy list of all rejected transactions identifying all fields in the transaction record.

It is useful for the application system to print a message of the cause for the reject. Dollar controls and item counts of the rejects should be generated by the application system.

A file completion check: This is a programmatic procedure to determine that all records from the file have been processed. There are a number of ways to complete this check, the simplest of which is an end-of-file marker that is inserted by a file management utility under control of the operating system.

Reconciliation, balancing and settlement: These are terms referring to procedures used to verify processing accuracy and completeness. Balancing refers to comparison of two numbers from independent sources to determine that the numbers match. Reconciliation is a comparison of totals and detailed reports from two sources to identify differences. For example, reconciling the transaction totals and item counts processed by the system to the transaction totals and item counts calculated during the input phase. If the totals do not match, an item-by-item comparison between the computer report and the source documents is needed to identify the transactions not processed. The term settlement is similar to reconciliation, but it is usually used to signify the reconciliation of the application system dollar totals to the entries made to the general ledger for that day. Ideally the general ledger should be supplied with dollar totals from the transaction generation area or the input area. The dollar totals processed by the application after processing is complete are compared to these independent totals supplied to the general ledger. This independent settlement works to ensure the completeness of processing—it shows that the application received and processed all transactions that were generated.

Input/output verification: This entails comparing the information output by a computer system to the input documents. This is an expensive control because of its labor intensity that tends to be over-recommended by auditors. It is aimed mainly at nonmonetary data such as name and address changes, which cannot be reconciled by dollar totals and item counts.

Hardcopy reports: These should be generated by the application to reflect all the processing aspects of each individual program in the system. Even though computer reports may be thought of as output controls, their purpose is to verify the accuracy and completeness of the processing phase. These reports provide the audit trail for all application processing. The minimum acceptable reports are:

- Trail balance—a list of all accounts or master records from the master file that lists critical data from the master file including the updated balance. The trial balance should include a dollar control total of all balances and item count of all accounts on the master.

- Transaction journal—a listing of all processed input transactions. The key term is "processed" because the rejects are not usually included in the transaction journal. They should not have any effect on the master file records, for they were rejected. This report should include all data from the input records, that is, a picture of the source document. Control totals and item counts should also be printed.

- Posting Totals—This is a short report, usually one or two pages, that identifies dollar totals and items counts processed by the system for each transaction code or processing category. The design and content of this report is strictly dependent upon user needs and, by inference, system design. This report must include dollar control totals and items counts for *all* processing aspects. This report is used for reconciliation, balancing, and settlement.

- Errors reports—These reports were previously discussed under error-handling procedures.

- Management information reports—These reports are not necessarily vital to prove accuracy and completeness of processing, but they are necessary for the completion of business activities. Computer reports are classified into three categories: control, exception, and information reports.

11.2.3 Data Storage and Retrieval

This focuses on application system access and usage of tape or disk files. Data storage and retrieval techniques are usually under total control of the application system through the use of job control language. A program and the jcl call the files needed at the appropriate processing point.

11.2.3.1 DATA STORAGE AND RETRIEVAL ACTIVITIES

These activities relate to file handling.

- Data library—these procedures were discussed in Chapter 7.
- Computer operator interface—the procedure executed by a computer operator to support application processing.
- File access—authorization for file use through the use of passwords, and identification of the correct file by programmatic and jcl verification of the internal file label and header records.
- File maintenance—relates to on-line update of on-line files for activities other than monetary transactions, such as name and address changes.
- Backup files—copying files and moving files to off-site storage for protection from file destruction (see Chapters 7 and 8).
- Error handling—this relates to correction of file handling errors, preventive, and detective controls are discussed above.

11.2.3.2 CONTROL OVER DATA STORAGE AND RETRIEVAL

Data file library and computer operator procedures and documentation were discussed in Chapters 7 and 8.

Label checking: This is a programmatic reading of the internal file label located at the beginning of a tape file or in the directory of a disk file. The internal label identifies the file name, creation date, and other critical information to permit specific identification of the file by the program. If the loaded file does not match the programmatic specifications then the program should send a message to the computer console about the error.

Data Set cataloging: This includes jcl functions to call and identify specific files during specific points in the application processing job stream.

Online system control: This requires logging of entered transactions and master file images for and after the transaction is processed.

File handling error correction: These procedures refer to procedures executed to correct file errors, interactive corrections between the application system and the computer operator. For example, assume that the program calls the wrong file, or the operator mounts the wrong file, even though the correct one was requested. The application system and file management utilities communicate with the computer operator via messages displayed on the computer operator's CRT. The application system and file management utilities should tell the operator whether a wrong file was mounted. If the wrong file was called by the programs, the error may not be detected until the user reviews the output; the correction procedure in this case is complete rerun. Error correction for loading the wrong file is the operator's loading of the correct file and entering an application-acceptable command to restart the file reading process.

Application system abnormal endings can occur for various reasons. The operator can correct these by executing restart/recovery procedures specified in operator's run manual for the specific application; each application will require different procedures.

Checkpoint/restart techniques: permit use of previously completed processing results, thereby avoiding a costly complete rerun of all application programs.

11.2.4   Output Phase

This phase involves the creation of computer reports in three categories; control, exception, and management information. Control and exception reports are used to verify processing accuracy and completeness. Specifically, the exception reports are used for correction of processing errors and management information reports for completion of business activities.

11.2.4.1   ACTIVITIES OF THE OUTPUT PHASE

Some textbooks include user-balancing and reconciliation procedures as part of the output phase. In this book, they are included within the processing controls because the reports are used to verify processing accuracy and completeness. The procedures discussed in the output phase are those executed to control the application system output.

The distinction between processing and output control is not highly critical as long as the reader understands the concepts and the auditor evaluates the procedures executed by the user and data processing.

The activities of the output phase are the following:

- Output distribution—all generated reports are delivered to the correct user;
- Records retention—secure storage of critical records in a manner that permits efficient retrieval, routine destruction of outdated records, and elimination of application generated reports that are no longer used; and
- Sensitive documents—checks or other negotiable items of value.

11.2.4.2   CONTROLS OVER OUTPUT

Schedule of reports: This is a list of all reports that should be generated by the application. The program prints reports as it is coded to do. However, program maintenance could inadvertently delete a report. A manual procedure must be executed by data center personnel or the application user to detect missing reports. The error is corrected by notifying the programmer, who corrects the program.

Distribution list: This specifies the report titles, frequency of generation, the owner, and the estimated pick-up time. Computer operations personnel should execute procedures to ensure that only the authorized user obtained the reports. The distribution list also serves to identify reports remaining in the data center that have not been picked up. Data center operations personnel can call the authorized user to move the reports along.

Controlled pick-up: This involves secure storage or custody of reports waiting for pick up. Access to the area should be limited to authorized personnel only.

Sensitive document procedures: These are needed for checks and other negotiable items to protect against theft. These procedures include reconciliation of beginning and ending sequence numbers, such as the sequence numbers on individual checks. In addition, any blank checks used during the printing sequence should be voided. The user should maintain an accurate log of the sequence or control numbers of sensitive documents.

NOTES

1. Weber, Ron *EDP Auditing, Conceptual Foundations and Practice.* McGraw-Hill, New York, 1982, 286–287.

2. *System Auditability and Control Studies.* Institute of Internal Auditors, Altamonte Springs, FL, 1977.

Application Audit[1]

12.1 INTRODUCTION

The programming department (see Chapter 6) is charged with creating and maintaining the application programs. Accessing these programs to make required changes is extremely sensitive, because it is difficult to verify that the change programs do not contain unauthorized code (see Chapter 10). Adequate administrative controls must be enforced to ensure controlled maintenance, systematic systems development, sufficient documentation, realistic long-range planning, efficient programming and processing, and high personnel productivity.

Systems software (see Chapter 14) executes application program logic, which in turn updates data files. Thus, if the system software can be purposefully modified, it can process application logic, and thus the files, in any manner a perpetrator of fraud sees fit. Administrative controls are necessary to prevent unauthorized use of system software. This does not completely obviate the problem, however, because systems programmers must have direct computer access to do their jobs. Detection controls and strict separation of duties are a must.

Database administration (see Chapter 13) poses another set of problems, primarily because of the technical expertise required to fully understand the processing environment. The establishment of database files to be used by the application programs must be properly controlled.

To round out the audit of the EDP environment, the auditor must concentrate on the computer applications themselves. These can be separated into two distinct categories, each with its own special problems: existing applications and those being developed. It is best to review a computer system during its developmental phase because it is easier to correct a problem before it is implemented than after. The auditor should be involved in the development process (see Chapter 17) from the proposal justification stage to the conversion of the production system. The auditor is responsible for reviewing both the programmatic and external controls of the systems being developed and monitoring the administrative systems development process.

This chapter discusses the review of application systems in terms of the system's efficiency and effectiveness, and the manual and automated procedures that prove accuracy and completeness.

12.2 PLANNING AND PREPARATION

The entire data processing function revolves around the live application systems, because they process the financial transactions that form the financial statements. The scope of the application audit should be discussed with the financial audit staff to avoid any unnecessary overlap of review and testing.

An application system can be examined in terms of its input, processing, and output. Because transactions are the basic "drivers" of application systems, all transaction codes should be formally documented in the workpapers for future reference. System output is the ultimate subject of the audit, because the results of system processing are summarized in the generated output. Application systems must have both programmatic and external controls to ensure that the accuracy and completeness of system processing can be proven on a daily basis.

The purpose of the planning phase is to gain a general understanding of the application, identify the major functions of the application, prepare the scope summary, and determine budget hours. Figure 12–1 lists the areas of concern covered in this chapter. In practice, these transactions would be those actually

FIGURE 12–1   Audit Concerns

Audit Activity Code	Transaction/Area
A	Input
B	Processing
C	Data Storage and Retrieval
D	Output
E	Documentation
F	User Satisfaction

input by the user to process the daily work. Because these vary for each system, Figures 12-1 and 12-2 deal with the elements present in all applications.

The auditor should review previous workpapers, permanent files, and pending files, and should discuss the audit approach to the S&P project leader responsible for the application. The auditor should identify the number, type, and purpose of the application's programs. This can be accomplished by using an on-line search of program source libraries; purchased package applications may have unique libraries. The program type should be documented in the application system documentation. The purpose of each program should be briefly explained, by reference to the application documentation.

The purpose and complexity of the application's batch jcl job streams can be determined by reviewing the data center run schedule and the on-line library containing the jcl. The jcl library modules can be compared to the run schedules to identify any special processing. The purpose of each jobstream, including

FIGURE 12-2   Scope Summary

Risks/Exposures

1. Errors and omissions
2. Unauthorized transactions
3. Inaccurate processing
4. Incomplete processing
5. Lost files
6. File destruction
7. Inadequate procedures

Control Objectives

1. Procedures are adequate to ensure that application processing is accurate and complete
2. Ensure that application processing is efficient and effective

Audit Objectives—Specific

Determine that adequate procedures exist to ensure:

1. The accuracy and completeness of processing
2. That application processing is efficient and effective

special processing should be briefly explained. Special processing is any processing other than daily execution, for example, month-end, year-end, statement runs, and file purges.

The complexity of the data files can be determined by briefly documenting the purpose of each file and identifying any database sharing with other applications. File sharing can be identified by scanning the database control libraries for each application database name (see Chapter 13). With database sharing, the application's capabilities can be determined by reviewing the database program specifications, specifically programs that cross applications with data update capabilities. These should be considered for the preliminary review phase, and included as a transaction area of concern in Part 1 of the scope memo. The program access control specifications define access using get, insert, replace, delete, all functions, read only, load, and other special functions, specific to each DBMS type.

For an on-line application, the on-line transaction codes and their purposes should be documented. These can be identified by reviewing the transaction definition library. The on-line transaction code's purpose and function should be explained in the application documentation.

Internally generated transactions should be identified and documented, as being either monetary or nonmonetary, through interviews with the programmer and review of the documentation. An audit decision is needed as to whether or not the transactions will be reviewed.

Major changes made to the application since the last audit, should be identified and discussed with the programmer or analyst to determine the nature of the changes, and why they were made. This should include any major changes planned for implementation within the next 12 months. A major change is one that affects the field size or content, a calculation, control report content, methods of data input, update or retrieval, or that creates a new transaction code.

The planning phase is concluded by preparing a brief overview of the application and describing the flow of processing, type of input, and method of updating.

12.3 EXECUTION OF PRELIMINARY REVIEW

The objective of this phase is to document the flow of transactions through the data processing environment, and to identify existing and nonexisting internal controls. The application audit focuses on the application system, even though the compliance testing programs described later in this chapter cover both the manual and automated environment. The compliance testing programs are so designed to give the EDP auditor a tool to examine the complete environment—an integrated audit program. If the EDP audit is limited to the application system then the auditor needs only refer to the elements regarding programmatic procedures. The manual environment, however, must be reviewed by someone else in the audit group or incomplete information will result.

12.3.1 Batch Processing

The auditor should prepare flowcharts of the application's programs. This can be accomplished through review of the jcl and application documentation or with a flowcharting package that uses the jcl as input. The flowchart should identify the point(s) where the transactions being audited enter the jobstream and should report names and numbers. If the flowcharts are prepared using the jcl from the production environment, a transaction review is unnecessary because the jcl represents the actual procedures being performed.

An ICQ is usually used to evaluate the control environment—to identify existing and nonexisting controls. The elements of the application ICQ are incorporated into the compliance testing program later in this chapter. The ICQ is completed by interviewing the user, analyst, and programmer. The auditor should identify the existing and nonexisting internal controls.

12.3.2 On-line Processing

The auditor should prepare a flowchart of the on-line transactions processed for each transaction being audited. The flowchart should identify the input screen contents, the names of the programs executed, the data files that are modified, the output screen contents, if any, the points where the manual processes interface with on-line input/output, and the points where on-line processing interfaces with batch processing, if any. The audit programs in this chapter and Chapter 16 can be used to evaluate the on-line environment by extracting needed elements from the programs. The auditor should identify the existing and nonexisting internal controls.

12.3.3   Key-to-disk Processing

The auditor should prepare a flowchart of the key-to-disk processing for the transactions being audited. This flowchart must identify the input received, the data files created, the points where the manual procedures interface with key-to-disk processing, and the points where key-to-disk processing interfaces with batch processing.

The input sections of the compliance testing program can be used to evaluate the controls by reviewing application documentation and interviewing the application programmer, key-to-disk supervisor, or user. The auditor should identify the existing and nonexisting internal controls.

12.4   COMPLIANCE TESTING

The audit programs shown in Figures 12–3 through 12–12 describe the elements of the user area and the application system that can be tested. These programs include elements that would ordinarily be separated into an ICQ for identification of controls and a compliance testing program. They are combined to simplify, it is hoped, the explanations of audit requirements. These programs differ from others because the key controls and scope are not identified for each separate audit program. The reason for this is that the key controls are the object of the test procedures; listing them would be redundant. The scope generally includes all transactions that occurred during the period being examined.

In reviewing the audit programs, narrative explanations are not given for procedures that are self-explanatory. The test procedures are worded from the standpoint of what the user or the system should do. The auditor's job is to determine that the described procedure is performed by the user or the application.

12.4.1   Input Phase

The four sections that follow explain the audit procedures that should be considered in the input phase of application processing.

12.4.1.1   TRANSACTION GENERATION

Chapter 11 explained the differentiation between direct contact customer-generated transactions and company-generated transactions for the customer; the customer should not be relied on as part of the control without his or her direct involvement. For this reason, the area where internal transaction source data is generated should be separated from input, and from reconciliation. The area generating the transactions will generally prepare the source documents.

The auditor wants to determine that the user's procedures ensure that transactions originate in a consistent and orderly fashion and that errors, omissions, and the creation of unauthorized input are prevented.

The auditor should evaluate the documented procedures for the origination and control of source documents. They should include document preparation, cutoff times, transaction authorization, error handling, and document review (see Figure 12–3). Also, source documents should be reviewed for completeness.

Verification of approval before input of sensitive documents includes identifying any conflicting transactions that require the transaction and source document generation to be separated. For example, the generation of a monetary entry to the application should be separated from the generation of a monetary entry to the general ledger. The general ledger is the independent control against which application processing is compared. This separation reduces the risk of fraudulent transactions.

FIGURE 12-3 **Transaction Origination**

Audit Test Objective

Determine that user procedures are adequate to ensure accurate data origination and preparation, and all transactions are included

Compliance Testing

Verify:

1. Documented procedures adequately describe all functions
2. Source documents are reviewed for completeness
3. Sensitive transactions are approved before input
4. Transmittal documents are used to control the movement of input documents between the user and data entry
5. Timely transmittal and receipt of transactions or batches should be logged and monitored
6. Control totals are independently generated for each batch or group of transactions
7. Input documents are securely stored to permit reconstruction
8. Located errors are corrected and resubmitted to data entry on a timely basis

A separate person or function may prepare the source documents for sending to the input function by grouping the transactions in batches, logging the batches, and reviewing the accuracy of the documents. Verifying that transmittal documents are used to control the movement of input documents between the user and data entry and that timely transmittal and receipt of transactions or batches is logged and monitored review the procedures that ensure timely movement to data entry and back to the user. This includes assigning a unique sequence number to each batch on a transmittal document attached to the batch. This helps the user control data omissions.

Verifying that control totals are independently generated for each batch or group of transactions permits the user to reconcile data sent to data entry against what was processed by the system in order to control data errors and omissions. Verifying that input documents are securely stored to permit reconstruction reviews a procedure that may only be necessary if tape or disk files of input transactions are not created. In any event, these files may not include data that was omitted or may include data with errors.

If the accuracy of the data on the files is assured, then retention of the input documents is not as critical.

Making sure that located errors are corrected and resubmitted to data entry on a timely basis focuses on the procedures for handling errors found in source documents by the origination function that can be corrected before transmittal to data entry. Errors found by data entry and returned for correction must be controlled separately from regular transactions and resubmitted to data entry in a timely manner. Error-handling procedures should be sufficiently documented, covering all reasonable types of errors that may occur. Correction procedures should be adequately explained. The data entry procedures of the corrected input should be specified.

12.4.1.2   DATA ENTRY

The data input area may be audited separately. If the controls were found to be adequate, these procedures may be unnecessary. Making sure documented procedures describe all functions reveals the purpose of batching documents, of using dollar control totals, of the logging of control totals, and the procedures for reconciliation of control totals, (see Figure 12–4).

Making sure batch and control totals are logically recorded for reconciliation and that control totals are prepared before data is entered reviews the adequacy of control totals. The source documents should be cancelled after they are entered to prevent erroneous reentry.

Provision of dollar and item count control totals and verification of reconciliations' being performed after each posting run or daily for realtime posting examine the control reports generated by the system. The auditor should examine the reconciliation of input to output, which is necessary for the user to prove application processing accuracy. The reconciliation should adequately prove that all data entered was posted. The auditor should also verify that reconciliations are performed and that independently prepared control totals are used. Control totals can be prepared in transaction generation or input preparation activities. These

FIGURE 12–4 Data Entry

Audit Test Objective

To determine that the controls are adequate to ensure that data is entered in its correct form

Compliance Testing

Verify:

1. Documented procedures describe all functions
2. Batch and control totals are recorded in a logical fashion for reconciliation
3. If cash totals are used, that they are created and used accurately
4. Control totals are prepared before data is entered
5. The reports provide the detail of all items as they were entered
6. Dollar and item count control totals are provided for each major transaction
7. Reconciliations are performed after each posting run or daily for on-line realtime posting
8. The output reports are reconciled to independently prepared control totals

---

control totals and item counts are calculated independently of key-to-disk or application systems calculations to provide a more accurate verification.

12.4.1.3 DATA EDITS

The application system user's objective is to ensure that the application or key-to-disk programs perform sufficient edit checks, where practical, to prevent the input of erroneous data. However, the user seldom has direct authority over the functions of the application or key-to-disk programs. Edit needs must be obtained by formal request. The auditor plays an additional role, in this situation, by recommending improved edit controls, if needed. Sometimes the audit report can accomplish changes that the user has difficulty accomplishing.

Making sure that punch card input is verified by another operator and that the input formats are documented and standardized focuses on card input accuracy controls. Keypunch machines are mechanical and cannot be programmed to edit data. Drum cards can be used to control some errors, but the best accuracy check is key-verification, whereby a second person key-punches the cards a second time. The machine does not physically punch the card a second time, but senses the holes in the card and compares it to the operator's keystrokes. When an error is detected, the card is punched, destroying the card. A system card reader will then reject these cards (see Figure 12–5).

Programmed keying formats are formatted displays on a CRT to guide the operator as to what data fits where. These can be used in any system that is programmable. The auditor should make sure that keying formats are used for on-line, key-to-tape, and key-to-disk data entry.

The data edits can be programmed in key-to-disk or the application system. Verifying the accuracy of the data edits can be accomplished with test decks for batch system input (see Chapter 3) or a set of test input transactions for terminal input. The data edits include check digit routines, character checking (for example, tests for sign, numeric data, alphanumeric data, and for blanks or control codes), field checks and record checks (see Chapter 11, Section 11.2.2.2). Transaction dates should be verified and rejected by the system when and if the dates are beyond an acceptable range. This prevents abuse of back-and forward-dating of transactions, which can be used to cover errors or fraudulent activity.

FIGURE 12–5   Data Edits

Audit Test Objective

To determine the adequacy and accuracy of data edit techniques utilized

Compliance Testing

Verify:

1. Punch card input is key-verified by another operator
2. The input formats for card input should be documented and standardized
3. Programmed keying formats are used for on-line, key-to-tape, and key-to-disk data entry
4. Verify the accuracy and adequacy of the data edits

Data edits are a key defense against processing errors. If audit budget time is short, the data edits should be tested to accomplish minimum coverage.

12.4.1.4 ERROR HANDLING

This audit activity focuses on handling errors detected during the data entry phase. The audit procedures focus on error handling by application system input programs for batch or on-line batch processing. With on-line realtime processing, errors should be detected by the on-line application program and returned to the operator for correction and immediate resubmission. This makes the audit of edit functions even more critical (see Figure 12–6).

The application should generate an input error report that represents the results of the edits performed in the initial input program. The edits should be designed to edit all data in the transaction, rather than stopping at the first error, which is sometimes the case (see Chapter 11, section 11.2.2). The auditor is required to evaluate the content of the reports. They can be tested by entering test transactions that fail the edits, then locating the transactions on the reports to determine how they were reported. The control totals are necessary for reconciliation

FIGURE 12–6 Error Handling

Audit Test Objective

To evaluate the adequacy of error detection, correction and reentry procedures

Compliance Testing

Verify:

1. An input edit error report identifies all transactions in error
2. The report lists all errors in each transaction
3. Control totals and item counts of the transaction in error are printed on the report
4. Errors are researched and corrected documents are reentered on a timely basis
5. Reentered items are subject to the same control and edit procedures as original data

---

of processing. Moreover error correction effectiveness must be examined. Timely correction is usually considered as one to two days.

12.4.2 Processing

Manual user procedures and programmatic functions should ensure the consistent handling of transactions. Transactions must be accurate and complete, errors must be recognized and rejected, and reports must be generated to reflect the effects of processing.

12.4.2.1 TRANSACTION IDENTIFICATION

Verifying transaction identification focuses on the techniques used to direct transactions toward specific sections of programming logic and is accomplished through documentation research and interview of the programmer responsible for the system. The auditor is also required to judge the quality of the documentation. The auditor is in a good position to do this because of his or her inexperience with the system. If the auditor understands how processing is accomplished, then the documentation is of good quality. Making sure transactions are performed as documented can be accomplished through review of actual transactions, through the use of the test transactions specified in the input phase, and by interviewing the user. If a transaction is malfunctioning, the user will say so (see Figure 12–7).

12.4.2.2 INTERNALLY GENERATED TRANSACTIONS

Internally generated transactions occur as the result of preestablished criteria recognized by the program. Interest receivable or payable calculations are examples. The user should verify that calculations are performed accurately. Making sure that all internally generated transactions are printed on hard copy for direct feedback to the user, that control totals of these transactions are generated, and that the program uses automatic balance procedures for passing these transactions between

FIGURE 12–7   Processing Phase

Audit Test Objective

Determine that programmatic procedures are used to ensure processing accuracy and completeness

Compliance Testing

The means by which transactions are identified and handled by the system should be reviewed

Verify:

Transaction Identification

1. Transactions are identified by a unique code which directs proper application program processing
2. User and application documentation manuals fully explain transaction function and usage
3. Transactions perform as documented

Internally Generated Transactions

4. All internally generated transactions are printed on hard copy for direct feedback to the user
5. Control totals of these transactions are generated
6. The system uses automatic balance procedures for passing these transactions between programs or modules

Computation and Logic

7. Control totals are passed between jobs and programs
8. The system balances dollar totals of data received to data it processes
9. The system accounts for all transaction records received
10. File control totals are used to balance a program run
11. File completion checks are used to ensure that all records have been processed
12. Account numbers are verified by the program

---

programs or modules require the auditor to test these calculations by tracing the transactions to the appropriate control totals, account records, and output reports. The auditor should also determine that internally generated transactions occur as a result of valid and expected conditions. It is important to note that these tracing tests can be automated using audit software. Although research, programming, and testing time is required to develop the tool, the resulting automated programs can be used in future audits. The most commonly used automated technique is simulation (see Chapter 3).

12.4.2.3   COMPUTATION AND LOGIC

The auditor must also focus on the computation and logic of application system programs, primarily the update program (Figure 12–7 procedures 7–12). The extent of audit testing of programmatic balancing depends on application program sophistication. Ideally, the application system should test the equality of the transaction dollar totals processed by each program to the transaction dollar total it received. If the totals do not match, then the program prints a message to a hard copy report. This helps the user determine where processing errors occurred. To accomplish the balancing technique the program must generate control totals.

To verify that the system accounts for all transactions received, the update program should use sequence-checking, like the input program, to ensure that all input transactions were processed.

Ensuring that file control totals are used to balance a program run, programmatic procedures at completion of the run must be examined. For example, the previous day master file dollar total is added to the net effect of today's transactions, which should equal the new master file dollar total. Any exception would be disclosed by a message printed on an error report. File completion checks are usually accomplished by end-of-file routines that are an integral part of programming languages, however, they must be used. The auditor should verify that this technique, or another acceptable one, is, in fact, used.

Verification of account numbers was mentioned in the input phase, but it can only be used there if the master file is available to the program; this complicates programming. The update program has access to the master file and is the one place that the account number associated with the transaction is an open, "live" account. This is usually automatic if the program is coded to match accounts between the master and transaction file. However, implied in this audit review is the determination that non-matching conditions are printed on a hard copy error report.

12.4.2.4 COMPUTER OPERATIONS

The application audit provides additional information to the auditor to improve his or her focus on computer operator support of application processing (see Chapter 8). One critical function is the recovery of files and restart of an abnormally ended job run, with partially created files. Daily processing of a single application may require two to three hours to complete; if it aborts half-way through the file, processing is lost. Checkpoint/restart techniques and recovery programs can be used to capture partially completed files and permit restart at the point of failure. The time saving is obvious. The auditor is required to test or observe a test of these recovery programs. The run books should completely explain the procedures the operator should follow to accomplish recovery (see Figure 12–8).

The effectiveness and efficiency of operator support is directly dependent on the quality of the documented procedures. The run book is the programmer's instructions of how to operate the application. It is important to focus on the adequacy of this documentation, which should explain system startup, error and system messages, system shutdown procedures, job status reporting, console message instructions, error message instructions and

FIGURE 12–8 Computer Operations

Audit Test Objective

Determine that the computer operators can adequately support application processing, and recover the system from failure

Compliance Testing

Verify:

1. Recovery procedures are adequate
2. Operator run documentation is adequate
3. The job control language is accurate

responses, program halt instructions, rerun procedures, check-point and restart instructions, job setup instructions, and printing instructions.

The job control language is used by the operator to start application processing. It will exist in either punched card form or in on-line production libraries accessible by the operator's console command. The auditor should compare the current jcl listing, from the system documentation to the production jcl job stream maintained in the data center. The accuracy of the latest application runs using these job streams should be determined. Any abnormal program endings should be documented and re-searched. The live jcl should be reviewed for any cards (lines in an on-line library) that could execute a program from a library other than the production program library. If found, the auditor should determine why another library is being accessed and bring this to the attention of management immediately, for this could be an unauthorized library usage (see Chapter 10). The auditor should determine which jcl steps are used to ensure that the correct files are read and created.

12.4.2.5   ERROR HANDLING

Making sure error reports identify fields in error, the error condition, and the entire transaction record is accomplished by reviewing the reports generated by the system. The transaction in error should be rejected and reported; processing of other records should continue. Out-of-balance conditions should be flagged. Flagging means marking with a special character so the errors stand out on the report.

Error suspense files should be cleared daily. Rejected financial transactions typically require an accounting entry into a suspense account to keep the application and general ledger in balance. These suspense accounts should be adjusted when the errors are corrected and accepted by the system. With an automated suspense error file, each error should be assigned a sequential number to facilitate tracing. Records should be corrected, reentered, and reversed from the error file on a daily basis (see Figure 12–9).

FIGURE 12-9   Error Handling

Audit Test Objective

Determine the adequacy of error-handling procedures and reports

Compliance Testing

Verify:

1. Error reports identify fields in error, the error condition, and the entire transaction record
2. Processing of a transaction record discontinues when an error occurs
3. Out-of-balance conditions are flagged
4. Error suspense files are cleared daily
5. Unposted items are corrected and reentered on a timely basis
6. A trend analysis of the error conditions is performed

Some application systems write error transactions to a file in which the transaction stays until it is corrected. These transactions represent an accounting entry that affects general ledger. If the errors are not researched, corrected, and removed from the file with the appropriate accounting entries, the transactions can build up, and their resolution becomes very difficult. The older the items get, the colder the audit trail becomes. A credit card company and a major bank permitted this scenario to occur. Internal auditors were used in both cases to try to unravel the mess, but to no avail. Each company charged off approximately $1,000,000.

A test of all rejects and unposted items on selected day(s) should be compared to their disposition, noting the amount of time taken for final resolution of discrepancies. A timely basis implies one to two days maximum. A user procedure that can determine whether the errors are the result of incorrect programming logic should be performed. The analysis requires that causes of all error conditions are documented.

12.4.2.6   REPORTS AND RECONCILIATION

The user's control objective is to ensure that the application generates reports that accurately reflect processing. Making sure that the results of each processing aspect of each program are reflected in the reports and that exception reports are generated, showing rejected and unposted items is accomplished by reviewing the reports. Verifying that posting total reports are generated ensures control totals for each transaction (see Chapter 11). Ensuring that a report containing the batch header records and corresponding detail records of each batch is generated requires the user to research error conditions and imbalances found by the reconciliation. Adequate reports are necessary for verification of processing completeness and accuracy, which should be performed for each processing cycle (see Figure 12–10).

To test the reports, independent totals, generated by an audit software program, should be traced to all control total reports. The current day's transaction totals should be added to an independent file foot on the previous day's master and compared to the total of the file foot for the current day's master. A sample of input transactions (as close to the point of origin as possible) should be traced to all appropriate reports and files, for example, history, statement, and transaction. The dollar totals of transactions on critical reports can be tested by simulating the report

FIGURE 12–10   Reports and Reconciliation

Audit Test Objective

To assess the adequacy of programmatic report generation, and the reconciliation process

Compliance Testing

Verify:

1. That the results of each processing aspect of each program are reflected in the reports

2. That exception reports are generated, showing rejected and unposted items

3. That posting total reports are generated

4. That a report containing the batch header records and corresponding detail records of each batch is generated

5. That reports are printed in a logical format to promote efficiency and speed in the reconciliation and settlement process

6. That independently prepared input dollar and item count totals are used to perform a reconciliation of input to output for each run

with audit software. A sample of detail items on critical reports should be traced to their origin. It is best that these detail items not be the same items selected in the previous sample.

12.4.3   Data Storage and Retrieval

Data storage and retrieval procedures prevent processing errors and maintain an optimum operating efficiency. They involve the data library, computer operator, and programmatic procedures. Operating procedures for handling the application files should be documented in the tape library (see Chapter 7). The procedures should include daily, weekly, and monthly setup instructions, file rotation, and backup.

Separate program libraries should be established, one for production and one for test programs (see Chapter 10). File access procedures include restricting access to authorized programs, which is be accomplished by security software (see Chapter 9). The access rules, procedures, and controls apply to the batch application processing environment (see Chapter 9). The programmatic procedures that should be examined are discussed below (see Figure 12–11).

The internal file label information can be printed with an installation utility for auditor inspection. Programmatic reading

FIGURE 12–11   **Data Storage and Retrieval**

Audit Test Objective

Determine that procedures are adequate to ensure accurate file use

Compliance Testing

Verify:

1. The internal file label contains the file ID, volume/serial number, creation date, version/generation number, scratch date, and necessary security information
2. The program and jcl read the internal label for input file identification
3. A program cannot be forced into read status by operators using an ignore-label command
4. The jcl correctly catalogues the file as a generation data set
5. The adequacy of the backup files

of the label information is vital to prevent the use of incorrect files. An operator can easily mount the incorrect file in the tape or disk drive. The ignore or bypass label command is dangerous, but sometimes necessary to get past a corrupted label on the correct file. However, bypassing the label forces the program to accept the file whether it is the correct one or not. Making sure an ignore-label command cannot be used can be tested by examining a sample of computer console logs or processing a job accounting utility file with an audit software program. Ensuring that the jcl correctly catalogues the file as a generation data set is also crucial. The generation data set is an archiving feature to programmatically control the grandfather-father-son scheme (see Chapter 7).

Verifying the adequacy of the backup files can be accomplished by a simulated disaster test. For example, by assuming a disaster has occurred that affects various elements of the application, the auditor can determine if the backup files are adequate to restore the system to its proper status (see Chapter 8).

12.4.4 Output Phase

Verifying that output handling procedures are documented in the operations manual focuses on data center procedures for distributing reports to authorized users. These procedures can be tested by comparing the documentation to actual activities via observation of data center personnel. These procedures should specify which reports are to go to which user, how many copies, on what output form they should be printed, and how they should be prepared (for example, bursted and decollated). It is important as well to verify that the output handling procedures include a schedule of reports to be generated, a distribution list, and the name of the user authorized to pick them up. The distribution list is usually prepared by the programmer and user and is the only method by which data center personnel know who gets what reports. (See Figure 12–12.)

Verifying the control of sensitive documents refers to checks and other negotiable items, such as stock certificates. Their usage for printing must be controlled through running logs that record the serial numbers of documents used. Any blank documents

FIGURE 12–12   Output Phase

Audit Test Objective

Determine that the procedures for handling generated output ensure authorized use

Compliance Testing

Verify:

1. That the output-handling procedures are documented in the operations manual
2. That the output-handling procedures include a schedule of reports to be generated, a distribution list, and the name of user authorized to pick them up
3. Procedures for control of sensitive documents are adequate

within the sequence used must be marked "voided" to prevent unauthorized use. The user should reconcile the beginning and ending sequence numbers with the series used each time these documents are used in a print run. The documents should be stored by data center personnel in a locked area. Only a minimal working supply should be kept in the data center; the bulk supply should be stored in a vault.

12.4.5   Documentation

The quality of documentation has been extensively discussed throughout this book because of its contribution to efficiency and effectiveness. In application processing, the control objective is to ensure that the systems documentation adequately explains the function of the system, so that any reasonably qualified programmer or analyst can locate and correct program problems.

The auditor should determine the adequacy of the application system documentation, that is, the programmers tool, which should include; a generalized system flowchart, program flowcharts, run setup instructions, file and record layouts, tape library procedures, explanations of programmatic edits, an index of reports, explanations of transaction codes and their function, internally generated transactions, their function, and the criteria governing their occurrence, and restart and recovery procedures.

A generalized flowchart of the system should accurately reflect the processing scheme. Program narratives for each program should explain the program's functions in a complete and concise manner. All files that are used by the application should be completely documented. All reports generated by the system should be documented and examples should be shown. All jcl job streams should be completed and documented. The functions of all transaction codes should be explained. All internally generated transactions and calculations should be completely explained (see Chapter 6).

12.4.6   User Satisfaction

The auditor should listen for any user comments during the audit that convey their opinion of system adequacy. An appropriate person in the user department can be interviewed to determine:

- whether the application is reliable,
- whether down time and/or errors are prevalent,
- the number of outstanding maintenance change requests,
- whether any pending requests should be given a higher priority than is currently assigned,
- whether communication with the analyst is satisfactory,
- whether the system satisfies the needs of the user, and
- whether generated management information reports are adequate and useful for decision-making purposes.

Negative answers to these questions should be researched and reported to user and S&P management to correct any problems.

NOTES

1. See Mullen, Jack B. "Auditing Applications and Maintenance." Adapted from *EDP Auditing* (New York: Auerbach Publishers). © 1986, Warren, Gorham & Lamont, Inc. Used with permission.

13

Database
Administration

13.1 INTRODUCTION

This is the first examination of the advanced environmental audits, referred to as such because of the technical complexity of the database administration's function. The database administration's function is highly specialized, utilizing specialized and complicated software to perform a deceptively simple function— to control data file access.

A database management system (DBMS)—examples include IBM-IMS[1] (information management system) and CA-IDMS[2] (integrated data management system)—create, read, and update specialized data files through direct access techniques. Database files are very different from other tape or disk files created and accessed by conventional means. Each record of a sequential file must be read to get to the record that is needed. When a conventional file is updated, the entire file must be accessed and all data re-sorted to update just one record. A database management system can directly modify a single field within a segment.

Database management systems use a main control program to access the database files. All programs designed to read or update a DBMS file must tell this control program what it wants to read or write, so that the control program can do so. The application program must use a special message system to communicate with the control program. In comparison, the non–database file can be directly read or updated by the application program.

The DBMS control program, through the use of a "key-field" and special calculation, can find and directly access any data needed in the database file.

A DBMS offers several benefits. Data that resides in one location can be shared, accessed, read, or updated by numerous users. A single set of data can be updated by different programs or methods in different locations. With conventional data storage, each user or program must create a separate file, with each file containing many of the same fields, which causes overlap redundancy and increases the amount of storage space needed. Because the DBMS stores the data in one location, it offers reduced data redundancy and reduced need for storage space. Random access permits faster processing because the DBMS can directly access the data needed without having to read an entire file.

When the data is located in one place, data management is more efficient, because multiple files with the same data elements do not have to be verified for agreement.

Weber[3] cited four objectives for benefit of the DBMS: 1) "shareability"—multiple users with different functions can access the data, 2) availability—the data can be extracted and assimilated into the needed form for each user, 3) "evolvability"—when the data is in one place, it can be changed more easily to meet changing needs, and 4) database integrity—data is unimpaired, complete, and accurate.

13.1.2 Overview and Concepts

There are numerous vendors of DBMSs and each has its own terminology with which to identify the function and concepts needed to understand and operate the DBMS. The terminology used in this chapter comes from IBM-IMS, but DBMSs will be explained in general terms to assist the auditor in understanding the one used in his or her company.

Ron Weber[4] defined five functions of the database administrator: 1) defining, creating, and retiring data, 2) making the database available to users, 3) informing and servicing users, 4) maintaining database integrity, and 5) monitoring operations.

Due to the specialized nature of the DBMS it is vital for a company to have a qualified person perform the duties of a database administrator (DBA). The DBA's major objective is to define the control elements of the DBMS.

The DBA is responsible for defining the segments of the database, which is a collection of data that share some common attributes, for example, customer identification data, all orders for a particular product, or all the transactions within a certain period.

A segment definition is much like a file layout (see Chapter 5), which defines the field names, data type, start position, and field size. A database definition identifies the segment's name, size, and key-field for each segment. The key-field is one field within each segment that is used as the means to locate its needed data.

Access to data is accomplished by a calculation based on this key-field. Because the calculation is always the same, the system can find the data relating to each key-field. All of the segments in the database relate to each other by some common trait.

Another of the DBA's functions is to define the relationships of the segments within the database. In IBM-IMS, these relationships are defined as root, parent, and child. The root segment is the highest-level segment within the database. The parent can be a subordinate segment of the root, and the child is a subordinate segment of the parent. There can be multiple children for each parent, and multiple parents under each root. This root-parent-child construction is common to such hierarchical database structures as IMS.

Data in subordinate segments can only be retrieved through its root-parent relationship. This structure does not permit backward access of segments through a child-parent-root definition. The organization of a hierarchical database looks like a corporate organization chart.

Another major database type is the network structure that permits access to data elements by connection with any other member. CA-IDMS is a network database and uses terms like "set" and "member" instead of parent and child. In a hierarchical database structure, each child can only have one parent, whereas in the network database structure, each child can have multiple parents: network architecture is more complex.

The third major database type is the relational structure, which uses a table-type format similar in appearance to a microcomputer spreadsheet containing columns and rows. The relational database structure is the easiest of the three types to initialize and maintain. The rows and columns used establish relationships at the data level, eliminating the need for pointers. Relational database structures are common among the microcomputer packages.

The database administrator controls the definition, creation, and storage of a program specification block (PSB), and program control block (PCB). These terms relate to the hierarchical database structure of IBM-IMS. A PSB defines the logical picture or view of a database. A program control block specifies the picture of the database and the program functions allowed within that view. The PCB definition includes the segment name, the root-parent-child relationship, and the program functions permitted (such as read, write, or delete).

An application program can only access the database through the use of the DBD, PSB, PCB, and the key-field. The terms used in the preceeding paragraph relate to IBM-IMS, but similar controls are needed in other database structures to access application programs.

13.2 PLANNING AND PREPARATION

The areas of audit concern within the database administration function are organization, database control libraries, backup and recovery, system reporting, interface requirements, and documentation (see Figure 13–1). These both comprise and delineate the organizational position of the database administrator within the data processing department. The database control libraries execute programmatic control over access to all databases, by defining the access permissible to specific application programs and by creating an audit trail.

For the purposes of this chapter, the term "database" refers to a collection of data that belongs to a specific application or user. Examples of a database are accounts payable, investments, and

FIGURE 13–1   Identification of Audit Concerns

Audit Activity Code	Transaction/Area
A	Organization
B	Database control libraries
C	Backup/recovery
D	System reporting
E	Interface requirements
F	Documentation

FIGURE 13–2   Scope Summary

Risks and Exposures

1. Accidental or erroneous destruction of data by authorized users
2. Intentional or deliberate destruction of data by authorized or unauthorized users
3. Loss of data
4. Inaccurate reporting
5. Inaccurate information loaded to the database

Control Objectives

Verify that procedures exist to ensure:

1. Access to databases is properly restricted
2. Database information is backed up on a timely basis
3. Recovery procedures are documented and tested
4. Policies and procedures are adequately documented
5. Only authorized changes (additions, deletions) are made to database control libraries
6. Only authorized reports are produced

Key Controls

1. Restricted access
2. Authorization
3. Supervision
4. Comparison
5. Validity

Audit Objectives

To determine:

1. That adequate controls exist over the maintenance of control library members including additions, deletions, and modifications
2. That adequate controls exist over access to the control library
3. The utilization of database reporting software and authorization for its use

Preliminary Review

Activity Code	Transaction/Area	Budget Hours	
		Audit Time	Review Time
A	Organization	10	1
B	Database control libraries	25	3
C	Backup/Recovery	10	2
D	System reporting	15	2
E	Interface requirements	10	2
F	Documentation	7	1

checking accounts. The databas*es* refer to all of the databases within a company.

Backup and recovery includes required logging of transactions, database images, and database messages to permit recovery via checkpoint/restart programs.

An increased number of DBMS packages can be accessed with a generalized reporting system that is specifically designed for the DBMS. This system is similar to the audit software packages (see Chapter 5), but such systems frequently do not provide for sophisticated program logic, limiting their use as a processing tool.

Interface requirements include the means for the application programs to talk to the database control program, and other techniques to control and organize the database structure and data.

The risks and exposures indicate the potential for the destruction or loss of data, for inaccurate reporting with the generalized report package, and for inaccurate information residing in the control libraries. The control objectives, key controls, and audit objectives are self-explanatory, but they will be reinforced with explanations in this chapter's preliminary review and compliance testing sections, (see Figure 13–2).

13.3   EXECUTION OF PRELIMINARY REVIEW

In the case of DBMS audits, the EDP auditor will only perform preliminary review procedures, because compliance testing may not be necessary. The EDP auditor, upon completion of his or her preliminary review, will then determine whether compliance testing is necessary.

13.3.1   Organizational Structure

There are two special audit issues that must be addressed in the database administration audit, 1) placement of the database administrator in the data processing organization structure, and

2) segregation of database administration functions from all other data processing functions.

To properly accomplish control and business objectives, the database administrator must be placed high enough in the data processing hierarchy to have independence from, and exercise control over, access to the databases by system programmers, application analysts, and application programmers. The database administrator should have final say on access to, design of, and definition of, database structures. The auditor's objective is to determine that the database administrator has sufficient authority to exercise control over database activities.

13.3.2 Database Control Library

These libraries contain the definitions of the database, the program specifications defining the logical views of the database, and the controls specifications that define application program functions that can be performed. The DBA should have sole control over these database libraries. To operate properly, all DBMSs will extract the definitions and specifications from a control library as input to a generation or initialization program that translates the definitions and specifications to machine-readable code for use by the DBMS software, the operating system, and application programs. The information in these libraries is extremely sensitive because errors and omissions of critical information could cause database failure.

Determining the procedures for authorization and update of the control libraries focuses on the procedures to add and delete specifications to and from these libraries (see Figure 13–3). The questions that the auditor will answer during the preliminary review involve; how are the creation of and changes to these definitions and specifications controlled? What controls exist to ensure that source library information is properly converted to the object libraries containing machine-readable code? How are the validity and accuracy of the definitions and specifications verified? Does the procedure documentation adequately explain all procedures?

FIGURE 13–3   Database Control Libraries

Audit Test Objectives

To determine that the controls over production changes to the libraries are adequate

Key Controls

1. Authorization
2. Access control
3. Single authorized library

Scope

All library member creations, updates, and deletions that occurred during the audit period

Audit Procedures

Preliminary Review

1. Determine the procedures for authorization and update of the control libraries

Compliance Testing

1. Select a sample of library updates
   Verify that:
   a. The request for library update is authorized by the appropriate personnel
   b. The information on the updated library module agrees to the information specified
   c. The system message on the update report states the module was updated successfully
2. Select a sample of deleted library members
   Verify that:
   a. The request for the deletion was authorized
   b. The deleted module name on the delete report agrees to the module name on the authorization form
   c. The system message on the delete report states the module was deleted successfully
3. Select a sample of months. For each month selected obtain a system generation master list that identifies all of the on-line transactions to be added to the system. For each transaction on the master list obtain the request for the transaction
   Verify that:
   a. The transaction request forms are authorized
   b. Each identified transaction was requested by the appropriate person
   c. All condition codes are acceptable and updates are authorized by the DBA
   d. The changes that appear on the output agree to what was requested on the request form, for all transactions

13.3.3   Backup and Recovery

Database recovery is accomplished by utilizing copies of database segment after-images. These are pictures of the records after they have been updated by a transaction. However, when a database is being used for on-line transaction processing, the images or records constantly change, complicating the backup strategy. The DBMSs contain utilities that log the before- and after-images of the segments, log the transactions that were entered against the database, and log the database system messages. Should the on-line database system fail, checkpoint/restart programs can be used to read these log files and reconstruct the database.

The auditor is directed to determine the files that must be copied, and the procedure for creating backup files as it relates to inclusion in the routine data center run schedule. In summary, the creation of backup files should be automatic—a routine function of the computer operator (see Figure 13–4).

FIGURE 13–4   Backup and Recovery

Audit Test Objective

Determine the adequacy of backup and recovery of the database files

Key Controls

1. Schedules backup copy programs
2. Checkpoint restart techniques
3. Testing of recovery strategy

Scope

All database files

Audit Procedures

Preliminary Review

Determine:

1. Which files must be copied
2. The procedures for creating backup files

Compliance Testing

Verify that:

1. The creation of backup copies is part of the routine data center job schedules
2. The database recovery programs are routinely tested

13.3.4   System Reporting

DBMSs frequently have a generalized report writer that is specifically designed for quick report generation of database files. These reports can become part of the routine production work and should, therefore, be subjected to the same authorization procedures as are request for changes to application programs. The auditor is directed to determine how requests for reports are documented, and how they are authorized. The authorization includes an approval from the requestor's manager, which is necessary because the user is requesting the expenditure of data processing resources. The other element of authorization is the DBA's approval to code and implement the report program (see Figure 13–5).

Inasmuch as these reports will typically be production jobs and the reports will be used for business purposes, the accuracy of the report must be verified before it is turned over to the user

FIGURE 13–5   System Reporting

Audit Test Objectives

To determine that all reports are properly authorized and that the reports produced contain the selection criteria requested

Key Controls

1. Authorization of request
2. Specifications of the request
3. Verification of report accuracy

Scope

All reports produced during audit period

Preliminary Review

1. Determine the procedures for request, authorization, accuracy verification of the reports

Compliance Testing

Verify that:

1. The report generation request was authorized. Compare signature to authorized signature list
2. The report matches requested criteria
3. The completion of the review of report accuracy and validity

for business use. Some users will accept computer reports as totally accurate and may not validate report contents. Furthermore, the user may not understand how the report is created insofar as the criteria used for selection and the database segments selected. These two considerations make it vital that the auditor determine the report verification procedures executed by the DBA group.

13.3.5   Interface Requirements

During preliminary review the auditor will focus on determining the controls that exist to ensure that only authorized reports are produced. Because report creation requires the use of limited EDP resources, the auditor should determine the priority identification system that helps the DBA determine which jobs to work on first.

This area of concern will not include an audit program because the elements of the interface requirements can vary based on the company and the DBMS in use. Furthermore, this section is designed to give the reader ideas of what to look for in his or her company. Depending on the results of the research, the EDP auditor may or may not need to define compliance testing.

DBMSs have very specific rules for application programs to follow, to the extent that special programs exist as part of the DBMS, or by purchase from a separate vendor to interface with the DBMS. The EDP auditor should acquaint himself with the various interfaces to determine if they present any exposure to the organization.

A DBMS will typically use a message system for design of on-line screens and other messages, returned to the terminal or printed on reports, that occur as a result of interface with the database system. These messages are typically stored in a program style library accessible by production programs. Due to this production access, the auditor must ensure that access to this library is controlled and that changes, additions, and deletions to the library are authorized, reviewed prior to addition or deletion from the library, and that the update to the library is verified for accuracy.

A data manipulation language (DML) provides the interface between an application program and the DBMS. The application program uses the DML to execute such program instructions as opening the file, reading the record, or writing a record. DL/I[5] is the DML used by IBM-IMS. CA-IDMS and other network databases use the CODASYL standards to define their DML interface requirements.

A data description language (DDL) is used to define the elements of the database—the (DBD) database definition. This interface language permits the definition of the schema and subschema used by the CA-IDMS database product, complying with the CODASYL standards.

The DBA can use a data dictionary (DD) to document the characteristics of all the fields in the database, including data types, permitted values, and relationship to other fields. According to Murphy *et al.*, "DD's are classified as passive or active. Active DD's are updated automatically when the DBMS is changed. A passive DD is not integrated with the DBMS and must be maintained separately. IBM-IMS has a passive DD, while CA-IDMS has an active integrated DD, DB2 has the DB2 Catalog that performs some active DD functions."[6]

Prototyping and Computer Aided System Engineering (CASE) are two techniques used for more efficient design and development of computer programs. Although these are not mandatory for interface to a DBMS nor critical to the function of a DBMS, they are programmer productivity tools that add an additional level of complexity and control complication to the environment. The auditor should determine if his or her installation uses these tools, and through discussions with the DBA and system software programming manager identify the effect of these tools on the control over database control libraries.

13.3.6   Documentation

The procedures for maintaining a DBMS are highly technical and very specific, requiring excellent procedure documentation for database administration employees to follow. The auditor should ensure that these documented procedures exist, and verify their accuracy and adequacy by following the procedures to perform a walk-through with the DBA. Any procedural documentation that contains weak or missing explanations should be fixed.

The documentation covering the technical components of the DBMS are documented by the vendors of the various products. Because these products have existed for at least 15 years, the vendor documentation is generally very good. However, the auditor should determine that the database administration group has copies of all the necessary vendor documentation and that each database administration employee has ready access to it.

13.4 COMPLIANCE TESTING

The compliance testing procedures (see Figures 13–3 through 13–5) focus on database control libraries, backup and recovery, and system reporting.

The transaction covering interface requirements may or may not have compliance testing requirements in the EDP auditor's installation. This area was identified as a separate transaction to highlight the importance of the special software and rules needed for interface with a DBMS.

13.4.1 Database Control Library

The database control libraries contain the definitions and specifications of the databases. Before the DBMS can recognize these definitions and specifications, the components in the database control libraries must be initialized or generated with special DBMS procedures. Within IBM-IMS these procedures are known as DBDGEN, PSBGEN, and ACBGEN. The CA-IDMS DBMS requires similar functional procedures that use different names.

The DBDGEN generates the database definitions, which is similar in structure to a standard file layout. The PSBGEN generates the program specification blocks that define the logical views of the database(s). The ACBGEN generates the application control blocks, which defines the database and programs for use by an on-line system. Owing to the technical complexity of these definitions and specifications, the access and authorization control implications are important.

Changes to the database control libraries is typically performed through an on-line programming system. The sensitive nature of these libraries demands preventive access control over these libraries. This is typically accomplished with a security software system such as CA-Topsecret or IBM-RACF.

With regard to user and DBA authorization to update the components of the control libraries, the DBA must review the request forms identified to ensure that they are complete and prepared by an authorized person, one that is technically competent. DBA procedures should identify the S&P personnel who are authorized to request changes to the database. Incomplete or inaccurate requests can cause errors in the generation of the database. DBA must check the update report to determine that the library update was properly accepted and processed. The erroneous deletion of a control library member could cause one or a series of application programs to fail, because the applications interface specifications are no longer defined to the database. The database control program would, therefore, abort any attempt by the application program(s) to access the database.

The procedures for authorization to delete a library member must be examined and verification that the delete was properly performed, in other words, the wrong member was not deleted accidentally, must be provided. Before a definition or specification is deleted from the control library, the DBA should research all specifications that reference the database definition to ensure that the deletion of the DBD will not have any adverse effect on processing.

The procedures to generate the database using the components in the control libraries and add on-line transactions to the database for use by the on-line system must be verified and so must DBA procedures that validate system acceptance of the transaction definitions. Even though the specifications and definitions were included in the executed GEN (generation or initialization), their acceptance by the system can only be validated by review of the condition codes printed on the GEN output report. DBA verification that the requested specifications and definitions were updated to the system must also be examined.

13.4.2 Backup and Recovery

Programs or utilities used to create backup copies of databases should be included as a standard job in the data center run schedule. The auditor's verification of the creation of backup copies must be provided. Backup copies could be generated for daily, monthly, quarterly, and yearly processing cycles.

DBMS products are usually accompanied by a utility program that can accomplish checkpoint restart and recovery of database. A database administration employee or the DBA should verify that the backup utility program was executed properly by verifying the condition codes on the utility run report.

There is also a focus on testing of the recovery programs, which is important to ensure their proper function. A database failure when recovery is needed is a bad time to discover that the recovery programs do not work. Testing these recovery programs on a monthly or quarterly basis is suggested.

13.4.3 System Reporting

Because the reports created by the generalized report writer are production jobs competing for EDP resources, the request for the report must be authorized. The DBA should ensure that the request originates or is approved by the authorized user liaison.

These reports could be used by the business function for control purposes or management information. A database administration employee should match the report to the request to determine that it satisfies the users' needs. The data on the report should be checked for reasonableness to validate the accuracy of the information from the standpoint that the proper fields were selected and the selection criteria is accurate.

NOTES

1. IBM and IMS are registered trademarks of International Business Machines, Inc.

2. CA-IDMS is a registered trademark of Computer Associates, Inc.

3. Weber, Ron, *EDP Auditing—Conceptual Foundations and Practices*. New York: McGraw-Hill, Inc., 1982, pp. 165–166.

4. Ibid., pp. 168–171.

5. DL/I is a registered trademark of International Business Machines, Inc.

6. Murphy, Michael A. and Ley, Xenia. *Handbook of EDP Auditing*, 2nd ed., Boston: Warren, Gorham & Lamont, Inc., 1989, pp. 28–11.

14

System Software Function[1]

14.1   INTRODUCTION

This chapter delves into the system software function, one of the most fundamentally important areas of data processing. The operating system processes all other application and utility programs used by the organization. This makes the systems programmer one of the most important, and arcane, members of the organization.

The data processing area has traditionally been divided into environmental and application audit areas, with the latter's being dependent on environmental controls as well as its own. Environmental weaknesses are pervasive and cannot be compensated for by application controls, no matter how numerous or extensive. The systems software function is a key element in the environmental control scheme.

The systems programmer's job is highly technical, requiring the special skills and training needed to code and implement changes to systems software and to install packaged software. All computer programs are effected in some way by the systems programmer.

The high-level technological background needed for the systems software function is conducive to a natural segregation from the application programming function, but it also presents a major control problem for management. The systems programmer is difficult to supervise because management generally does not understand the function well enough to detect irregularities. Operating system code is voluminous and the interrelationships of its various functions and programs are complicated. This makes a review for errors, fraud, or irregularities impractical. Errors and omissions can be found by sufficient testing, but fraudulent code executed under chosen conditions can only be detected by code review.

14.2   PLANNING AND PREPARATION

The computer software within the system programmers' responsibility is referred to as system software and specifically includes:

- The mainframe operating system,
- Systems programs and utilities,
- Application utilities,
- Programming tools and languages,
- Job entry systems,
- On-line networks and dial-up links,
- Security software, and
- Program and file libraries.

Specific job duties of the systems programmer vary depending on the installation's requirements but the generic responsibilities are to:

- Evaluate, modify, and install software packages,
- Write and maintain systems programs,
- Investigate and resolve hardware and software problems,
- Maintain up-to-date knowledge of system programming techniques and innovations, and
- Provide technical support for data processing activities.

Software packages: These are any vendor-packaged software, such as utilities, programming aids, and application programs. The systems programmer must evaluate these to determine their compatibility with the environment and the practical cost benefit. Judgment errors are costly if not detected prior to purchase and installation. Before implementation, the systems programmer must establish program library and installation conventions. Disk space must be estimated and allocated, and the table of contents modified. Operating system security must be defined to accept the new programs, and software security access rules must be defined to permit user access. Database definitions and program specification blocks must be written and implemented and the data dictionary updated.

Errors or omissions in any of these activities prevent applications from running properly and consume expensive computer resources unnecessarily. Fraud and irregularities are viable concerns, but errors and omissions are more prevalent. Matching of a properly trained person to the complexity of the job, supervision, review, and extensive testing are vital elements of risk reduction.

Operating systems: These systems, such as MVS[2] (Multiple Virtual Storage), DOS[R] (Disk Operating System), and UNIX[3] control and supervise CPU (Central Processing Unit) and computer resources and programs. The systems programmer tunes the operating system, using internal and vendor-supplied enhancements to maintain peak operating efficiency. These changes should be implemented with a vendor-supplied system modification program. Errors in these tasks can cause partial or complete operating system failure that require restart-and-recovery.

System monitor programs accomplish such tasks as dynamic job scheduling, error checking, resource priority assignments, diagnostics of program code and hardware, and redundant file management. The systems programmer uses these to evaluate system performance and resource usage to identify areas that need fine tuning in order to maximize efficiency and processing capability. Dumping and tracing programs provide printouts of the values in control registers and core to diagnose causes of program and system failures.

Teleprocessing monitors, such as the IMS DB/DC[4] (Information Management System Data Base/Data Communications) and TSO/CICS[5] (Time Sharing Option/Customer Information Control System) support on-line interaction between the mainframe and individual terminals or microcomputers. Errors in these programs can degrade on-line network performance, create file update errors, or fail to execute interactive programs.

Control programs include security software, accounting programs, on-line documentation, file management, and library management. Program errors can negate on-line access control, affect the accuracy of monetary chargeback, and lose track of tape and disk files.

Utility programs help structure and modify data used in the system and in data sets. Other utilities prepare peripheral equipment for interface with the system. These programs initialize and change DASD (Direct Access Storage Device) setups, list system control data, copy data sets, change access methods and dump and restore data files. Some utilities can be used as subroutines or individual jobs while others can only operate independently. System utility programs, which are called by the system, must reside in authorized libraries. Utility usage must be controlled by the security software system to provide a record of what data sets and programs were accesses. The utility programs should print reports of the functions used.

Database management systems such as CA-IDMS and IBM MS, create, access and change database files. Application programs directly access and maintain all non-DBMS (Database Management System) files, but must use a DBMS interface for database file handling. Maintenance of the DBMS interface program is both a highly complex task and a dangerous one: errors and omissions could destroy file integrity.

Systems programming aids consist of utilities that automate such routine and redundant tasks in system development as sorting, purging, and file identification. This group of programs is highly sensitive because it includes the utility needed to install operating system "fixes."

Performance monitoring software, also a systems programming aid, measures CPU utilization and uptime, on-line network efficiency and utilization, and disk usage and availability. Application software includes compiler and assembler utilities that translate source codes to machine codes for execution.

Checkpoint restart programs can determine what needs to be recovered and do so unassisted. They execute according to chosen conditions throughout the processing period to provide file backup, data, and program checkpoints for automated restart and recovery.

Long- and short-range planning is vital to provide a stable and continuous processing environment. Computer resource usage must be monitored to ensure that sufficient processing and storage capacity is available. New application implementation and enhancements must be planned in advance so that hardware ordering lead times and deadlines can be met. CPU usage must be monitored for contention problems (competition for resources), and job scheduling should be monitored to ensure that job overruns do not become a habit.

14.2.1   Identification of Transactions

Figure 14–1 lists the areas of concern to be covered in a full-scope audit. The high level of risk in the function demands audit consideration each year.

14.2.2   Risks and Exposures

The specific control concerns can be translated into five broad risks and exposures listed in Figure 14–2. Inadequate control

FIGURE 14–1   Identification of Transactions

Activity	Transaction/Area	Include Exclude	Reason
A	Administration	I	Satisfy Audit Objective 1
B	On-Line Access Control	I	Satisfy Audit Objective 5
C	Operating System Maintenance	I	Satisfy Audit Objectives 1, 3, 4
D	Systems Software Maintenance	I	Satisfy Audit Objectives 1, 3, 4
E	New Software Installation	I	Satisfy Audit Objectives 1, 3, 4
F	Backup Procedures and Testing	I	Satisfy Audit Objective 6
G	Installation Standards	I	Satisfy Audit Objectives 2, 3

over systems programmers can permit errors, omissions, and fraud to occur and remain undetected, contributing to loss, alteration or misuse of data. Significant errors that affect the entire environment can cause the system to fail, causing major waste and time loss.

Subtle, or less obvious, errors can create incorrect data that misinforms management, permitting the erroneous management decisions that contribute to competitive disadvantage.

14.2.3 Control Objectives

Management is responsible for maintaining an adequate internal control system within the systems software function. In so doing, management accomplishes the control objectives, namely ensuring that all job responsibilities are specifically defined and documented, tasks are assigned to systems programmers based on their ability to properly complete the task, and the work is adequately supervised and reviewed.

It is also necessary to evaluate new systems and changes to existing systems in terms of their cost benefit and their operational and functional fit prior to purchase. Mainframe performance, DASD resources, and the terminal network should be monitored daily to ensure that the system can process all scheduled work.

Moreover all modifications to system programs and software should be authorized, reviewed, tested and approved; short-range and long-range resource plans should be maintained to prevent the unavailability of hardware and software; authorized system access and a workable disaster recovery plan should be protected (see Figure 14–2).

14.2.4 Key Controls

The key controls relevant to the systems software are simple controls that are also used in nontechnical functions. When used properly they work well to control a high-tech function. These have all been explained in previous chapters.

FIGURE 14-2   Scope Summary

Risks/Exposures

1. Loss, alteration or misuse of data
2. Business interruption
3. Misinformation to management
4. Excessive costs
5. Competitive disadvantage

Control Objectives

1. Job responsibilities should be specifically defined and adequately supervised and reviewed
2. The system should perform efficiently and effectively
3. The system should be reliable and data integrity should be maintained
4. Organizational needs should be satisfied on a timely basis
5. The system should be protected against disaster

Key Controls

1. Restricted access
2. Audit trails
3. Authorization of changes
4. Job descriptions
5. Logging and review of critical events
6. Segregation of duties
7. Procedures and operator manuals
8. Documentation of program changes
9. Hiring and screening procedures
10. Management review and approval
11. Backup and recovery procedures

Audit Objectives

Determine that adequate controls exist to:

1. Ensure that work is supervised and changes are authorized
2. Ensure that system performance is maintained
3. Ensure system reliability and integrity
4. Ensure that organizational needs are satisfied
5. Protect the system from unauthorized access
6. Protect the system from disaster

FIGURE 14–2   *(Continued)*

Preliminary Review

Activity Code	Transaction/Area	Audit Time	Review Time
		Budget Hours	
A	Administration	5	1
B	Security access control	7	1
C	Operating system maintenance	10	2
D	System software maintenance	10	1
E	New software installation	10	1
F	Backup procedures and testing	7	.5
G	Installation standards	3	.5

14.2.5   Audit Objectives

The audit objectives must be refined in compliance testing. A time-consuming audit task is that of identifying and quantifying the existing systems software: operating system programs, control programs, systems programming aids and application-related software that falls within the responsibility of the systems programming group. The procedures in each area are to be measured against the control objectives. In the first audit of the area, this task will consume significant time.

14.2.6   Completing Audit Planning

Decisions are needed on audit staff assignments, training time, and research time. Adequately experienced staff should be selected to make the research proceed as effectively and efficiently as possible.

The external auditors should be consulted about their scope requirements. This will be needed in the external auditor's annual general control evaluation to permit financial statement sign off. A company may be able to reduce external audit fees by conducting the internal audit using the external auditor's objectives and testing. The systems software audit has a profound effect on external audit procedures for companies needing an internal control "comfort" letter for distribution to customers.

14.3   EXECUTION OF PRELIMINARY SURVEY

All available audit material should be researched to identify the standard controls needed in the systems programming area, all of which may not be appropriate, but they provide a benchmark for evaluation.

The internal control evaluation measures the control procedures in the actual environment against the standard control objectives. Exceptions to the standards become potential control weaknesses, but a standard control may not be practical in every environment.

Nothing irritates data processing managers more than a textbook audit or a cookbook approach. Audit findings and recommendations for improvement must be tailored to fit the specific environment, and consider effectiveness, efficiency, and practicality of recommended changes in procedures.

The initial audit research time spent on quantifying systems programmer duties and responsibilities is significant. Specifically, an installation with two mainframes could easily have 120 different programs that the systems programming group is responsible for maintaining.

The complexity of the systems programmer's job responsibilities create control concerns for the auditor and for management. The systems software group is a highly technical one, and few people outside its realm fully understand the function. This makes properly supervising and managing it difficult. An effective audit requires significant knowledge and technical skill in order to understand the potential risks of systems software interrelationships. The audit team needs at least one person who is as knowledgeable as the systems programmers, to ensure the audit's accuracy.

14.3.1   Administration

The administrative audit deals with management and supervisory control of the work. The extent of control management has over individual accountability for work duties must be examined,

FIGURE 14–3 **Administration**

Audit Test Objective

Determine that:

1. All job responsibilities are specifically defined and documented
2. Tasks are assigned to systems programmers based on their ability to properly complete the task
3. The work is adequately supervised and reviewed

Key Controls

1. Periodic job assignment
2. Review of all production updates
3. Adequate training

Scope

All work assignments which occurred during the period being examined

Audit Procedures

Preliminary Review

1. Determine that an inventory list of all software is maintained
2. Determine that all systems software programs on the inventory list are assigned to a systems programmer who is accountable for the operation, maintenance and support of each program
3. Review the resumes, job applications and seminar attendance of each programmer to assess that they are adequately trained to handle the programs for which they are responsible
4. Review the work assignment methodology

Compliance Testing

1. Trace a sample of programs from this list to system data sets to determine that these programs are on the system
2. Select a sample of programs from system data sets and trace them to the inventory list to ensure they are included
3. Verify that assignments are made periodically (daily, weekly, biweekly, monthly) to the systems programmer by the system programming manager or supervisor
4. Verify that a supervisor or manager reviews work progress frequently on a schedule that fits the organization
5. Select a sample of work assignments completed during the period
   a. Trace them to periodic progress reports and other documentation to determine that the assignments were reviewed and approved by a manager or supervisor

for the absence of accountability could permit the systems to fall into disrepair. Also, ongoing training is vital to keep the systems programmers' technical skills sharp. Management's evaluation of staff qualifications and training must be reviewed too.

Moreover, interviewing the manager and supervisor to determine how work is assigned and progress is monitored must be included in the preliminary review as well. Supervision is a key control in reducing the risk of fraudulent practices (see Figure 14–3).

14.3.2   On-line Access Control

The demands of the system programmer's job dictate the need for on-line access to the systems software, which makes restricted physical access an ineffective control. The systems programmer's access to shared resources compounds the effect of errors and omissions. Improper access control could permit a copy of the operating system to be modified with illegitimate code. When this modified copy is loaded, the illegitimate code becomes part of the resident operating system. Proper preventive and detection controls provided by a security software package can reduce the risk of this maneuver.

Improper security software access profiles can permit the systems programmer to turn off the security software. The systems programmer has the authority and techniques to generate operating system modifications. Without security software control, the systems programmer is free to make changes to any data set or program without detection.

To control this situation, the security software can be specifically coded to monitor and record all the systems programmer's actions and accesses. Security software deactivation by the systems programmer can be stopped by coding deactivation and startup under a restricted security profile. This profile would permit only the data security administrator to activate and deactivate the security system, providing constant monitoring of the systems programmer's activities. The auditor must determine the definition of these access profiles.

FIGURE 14–4   On-Line Access Control

Audit Test Objective

To determine that on-line access cannot be gained to system resources without authorization

Key Controls

1. On-line access control system
2. Security profile definitions
3. Track use of emergency access profiles

Scope

All systems programmers

Audit Procedures

Preliminary Review

1. Review the security access profiles for each system programmer. Determine the extent of system programmers' on-line access to test and production systems
2. Determine the rules for emergency access

Compliance Testing

1. Review systems programmers' access rules to determine that they can only access the functions that have been approved by systems software management
2. Verify that the defined access levels do, in fact, access only the program libraries and functions that management intends
3. Design and perform tests that violate access rules
4. Review access profile definitions to determine that programmers do not have access to production facilities or transactions
5. Determine that all uses of emergency access levels are reviewed and approved, in writing, by system software management within two days of the actual usage

---

The systems programmer needs only limited access ("read-only") to application program libraries and application job control language. The data security administrator can provide an emergency access profile for the systems programmer to change application program code and jcl when needed. The auditor must review the emergency access provisions with management and with the data security administrator.

14.3.3   Maintenance and Installation

Operating systems, systems software maintenance, and new software installation involve the technical aspects of the systems programmer's job. The preliminary review procedures are essentially the same for all, and can be performed simultaneously through interviews of management and the supervisor. Inadequate controls in these high-risk functions can affect the entire data processing environment because errors, omissions, or fraud would affect every application system (see Figure 14–5).

Programming errors and omissions can be costly. Management must implement an effective means for review and testing of changes. Inadequate testing usually occurs in a time crunch. Ideally a systems software supervisor should perform a technical review of all changes, but this can create a bottleneck, reducing productivity. Another systems programmer can be assigned to review for errors and omissions, which facilitates cross training, backup for personnel turnover and absences, and some protection against fraud as collusion would be required.

Exhaustive testing using a test environment is vital to detecting errors. Upon implementation of the changes, a copy of the functioning systems software should be saved for backup and recovery should the implemented changes prove incorrect (see Figure 14–6).

Some companies duplicate the operating system and "freeze" it, then implement the changes to the copy. After passing a systems programmer's test, the systems development staff test it against their criteria, then the users test the system. In addition, all changes are logged and saved for research if needed. This process may seem costly, but the operating system is the backbone of the data processing environment (see Figure 14–7).

Inadequate documentation of systems software can cripple the installation. Documentation standards should be established for all existing systems software and for changes to the systems software. These standards should be strictly enforced. Management's review of software changes should include a review of

FIGURE 14–5 **Operating System Maintenance**

Audit Test Objective

To determine that additions and modifications to the operating system are authorized, tested and approved

Key Controls

1. Authorization of changes
2. Review of all changes
3. Changes to a test system

Scope

All operating system changes that occurred during the period being examined

Audit Procedures

Preliminary Review

1. Determine maintenance authorization procedures and requirements

Compliance Testing

1. Select a sample of operating system changes made during the audit period and trace them to an authorization form to prove the change was approved by management. Determine that:

   a. The change specifications were adequately defined and described by an experienced person and approved by systems software management

   b. All additions and modifications to the operating system were completed by using a vendor-supplied system modification program

   c. The changes were made to a "frozen" version of the operating system separate from the production environment

   d. The changes were tested in an environment separate from the production environment and the test results were reviewed by systems software management, and used in a test environment by appropriate S&P personnel

   e. All modifications were documented according to installation standards and filed in a manual

   f. Recovery procedures for the removal of changes were documented

   g. Authorized programs added to the system control program were reviewed to ensure that they do not compromise system integrity

2. Determine that the implementation to production was approved by S&P management and that all S&P personnel were notified in advance of the cutover to production

FIGURE 14–6 System Software Maintenance

Audit Test Objective

To determine that additions and modifications to system software programs are authorized

Key Controls

1. Authorization of changes
2. Review of all changes
3. Changes to a test system
4. Testing

Scope

All system software program changes that occurred during the period being examined

Audit Procedures

Preliminary Review

1. Determine maintenance authorization procedures and requirements

Compliance Testing

1. Select a sample of system software changes made during the audit period and trace to an authorization form to prove the change was approved by management. Determine that:
   a. The change specifications were adequately defined and the impact of the change was evaluated by an experienced person and approved by system software management
   b. Acquisition or programming costs were identified, documented, and approved by system software management
   c. The changes were made to a copy of the software and reviewed by another qualified system programmer
   d. The changes were tested in an environment separate from the production environment and the test results were reviewed by systems software management, and used in a test environment by all relevant S&P personnel
   e. All modifications were documented according to installation standards, and filed in an organized manual
   f. Program usage instructions were changed in all applicable documentation
   g. Recovery procedures for the removal of changes were documented
   h. Authorized programs added to the system control program were reviewed to ensure that they do not compromise system integrity
2. Determine that the implementation to production was approved by systems and programming management and all S&P personnel were notified in advance of the cutover to production

FIGURE 14-7 **New Software Installation**

Audit Test Objective

To determine that new software is evaluated and installed properly

Key Controls

1. Authorized workorder
2. Review of all production updates
3. Independent comparison of changes to specifications
4. Testing

Scope

All new software purchased or implemented during the period being examined

Audit Procedures

Preliminary Review

1. Determine procedures and requirements for new software installation

Compliance Testing

1. Select a sample of new software purchased or implemented during the audit period. Determine that:

   a. The impact of any new release or change was evaluated prior to the decision to implement

   b. Acquisition and programming costs were isolated and documented, then reviewed and approved by management prior to the decision to purchase

   c. The work was assigned to one systems programmer, as a primary responsibility, and that a second systems programmer was assigned as a backup and reviewer

   d. Program libraries were established in a test environment for source and object code and jcl parameters

   e. Program and functional testing were performed by the systems programmer, and that the results were reviewed by the systems programmer and systems software manager

   f. Testing was reperformed after changes were made

   g. Documentation was modified according to installation standards and placed in a centralized location

   h. The user community was notified in writing, and via the on-line programming system, of the impending change

documentation for accuracy and completeness. The retention of the documentation should be centralized and indexed to promote efficient research.

Fraud and embezzlement are a major concern of the auditor. Unfortunately, if systems programmers want to defraud their company, they can. Due to their high level of technical knowledge, absolute prevention of systems programmer fraud would be extremely costly. There is always a way around any preventive measure. A practical approach is to provide efficient and effective preventive controls and rely heavily on detection controls. Good backup procedures will enable discovery.

14.3.4   Installation Standards

The installation should develop and maintain systems software standards to maintain control, efficiency, and effectiveness. The absence of standards permits confusion and degrades productivity (see Figure 14–8).

The systems software group must continually evaluate system performance to ensure adequate operation. Performance evaluation elements must be identified to determine whether this evaluation includes all the necessary elements and whether it is performed on a sufficiently frequent basis. Installation standards should be established by the systems software group for all application programmers to follow. The audit should determine that all necessary elements are included.

Restricted-use programs perform specialized functions that could have a disastrous effect on the environment if not controlled—for example, a "zap" program can change data or program code on a file to anything the user wishes. The program accepts user input and inserts it in place of the original data. Reports or other audit trails may not be created by a zap program. Other sensitive utilities exist that accomplish a variety of functions, such as reorganizing files and recovering data and programs. Interviews of systems software programmers must be accomplished and discussions must be held with the operating system vendor.

FIGURE 14–8 **Installation Standards**

Audit Test Objective

To determine that system operation standards have been developed and are adhered to

Key Controls

1. Documented standards
2. Authorization for use of sensitive functions
3. Password control

Scope

All system operation standards

Audit Procedures

Preliminary Review

Examine:

1. Responsibilities for system performance evaluation
2. The sensitive programs that exist
3. Responsibilities for maintenance of documentation
4. Procedures for reviewing new applications to determine the default specifications needed

Compliance Testing

1. Verify the execution of control procedures for sensitive programs:
    a. They should be stored in restricted-use libraries
    b. Determine that access to the library or individual program is password controlled
2. Identify the installation-written programs that run in the supervisor state:
    a. Determine that they are stored in libraries authorized by systems software management
    b. Determine that management specifically authorized the inclusion of the program for use in the supervisor state
3. Select a sample of daily computer console logs printed during the audit period:
    a. Examine the log for bypass label processing and trace to a written authorization for use

The efficiency and effectiveness of the systems software function is dependent on accurate, complete, and current documentation. Much of this documentation is vendor supplied, but the installation must organize it so that it is readily available and permits easy location of the topic needed. The auditor should determine what management requirements and systems software's procedures should be for maintaining the documentation.

All vendor supplied programs are designed to be as fully automatic as possible, but they all require initialization of specific parameters, attributes, and options. In the absence of the installation's specifying these parameters, the programs are coded to use defaulted values established by the vendor. The vendor-supplied default values may be incorrect for the installation, causing abends, wasted processing, or unnecessary use of resources. Therefore, procedures that ensure that all new applications get reviewed by the systems software group should be examined.

14.4 COMPLIANCE TESTING

Using the information gained from the preliminary review, the auditor can design and complete tests for the existing control procedures. The tests should cover the events from the audit period to determine that the controls were functioning throughout the period instead of at just one particular time.

It is beneficial to review the preliminary survey results with the external auditors. This is because a weak control environment may dictate using larger test samples of transactions to provide the external auditors with enough information for "reasonable assurance" that the control system is sound. This reasonable assurance permits the external auditors to sign off on the financial statements or internal control opinion letter. The larger sample sizes increase internal audit staffing needs and the amount of time needed to complete the audit. In addition, the timing of compliance testing may have to be moved closer to year's end so that there is enough information for the external auditors to assess the level of reasonable assurance.

14.4.1 Administration

Figure 14–3 describes the audit tests for evaluating the adequacy of management and supervision. Most managers do not understand the function, which makes it difficult to supervise. Close supervision by a systems software supervisor reduces the risk of misunderstandings or oversights.

The accuracy of the inventory list must be verified to ensure the quality of the accountability. The listing of system data sets can be found on the volume table of contents or data set directory listing.

Application programmers frequently need assistance from the systems software unit to determine causes of program failures. Any installation uses numerous utilities and systems programs that assist personnel in programming, because systems programmers cannot possibly know all systems. Each systems programmer must be assigned accountability for a group of systems, which makes him or her a source for answers and quick repair to keep the system operating smoothly.

The completion and quality of work assignments procedures must be verified. Work assignments to the systems programmer should be made periodically (daily, weekly, biweekly, monthly). This provides a "time window" for providing some access control: that is, if the systems programmer has a week to complete a change project on a specific program, then the next week there should be no "change access" to that program. Individual work tasks are more effectively managed with a specific completion date.

14.4.2 On-line Access Controls

Security access evaluates the systems programmer's authority to access programs, utilities, and software via the on-line system. The nature of the job requires extensive on-line access, which must be closely monitored by data security administration and system programming management (see Figure 14–4).

The audit procedures that evaluate the adequacy of systems programmer's access control must be examined. Their on-line access presents a control dilemma. On the one hand, the demands of their job require access to all elements of the operating system, systems programs, and utilities. On the other hand, this extensive access exposes the organization to excessive risk. Limiting programmer's access can reduce their productivity and delay the quick fixes needed to keep the system running. A security software package is the only effective on-line access control mechanism over system programmers.

Programmer's knowledge provides the means to circumvent most controls. Therefore the on-line access definitions for each system programmer should be reviewed. Systems programmers' access can be coded as read-only access, with emergency access profiles available for activation by the security administrator or systems software manager. All data processing resources, terminals, transactions, programs, and files should be defined to the security access system. Systems software management must authorize the access levels available to systems programmers. All systems programmers' access profiles should have a tracking attribute defined for them. This is sometimes referred to as an audit attribute, which permits management to trace and track all system programmers' accesses and changes.

The demands of the systems programmer's job require access to all elements of the operating system, systems programs, and utilities. However, programmers do not need routine access to any application program libraries because these are the responsibility of application programmers and analysts. If needed, application libraries can be accessed under emergency access profiles.

Daily management review of these access reports provides an excellent detection control mechanism, but the human element— the reviewer—must be watched because he or she can be the weakness that permits a break in the system.

14.4.3   Operating System Maintenance

The operating system is a highly technical and specialized piece of software and is vendor supplied in most installations. Even if the systems programmers know how, changes to the operating system should be limited to vendor-supplied material. Changes designed in-house should be reviewed and approved by the vendor's operating system technicians (see Figure 14–5).

Due to the pervasive effect of errors, operating system changes should be strictly controlled and limited to as few releases per year as possible. Some companies limit operating system changes to two releases per year, except for emergencies. These changes are tightly controlled, reviewed by different groups, supervised, and extensively tested for several months prior to implementation. All users acknowledge the coming change and their review of test results in writing.

The testing should be exhaustive and include participation by application programming personnel to be absolutely sure that the system will operate successfully before going into production. The failure of a new operating system release could result in lost data. The operating system is the most critical software in any environment. Although it is always difficult and expensive to guarantee that a new system will operate properly, a new operating system must be as close to guaranteed as possible.

14.4.4   Systems Software Maintenance

Systems software includes all of the other programs, other than the operating system, that are within the scope of the systems programmer's responsibility. The programmer will change the program code that many users will be executing. The changes can be in good faith, but still contain errors that are not detected by review or program testing. Or, changes may be erroneous or fraudulent. The following standards are suggestions for "ideal" control, and the auditor must evaluate the efficiency, effectiveness, and practicality of each control in its environment. The testing procedures are essentially the same as for operating system maintenance, because the control procedures are the same.

The impact of any new release or change should be studied before deciding to use it. This reduces the risk of implementing changes that adversely affect existing programs and systems.

Acquisition or programming costs should be identified, documented, reviewed, and approved by management.

An ideal control situation would have all systems software code secured, for read-only access, by a control group. The control group would release a copy of the code to the systems programmer only when needed for modification. (This extent of control would be unusual. The author knows of no installation that exercises this much control over systems programmer access, because such tight control can degrade productivity.)

Audit testing verifies that changes are made to a copy of the program, the changed code is reviewed by a supervisor or at least another qualified systems programmer, and the initial functional testing is performed in a test environment segregated from production. Changes should be documented, and the program usage instructions changed for insertion in systems software, data center, and application programmer documentation as appropriate. The documentation should be organized, readily available, and centrally located as well as being reviewed by a supervisor. The user community should be notified in writing and via the on-line programming system of any impending change, for user programs and functions may be adversely affected by implementation. The advance notification reduces the risk of wasted debugging and research time for extraneous causes of malfunctions.

Once the code is error free, it can be released to production for linkage, preferably by a control group or a system programmer responsible for updates. This eliminates the need for routine access to the production update function by all system programmers.

14.4.5 New Software Installation

The system software staff should monitor relevant computer publications and periodicals to maintain an awareness of the quality and availability of new products, new releases to owned products, and the financial soundness of new and existing vendors. A major new release is essentially a major enhancement to an existing product or a complete replacement of all program codes. The responsible programmer and supervisor should review the new release documentation and decide on acceptance or rejection of the release.

This documentation review should include the following critical factors important to the installation:

- The need for new functions supplied,
- The functions that are being deleted,
- Indications as to whether the product, without implementation of the new release, will still be supported by the vendor, and
- The effect on other functioning systems of the new release.

Upon completion of the evaluation, the programmer and the supervisor should prepare a brief documented recommendation and submit it to the manager for final approval.

After approval, the responsible programmer should determine and document the tasks, resources, and the period of time needed to implement the new release. This plan should be used by the manager to measure progress via daily or weekly progress reports from the programmer. A test system should be established that approximates the production environment. The manager should be advised at least weekly of the test results and progress.

Acquisition and programming costs should be isolated and documented, then reviewed and approved by management prior to the decision to purchase. This reduces the risk of programming and implementation costs exceeding the benefit. The work should be assigned to one systems programmer as a primary responsibility and to a second systems programmer as backup and reviewer in case the first programmer quits, and to improve the quality of the final product.

Test program libraries should be established for source and object code, and jcl parameters maintained, to keep the development environment from adversely affecting production. Program and functional testing is usually performed by the primary systems programmer. The results should be reviewed by the secondary systems programmer and systems software manager. A representative group of users, probably application analysts and programmers, should review the test results. Changes will ordinarily be needed, and all testing relevant to the functions changed should be reperformed.

Once the code is error free, the software can be migrated to the production environment. This should be accomplished under strict supervision. The production processing environment should be monitored to ensure that any unusual events are researched. This will prevent potential production problems from becoming too serious.

14.4.6   Installation Standards

The installation standards to be adhered to include system performance evaluation, maintaining system operation standards, documentation standards, installation specifications, and utility program and dial-up network standards.

14.4.6.1   SYSTEM PERFORMANCE EVALUATION

The systems programmer should follow management-established criteria to monitor the performance of hardware and software. These criteria should evaluate power, capability, and timeliness (see Chapter 6). Performance measurement of hardware, systems software, and on-line systems is usually delegated to the systems programming group because of the technical knowledge required to interpret properly the statistics.

Tracking the hardware and systems software costs is the responsibility of the systems software group. Hardware and systems software is used by all users and, ideally, should be charged back to the users on a pro rata basis. This is a simple exercise done in conjunction with the accounting department. Nonetheless, the auditor should determine that the accounting mechanisms are adequate to capture and report all costs accurately to the accounting department.

14.4.6.2 SYSTEM OPERATION STANDARDS

Restricted-use programs perform specialized functions that could have a disastrous effect on the environment if not controlled. Reports or other audit trails may not be created. Other sensitive utilities exist that accomplish a variety of functions, such as reorganizing files and recovering data and programs.

The usage of these sensitive programs should be subject to password control. They are executed on an as-needed basis, so they need never be part of a production processing job stream. One control technique is to provide the password for program usage to a data center systems operator who alone knows this password. When the sensitive program is executed, the job will stop and prompt the operator for the password before continuing. The operator can be given a written authorization signed by the user programmer and the appropriate data processing manager. The operator may only enter the password if written authorization has been granted (see Figure 14–8).

The "supervisor program," which is a component of the central processing unit, controls and directs the usage of the CPU. A program cannot gain access to the CPU without the direction of the supervisor program. Installation-written programs that execute in the supervisor state are very sensitive and should be stored in authorized libraries, largely because the "supervisor" only uses specific libraries.

Tape and disk files have internal labels identifying their names, which can be read by the system. The rules of jcl require that the file name be specified. The system will then call for that file and check the internal label. If the label name does not match the one specified in the jcl, the system will stop the program. This control ensures the use of the proper file. Bypass label processing overrides this control and permits the system to read any file specified by the operator. This practice could permit the use of the wrong file, producing erroneous results. The auditor must verify that bypass label processing is limited and authorized to prevent routine overriding of this control.

Tape-read errors and damaged internal labels are justified usages of bypass label processing.

14.4.6.3 DOCUMENTATION STANDARDS

The documentation of changes made to systems programs is solely the installation's responsibility. Complete standards should be developed that specify how changes are documented. The standards should require a code listing, a narrative explanation of the need and effect of the change, and a list of the operational procedures needed to execute the program (or an explanation of how the program is automatically executed). The supervisory review of the change documentation should be evidenced by initials or a signature. Documentation standards should be developed with the objective of reducing dependency on human handling for obtaining instructions.

Change control procedures should be documented that explain how to complete a change, who should review it, how it should be tested, who should authorize implementation, and how implementation should be accomplished.

14.4.6.4 INSTALLATION SPECIFICATIONS

All vendor supplied programs are designed to be as fully automatic as possible; they all require however, initialization of specific parameters, attributes, and options by the installation. In the absence of the installation's specifying these parameters, the programs are coded to use defaulted values established by the vendor. The vendor-supplied default values may be incorrect for the installation, causing abends, wasted processing, or unnecessary resource usage.

Systems software documentation should clearly and concisely explain the values supplied for the installation and the justification for it, when needed. These installation specifications are particularly critical for the operating system, DBMS, on-line system, security software, and utility programs. Incorrect specifications can cause system failure or inefficient processing.

14.4.6.5 STANDARDS FOR UTILITY PROGRAMS

All installations have sensitive utilities that can perform a variety of programming repair tasks that assist in system recovery or reconstruction of files. These programs can change data files, program files, and file labels without leaving any evidence that a change was made. These sensitive utilities should be placed in a password-protected library and be executable only when a computer operator has advance written authorization from the appropriate data processing manager and enters a password.

These programs, as delivered by the vendor, have no automatic or inherent control defined for them. The installation must define and install the security mechanisms, using a security software product or other means.

It is the responsibility of the systems software group to ensure that these sensitive utilities are installed and used within the appropriate security guidelines and standards.

14.4.6.6 STANDARDS FOR DIAL-UP NETWORKS

The use of microcomputers for dial-up mainframe access has exploded in the past five years. File transfer from and to the mainframe has been cumbersome in the recent past, but improvements in file transfer capability are gaining momentum. Unfortunately, the security of all mainframe installations has not kept pace as well as it should have.

For file transfer to operate, the mainframes must have the software capability for dial-up access and file transfer. However, one exposure can exist even if the mainframe does not have resident dial-up and file transfer software. This exposure takes the form of an asynchronous port that is accessible by a phone line. Some installations have terminal network controllers with dial-up synchronous ports that cannot be accessed by a microcomputer without a protocol converter, as microcomputers use asynchronous protocol. However, some vendors deliver these network controllers with one port coded to accept asynchronous protocol, though the rest of the ports are synchronous. If this controller is connected to a dial-up link, then a microcomputer can dial up the mainframe via this asynchronous port, and, by using terminal emulation software, the microcomputer can tap into the network monitor.

Installation standards should protect the installation from this type of inadvertent trap. The systems programmer will know of this risk and take steps to reduce it.

14.5 EVALUATION OF RESULTS AND REPORT

Management's lack of technical knowledge can result in inadequate supervision that can produce significant control weaknesses and reduce the "auditability" of the system programmer. The control weakness that usually exist are inadequate:

- physical or on-line access control,
- organization of documentation for vendor-supplied software,
- documentation of changes to existing systems,
- control over changes to existing systems,
- test planning and segregation of the test environment,
- segregation of duties among the system programming staff,
- review of completed work and lack of cross-training or cross-review,
- backup copies of completed work, and
- disaster recovery procedures.

The exceptions disclosed via audit testing should be carefully evaluated to ensure that they do, in fact, cause additional risk. Due to the pervasive effect of any control weaknesses, the importance of the exceptions must be carefully measured and extenuating circumstances extensively researched. Major control weaknesses can invalidate the control structure of the EDP organization and, possibly, lead to a disclaimer of opinion on the financial statements by the external auditors. Furthermore, obtaining a clean opinion for an AICPA's Statement on Auditing Standards No. 30 or No. 44 internal control review could be impossible, which could threaten customer relationships.

The control weaknesses should be reported including complete explanations that describe the condition, cause, effect, and recommendation. A draft of the report should be reviewed with the systems software manager to correct any misunderstandings. The auditor's objective is to ensure that systems software management understands the findings and recommendations. Management does not have to approve of the report; it seldom does. It is important, however, that recommended solutions are practical and cost effective.

Executive management should be advised of the pervasive effect of systems programmer control weaknesses and their related effect on the financial statement opinion, third-party internal control opinion, external audit fees, and internal audit staffing.

NOTES

1. See Mullen, Jack B. "Auditing the Systems Software Function." Reprinted from *EDP Auditing* (New York: Auerbach Publishers). © 1990, Warren, Gorham & Lamont, Inc. Used with permission.

2. MVS is a registered trademark of International Business Machines.

3. UNIX is a registered trademark of American Telephone and Telegraph (ATT).

4. IMS and DB/DC are registered trademarks of International Business Machines.

5. TCO/CICS are registered trademarks of International Business Machines.

15

Service Bureaus and Out-Sourcing

15.1 INTRODUCTION

The audit of service-bureau-related activities differs from the control review audits discussed previously because the service bureau (servicer) is independent of the company (servicee)—not controlled by company management. The service bureau may have its own internal audit staff and external auditor. Even when the contract with the service bureau has a right-to-audit clause, the servicee auditor may not have routine access.

Service bureaus provide data processing services on a contract basis. These services vary from servicing one application to providing all data processing services. The service bureau has numerous customers—if it allows internal audit access by one customer company, it would have to allow auditors from all customers, which would be extremely disruptive.

When a company out-sources all data processing to a service bureau it may not need an EDP auditor. The terms service bureau and out-sourcing generally mean the same thing in this chapter. Therefore, the financial auditors need to review service-bureau-related activities. Even though the user company has no internal data processing department, many EDP-audit- and control-related concerns still exist.

Because of the high personnel cost needed to support data processing, many companies, regardless of size, are turning to out-sourcing all or part of their data processing activities. The auditor should ensure that a complete cost benefit evaluation is performed, covering at least five years. The initial costs of out-sourcing may initially be low, but they could escalate in later years, exceeding what in-house costs would have been. Data processing costs can increase as the servicee's business grows, or the servicee may need specialized processing for competitive advantage that the service bureau cannot provide.

Contract terms, financial stability, and processing control are the auditor's main service bureau concerns. Both the servicer and the servicee have specific responsibilities that maintain an efficient and effective business relationship. The servicee must be extremely careful with out-sourcing any data processing work, because it has relinquished control of a strategic business activity.

15.2 PLANNING AND PREPARATION

The number of out-sourcing providers is growing because companies are finding escalating data processing costs and management of such activities increasingly difficult to handle. The personnel costs and lack of availability of qualified personnel are forcing management to seek alternatives to in-house data processing.

A multitude of varying services exists in the marketplace. A company can use contract programmers to complete maintenance on all or some of their application programs. Many out-sourcing firms specialize in design, development, programming, and implementation of new systems. One or several applications may require significant enhancements that could be out-sourced to contract programmers or a system development contractor. Some companies are selling all of their computer hardware and buying computer time on a service bureau computer, while keeping all application maintenance responsibility. This frees up the capital used to purchase computer hardware. The most pervasive approach is to out-source the entire data processing function, eliminating the need for in-house hardware, software, and technical personnel.

Figure 15–1 lists some of the audit concerns with service bureaus and out-sourcing. Each of these areas of concern could have numerous audit issues for the EDP auditor to deal with. Such are the major risks and exposures of poor service, lost data and programs, inaccurate processing, overcharging, and improper management decisions. As the EDP auditor examines these areas of concern, more risks and exposures may be discovered that the EDP auditor would then need to address with review and testing (see Figure 15–2).

FIGURE 15-1   Audit Transactions

Audit Activity Code	Transaction/Area
A	Evaluation of alternative
B	Contract
C	Data
D	Programs
E	Backup and recovery
F	Service level
G	Contingency planning
H	Costs
I	Audit coverage

FIGURE 15-2   Scope Summary

Risks/Exposures

1. Poor service
2. Lost data and programs
3. Inaccurate processing
4. Overcharging
5. Improper management decisions

Control Objectives

Determines that procedures exist to ensure:

1. Accurate processing
2. Service levels comply with contract terms and meet the needs of the service
3. Adequate backup in case of a disaster or bankruptcy of the servicer
4. Payment of only authorized fees to the servicer
5. Sufficient information for management to make an informed decision

Key Controls

1. Monitoring of service levels
2. Daily settlements and data transmittal monitoring
3. Ownership and possession of data files and programs
4. Verification of fees
5. Adequate evaluation of alternative processing

Audit Objectives

Determine that adequate controls exist to ensure the servicer provides adequate service, continuation of processing, and adequate initial and ongoing evaluation

The control objectives—accurate processing, compliance with contract terms, adequate backup in case of disaster or servicer bankruptcy, payment of only authorized fees, and sufficient information for management to make informed decisions—are management's major concerns when dealing with a servicer. These control objectives have a one-for-one relationship with the key controls. The EDP auditor may find that other control objectives and key controls are necessary as he or she completes his or her work. The audit objectives used here are general, to permit the auditor to focus on specific company needs.

15.3   AUDIT CONCERNS

This chapter departs from the standard structure of the other chapters because there are so many possible variables. For example, the company may not out-source any data processing services at all. In addition, there are so many out-sourcing alternatives that assembling the audit programs in some rational order to cover all alternatives is more confusing than not. This chapter is designed to give the EDP auditor a structure around which to customize the preliminary review and the compliance testing procedures that will meet his or her needs. The EDP audit methodology described in Chapter 3 forms a foundation for this chapter that enables the auditor to customize particular audit programs.

15.3.1   Evaluating the Out-Sourcing Alternative

The auditor's objective is to make sure that a proper evaluation was performed that produced enough information for management to make proper decisions. This evaluation should take the form of the feasibility study that analyzes the costs and benefits of the alternatives, user requirements that specifically identify the user's needs, and a recommendation to management (see Chapter 17). The audit review elements should be used to evaluate the out-sourcing alternatives.

15.3.1.1   CRITERIA FOR CHANGE

The reasons for using the out-sourcing alternative are as numerous as there are companies, but the criteria and justification for using them must make logical business sense. The reasons for doing so include: cost reduction, continuity of processing, elimination of a management problem, unavailability of skilled technicians, and the fact that the current system can no longer service the company. Whatever the reason, the single most important criterion is to satisfy an unmet need.

15.3.1.2   SERVICER EVALUATION CRITERIA

Management must develop evaluation criteria that measures the quality of the service. Suggested criteria include: the servicer's financial stability, its reputation, flexibility, vis-à-vis specific needs, cost, advance planning and expansion flexibility, handling of ownership of data files and programs, its conversion plan, and its contingency plan. The importance of each of these criteria will depend upon management's focus—some may not be important at all. The auditor must determine which criteria are important to management (see Figure 15–3). Based on this determination, the auditor must judge whether the selected criteria are appropriate, and whether the evaluation properly addresses the criteria.

Financial Stability: This indicates the servicer's ability to remain in business and maintain its computer facilities well enough to provide proper service. Certified financial statements from a reputable outside accounting firm for the past three to five years will provide the basic information needed for such a management decision. The servicer's creditworthiness, however, is not usually indicated by financial statements. A servicer with marginal financial performance should be avoided, in particular for ongoing data processing service. This may not be of critical importance for contract programming or other short-term services and one-time deals.

FIGURE 15–3   **Audit Program**

Audit Objective

To determine the arrangements and relationship with a service bureau or out-sourcing alternative

Key Controls

1. Evaluation of alternatives
2. Contract with the servicer
3. Servicer security
4. Established procedures
5. Backup and recovery
6. Service, performance, and cost monitoring
7. Contingency planning
8. Audit coverage

Audit Procedures

1. Determine which criteria are important to management
2. Determine how each criteria is evaluated; verify that the evaluation of the criteria is adequate and accurate
3. Determine that the contract contains all necessary elements
4. Determine procedures for storage and control of backup files
5. Determine the extent of security necessary to protect customer privacy, competitive advantage, and proprietary information
6. Verify the adequacy of settlements and reconciliations of processing accuracy
7. Determine that adequate backup and recovery is provided for
8. Verify that performance and service levels are monitored
9. Determine the adequacy of the contingency plan
10. Determine fee-charging methodology and verify that services and costs are being monitored
11. Determine the quality of internal and external audit coverage

Although the external auditor's examination addresses the servicer's contingent liabilities and lawsuits, it is possible for such an auditor to be misled by erroneous management information. The loss of a significant lawsuit could bankrupt what appears to be a financial stable company.

Service Reputation: This involves several factors, such as processing turnaround time, responsiveness to changes, processing accuracy, and the level of internal control. Eager to get new business, the servicer may claim excellence in all categories, but in actual practice the quality may be less than the servicee desires. The best technique for checking reputation is that of talking with current and previous customers of the servicer. Talking to previous customers is vital, if for nothing else than to determine why they no longer use the servicer. A servicer will always provide lists of customers or contacts, but the true test comes from talking with customers who are no longer on the servicer-supplied list.

Processing turnaround time deals with the ability to meet daily deadlines, which is important because servicee employees need the computer output to perform their jobs. Late or absent output will reduce productivity. Responsiveness to change deals with the servicer's quality and speed in servicing a request for change in processing schedules, requirements, and reports. Processing accuracy focuses on the consistent correctness of the daily service. The level of internal control can indicate the servicer's commitment to quality. This can be determined by reviewing the internal control letter from an external auditor of the servicer and interviews of the servicer's internal auditor, if one exists.

Flexibility of Offering: This involves the type of service that the out-sourcing company is willing to provide the servicee. If the servicee is seeking programming assistance, there is no need to talk to a servicer that only offers computer processing services. A more subtle variation involves the ownership of programs. The servicee may want to retain maintenance and support of application programs, but just rent computer hardware and operating system time. A computer processor servicer may not want to relinquish control over programs. If this is the case, there is no need to consider this servicer. In another example, the servicee may want on-line processing, but the servicer may not be willing to "gear up" to meet that need. The formal evaluation should only include servicers that provide the needed service.

Satisfaction of Company Needs: This is closely related to flexibility of offering, but it is different in that it involves the specifics of the required service. For example, the servicer may provide a specific application, but the servicer's standard reports do not provide all the information needed by the servicee. Or, the servicer's input requirements and processing scheme would force the servicee to completely change all manual procedures. This boils down to whether or not the servicer uses a general purpose program for all its customers or provides custom processing for each.

Costs: The cost of the service is obviously an extremely important element because it affects servicee net income and forms the basis for comparison to existing data processing costs. The most important cost elements are the escalation clauses that increase the cost from year to year, and the servicer's charging methodology. If the servicer charges on a fixed-cost basis, then future costs are more predictable, but if the basis is variable— based on transaction volume—then management must ensure that future estimates of volume are accurate. If the servicee's business grows beyond expectations, management could be faced with excessive increases in EDP costs. These may exceed what in-house costs would have been.

Advance Planning and Expansion Flexibility: This involves the computer processing servicer's ability to meet the servicee's future needs. If the servicer's planning is haphazard, or its technology is not in state-of-the-art condition, the servicee could be faced with a resource crisis in the future. Servicers that use old technology may prevent the servicee from easily moving its processing to another out-source provider.

Ownership of Data Files and Programs: This can be tricky, because although the data obviously belongs to the servicee, the programs could belong to either party. Program ownership relates to the flexibility of the service offering. A key point here is not just ownership, but also possession of data files and programs. If the servicee receives copies of data files daily, and copies of programs as they are changed, then the servicee has the flexibility to switch to another out-source provider. This should be verified.

A major exposure here can be servicer bankruptcy, which can result in a lockup of its facilities. In such a case, the servicee may only be able to obtain possession of the data files through a court action, which may take three to six weeks. Companies cannot run for three days without daily computer processing, much less three weeks.

Conversion Time: This is important because the servicee may have an immediate resource crisis, such as imminent conversion (moving all data from one system to another), to continue processing. The servicer offering extended conversion times should be eliminated from consideration, if time is apt to be critical.

Contingency Plan: This provides for continuity of processing. A servicer without a viable contingency plan and a sound methodology for routine updating and testing of the plan should be avoided. To determine the adequacy of the evaluation, the auditor should interview the knowledgeable parties and review the contract (see Figure 15–3).

15.3.2   Contract with the Servicer

The necessary elements of the contract with the servicer should be addressed. The contract is the most important element in controlling and managing the servicer, providing that it contains the means to accomplish control. Generally speaking, there is no standard contract for out-sourcing because the needs of each company differ. The auditor should determine, through interviews with management and users, the contract elements necessary for the company's best interest. The key thing to remember is that when a company switches to a servicer for all data processing needs, there will be nothing to fall back on—internal data processing support will have been eliminated. Some of the contract elements deserving auditor consideration are discussed below.

The procedures describing the deadlines for completion of the daily procedures and how the processing work will be completed should be explained, insofar as who will perform specific procedures (the servicer or the servicee). For example, if the servicee needs all daily computer reports by 8 A.M. to keep its people working, then the 8 A.M. deadline should be specified in the contract, with penalties for missing the deadlines. Another potential question is, who will reconcile and settle transaction processing to ensure that all transactions received were processed? Processing accuracy and completeness verification is the servicee's responsibility, but control over data transmittal to the servicer could be placed in either party's hands.

When a servicer is responsible for the processing of one or all applications, it has an implied responsibility for maintaining backups of programs and data, and for the recovery of the application processing in the event of failure or disaster. Even though these responsibilities are implied, however, the servicee should not rely on blind faith. The responsibility for creating backups of data and program files must be specified in the contract in terms of what should be copied and how frequently. The recovery aspects should be explained, identifying the specific responsibilities of the servicer and if the service participates.

Combined with the concern for backup and recovery are the issues of legal ownership and actual physical possession of data files and programs. The programs may belong to either party depending on the needs of the servicee. Some companies retain the application maintenance responsibilities but just rent computer time, making the servicee the owner of the programs. The servicee definitely owns the data, but the key issue is who has possession of the data and program files. Obviously the servicer needs possession to accomplish processing, but who has possession of the backup copies? If a servicer were to go bankrupt and its facility was locked up, the servicee could only gain access to its own data and programs through a court action during which time the servicee could be driven out of business. The contract could specify that backup copies of current data and programs are shipped or transmitted to the servicee daily, giving the servicee the flexibility to move to another service provider.

The data and programs of any given servicee could contain proprietary or secret information. The contract should explain the security and protection measures required of the servicer, with penalties for violation.

Performance parameters are another consideration worth EDP audit focus. The contract could specify specific up-time and on-line response time parameters, with penalties for noncompliance.

Some service providers charge one fee for 90-percent availability and up-time, a higher fee for 95 percent, and a still higher fee for 98 percent availability and up-time. With this arrangement the servicee will need to monitor the servicer's actual performance to ensure the accuracy of servicer's billing. The servicee should also consider requiring penalties for substandard performance levels, for example, availability and up-time that is less than 80 percent.

The most obvious contract element is the cost of the service. This can vary with each company's needs, and with the type and quantity of processing needed. The servicee auditor's key concern is that someone in his or her company is monitoring the actual basis for servicer charging and verifies that the servicer's bill is accurate.

The contract must define the parameters for termination of the relationship by either party. If the servicee is relying on the service provider for application processing, then the servicee would require at least six months' notice to provide for an alternative. It is not a simple task to just pick up and move application processing from one servicer to another. Because the termination of the relationship can detrimentally affect the servicee's continuity of processing, stringent penalties for noncompliance with these contract terms should be considered.

Auditors are not attorneys, and the converse is also true—the auditor should ensure that a knowledgeable attorney has reviewed the contract to identify the responsibilities of both parties and any legal traps that may exist.

15.3.3   Servicee Data

The servicee definitely owns the data because the company's business generates it; however, as mentioned previously, possession of the data files permits the servicee to move easily to another service provider and protects the servicee from loss of data. In addition, possession of backup files by the servicee serves as an off-site storage location for the servicer. If the servicee has possession of backup files then procedures for storage and control of backup files must be reviewed by the auditor.

These procedures and controls are similar to those discussed in Chapter 7 regarding the data library. If the servicee receives copies of the backup files, then it needs to provide secure storage, environmental control, and inventory control in order to know what files need to be shipped back to the servicer on a daily basis. The rotation of these files will most likely follow the rules for generation data sets.

The auditor is required to determine the needs for customer privacy, competitive advantage, and proprietary information. As stated, the contract should specify that the servicer must protect these elements. The auditor may want to determine, through conversations with the servicer, the actual extent of security measures taken to protect the servicee's data.

15.3.4   Computer Programs

The concerns for ownership and possession of computer programs are identical to those described in the servicee data section with one difference—when the servicee maintains the application maintenance responsibility. If the servicee has possession of programs that the servicer makes routine changes to, then the servicee must have procedures for storage and control of these program files, as stated in the servicee data section.

The servicer could have responsibility for application maintenance of the programs and still grant the servicee ownership rights to those programs, which would protect the servicee in the event of losing the service provider.

If the auditor has the opportunity to review the program change control environment of the service provider, he or she can use the audit programs provided in Chapter 10.

15.3.5   Processing Accuracy

In most cases, even though the servicer may have responsibility for reconciliation and settlement of daily transaction processing, the servicee must perform reconciliations and settlements to verify the accuracy of daily processing.

Because the daily transactions occur under the control of the servicee, procedures must exist for manual or automated transmittal of data to the servicer computer center. Logs of the data that have been sent must be maintained and compared to what was received by the servicer. The controls and audit procedures over data transmittal are essentially the same as those regarding data transmittal to the data preparation area or to the computer center (see Chapter 12). These audit procedures can be used to verify the adequacy of data transmittal procedures.

15.3.6   Backup and Recovery

The auditor must examine the provisions for backup and recovery executed by the service provider. Even though the contract may specify all necessary provisions, it is important for the auditor to determine actual practices. This can be done via discussion with service bureau management or its auditor, and by requesting permission to observe a test of application or system recovery. This is not an unrealistic request and will provide the servicee auditor with an additional level of comfort.

15.3.7   Service Level

Making sure that performance and service levels are monitored focuses on procedures performed by the servicee. This is important because the performance and service levels may relate to how fees are charged by the service provider. It is also critical to accomplishing the company's objectives.

A group or person in the servicee company should monitor the level of user satisfaction with the service being provided, and how the service level affects the users' goals and objectives in accomplishing both the short- and long-range objectives. This monitoring will also provide a means for the servicee to detect changing needs of the organization in time to provide for additional service.

15.3.8   Contingency Planning

A service provider without a documented and tested contingency plan should be avoided. The auditor should evaluate the contingency plan at the service bureau and in his or her own company. The service bureau must have processing alternatives, if nothing other than a backup service bureau that can handle the systems (see Chapter 8).

The servicee must protect itself against potential disaster, and against the bankruptcy of the service provider. The servicee should identify and have standby agreements with another, backup service provider. The company's primary service provider could, after all, go bankrupt or simply go out of business, as well as possibly being destroyed by fire or other disaster. These contingency considerations are a primary reason for maintaining possession of backup data and program files.

15.3.9   Costs

There are two elements of out-sourcing cost: 1) the methodology used by the service bureau to charge fees, and 2) the extent of monitoring and verification of the fees charged (see Figure 15–3).

Fees can be structured based on fixed or variable rates. Variable rate charging can relate to transaction volume, number of programs executed, or number of additional reports required by the servicee. These must be watched closely by the servicee, who should have a person or group that logs the number of variable items and verifies those items to the bill when it arrives from the servicer.

The servicee must watch for escalation clauses that increase the fees based on some inflation rate increase over a period of time. Price escalation can increase the cost of the service to the point at which the service provider is charging more than it would cost to process the data in-house. The only effective time to limit or negate an escalation clause is during contract negotiations. Price escalation, variable cost items, increases in volume, and requests for special processing must be estimated for at least three to five years from the contract date. It is imperative to perform a feasibility study of the out-sourcing alternative at each contract negotiation date.

Numerous factors affect the way a company does business which, in turn, affect the data processing services needed. Application programs need maintenance to permit the servicee to keep pace with the economy, its customers, and regulatory requirements. The servicee will have to pay the service provider to do this if the programs are owned by the servicer. This may be done under a separate contract or under the existing contract. Either way, these maintenance costs need to be monitored very closely.

Program maintenance for a single application or all applications could be out-sourced by a company whose processing is performed in-house. This is commonly known as contract programming, which consists of at least two types: 1) Contract programmers are hired and managed by in-house managers, or 2) the maintenance is out-sourced to a company that manages a group of programmers. In either case, the requirements of the work to be done, agreement on the end product, delivery date, and costs must be established in the contract. The servicee must monitor the services performed closely to ensure that the fees charged are accurate.

A data processing service provider will typically offer specific reports for each application. However, the servicee will frequently want special reports on either a one-time, or only periodic, basis. The servicer provider charges extra for these special reports, so the servicee must ensure that the reports are received, that they are accurate, and that the charge is fair.

15.3.10   Audit Coverage

Procedure 11 in Figure 15–3 involves interviewing the external and internal auditors of the service provider. If a servicer internal audit staff exists, the servicee auditor can interview the service provider's auditor, and most likely be granted an opportunity to review audit workpapers. Although all areas of the servicer provider's are important, the servicee auditor should focus on the audits that cover the procedures that protect the servicee's business. Specifically, these are the data library, data center review, and application program maintenance, if the servicer is providing maintenance (see Chapters 7, 8, and 10).

The contract should include the delivery of an internal control letter prepared by an external audit firm and a right-to-audit clause for the servicee's protection. A blanket right-to-audit clause is preferred, but anything is better than nothing. This clause gives the servicee the opportunity to send its own audit team into the servicer's installation and conduct reviews as the team sees fit to protect its company's interest.

Although financial statements prepared by the external audit firm provide reassurance and information about the service provider's financial stability, such certified financial statements do not provide enough information about the servicer's internal control system to rely on. Without an internal audit staff or right-to-audit by servicee auditors clause, a SAS No. 44 report is the only audit product that can provide reasonable assurance about the servicer's internal control system.

Compliance with SAS No. 44[1] requires that numerous criteria be met; the most significant of these for the servicee are the system description of application programs and controls, the opinion on the adequacy of those controls, and comments and recommendations on internal control weaknesses that exist within the service bureau. These three elements permit the servicee auditor to get an adequate picture of the condition of the internal control system at a service bureau.

15.3.11   Conclusion

The foregoing discussion gives the servicee auditor enough information to begin customizing an audit program of service bureaus and out-sourcing alternatives. If the opportunity arises for the servicee auditor to evaluate service bureau processing, various chapters in this book can be used to customize the necessary audit programs to audit all aspects of the service bureau.

NOTES

1. The AICPA's Statements on Auditing Standards No. 30 and No. 44 govern the external auditor's review of internal control and his or her report thereon. This is over and above audit standards for financial statement audits because it is considered a "special" report.

16

On-Line
Transaction Systems[1]

16.1   INTRODUCTION

The audit of on-line transaction processing appears deceptively simple and short. Actually it covers the review and testing requirements for a part of an application system. The auditor has two primary concerns with the on-line transaction systems: 1) the security of the on-line terminals or microcomputers, and 2) the accuracy of application processing.

Limitation of physical access to a terminal is primarily a fraud, theft, and sabotage control. Physical controls serve by further frustrating the would-be hacker. Logical (on-line) controls prevent and detect unauthorized access by anyone—inside or outside the company.

Unauthorized transactions can be effected by using an existing terminal or hard-wire tapping into the network with another terminal. Physical security can control a hard-wired tap into a cable, but preventing a tap by other means, such as a dial-up terminal, requires logical access control.

The supervisor of the terminal area should be assigned the responsibility for its physical security—this should be included in his or her job description. Equipment sabotage is prevented by good physical security (damage to one area's terminals should not threaten the entire on-line system). A key ingredient for effective physical security is a realization among the employees that physical security does, in fact, exist (see Chapter 9).

Although auditors are ever mindful of the potential for fraud, the fact remains that the largest dollar loss can be caused by input and processing errors and omissions. This is the focus of this type of audit and it should be used in conjunction with the application audit (see Chapter 12).

16.2   PLANNING AND PREPARATION

On-line transaction systems have melded the application control phases of transaction origination, data preparation, data input, and processing into one phase performed at electronic speed. The traditional control—segregating these phases even with on-line systems—is, however, still recommended. In daily life, these phases appear as one—as with an airline ticket computer system, a retail store computer system, and a 24-hour teller machine, to name a few. The phases are not segregated in these situations.

There is one key difference between these examples and the on-line system that requires segregation, however—direct contact with the customer. That is, the customer is part of the control system in helping to authorize the transaction.

Transactions generated within a company without direct customer contact need segregation, even though a customer may have called or written a letter to originate the transactions.

When a customer is physically present, he or she is part of the control, but if not physically present, the company cannot and should not rely only on customer contact as a control.

16.2.1   Identification of Transactions

The controls over the accuracy of data entered into the system center around reconciliations, settlements, programmatic edits, and input-output verification. Operator training and documentation, which are necessary to reduce the risk of errors and omissions, must also be reviewed—operator training is frequently overlooked by auditors (see Figure 16–1).

FIGURE 16–1   Identification of Audit Transactions

Audit Activity Code	Transaction/Area	Include Exclude	Reason
A	Data Input	I	Satisfies Audit Objective 1
B	Processing Accuracy	I	Satisfies Audit Objective 1
C	Operator Training	I	Satisfies Audit Objective 2
D	Documentation	I	Satisfies Audit Objective 3

16.2.2 Risks and Exposures

Unauthorized transactions, input errors and omissions, hardware damage, inaccurate processing, erroneous output, and computer abuse or fraud relate to the on-line entry and processing of data portions of the application system. Hardware damage can be reduced by physical access controls. Computer abuse deals with input of unauthorized transactions and is partially controlled by the logical access controls. These various risks are dealt with via personnel, training, and repair controls (see Figure 16–2).

16.2.3 Control Objectives

Management's concerns with on-line processing are largely a part of the application processing control concern. Ensuring that processing accuracy is verified daily relates specifically to the on-line application system (see Chapter 12). The other control objectives—restricted access to terminals, monitored terminal activity, current, complete system user documentation, and verified operator excellence—are directly related to on-line terminal input.

16.2.4 Audit Objectives

The audit objectives again relate to on-line terminal input and become part of the application audit objectives. The audit time budget for the preliminary review transactions are estimates of the amount of time needed to review and document the functions performed via on-line terminals or microcomputers in entering transactions (see Figure 16–2).

16.3 EXECUTION OF PRELIMINARY REVIEW

The execution of the preliminary review involves data input, processing accuracy, operator training, and documentation.

FIGURE 16–2   Scope Summary

Risks/Exposures

1. Unauthorized transactions
2. Input errors and omissions
3. Hardware damage
4. Inaccurate processing
5. Erroneous output
6. Computer abuse/fraud

Control Objectives

Ensure that:

1. Access to the terminal area is restricted
2. Terminal activity must be reported and monitored
3. System and user documentation is current and complete
4. Processing accuracy is verified on a daily basis
5. Terminal operators possess adequate expertise to operate terminals

Key Controls

1. Physical access is restricted and monitored
2. Restart-and-recovery procedures
3. Reconcilements, batch controls, control totals
4. Operator training and documentation

Audit Objectives

Determine that adequate controls exist to:

1. Promote accuracy, efficiency and effectiveness
2. Ensure that terminal operators possess an adequate level of expertise in operating the terminals
3. Keep documentation current

Preliminary Review

Activity Code	Transaction/Area	Budget Hours	
		Audit Time	Review Time
A	Data input	10	2
B	Processing accuracy	10	1
C	Operator training	8	1
D	Documentation	10	1

16.3.1 Data Input

Data errors and omissions can be extremely costly in terms of program reruns, extensive research to correct errors, and loss of customer goodwill. Data input and processing accuracy functions reduce the risks that data errors and omissions will have a significant effect on business.

Figure 16–3 generally describes the steps to evaluate the terminal data entry function. The entry functions should be designed to promote data accuracy, operator efficiency, and functional effectiveness. To check for this, make sure that the system: prompts the operator for the next input item, uses formatted input screens, supplies standard information, uses menu screens, uses a limited number of passwords, and uses display features that reduce fatigue. System prompting leads the operator to the next input item. The on-line system should use formatted input screens to eliminate operator guesswork about field data. The formatted screens should tell the operator about the field size, data type, and field contents. All transaction standard information should be precoded on the screen or supplied by the system; repetitive input of standard data is redundant and time consuming. Menu screens lead the operator and dramatically improve operator efficiency because this way the operator does not have to remember all system functions. The greater the reliance upon the operator's memory the longer the learning curve. Many of the current microcomputer packages use menu screens, increasing "user-friendliness" and reducing the amount of time needed to learn the system.

The on-line system should rely on as few passwords as possible. Some on-line systems rely on a different password for each transaction forcing the operators to write them on paper, which threatens the integrity of access control. Multiple passwords also increase the number of keystrokes for each transaction, increasing the potential data error factor.

Operator fatigue increases error rates and can be reduced by designing system displays and the work environment to limit fatigue. Long work sessions encourage eye fatigue and can be

FIGURE 16–3   Data Input

Audit Test Objective

To determine that terminal data entry functions are designed to promote accuracy, efficiency, and effectiveness

Key Controls

1. Prompting of the operator
2. Formatted screens
3. On-line help screens
4. Front-end data edits

Scope

All data entry terminals in the installation

Audit Procedures

Preliminary Review

1. Select a sample of terminals throughout the installation. Observe operators during data input to determine that the system:
   a. Prompts the operator for next input item
   b. Uses formatted input screens
   c. Supplies standard information
   d. Uses menu screens
   e. Uses a limited number of passwords
   f. Uses display features that reduce fatigue
2. Review a sample of programs and their documentation and develop tests to determine that:
   a. The on-line entry programs validate critical fields
   b. Determine the input fields that have required edits
   c. The operator is informed by the system of failed validation checks
   d. The system provides error correction and resubmission functions for the correction of data
   e. The system provides the operator access to on-line help screens

Compliance Testing

Verify that:

1. Required edits exist in the programs, that they work properly, and that all edits needed are installed
2. Resubmitted data is edited the same as original input and is processed properly

reduced by frequent breaks, using large print on the screens, flashing fields, or different colors. Erroneous data should be displayed in flashing fields or in a color different from the rest of the display.

Reviewing a sample of the programs and their documentation deals with editing performed by the application input programs that screen out errors and omitted data. Most organizations cannot afford to edit every field, so installation management must decide which data fields are critical and perform edits on the entered data for those fields. The system accepts accurate data or rejects erroneous data, sending an error message back to the operator who can correct and resubmit it.

Computer files are made up of records that consist of fields. The fields are comprised of individual characters. Field checks can be performed independent of data in other fields, including such edits as check digit routines, tests for missing data, range, and field size. Record checks depend on data in other fields within the file and include edits for reasonableness, validity of sign, data type, and field size. Batch checks include edits for transaction type, sequence, item counts, and dollar control totals (these edits are covered in more detail in Chapters 11 and 12 on application audit).

The system should inform the operator of data errors found by the validation routines using a message code or explanation and showing the erroneous data highlighted. Obviously, the system should reject the invalid data and ask the operator for reinput. The system should validate the corrected data with the same edit checks as the original data. Some systems read the data in the record until the first error is found, leaving some of the data unedited. If the system does not edit all of the data again, some data will enter the system unchecked, increasing the likelihood of errors. Operator efficiency can be improved by on-line help screens, which explain the use of transaction codes and provide explanations of error messages.

Prompting of the operator, formatted screens, and help screens can help the operator, but they also increase the risk of successful unauthorized access.

16.3.2 Processing Accuracy

Processing accuracy must be verified at least daily by reconcilement of processing results to an independent control source. The key concern is the transaction effect on the master file records.

The audit of an on-line transaction system is geared primarily to the review of data edits, the system response to data errors

FIGURE 16–4 Processing Accuracy

Audit Test Objective

To determine that procedures exist to verify processing accuracy

Key Controls

1. Daily reconcilements
2. Settlement to general ledger
3. Informative application reports
4. Programmatic data edit routines
5. Control totals and batching

Scope

All settlements performed for all on-line applications in the installation during the audit period

Audit Procedures

Preliminary Review

Determine:

1. The error edit override features
2. The item count and dollar control totals used to balance input transactions
3. The programmatic procedures to detect out-of-balance conditions between dollar control totals and accumulated input transaction totals

Compliance Testing

1. Select a sample of work days during the audit period—for the applications and work days selected, verify that:
    a. Reconcilements are properly performed on a daily basis
    b. Total transaction dollar amounts processed by the on-line system are settled to general ledger or other independent control on a daily basis
    c. Reports are generated detailing transactions processed and appropriate control totals
2. Adequacy and accuracy of output screens

---

found by the edits, and the settlement of daily transaction processing. The on-line application program's ability to permit a terminal operator to override a programmatic edit is of critical importance. The auditor should determine what edit override features exist in the on-line application programs through discussions with the programmer, review of program documentation, and review of program code, (see Figure 16–4). Some on-line applications are designed to accumulate item counts of transactions and dollar control totals for execution of programmatic balancing procedures (see Section 16.4.2). The auditor must also determine how the user or the system accomplishes the control over processing accuracy and completeness.

16.3.3 Operator Training

The auditor must determine whether the auditee is using structured training or relying on supervisors or other experienced personnel to train its people. If the auditor discovers that structured training is used, then the compliance testing procedures should be completed. The auditor can complete the preliminary review by determining exactly how new employees are trained in terminal use and how effective that training is (see Figure 16–5).

16.3.4 Documentation

Documentation can be the most neglected element of any system simply because of the extra time and energy needed to create it. The motivation is to implement a workable system and maintain it. Many companies don't realize the time savings afforded by good documentation because it is difficult to quantify. The documentation must be sufficient to permit diagnosis and correction of system problems.

The user saves tremendous time with good operating procedures, especially when new personnel are learning the system. Poor documentation will force an experienced employee into babysitting the trainee at the high cost of lowered productivity.

The preliminary review procedure in Figure 16–6 directs the auditor to simply determine the documentation required by management standards and locate the documentation that does

FIGURE 16–5 **Operator Training**

Audit Test Objective

Deter.nine that terminal operators are adequately trained and have achieved an adequate level of expertise

Key Controls

1. Specific job descriptions
2. Formalized training of terminal operation
3. Computer-aided instructions
4. Terminal operations manuals

Scope

All operators in the installation

Audit Procedures

Preliminary Review

Determine:

1. Whether the audit area relies on experienced personnel to train new people or uses structured training

Compliance Testing

1. Using the a sample of operators, determine that they are properly trained
   a. Evaluate training by attending a class and reviewing course content
   b. Determine relevance and applicability of training material by comparing it to actual usage
   c. Determine whether the training classes use actual terminal usage

indeed exist. Implied in this procedure is the auditor's responsibility to determine the adequacy of the documentation, whether it is available to the terminal users, and if the documentation is of any true benefit to the terminal users. The typical weaknesses in documentation are explanatory procedures prepared once and then never updated. In addition, the documentation may not be readily available to the operators, or it may be written in such a complicated form that the terminal users do not use it.

16.4 COMPLIANCE TESTING

The compliance testing primarily focuses on the programmatic edits and programmatic balancing performed by the on-line

FIGURE 16–6   Documentation

Audit Test Objective

To determine that the system and user documentation is adequate and kept current

Key Controls

1. Documentation is a key control

Scope

Systems manual, users manual, and data center run manual

Audit Procedures

Preliminary Review

1. Determine the documentation required by standards and locate the documentation that exists

Compliance Testing

Verify:

1. The terminal users manual explains:
    a. On-line access security procedures
    b. Obtaining forgotten or expired password
    c. Usage of all transactions
    d. Terminal operator responsibilities and procedures of restart and recovery
2. The on-line system manual explains:
    a. The configuration of on-line hardware components
    b. On-line software type and function
3. The data center run manual is adequate

application. Manual edits and balancing procedures performed by the auditee are covered either in the application audit or the financial audit of the area.

16.4.1   Data Input

Some programmatic edits will undoubtedly have been designed into the system, and these should be tested to determine that they work according to specifications. Moreover, the auditor must judge whether other programmatic edits are needed. This can be accomplished by reviewing the fields entered by each transaction and judging whether or not the data is critical enough to need additional programmatic edits. The criteria for required edits is the importance of the data to the company's business activities, to customer service, or regulatory reporting. The cost of additional edits must be balanced against the benefit derived from reduced errors and omissions.

Making sure resubmitted data is correct and processed properly is also important. The auditor must be careful to determine how the programmatic edit function works. For example, if an error is detected by the system and returns an error message to the operator, then the operator is given the opportunity to correct the data and enter the transaction again. The auditor's major concern is whether the resubmitted transaction is edited again according to the same edit criteria as the first transaction.

The concern is that erroneous data can enter the system if flawed editing occurs. Some systems may be designed to edit each field in the transaction until an error is detected. Upon detection, an error message is returned to the operator, who then corrects and resubmits the transaction. If the resubmitted transaction is not edited according to the original criteria, the fields in the transaction that followed the field originally in error will not be edited at all, thus permitting erroneous data to enter the system.

16.4.2 Processing Accuracy

The audit of processing accuracy verification falls within the EDP application audit scope. It also falls within the audit of an on-line transaction system. Auditing processing accuracy should not be performed if a limited review of the on-line system, the "audit of on-line security," is done. Processing accuracy does not fall within the scope of that audit. In any event, the audit of processing accuracy needs only to be performed once per audit cycle, either in the individual audits of the various application or when performing an audit of "on-line transaction systems." Another good time to review processing accuracy in the on-line audit occurs when settlement is done as a part of the on-line data entry function. For example, a credit-card-processing system utilizes on-line batch proofs in a memo-posting system combined with on-line realtime update of the master file. Transactions are batched and given to operators for keying. The batch total is entered first with a special transaction code. The dollar amount of each entered transaction is accumulated and compared to the batch total at the end of the batch by an on-line zero proofing technique. The on-line application programs prevent operator release of the transaction to on-line master file update until the transaction totals equal the batch total. Only the supervisor's entry of his or her sign-on key and a special transaction code can override this proof control. If overridden, the batch is placed on a separate file for later research and resolution.

The daily reconcilements must be reviewed. Input dollar control totals and item counts should be prepared for all transactions processed. This is more easily done for batches of transactions, or all transactions at a local branch, or some other natural grouping. These can be generated manually or by an on-line input program that is separate from the programs that update the transactions to the master file.

The system or user should balance the number and dollar amount of records on the opening of the master file, with the changes made during the day to the closing balance. The system can use master file control records to balance the posting of the day's transactions.

Testing focuses on output control totals, and item counts of all transactions processed should be generated by the application or on-line programs. The input control totals and item counts are reconciled to the output control totals and item counts, which proves that all transactions were posted to the master file in the correct amounts. It does not prove that they were posted to the correct accounts.

Rejected or unposted items are transactions that could not be posted to the master file; unless they are caught in some way by the on-line system or through reconcilement, they will literally disappear. Rejected items, under the right circumstances, can provide a means to embezzle money from the system. Therefore, rejected items must be tightly monitored and controlled, and quickly resolved. Rejected items should be identified in specific detail either in the on-line system or externally by some other manual or automated means. Daily control totals should be developed for rejects because this total is needed to fully reconcile the processing for a day. A person or group of people should be held accountable for immediately researching, correcting, and reentering these items into the system.

The settlement of the on-line or application processing to general ledger must also be dealt with. What is the difference between a reconcilement and a settlement?—These terms are often used interchangeably, but for the purpose of these procedures, a reconcilement is the comparison of two independently generated dollar totals to prove the processing accuracy of the application or on-line system. A settlement is comparing the dollars processed by the on-line system to the dollars posted to general ledger for the on-line system.

The general ledger should receive dollar control totals from a source other than the application or on-line processing group, say, a branch, an office, a department, or some other grouping. This independent verification provides a second external check on processing accuracy. Ideally the on-line processing should compare to the general ledger exactly, but, unfortunately, this is not always the case. Unreconcilable differences will occur that show that the transactions were not processed in the same way by the on-line system. These differences also provide a means for embezzlement, so they should be identified in detail with the daily dollar control totals generated. They should be researched and resolved quickly, within three days. Proper agreement or settlement to the general ledger is absolutely vital because the general ledger represents the company's financial statements.

16.4.3 Operator Training

Better-trained operators make fewer input errors. This is enabled by having their jobs clearly defined and providing them with formal training.

Elaborate examples are on-line systems programmed with training courses and achievement tests. The operator is only given authorization by the on-line system to use a particular transaction when he successfully completes the training course and passes the achievement test. Obviously, the cost of such a system would be very high, but that can be justified.

The training should include a review of the terminal operator's manual, a "walk through" of the transactions he or she will use, and hands-on usage of a test terminal. Operator training is often overlooked by management and the auditor, but increased productivity can be gained with even rudimentary training. Operator inexperience causes errors and omissions, reducing productivity. Companies tend to rely on experienced personnel (who already have their own jobs to perform new employes to train). In this situation, the absence of formal operator training reduces the productivity of both trainer and trainee. Productivity can be reduced by yet another factor—inadequate documentation. It is impossible to quantify the extent of reduced productivity for every installation, but the auditor can examine these elements and subjectively determine the extent of reduced productivity.

The auditor can evaluate training by attending a class, reviewing the course content, and compare learned information against actual terminal usage. The auditor should determine the relevance and applicability of the training material. The key training element for the new terminal operator is actual terminal usage, which is what develops self-confidence.

16.4.4 Documentation

Documentation is a valuable training aid for new employees, providing them with their own reference for answering questions instead of relying solely on experienced personnel who have other work to complete.

The terminal operator's manual should cover seven groups of activities: 1) terminal usage, 2) password maintenance, 3) transaction usage, 4) monetary balancing, 5) output handling, 6) error processing, and 7) restart-and-recovery.

Detailed explanations should be provided for the following: 1) signing on and signing off the system—the data required and the screen format, 2) the period of time allowed for automatic sign-off of an inactive user by the system, 3) the rules for not leaving an active terminal unattended, 4) explicit instructions on how to change a password, how often it changes, and what to do if a password is forgotten, 5) how to use transactions assigned to the area or terminal that the operator is assigned to, examples of input formats, data content of the transaction, output screen examples with field definitions, the definitions of error messages and their associated corrective procedures, and 6) the procedures for restarting the terminal and recovering lost data.

The adequacy of an on-line application system manual used by programmers to support the user and identify and correct processing problems must be reviewed. This manual should include: 1) system and program flowcharts, 2) a description of the on-line system configuration, 3) computer setup and data center operator instructions, 4) file layouts, 5) tape library procedures, 6) programmatic controls, 7) explanations of reports and screens, 8) transaction code definitions, and 9) restart-and-recovery procedures.

The system and program flowcharts explain the overall functions of the system and of the individual programs; they also identify all of the application programs. The system configuration describes the network hardware components, on-line software, and type. The operator procedures explain the execution and support instructions for data center computer operators to follow. These are vital to consistent and accurate execution of the programs (see Chapter 8). File layouts are the descriptions and name of each field in a file, its start position, size, and data type. These are necessary to write program code to access the fields on a file. The tape library procedures are vital to data library operations (see Chapter 7). These specify what files are generated, when, and by what programs. They are necessary to provide file backup. The programmatic controls are the data edits and balancing techniques used by the programs to detect input errors and out-of-balance conditions. Explanations of reports and screens describe the fields and their position on computer-printed reports or terminal screens. The transaction code definitions describe all of the batch or on-line code identifiers to specify processing for a given transaction. Restart-and-recovery procedures explain how to recover partially processed files to avoid completer reruns and provide the procedures for the computer operator to follow to restart the programs.

The data center run manuals, which explain the system support requirements necessary to keep the on-line system running, must also be reviewed. These should include explanations of: system startup, terminal backup assignments, error and system message explanations, system shutdown procedures, job and system status reporting, console and error message instructions, checkpoint and restart-and-recovery instructions, and job setup instructions.

16.5   CONCLUSION

The audit of on-line transaction processing deals with the hands on, day-to-day tasks and utilities that make business, and the part EDP auditing plays in business, keep on going. The details and specifics provided above should enable orderly and successful on-line transaction processing audits.

NOTES

1. Mullen,   Jack B. "Auditing Online Terminal Security." Adapted from *EDP Auditing* (New York: Auerbach Publishers). © 1990, Warren, Gorham & Lamont, Inc. Used with permission.

Auditing Systems in Development

17.1 INTRODUCTION[1]

Auditing computer systems while they are in development involves two elements: 1) evaluation of compliance with the administrative procedures and guidelines in each phase of the development process, and 2) an analysis of the internal controls programmed into the system and the manual controls executed by the user area. The system development audit approach described here applies to all systems purchased as complete packages or developed by the company's programming staff.

New computer systems can be implemented either by purchasing a software package that meets the company's requirements, by modifying a purchased package to meet the company's needs, or by in-house design and programming. Whatever the method, project administration activities should be consistent for each project. The installation should have documented guidelines standardizing requirements in each phase of development. System development guidelines should cover the administrative tasks that must be performed, including:

- Defining the job,
- Organizing and staffing,
- Time and cost estimating,
- Breaking down and assigning job steps,
- Procedures for implementing necessary changes,

- Criteria for acceptance, and
- Minimum standards for communication.

These guidelines, in turn, provide each project leader with standard development and reporting conventions. Thus, the manager of several projects can evaluate the performance of the project leaders by concentrating on the progress of major events.

Each phase, from proposal to implementation, requires that specific facts be gathered and built upon as each step gives way to the next. System development administrative controls ensure that these facts are gathered, documented, and that all required tasks are completed.

The greatest difficulty is with in-house designed systems. The auditor is reviewing a system that does not exist—there is no evidential matter produced by the system on which to perform compliance testing.

Therefore, the system development control review requires the auditor's judgment to ascertain how, when, and why to react to apparent problems. The timing of reporting exceptions is highly critical, because the circumstances of an exception could change quickly. The auditor must immediately research a problem and bring it to management's attention. Less time is required to correct problems early in the system development life cycle than during a later phase.

The development process should be planned and organized to progress in phases with appropriate checkpoints for management review and sign-off. This provides management with the opportunity to stop a project that may prove to be inadequate.

17.2   EXECUTION OF AUDIT EVALUATION

The phases of development in an in-house design include: feasibility study, user requirements, general design, detailed design, program specifications, programming, program testing, system testing, conversion, and maintenance.

The phases of development for a purchased package include; feasibility, user requirements, general design, package evaluation, package acceptance testing, package modifications (optional), program specifications (for modifications), programming (for modifications), program testing (for modifications), system testing, conversion, and maintenance.

Audit concerns are described in the following sections that cover the administrative requirements and the phases of the Systems Development Life Cycle (SDLC). These audit concerns can also be used to evaluate the system development guidelines (see Chapter 6).

17.2.1 Justification Proposal

The process by which management approves system development projects varies with each company. The justification proposal and the feasibility phase may be combined in some companies.

The auditor must verify compliance with management requirements for completion of the justification proposal (see Figure 17–1). This proposal should contain enough relevant information, supported by enough research, to support all facts and assumptions. Representatives from the user area, programming, and other appropriate EDP areas should be consulted for input in formulating this proposal.

The proposal provides information for senior management to use to decide whether or not to proceed with purchasing or designing a new system. The decision may be based on cost effectiveness, increased customer service, competitive advantage, or other factors. The factors upon which the decision should be based should be included in the proposal.

At least three alternatives should be researched and explained in the justification. One alternative is always to keep the existing system; it provides a basis for comparison. At least two alternate approaches should be considered. Problems of development that could include the need for additional hardware or system software to support a purchased package that the installation does not currently use must also be verified.

FIGURE 17–1   Justification Proposal

Audit Objective

To determine whether the justification proposal is accurate and contains all relevant data

Audit Review

Evaluate the documented justification proposal

1. The scope and purpose of the system should be completely defined
2. User requirements should be generally defined
3. Desired improvements and the benefits resulting from the new system should be explained and supported by adequate evidence
4. All reasonable alternatives should be explained in terms that easily show the most cost-effective approach
5. Costs and benefits should be accurately calculated and presented in a comparative analysis
6. A reasonable estimate of the time required to develop the proposed system should be disclosed
7. All existing and anticipated problems of development should be disclosed

The scope and the purpose of the system—what the system will do, who will use it, and why the company needs it must be addressed. The user requirements are the foundation for analysis of the system. The user requirements are one of the most important elements of the design process. They are always needed for in-house design or package purchase.

By interviewing the user and other appropriate personnel, the auditor should determine that all concerned parties participated in the preparation of the proposal and whether or not the new system reduces internal control in a particular audit area. For example, the system may not contain as many edits of critical input data as does the existing system.

17.2.2   Feasibility Study

The feasibility study and justification proposal may be combined into one activity. This is acceptable as long as senior management approved the completion of a feasibility study. Management requires that an adequate investigation be conducted to prove the feasibility, or lack thereof, of the proposed system.

The feasibility study must be evaluated in terms of whether it was logically developed and the problem was factually presented through an in-depth review of the feasibility documentation and interviews of appropriate personnel.

The auditor must determine:

- Whether the final recommendations of the study are accurate and based on facts,
- Whether the proposed system meets the user's needs, and
- Whether the design schedule can be met.

It may be found that accomplishing the input requirements of the new system would be impossible. For example, input to the new system may require a tcom monitor system that the company's computers cannot support. The system flowcharts depict the major components of the application and show how the data is processed. This may reveal that the new system would cause scheduling conflicts with existing applications in the data center (see Figure 17–2).

A general schedule of this project should be completed by the S&P project leader, and management should review it to determine that there will be enough personnel to handle the project.

Problems created by the goals and objectives of the project must also be addressed. For example, the system may be ready for implementation during the company's busy season. Because this is known in advance, the schedule can be changed accordingly. The auditor's focus is to ensure that the planners do not delude themselves. People frequently cut time and cost estimates to satisfy senior management, or they plan without providing any leeway for slippage.

17.2.3   User Requirements

The objective of this phase is to adequately identify and document the user requirements that will provide the basis for the

FIGURE 17–2 **Feasibility**

Audit Objective

To determine whether the content of the feasibility study is accurate

Audit Review

1. Input/output requirements should be clearly defined
2. System flows should be clearly and logically presented
3. Anticipated costs and benefits for all alternatives should be reasonably supported and comparatively presented
4. All existing and anticipated project problems should be accurately disclosed and solutions recommended
5. All interdependencies of this project schedule with other project schedules should be described
6. A preliminary implementation plan should be prepared; this plan should outline the start and target dates as well as estimated hours for each of the following phases:

   User requirement preparation

   Package evaluation or design specification

   Functional or package modification specifications

   Programming

   Testing

   The expectations of the project

   Major events

   Manpower estimates
7. The feasibility study should address the problems implied by the goals and objectives cited in the proposal
8. The estimated schedule, costs, and personnel requirements should be conservative but realistic

system design or package evaluation. The auditor should ensure that the project leader determines that the proposed system processing satisfies the needs of the user. The auditor should ensure that the user completely reviews the developed user specifications and requirements. EDP guidelines will usually require the user to approve the documented user requirements and formally to approve continuation (see Figure 17–3).

Determining the adequacy of the requirements definition must be focused on. The user requirements are essentially the

FIGURE 17–3 **User Requirements**

Audit Objective

To determine whether the user requirements contain all elements necessary for system processing and control

Audit Review

Evaluate the user requirements and their development to determine whether:

1. The user requirements are sufficiently defined to serve as the primary package selection or design criteria

2. The information required to be generated by the system on reports should be presented in a detailed, accurate, and useful form

3. The specifications describe how input will be controlled and reflected on computer reports

4. All applicable legal requirements are satisfied by the system

5. System controls are defined for:

   Input and source document control

   Programmatic edits

   Output and balancing controls

6. Error correction procedures are defined

7. A conversion plan is properly defined

8. All necessary documentation is completed and complies with in-house guidelines

---

shopping list of everything users want the new system to do. This phase is the most overlooked and underdeveloped phase of most development projects, especially when considering purchased packages. The one major requirement is the computer reports generated by the new system. The reports from the existing system can be used as a foundation for developing the specifications for the new reports. Data input and its control through the use of computer reports must be checked. Invariably, new systems, especially purchased packages, will require the user to change the manual input procedures, reconcilements, settlements, and comparisons. The user specifications should identify how the control and information reports will group, classify, and report input entered into the system.

Verifying that all legal requirements are satisfied obviously requires the input of a lawyer or compliance officer. The legal requirements are usually known at the time of the system design. However, new legal requirements often force companies to purchase or design new systems just in order to comply.

Making sure system controls are defined for input and source document control, programmatic edits, and output and balancing controls is vital to the auditor in terms of his or her participation, because these include the definitions of controls the auditor would like to see programmed into the system. The more these controls are programmatically performed the less the company has to rely on human handling of the controls, which introduces a high risk of errors and omissions.

The user already has procedures for correcting errors and system data. With in-house design, the system can be designed around the user's procedures, but with a purchased package the user may have to make changes. The more a user has to change his or her manual procedure for a new system, the greater the risk of errors, omissions, and problems later on.

The project leader must develop a conversion plan. Although this seems premature, it is not, because the user usually verifies the converted data on the new system to control totals from the old system. The verification controls and the programs that will convert the data to the new system require consideration and planning during the user requirements phase.

Documented timetables of the implementation plan, documented forms, copies of existing computer reports, or output definitions, and of course the user's formal signature on the continuation approval documents are also included in this aspect of the feasibility study.

17.2.4   General Design

Management's objective is to provide a general design of the proposed system. The appropriate user manager should review and formally approve the general design. The development process should not continue to the next phase until this approval is obtained.

The EDP auditor must be careful not to perform the duties of data processing in the general design phase. The auditor is required only to research information to determine that the project leader and other members of EDP management and the user area have accomplished the necessary elements of the general design phase (see Figure 17–4).

The requirements of the feasibility study and user requirements phases, which are previous commitments, must be focused on. Senior management, having approved this commitment during the feasibility study phase and for the general design should have its requirements satisfied, or should know why not. Documentation and definition of input and output requirements are carryovers from the user requirements phase, whereas the structural definition of all anticipated files is new development and documentation work for the analyst and user. These definitions form the contents of all files processed by the new system.

The system's compliance with the existing user department standards and procedures must be verified. The objective is to change as few user procedures as possible. Concentrating on the data elements, reports, and files that make up the audit trail to prove system processing accuracy are key in making sure the system is auditable. The general design phase is the time to identify and plan for any mainframe, operating systems, or utilities needs. The analyst must estimate the time it will take to prepare detailed design specifications and program the system, and the number of people that will be needed to complete the project. It is vital that these items are documented.

The auditor should determine that the project leader has considered the effect of purchasing new hardware, system software, or utilities needed.

The user and project leader must identify all costs and benefits relating to the events occurring so far and those remaining. This is a rerun of the feasibility study data, which is also used as a basis of comparison of the new version of costs and benefits after the general design phase. This is the point in the project when user management must evaluate the revised costs and benefits

FIGURE 17–4   **General Design**

Audit Objective

To determine whether the general design was prepared from the user requirements, that EDP personnel ensured that user's needs were satisfied and that all the elements of the feasibility study were addressed

Audit Review

Review the general design for completeness; determine that the design does not intend to repeat the inefficiencies of a current system or procedure

1. The design satisfies the requirements cited in the feasibility study and user requirements
2. Input and output requirements are defined and documented
3. Structural definitions of all anticipated files are documented
4. General processing design specifications comply with the user department standards and procedures
5. The system is easily auditable
6. Computer hardware, software, time and personnel scheduling requirements are defined and documented
7. If the purchase of new hardware and/or system software is required, the auditor must ensure that the project leader has considered:

   Lead times for delivery

   Cost/benefit

   Required enhancements

   EDP management approval of new acquisition

   Scheduling requirements
8. Estimated user, EDP costs and benefits are documented. Reasonable cost estimates of the following factors are included:

   System development

   Testing

   Programmer, analyst, and user training

   Operations costs

   Maintenance costs

   Hardware and software enhancements

   Cost of supplies

   Development team manhours
9. Procedures for security and integrity of sensitive data elements are developed and documented
10. Interface requirements of this system with other systems are defined and documented

estimates to determine that the project should be continued or terminated.

Security—how data on files will be protected from on-line access for batch system access that may be erroneous—must be addressed.

Verifying interface requirements is a critical element in the general design phase that is often overlooked. The planning and development for interface with other systems must be completed in the general design phase, because these interface requirements could have a significant effect on programming and design costs.

17.2.5   Package Evaluation

Management's objective is to determine if the software package(s) under consideration for purchase will meet the organization's needs.

This section of the audit program breaks away from the in-house design phases to discuss the evaluation of a potential software package purchase. This audit program is included here because this is the point in the sequence of the SDLC phases where the evaluation of the package occurs. The SDLC phases discussed before this one must all be completed even for a software package being purchased.

It is tempting to skip over the user requirements and general design phases when a vendor package is considered because most people feel that they can evaluate the package "off the top of their heads." If the package is evaluated without adequate specifications and general design documentation, however, the risk of the system's not matching the company's needs is greatly increased. If the auditor finds this to be happening, a written recommendation should be issued to senior management that the user requirements and general design evaluation and documentation should be prepared before the package is evaluated for purchase (see Figure 17–5).

Making sure the system is compatible with existing hardware deserves an independent review by the auditor. With the pressure for a new system, some processing requirements may

FIGURE 17–5   Package Evaluation

Audit Objective

To determine whether the package evaluation process is thorough and complete, and EDP management ensures the feasibility study requirements and user specifications are satisfied

Audit Review

Determine that specific evaluation criteria were utilized and include:

1. The package is compatible with existing or proposed hardware, and its processing requirements are practical
2. Feasibility study objectives are satisfied
3. The user requirements are an integral part of the package evaluation criteria
4. At least three vendors are considered
5. Data storage types and access methods utilized by the package are compatible with those used by the installation
6. The package is capable of accomplishing the required processing
7. The package utilizes state-of-the-art programming techniques and is easily understood and modified
8. The programming language is the type used by the programming department; if not, a plan for programming support should be developed and documented
9. Vendor support of the package is an integral part of the contract for at least 30 days following implementation. Continual support of the package is strongly preferred
10. The package has a reputation for reliable operation at other EDP installations
11. The total implementation cost should be approved by management
12. The package should satisfy all user requirements; if not, the required modifications should be identified and documented
13. The cost for vendor and/or in-house modification is determined, as needed
14. Modification costs should be formally reported to and approved by management

be overlooked. At least three vendors should be considered. There may not be three vendors, but the point is, the auditor must insist that alternatives are explored.

Without documented, detailed user requirements, the audit concerns whether the package can do the required processing cannot be discerned. Just because the package performed processing at a similar installation does not mean it will satisfy another company's requirements.

Package use of a company-supported programming language must be verified. The systems software programming group can answer this question properly.

One critical difference between a purchased package and in-house design is the contract with the vendor. The EDP auditor must ensure that this contract has been reviewed in detail by an attorney who has identified critical commitments for the vendor and the purchaser.

Thirty-day vendor support must be adequate and should be free. Most vendors offer maintenance contracts for continual support that can and should be purchased. Also talking to other users of the package is important. It provides an infinite amount of information, which can be used in the company's evaluation of the package.

Generally, modifications on the heels of package installation should be avoided. Installation, implementation, and conversion create enough problems for EDP and the user to deal with. However, if modifications are necessary, they must be identified and documented in detail. A decision must be made as to whether the vendor will modify the system or whether they will be done by the in-house programming staff. In either event, the modifications will generate additional costs that must be identified and reported to management for approval.

17.2.6   Package Acceptance Testing

The requirements of this phase ensure that sufficient testing is performed to prove the package is acceptable. The documentation of test requirements, which are the key to evaluating the adequacy of the package, deserves focus. The requirements specify all the aspects of the system that will be tested and how they will be tested. The user requirements can be translated by the project leader and the user into package functions which must be tested (see Figure 17–6).

The test requirements focus on testing daily, weekly, and monthly job streams and other significant aspects of the system,

FIGURE 17–6   **Package Acceptance Testing**

Audit Objective

To determine whether an adequate acceptance test was performed

Audit Review

Evaluate the acceptance test plan and test results to determine:

1. Test requirements are documented and permit the auditor to determine that the testing will reveal that the package satisfies user requirements
2. The test requirements cover all aspects of systems processing
3. Acceptance criteria is documented and mutually agreed upon by the user and EDP
4. The input/output requirements of the package satisfy user needs
5. The package is compatible with current and/or proposed hardware and system software
6. The package is capable of the type of processing required by the user
7. The package easily interfaces with other systems or is easily modifiable to permit interface

---

to ensure that the company's hardware and software can handle the system(s) processing requirements.

The acceptance criteria sets the target for package performance. If the system meets these criteria, then it meets the company's needs.

17.2.7   Package Modifications

Management's objective is to ensure that needed modifications to the package are properly defined. Below is a step-by-step review of procedures (see Figure 17–7).

The auditor must focus on the analysts' preparation of detailed explanations, which should be written in sufficient detail to permit a programmer to write program code. A systems analyst should prepare the specifications with input from the user (the user may not have sufficient programming experience to adequately prepare the specifications). The modifications specifications should be reviewed by a qualified vendor representative, who should determine that the modified code will operate properly.

FIGURE 17–7   Package Modifications

Audit Objective

To determine whether modification specifications are adequately prepared

Audit Review

Review the modification specifications to determine whether:

1. Detailed explanations of the modifications are documented
2. The modifications were prepared by the user and system analyst
3. The modifications and their associated costs are formally approved by user and EDP management
4. Whether the vendor or the in-house programming staff will make the modifications
5. A plan for the completion of the modifications is documented, including manpower requirements, estimated hours, and reasonable start and target dates
6. The user has reviewed and formally approved all modifications, including those that will not be completed prior to installation
7. The modifications will satisfy user requirements, system objectives, and system benefits; if not, the requirements or benefits that will not be satisfied should be determined
8. The user agrees with the deficiencies cited and their effect(s) on system control and efficiency

Because the modifications will raise implementation costs, the senior EDP manager should formally approve with ratification approval by senior management.

User approval of the modifications is another focus. This is necessary because the modifications are being made to satisfy the user's needs. The communication between the analyst and the user regarding the modifications must be excellent. Any needed modifications that cannot be made must be identified by the analyst and approved by the user. These deficiencies and their effect on control and efficiency should be reported to user senior management. All system processing functions required by the user that will not be present in a new system must be communicated to senior management and all other affected areas.

17.2.8   Preliminary Implementation Plan

S&P standards should direct the project manager to define a preliminary implementation plan that accurately accounts for all activities that will occur during the remainder of the development project (see Figure 17–8).

The auditor's responsibility is essentially compliance testing of evidential matter. The requirements of this phase are essentially the same as those prescribed for project management (see Chapter 6). The development phases, work tasks, programs, and modules of programs must be identified. This phase is applicable to both package and in-house system implementation.

Benchmarks against which actual progress will be measured must be set. The number of programmers and other personnel that will be needed and when they will be needed must be identified.

A formal project team organizational structure must be established, and the project leader must be given adequate authority. If the project leader is not given the authority to assign and enforce work tasks then the project could flounder and miss the

---

FIGURE 17–8   Preliminary Implementation Plan

Audit Objective

Determine whether the remaining project elements are accurately planned

Audit Review

Determine the adequacy of the preliminary implementation plan by verifying:

1. All major events that will take place during subsequent phases are identified
2. Each task is assigned estimated hours, start, and target dates
3. Total manpower requirements are established
4. A formal project team organizational structure is established, including an appointed project leader who has the authority to ensure that assigned tasks are completed
5. A user liaison and other appropriate personnel are assigned to the project team with a commensurate reduction in their normal job duties
6. An implementation schedule is documented identifying the start and target dates for each major task

---

target date. The user liaison is necessary to coordinate all user activities and provide a communication channel between data processing and other user personnel. These liaisons are usually appointed from existing user staff and already have a full-time work schedule, so their time demands must be respected. If the system project responsibilities are added on top of existing ones, the completion of the project will likely suffer.

Establishing target and deadline dates focuses on the preparation of a gantt or pert chart (graphic "pictures" of the relationship of dependent tasks) that depicts the start and target date. These are charted in a single schedule to permit the identification of conflicts in relationships.

17.2.9   Recommendation to Management

The project manager and user should provide senior management with a thorough and adequate recommendation, based on project results to date, to permit them to evaluate the benefits of the proposed system and to decide upon continuation or termination.

The recommendation should reiterate all short- and long-term benefits of the system to refresh senior management on the need for the system. Management should formally approve or reject the continuation of the project before project team members proceed to the next phase.

Project team preparation of a recommendation to management to proceed or terminate the project is the major focus. This recommendation is prepared after the general design phase for an in-house project or after the acceptance testing phase of a package purchase. This is known as a "kill point"; it provides senior management with the opportunity to make a "go" or "no-go" decision before progressing to the time-intensive, detailed design phase for an in-house system, or to the modifications or implementation phases of a purchased package (see Figure 17–9).

Senior management must be informed as to how the system will satisfy the elements of the feasibility study. This is generally the first time that senior management will see any documented progress report on the system since having approved the

FIGURE 17–9   Recommendation to Management

Audit Objective

To ensure that the recommendation to management is complete and accurate in all respects

Audit Review

Evaluate the adequacy of the recommendation to management by determining:

1. The recommendation explains how the system's objectives and benefits, cited in the feasibility study, are satisfied
2. The recommendation contains:

   An overview of user requirements

   An overview of the results of the package acceptance test

   A schedule of the needed package modifications and their associated cost/benefit

   A preliminary implementation plan

   Time, personnel, and cost estimates for implementation
3. All elements of the cost summary are stated in consistent terms
4. All time constraints and their resulting effect on the implementation schedule are disclosed
5. Alternatives to purchasing the package are disclosed

feasibility study. If the management's objectives and benefits are not satisfied, the project may be terminated. The auditor can accomplish item 2 by reviewing the documented recommendation and comparing the elements in it to the documented results of prior phases.

The consistent measurement of cost estimates must be maintained. Costs are typically stated in one-time monthly or annual figures. It is important that the recommendations to senior management state all costs consistently to avoid confusion.

The time constraints involve things like peak business periods, conversions of other systems, or month-end, quarter-end or year-end processing. The experienced EDP auditor or other members of the audit management team will be aware of these types of significant events based on prior experience with the company. Reiterating the alternatives available to senior management should close out this recommendation to management.

17.2.10 Detailed Design

The administrative guidelines should ensure that the detailed design of the system to be developed in-house is complete in all material respects and is formally approved by the user and EDP managements.

The detailed design phase is the first major step in defining the processing aspects of the system because the detailed design will be used to write functional specifications for use by programmers in writing the program code.

This phase requires an auditor to use his or her judgment for the decision on system design. The auditor can accomplish this through discussions with the analyst, programmers, and users to get a "sense" as to whether the system design is logical (see Figure 17–10).

All the elements of the files that will be used and created by the system as well as the definitions of the input should be defined. The term "defined" implies the preparation of documentation.

The auditor is directed to focus on the completeness of the report definition and the definition of input to the system. The reports to be generated by the application may not be defined in terms of their actual appearance. All reports and their contents, however, should be defined during this phase.

Because the detailed design phase reveals numerous potential areas of input, processing, and output error, it requires testing. It is best for the analyst and user to record these necessary elements as work progresses.

The conversion plan is actually a preliminary schedule of the file data elements that require special treatment or control during the conversion.

The programmatic controls over input, processing, and output must be defined during this phase. The EDP auditor must insist that these are documented, and comprehensively review these controls for adequacy and effectiveness. The analyst and user will usually look to the auditor for input on control design.

FIGURE 17–10   Detail Design

Audit Objective

To determine whether the detail design includes all items specified in the user requirements and the general design

Audit Review

Review the design documentation to determine:

1. The design of the system is logical
2. All disk and tape files are completely described and documented
3. File design complies with S&P standards
4. Provisions are made to allow independent audit access
5. Sufficient audit trails should exist
6. All required access controls are included
7. All system input data formats are documented in detail and comply with S&P standards
8. All source documents are defined in detail
9. Source document validation techniques are defined
10. Control techniques for source documents and input are defined (e.g., batching, balancing)
11. Data preparation techniques are defined
12. All reports and their elements are defined
13. Essential elements of the testing plan are recorded
14. A conversion plan is defined
15. Processing and output controls are defined
16. Data center operator system support procedures are defined

17.2.11   Project Team Staffing

The project team should be adequately staffed to promote timely completion of the project. Generally speaking, it is better to have a few full-time project members than many part-time members because the reorientation and startup time for part-time people erodes progress.

Getting a "feel" for the morale and "attitude" of the individual project team members through participation in the project team meetings should be a priority. A pessimistic viewpoint toward completion of the project on the part of the project team members can cause project failure (see Figure 17–11).

It may be necessary to use less-experienced programmers, but the rate of progress should be watched by the EDP auditor to ensure that extensive supervision and review of the programmers' work by the project leader does not have a detrimental effect.

The project team members need to know their exact responsibilities. This should be reinforced by each individual's supervisor or manager. The project manager, usually a systems analyst, should know how to delegate and follow up on responsibilities assigned to other team members.

The project manager may not have the authority to resolve conflicts in system processing between two or more users of the system. Therefore, the EDP auditor should watch for these conflicts to ensure that the problem is pushed up into the decision-making levels of the organization for appropriate resolution. This can be a vital service for management.

FIGURE 17–11   Project Staffing

Audit Objective

To determine whether project team members are sufficiently experienced and have adequate authority to complete necessary project tasks

Audit Review

Evaluate the adequacy of the organization and staffing of the project team; determine whether:

1. A project environment should be established in which all parties involved believe it is in their best interest to achieve the project goals

2. The project team is staffed with qualified personnel from all affected departments

3. The responsibilities of each member are defined

4. A project manager with adequate supervisory experience is appointed

5. In the event that the system serves two or more users, an official decision authority should be appointed

6. Event targets are established to signal task completion and to permit periodic progress reviews

Project management and establishment of goals for completion are critical for morale purposes as well as for ensuring that the project will meet the target date.

17.2.12   Detailed Implementation Plan

A detailed implementation plan should be defined to guide each member of the project team in his or her activities. The auditor should determine whether project team members understand their assignments and are qualified to complete them. The required approval points are opportunities for the user or management to approve completed work or approve project continuation; these should be noted in the plan (see Figure 17–12).

FIGURE 17–12   **Detailed Implementation Plan**

Audit Objectives

Determine whether all necessary tasks are included in the plan and that respective time estimates are realistic

Audit Review

Determine the completeness and accuracy of the estimates. Verify:

1. All major activities in the preliminary implementation plan are broken down into individual manageable tasks
2. Each task has a start date, a target date, and estimated hours
3. Target dates are based on the estimated hours for each task
4. The plan covers all project phases and the activities to be performed by the user, EDP operations, and programming including:

    Functional specifications for in-house design or modification specifications for a purchased package

    Programming, all phases of testing, and conversion

    Training and documentation

    The impact of hardware or operating system modifications

    Terminal installation and forms design
5. All personnel receive specific assignments that are documented on the plan schedule

After completion of the detailed design for an in-house system or management approval to purchase a package, a detailed implementation plan should be defined that is tracked by a project monitoring system (see Chapter 6).

Project management aspects and division of activities and tasks must be defined. A manageable task can be defined as work required to complete in 20, 40, or 100 hours, or some other measure that is useful to the project team. The manageable task size, or time, is usually defined by EDP management.

The "calculation" of target dates is based on the start date plus estimated hours for completion compared to how much personnel time is available. The establishment of target dates by means other than calculation will not be realistic. The most critical element of the implementation plan is the assignment of tasks and activities to individual project team members for completion. The work will not get done unless the people know what they have to complete and when.

17.2.13   Program Specifications

The systems analyst's instructions to the programmer should be adequately documented and explain all necessary elements of the programs. It is important to note that the program specifications phase is the EDP auditor's last chance to determine that all necessary programmatic controls have been designed into the system. After the next phase of programming begins, the auditor may not have the opportunity to insert changes or additions to internal controls.

All elements of the detailed design should have program specifications written for them, and these must be understandable. This is best determined through interviews of the programmers after they have reviewed the specifications. What may be clear and concise to the auditor may not be understandable by the programmer. The EDP auditor must ensure that any known confusion is resolved by the project manager (see Figure 17–13).

There is another very critical element of in-house design or package modification. Because of time constraints, system

FIGURE 17-13   Program Specifications

Audit Objective

Determine whether the program specifications are adequately documented and understood by the programmer

Audit Review

Determine that program specifications are accurate and comply with S&P standards

1. Program specifications exist for each program in a format consistent with S&P standards

2. The explanations of the specifications are clear and concise to permit efficient coding of programs

3. All necessary controls are defined in the specifications

4. The user is formally notified in writing of all design specifications that have not been incorporated and must wait until after system implementation for inclusion into the system

functions required by the user may have to be eliminated until after the system is implemented. They can be included as part of application program maintenance. However, the auditor must determine that the user and his management is aware of all processing elements that will not be included. This can be accomplished by reviewing the exclusions with the user manager. The EDP auditor must exercise extra caution with the exclusion of these elements because the biggest exposure is miscommunication between EDP and the user in all levels of management.

17.2.14   Programming

Management must ensure that programming is completed efficiently and effectively and that programmers are adequately supervised. The auditor must remember that his or her function is only to monitor progress and point out weaknesses through the proper channels (see Figure 17-14).

The EDP auditor should determine that the program coding is being reviewed in detail. The checkpoints establish time targets for the programmers to meet. Tasks should be assigned so that all personnel are aware of what is expected of them.

FIGURE 17–14   Programming

Audit Objective

To determine that the programmers' activities are well managed and supervised

Audit Review

The programming phase should be monitored to ensure its proper management. Make sure that:

1. The person(s) responsible for writing the design and programming specifications reviews the coding for compliance with the specifications
2. Review checkpoints are established
3. The programming activities are defined to include, as a minimum:

   Activities that will occur, their timing, duration, and objectives

   Necessary resources, when they will be needed, and length of time needed

   The end products

   The functions of nonproject personnel

   Change procedures
4. A sufficient number of experienced programmers are assigned to the project to ensure completion of programming within the desired time frame
5. Time estimates are established for each programming task
6. Programming is broken down into tasks that require no more than 80 hours to complete
7. A system of task reporting and control should be established, and status reports are reviewed by supervisors on at least a weekly basis
8. A standardized approach for dealing with changes in original specifications should be developed; this must be in place to prevent over-budget situations and delays

---

Audit judgment, which may take several weeks of monitoring the programming phase for the auditor to determine that a problem exists, must be attained. This is accomplished by reviewing actual versus budgeted progress. Excessive slippage in this phase can indicate inadequate experience or insufficient staffing. The auditor must act through appropriate channels to resolve these problems, if they are found.

Sometimes changes are identified during programming. Regardless of the quality of the detailed design and functional specifications, a programmer may find a better way to code a program to provide more efficient operation. The project manager should develop an approach for reporting these ideas, discussion of the potential changes, and decision on their inclusion or exclusion. This approach must be efficient and effective to prevent the project from being bogged down.

17.2.15   Program Testing

Management must ensure that all programs are sufficiently tested to prove compliance with specifications. This first phase of testing can be defined as unit testing because it concentrates on individual programs or modules (see Figure 17–15).

The results of this testing are usually not reviewed by the user or even known about by other project team members, because it is performed as an integral part of the programmer's job—writing program code. This testing will reduce the errors detected in a later system test phase.

The EDP auditor is directed to examine the test methodology, which is usually specified by S&P guidelines. The critical point is

FIGURE 17–15   Program Testing

Audit Objective

Determine whether individual programs have been adequately tested before the beginning of program string or jobstream testing

Audit Review

Review program test activities to determine the adequacy of testing; determine whether:

1. A program testing plan is developed that includes the following minimum guidelines:

    Test objectives

    Scope of testing

    Procedures for accumulating test results

    A procedure for isolating and correcting errors

2. Each program module has been tested and completely debugged

3. All programs successfully compiled and tested are maintained in a secure central location

4. Test results that meet specifications are reviewed and approved by the user and the analyst

the logging of discovered errors that cannot be resolved. This can be accomplished by the project team manager through the use of a checklist of programs.

Users should review any test results from this phase that are appropriate. Specifications documented in the test that are satisfied by this phase can be reviewed by the user and released, potentially eliminating further testing in the system test phase.

17.2.16 Documentation

S&P guidelines must ensure that all programs and system processing are sufficiently explained in the system, data center run, and user manuals (see Figure 17–16). As the programmers complete coding and testing, they can begin to prepare user and system documentation. The development of user training programs should begin at this point.

FIGURE 17–16   Documentation

Audit Objective

To determine whether system documentation is adequate to communicate system functions and operating instructions to analysts, programmers, and users

Audit Review

Evaluate the adequacy of systems documentation. Verify that:

1. A user manual is prepared, containing:

    Overall system flowchart
    Transaction definitions, input formats, input procedures
    Batching, settlement, and control functions
    Output descriptions and each report's use

2. A system manual is prepared, containing:

    Generalized system and program flowcharts
    Computer set-up instructions
    Record layouts of all files
    File retention, set-up procedures
    Index of reports, transaction code definitions
    Internal and external controls

17.2.17   System Testing

The project team must ensure that all system functions are adequately tested before conversion to a production environment. All test results should be reviewed and approved by user representatives (see Figure 17–17).

These testing activities involve the user review of test results.

To determine the accuracy of system output, results frequently need to be predefined. This can be accomplished by project team members through manual documentation of

FIGURE 17–17   System Testing

Audit Objective

To determine that the system is adequately tested

Audit Review

Determine the adequacy of the test plan. Verify that:

1. Testing objectives are documented and formally approved by the user and EDP

2. Program functions to be tested are documented and agreed upon by the user and EDP

3. Predefined testing output results are clear and concise

4. Review of test results are assigned to specific personnel

5. A methodology for documentation and verification of test results is established. This method should allow for easy recognition of system problems detected during testing

6. A log of problems isolated during testing is maintained

7. A formal problem reporting method is developed to ensure that all necessary personnel are advised

8. Acceptance criteria for each test condition are approved by the user and the project manager prior to the beginning of testing

9. Test data includes invalid transactions that violate program edit and control procedures as well as valid transactions

10. Programs are subjected to volume tests that approximate the volume expected in the production environment to establish processing adequacy, efficiency, and effectiveness

11. The final phases of testing includes all system requirements and manual operations

12. All appropriate departments review and formally approve test results

results or comparison against existing system reports. Accuracy cannot be verified unless the reviewer knows what the results should be.

To keep the test phase rolling, specific reports of functions being tested should be assigned to specific personnel for review. It is important to communicate the need for program changes back to the programmers. The reporting between the project team members is necessary to ensure that all members agree that the problems detected do require correction.

The acceptance criteria should be established that tells everyone involved that the testing is complete. Without agreed-upon acceptance criteria, unnecessary testing could be conducted, wasting valuable time.

The test objective should adopt a "make it fail" approach to test all system functions. Volume testing is frequently overlooked or cut due to time constraints. Volume refers to the number of transactions processed by the system. The test environment typically uses fewer transactions than would be processed in reality. Without volume testing, the system could pass all acceptance criteria and be converted, only to fail when the normal daily volume of transactions is entered into the system.

The manual operations should be included in the systems test. The test, even though it meets all acceptance criteria, is not completed until all appropriate departments have reviewed the test results and approved them in writing.

17.2.18   Conversion

User and EDP management must ensure that the new system is implemented in a controlled manner (with provision for fall-back to the old system should the conversion fail) and that all necessary personnel can operate the system. The conversion phase transfers the data from the old system files to the new system (see Figure 17–18).

There should be a conversion plan that includes documentation of activities and functions necessary. This plan should be approved by user and EDP managements, signifying approval to convert the system. The time and manpower requirements are

FIGURE 17–18   Conversion

Audit Objective

Determine the conversion will be adequately controlled to prevent the loss of data

Audit Review

Determine that the conversion plan will reduce or eliminate the risk of losing any system data

1. A conversion play should be documented and approved by the user and EDP management
2. Time and manpower requirements are established
3. Management approved conversion of the system in writing
4. All affected personnel are trained in systems operation and manual interface requirements
5. Documentation is complete, including:

    Systems manual

    Operator's manual

    Terminal operator's manual

    Compiled listings

6. Management should consider tactfully advising customers of the conversion
7. The master and transaction files of the old system are retained for backup
8. An alternate list of procedures, to be followed if the conversion fails, is developed and documented
9. The last day's data from the old system are reconciled to general ledger prior to conversion to the new system
10. Individual nonmonetary account data are verified as necessary

---

necessary because system conversions are typically scheduled for weekends. The estimates will reveal how many people are needed to work on the conversion and how much time will be consumed, and whether the conversion can be accomplished during the weekend.

There should be management review of the cost benefit one final time prior to conversion. The benefit of the system could have changed due to the business environment, resulting in costs that exceed the benefits of the new system. If this occurs, the company may consider aborting conversion.

There should be training of user personnel and completion of all necessary documentation. The users cannot operate the new system unless they have been trained, and data center operators cannot support the system without documented procedures. The EDP auditor must insist upon the completion of the documentation before conversion.

Some companies notify their customers of a system conversion to forestall any problems that may occur with customer service. This is not necessary for control.

The conversion can fail for various reasons, forcing fall-back to the old system to provide time to correct the problems and try the conversion again.

Item 8 refers to the special procedures that should be defined which may be needed for fall-back to the old system.

To maintain control of converted data, reconciliations and settlements of the application to the general ledger must be performed before the conversion begins, because the reconciliation identifies items that may not be converted properly.

User verifications of converted nonmonetary data that can not be controlled by reconciliation of dollar control totals must be performed. These include name and address, dates, account types, and other critical identifiers.

17.2.19   Maintenance

EDP management should assign a competent programmer(s) for maintenance and modification.

With the new system running in a production environment, numerous details will most likely exist that need resolution. The EDP auditor's last activity in the conversion phase is to determine that these pending items will be resolved (see Figure 17–19).

It is desirable to assign a programmer or analyst who worked on the development project to maintain the system, to avoid a significant learning curve.

Any system funtions that were excluded from the functional specifications or programming phases should have been identified in those phases. The auditor should determine that a

FIGURE 17–19   Maintenance

Audit Objective

Determine whether adequate plans have been made for maintenance and modification of the new system

Audit Review

Review the activities for maintenance/modification; verify that:

1. A programmer and/or analyst who worked on the development project should be assigned to maintain the system
2. After conversion, that outstanding program changes are reviewed to develop an implementation plan
3. The system is running smoothly without an abnormal amount of operator and/or programmer intervention
4. The extent of user satisfaction with the system; any serious problems should be reported to EDP and user management

plan has been developed for specification, planning, and testing of these pending items.

The auditor is required to interview data center and programming personnel to determine the amount of operator and programmer intervention to keep the system running. Excessive intervention should be reported to management.

The auditor is also required to interview users to identify any problems they might have with the system. Any serious problems should be reported by the auditor to EDP and user managements.

17.3   SYSTEM CONTROL ANALYSIS— INTRODUCTION

The audit objective is to determine that adequate programmatic and manual procedures exist that ensure processing accuracy and completeness in input, processing, and output of the system being developed. Controls necessary for special system activities depend on the type of data and the processing method. It is the auditor's responsibility to identify specialized processing situations and make sure that necessary controls exist.

This review closely follows the application audit with one important distinction—a development system does not provide physical evidence of daily processing activities. Thus, the auditor is reviewing an *idea*.

This analysis should start in the early phases of the system development life cycle and should be completed before the preparation of modification specifications for purchased software. In-house designed systems require analysis during the design phase and completion prior to the preparation of functional specifications. This timing allows audit recommendations to be incorporated into the system design rather than being patched in after implementation.

17.3.1 Planning and Preliminary Review

A certain amount of information must be collected prior to the analysis of control procedures. The information needs are the same as those identified in the planning and preliminary audit phases of the application audit (see Chapter 12). The major items of interest are the following:

- The scope of the analysis should be reviewed with the financial auditors to obtain their opinion on controls for the application processing phases,
- The overall system function should be reviewed, using the audit flowcharting requirements,
- A list of transaction codes and an explanation of their functions should be obtained or prepared,
- An index of reports to be generated by the system should be obtained or prepared with explanations of each report's function.

This accumulated data will form the basis for analyzing system processing.

17.3.2 Application System Activities

Chapters 11 and 12 identified application processing activities for focus during an application audit. The compliance testing program in Chapter 12 can be used to identify the detailed audit information needs about the system. The following sections will provide an overview of what is necessary.

17.3.2.1 INPUT

The elements requiring audit attention are the following:

- Manual and automated control points,
- Documented user procedures,
- Control techniques (see Chapter 11, section 11.2.1.2),
- Efficient and effective forms design,
- Segregation from other conflicting functions,
- Review for input accuracy,
- Authorization and approval procedures,
- Monitoring of transmittal and receipt of data,
- Batching of transactions,
- Procedures to control lost data,
- Control totals and item counts,
- Transmittal documents,
- Input document retention and storage,
- Procedures for handling errors,
- A means of cross-reference between the transaction on computer files and the source document,
- Computer reports listing all input transactions,
- Verification that all data verification points are defined, and
- Verification that user documentation is adequate.

17.3.2.1.1   ON-LINE ENTRY

Determine the adequacy of internal and external controls over on-line entry (see Chapters 9 and 16). Review such elements as:

- Terminal location,
- Temperature and humidity control,
- On-line (logical) access control,
- Ensuring that error edit override features are limited or not allowed,
- Ensuring that terminals not operable during nonbusiness hours,
- Computer reports showing terminal activity,
- Ensuring that dollar control totals are used to balance input transactions,
- Procedures for correction of out-of-balance conditions,
- Message control system (see Chapter 9),
- Logging of transactions, file images, and system messages,
- Data encryption for critical data,
- Restart-and-recovery procedures,
- Ensuring the existence of a user's manual explaining terminal operation procedures, and
- Terminal operator training.

17.3.2.1.2   KEY-TO-DISK INPUT

To determine whether the transaction validation techniques are adquate, review the following elements:

- Preprogrammed keying formats and programmatic edit checks,
- Digit routines,
- Processing schedules for control of data receipt,

- Terminal software error detection,
- Preposting error reports,
- Verification that resubmitted data is edited the same as the original data, and
- Control totals for all rejected items.

17.3.2.2 PROCESSING

Determine whether adequate controls exist to prove processing accuracy and completeness by reviewing:

- Transaction identification,
- Internally generated transactions,
- Control totals for internally generated transactions,
- Run-to-run control totals,
- Overrides of programmatic controls,
- Manual or programmatic balancing of system,
- Computer operations instructions,
- Error reports, and
- Restart-and-recovery procedures,
- All processing aspects of each program are reported,
- Reconciliation performed for each run,
- Control totals reports reflect dollar totals and item counts for each transaction group.

17.3.2.3 DATA STORAGE AND RETRIEVAL

Determine adequacy of procedures for control of data storage and retrieval by reviewing:

- File library procedures (see Chapter 7),
- Separate production and test libraries (see Chapter 10),
- Access control of certain files (see Chapters 9 and 12),

- File labeling,
- Header and trailer labels,
- Limited use of "ignore label" commands,
- Verification that file access and errors are logged by the system,
- Off-site storage, and
- File recovery and backup procedures.

17.3.2.4   OUTPUT

Determine the adequacy of output procedures by reviewing:

- Output distribution procedures,
- Schedule of reports,
- Controlled pick-up, and
- Sensitive document procedures.

NOTES

1. See Mullen, Jack B. "Auditing Systems Development and Program Changes." Adapted from *EDP Auditing* (New York: Auerbach Publishers). © 1986, Warren, Gorham & Lamont, Inc. Used with permission.

18

Auditing Microcomputers

18.1 INTRODUCTION

Beginning with the use of word processors, microcomputer usage has exploded in the past five years. Today, microcomputers can effectively and efficiently compete with mainframe systems to the extent that many companies are replacing some mainframe applications with cheaper micro applications. Strategic business objectives have shifted, and the justification for computer systems has changed. The primary considerations are the micro's ability to facilitate the creation of additional income and to enable people to work smarter.

Mainframe application systems centralized transaction processing and other operations. Microcomputers have resurrected decentralized processing. The development of application processing systems is no longer the exclusive territory of the systems and programming department—it is in the hands of the user.

Systems and programming, in some businesses, has developed a perceived reputation of being unresponsive, unable to understand particular lines of business, too slow, and too costly. The end users are now beginning to replace mainframe systems with microcomputers. Businesses will trade off the cost of maintaining expensive mainframe processing for inexpensive microcomputer processing.

18.1.1   Effect on EDP Audit

Reduced system development control creates additional risks, particularly in the testing and conversion phases. The speed of system development on the microcomputer reduces the possibility for development of proper accounting controls. Companies need physical security and on-line access devices to install password control and change control over micro-based data and application programs. Fortunately, because of EDP audit experience with computer technology, many EDP auditors are microcomputer specialists who have much more knowledge than the end users.

Microcomputer software programs are being developed with capabilities that rival many mainframe applications. The future will see the development of even more powerful and faster microcomputers and more pressure to shift to end-user computing. Microcomputer networks are being developed at a rapid pace—for example, electronic mail is becoming the standard rather than the exception.

18.1.2   Overview—Microcomputer Uses

Several categories of microcomputer usage have emerged. An explanation of their functions and related audit issues follows.

Stand-alone processing: These installations have no link to the mainframe and represent the primary reason for first purchases. These systems are used for word processing, spreadsheet analysis, and other applications. The enduser performs input, processing, and output.

Some examples are accounts payable and receivables. When the Federal Reserve Bank discontinued use of the Bankwire II system for wire transfer, banks were forced to develop a quick alternative to maintain an on-line processing link with other banks. Microcomputers provided an excellent alternative.

Audit issues focus on financial application processing, file damage, errors and omissions, lost data, inaccurate, and incomplete processing. Other major uses are customized reporting and analysis for special or infrequent analyses of data such as investment yields, tax analysis, and merger and acquisition analysis.

Microcomputer analysis programs are viewed by some as presenting no more risk than would a calculator, pencil and pad of paper. There are significant differences, however. When using a calculator, the user validates the formula he or she is using each time the calculation is performed and, therefore, tests the accuracy of the formula and the data each time. The microcomputer holds the entire formula and recalculates that formula each time a single specific button on the keyboard is pressed.

The opportunity for validation and testing of the data and formula has disappeared because the microcomputer performs these calculations sight unseen to the user. As long as the formula or vital data within the microcomputer has not changed, the calculation will remain the same. The accuracy of the formula(s) and the data must be verified and access to the program(s) and data must be controlled.

A major risk is the effect on management decisions caused by inaccurate calculations resulting from inadequate validation or testing. Programs are written by nonprogrammers unfamiliar with the need for systematic program testing. The effect can be improper management decisions, lost income, excessive expense, or faulty buy/sell decisions, to name a few.

Decentralized input: This strategy uses a micro for uploading input data to a mainframe. This can be 1) straight input—data entered from the document to the micro, then to a mainframe, and 2) processed input—data from existing micro files or source documents with some processing performed by the microcomputer, such as data edits, categorization, or other calculations.

The exposure is that inaccurate micro processing and the use of mainframe on-line transaction codes for input can create a potential weak spot in the mainframe system. If an authorized microcomputer can access a mainframe transaction code (a shorthand instruction to direct mainframe processing), can an unauthorized micro do the same?

The auditor can examine the errors and omission risk by preparing test transactions or tracing a sample of transaction through the micro to the mainframe. The auditor should determine the edit routines used from a documentation and micro program review, or the execution of test transactions that should fail the edits. Lost data or duplication risk can be determined by evaluating input/output verification and determining that input documents are canceled. The enduser should provide procedures for error handling, transaction audit trails, and operator authorization to perform transactions.

Decentralized processing: This involves full processing by a microcomputer with the results being uploaded to the mainframe. Data can originate from downline load, micro diskette, source document input or a combination. For example, an investment portfolio management system that performs inventory and trading activity on the micro with ending daily balances up-loaded to the mainframe.

The risks are inaccurate, incomplete, and lost data. The auditor should evaluate input and processing control total generation and test the balancing, settlement and reconcilement procedures. The auditor can utilize a tracing test or use a micro file dump utility to dump master and transaction files for examination. Additionally, the auditor should test the microcomputer transaction reporting function and the master file posting routine. The use of simulation programs may be justified. The enduser should use the standard backup recovery procedures of creating backup files.

Decentralized output: This involves printing processes. Microcomputers can be used for printing output downloaded from a mainframe; straight printing, however, could be done by a remote printer. A more efficient use would be customized reporting and analysis.

The auditor's main concern is the mainframe link transactions. The auditor should determine the extent of authorization control and test the accuracy of downloaded data. The auditor can test authorization control by attempting other on-line transactions not defined for use by the specific microcomputer. Finally, the auditor should determine the validity checks performed by the enduser to ensure the accuracy of the printed special reports.

Customer dial-up access: This involves permitting customer access to mainframe information, permitting them to manage their business relationship more efficiently. Some examples are corporate customer access to their bank's demand-deposit information to execute wire transfers in order to move money to other company locations. Raw material suppliers provide access to their ordering and shipping information to manufacturing companies that want to track location, quantities, and costs of raw materials.

Possible controls for these systems include dial-back software or modems. The customer password and phone number is stored in the modem. The customer calls in and enters the password, and the modem terminates the phone call and then dials back the stored phone number corresponding to the correlated password. This establishes the dial-up link. Additional access controls can be used to control entry into mainframe and customer databases to limit customer access to their own account information only.

Programmatic procedures should exist to permit only authorized customer access to the dial-up link, use of specific transactions, and their accounts.

18.1.3 Environmental Issues

Certain audit and control issues apply to all microcomputers regardless of their function. Physical access control focuses on the risks and exposures of theft or sabotage, unauthorized access, violations of customer privacy, and unauthorized use of data (see Chapter 9).

Logical access control focuses on similar issues but is more effective in a micro-mainframe link environment. The most that physical security can accomplish is protection from theft or sabotage. Micro access control can be accomplished using the PC Audit Card,[1] password control provided in some software packages, and network security provided in some Local Area Network (LAN) systems.

Communication protocols were once a major concern because of the vast difference in data transmission quality. The synchronous protocol used by mainframes was superior to the asynchronous protocol used by microcomputers. New products, however, have introduced sophisticated data checking and correcting software to reduce this concern. The audit issue is whether the micro is using communication hardware and software of sufficient quality to produce quality data communications.

The major concern with the micro-to-mainframe link is the exposure to illicit hackers—people who try to break in to dial-up networks for the sake of vandalism or fraud. The big question is, can it happen? The answer is, yes it can, under certain conditions, first, however, the hacker must gain access to the data lines. Micros use asynchronous protocols, mainframes use synchronous protocols, therefore, they cannot "talk" to each other without interface software acting as an interpreter. The receiver software must be resident in the mainframe to process micro input, and it is via this receiver software that the hacker gains access. IRMA[2] boards that provide terminal emulation are one example of micro sending software that can accomplish a link because it converts the protocol from asynchronous to synchronous. MVS/TSO[3] or VM/CMS[4] are examples of mainframe receiver software.

The installation must provide access control protection for these systems. Some telecommunication access methods, such as VTAM[5] (virtual telecommunication access method) have inherent security procedures than can be used to restrict access. TSO and CMS provide sign-on security and user security exits. Furthermore, security software packages such as CA-Topsecret[6], CA-ACF2[7], and IBM-RACF[8] provide access protection. Other techniques available to frustrate the hacker are dial-back modems, phone computer screening of incoming calls, and dataset access control.

Sufficient protection is available to protect the micro-mainframe link. If a company gets hit by a hacker, they probably were not paying attention.

FIGURE 18–1   Identification of Audit Concerns

Audit Activity Code	Transaction/Area
A	Hardware/Software Security
B	Microcomputer Environment
C	Data File Backup Storage
D	User Micro Training
E	Documentation
F	Software License Agreements
G	Uploading/Downloading Data
H	User-Developed Applications

18.2   PLANNING AND PREPARATION

The EDP auditor will address the same issues in each company area that uses microcomputers—these areas are hardware and software security, microcomputer environment, data file backup storage, user micro training, documentation software license agreements, uploading/downloading data, and user developed applications. The planning phase objective is to document the microcomputer hardware and software used by the auditee, and the types of applications used, if any.

To document the micro equipment being used, the auditor should include micro storage capacity; storage device types such as hard disk, floppy diskettes, cartridge, cassette tape, and others; and peripherals such as printers, modems, power surge protectors, backup tape drives, and other equipment in use.

The auditor should identify the purchased micro software used by the auditee. If the purchased software is unique, its use should be briefly explained. All user-developed micro application programs should be identified, including a brief description of each program's function and purpose. The contents of the reports generated by purchased and user-developed software should be documented, including the type of management or financial decisions made based on this information.

The company should have a policy covering the purchase, use, and control of data in the microcomputer environment. If this exists, the EDP auditor should determine the enduser's familiarity with the policy.

18.3   EXECUTION OF AUDIT REVIEW

Compliance testing, for the most part, may not be necessary because the control evaluation conducted during the preliminary review will provide an adequate picture of the extent of control. The risks and exposures, control objectives, key controls, and audit objectives must be considered in each preliminary review transaction (see Figure 18–2).

FIGURE 18–2 **Scope Summary**

Risks/Exposures

1. Hardware and software destruction
2. Malicious damage
3. Poor physical handling of files
4. Theft of files
5. Inadequate documentation
6. Legal liability
7. Data misuse or fraud

Control Objectives

1. Protect hardware, software, and data from unauthorized access and damage
2. Provide for continuity of microcomputer system use

Key Controls

1. Restricted access
2. Temperature control
3. Adequate procedure documentation
4. Established accountability
5. Off-site storage of backup files

Audit Objectives

Determine that adequate controls exist to ensure:

1. Protection of microcomputer hardware, software, and data from destruction and unauthorized use

Preliminary Review

Activity Code	Transaction/Area	Audit Time	Review Time
		Budget Hours	
A	Hardware/Software Security	5	1
B	Microcomputer Environment	1	—
C	Data File Backup and Storage	7	1
D	User Micro Training	1	—
E	Documentation	7	1
F	Software License Agreements	7	1
G	Uploading/Downloading Data	4	1
H	User-Developed Applications	5	1

18.3.1   Hardware/Software Security

The restriction of physical access to the micro focuses on physical access control. Making sure equipment is immovable focuses on minimizing the risk of theft (micro equipment is valuable to a thief for resale). Micros are typically used in open areas and need some type of anchoring to reduce the ease of moving them (see Figure 18–3).

Making sure the unit has a lock focuses on the user's locking the system when it is not in use or under direct observation, such as after hours or during lunch. The key should be kept in a secure location, separate from the micro when not in use.

Making sure a password is needed includes documenting the security software used and the adequacy of its use. Access to password files should be restricted and consideration should be given to encrypting passwords stored on a hard disk or on diskettes. Only authorized persons should have the ability to delete the security software from the micro. If passwords are recorded, then the record should be kept in a secure location.

FIGURE 18–3   Hardware and Software Security

Audit Test Objective

To determine the security over microcomputer hardware and software

Key Controls

1.   Restricted access

Audit Procedures

Determine that:

1.   Physical access to the micro is restricted
2.   The equipment is anchored to a table or the floor to prevent it from being removed
3.   The micro system unit has a lock on it
4.   A password is needed for logical access to the micro
5.   The effect of short-term and long-term downtime of the micro
6.   The micro software is stored on floppy diskettes and kept in a secure location

Adapted from Wilmington Trust Co., Internal Audit Division

The auditor should determine that the password add/change/delete function of the security software is restricted to authorized users only. Passwords should be changed periodically. The security software should produce access logs listing user-ID, time and date of log-on/log-off, and violations, and the logs should be reviewed by management.

Some software packages such as Lotus 123[9] use passwords to restrict access to data files or software. The auditor should identify these uses.

Determining the effect of short- and long-term downtime focuses on whether downtime could result in loss of business, customer dissatisfaction, or loss of revenue. If so, backup or alternative processing plans should be established by the user.

Making sure that the micro software stored on floppy diskettes is kept in a secure location is also crucial. Examples of secure locations are a locked diskette box, locked in a desk or room, or file cabinet. Security should be considered for lunch hour and breaks, and required during nonbusiness hours (see Chapter 9).

18.3.2   Microcomputer Environment

Many people are not aware of the potential effect of dirt, smoke, heat, paper clips, and soft drinks on computer equipment and diskettes (see Figure 18–4). Smoking, food, and refreshments around the micro should be prohibited. Power surge protectors are vital protection against power spikes that typically occur during thunderstorms that might burn out microcomputers.

The auditor must also examine the user's file-handling techniques. Rough treatment of diskettes will cause lost data.

18.3.3   Data File Backup and Storage

Regardless of the user's file handling techniques, diskettes and hard disks malfunction, resulting in lost data. Backup copies of files will save the user from reconstruction. Reviewing the user's back-up copies of data files, observing the back-up data file

FIGURE 18–4   Microcomputer Environment

Audit Test Objective

To determine if the physical environment is adequate to protect hardware, software, and data from damage

Key Controls

1. Temperature control
2. Clean area
3. Protective procedures

Audit Procedures

Determine that:

1. The micro hardware is kept in a clean, temperature controlled area
2. A power surge protector is connected to each micro
3. Floppy diskettes are kept in protective jackets when not in use
4. Floppy diskettes are kept free from magnetic charges that could destroy data
5. Diskette labels are prepared using a felt-tipped marker or are prepared prior to placing them on the diskette

Adapted from Wilmington Trust Co., Internal Audit Division

storage environment and interviewing the micro user(s) is also a priority (see Figure 18–5).

A suggested backup frequency is at least weekly for hard disk files and monthly for floppy diskettes. A different diskette box, separate cabinet, or other place should be required and verified.

18.3.4   User Micro Training

Making sure that the user has sufficient training in microcomputer use can be done by interviewing the micro user(s). The extent of classroom training or self-instruction on all software, including the operating system software, should be determined. Training is a vital element and is often overlooked. With microcomputers in the hands of the endusers, the quality of training will vary with each manager and the time and budget constraints (see Figure 18–6).

The efficient use of microcomputers and personnel resources depends on the quality of training and knowledge. In

FIGURE 18–5 Data File Backup and Storage

Audit Test Objective

Determine that procedures are followed to ensure adequate protection of data

Key Controls

1. Backup copies are made
2. Secure storage of copies

Audit Procedures

Determine that:

1. Data files are backed up on a timely basis
2. Data files are backed up on a separate diskette, cartridge, or tape
3. Backup copies of data files are clearly labeled as backup including the date of backup
4. Backup copies of data files are stored separately from the original files
5. Access to the backup copies of data files is restricted when not in use

Adapted from Wilmington Trust Co., Internal Audit Division

FIGURE 18–6 User Training

Audit Test Objective

Determine that the user has sufficient training in microcomputer use

Key Controls

1. Instructions from trained personnel
2. Procedures and operation documentation

Audit Procedures

Determine:

1. The extent of training the user has received
   a. For operating the micro hardware
   b. How to backup software and data files stored on floppy diskettes or hard disk drives, if applicable

Adapted from Wilmington Trust Co., Internal Audit Division

some companies, the microcomputer development philosophy will force the "enduser" to develop any specialized applications, without support from a centralized EDP group. Some productivity may be gained in the long run. During the development phase, however, the enduser must forgo all or part of his or her existing job duties to dedicate sufficient time to development of the microcomputer application. The company will buy long-range savings in data processing and other costs at the short-term expense of existing job duties. This tradeoff is acceptable as long as an informed decision on this alternative is made by management.

If cross-training is not provided, the area may have only one person who understands the use of the system. Documentation of procedures, practices, and programs is extremely helpful but not a complete cure.

A microcomputer philosophy and development strategy should be established to optimize the development of microcomputers for the purpose of reducing mainframe-based development projects. Adequate training programs will help the company accomplish effective and efficient microcomputer development.

18.3.5 Documentation

Documenting all software used on the microcomputer can be accomplished by producing a list of the files stored on the hard

---

FIGURE 18–7 Documentation

Audit Test Objective

Determine that the user has adequate documentation of department procedures, and for microcomputer hardware and software operation

Key Controls

1. Organized, readily accessible documentation

Audit Procedures

1. Document all software used on the microcomputer

Determine:

2. That the manufacturer's hardware operation manual defines how to use the equipment, for each of microcomputers and all peripherals

3. That the user has the manufacturer's operating/reference manual for each set of purchased software

4. That the user has reviewed the manuals

Adapted from Wilmington Trust Co., Internal Audit Division

disk in addition to looking at the software stored on floppy diskettes. The floppy diskettes may be too voluminous or contain other data that the auditor does not care about; this makes listing the contents of the floppy's impractical (see Figure 18-7).

Ensuring that the manufacturer's hardware instruction manuals are adequate can be accomplished by reviewing the micro user's hardware and purchased software documentation and by interviewing the micro user(s). Audit should also ensure that each user has the manufacturer's operating/reference manual.

18.3.6 License Agreements

The license agreements that are important to avoid legal liability should be evaluated. It is advisable for the EDP audit group to keep a file of copies of software license agreements for reference (see Figure 18-8).

The auditor should identify the license agreement restrictions and any violations that may exist. This could save the company potential legal liability.

Another issue that should be addressed is the fact that some agreements do not permit copies of software to be made; additional copies violate these license agreements.

If the user has unauthorized copies, the EDP auditor should document the unauthorized copies the user has. If the user has any copies of purchased software for which he or she does not have the originals, it may be a violation of the license agreement, unless the user has a site-license agreement stating otherwise. The authorized copies of the purchased software should be labeled as specified by the license agreement; some license agreements, however, may not specify any conditions for labeling copies.

Most agreements require that the reference material not be copied and must be kept with the software to prove ownership: this should be verified.

Such restrictions as use by only one person, on one particular micro, on one micro at a time, and others should be verified.

Some companies have a policy that forbids the use of personally owned software or software developed on home computers to be used on company computers. This is a preventive control

---

FIGURE 18–8   Software License Agreements

Audit Test Objective

Determine that the user has not violated the license agreements

Key Controls

1. User awareness
2. User review of the agreements

Audit Procedures

1. Read a copy of the software license agreement for each unique set of micro software owned by user
   a. Briefly document the specific copy and use restrictions specified in the agreement
2. Identify and document any violations of software license agreements

Determine whether:

3. The user has only the authorized number of copies of purchased software
4. The user has an original reference/user manual from the software manufacturer for each set of purchased software
5. The software is used as specified by the agreement
6. The software has been modified by the user
   a. Is this allowed by the terms of the license agreement?
   b. Is the modified software labeled according to the agreement specifications, if applicable?
7. The user is in compliance with all license agreement terms
8. The user has only company-owned software on the micro

Adapted from Wilmington Trust Co., Internal Audit Division

over the introduction of viruses into company computers. Furthermore, this policy usually also prohibits the use of games on company computers. These policies are strictly related to each company, however. Any software forbidden by company policy should be identified.

18.3.7   Uploading/Downloading Data

Microcomputer links to mainframes present special control concerns. Interviewing the micro user will determine if the micro is being used to upload data stored on the micro to the mainframe computer or to download data stored on the mainframe computer to the microcomputer. This does not include using the micro as a straight terminal for inquiry. It is aimed at the physical transmission of data stored on the micro, using micro commands, to achieve storage on the mainframe (see Figure 18–9). The mainframe and micro files involved must be identified.

The immediate update of a mainframe production data file or storage of the data in a mainframe production transaction file should be verified. The data transmission method, which could be hard-wire connection, internal dial-up, external dial-up, or other method, must be determined as well. How the data is manipulated, processed, or altered by the microcomputer must be focused on and sensitive data, such as payroll information or proprietary information should be identified so that the auditor can determine the level of security needed.

FIGURE 18–9   Uploading/Downloading Data

Audit Test Objective

Determine the data loaded to or from the mainframe, the use of the data, and the security over the data

Key Controls

1.   Restricted access

Audit Procedures

Determine:

1.   The type of data being uploaded and/or downloaded
2.   The mainframe application system and files effected by the uploading and/or downloading
3.   The type of mainframe processing that results from the uploading of the data to the mainframe
4.   The data transmission method
5.   How the micro user verifies that all data transmitted/received by the micro is received/sent by the mainframe
6.   The microcomputer software product used to facilitate the uploading/downloading of data
7.   The use of data downloaded from the mainframe system to the micro
8.   The sensitivity of data downloaded to the microcomputer

Adapted from Wilmington Trust Co., Internal Audit Division

18.3.8 User Developed Applications

The accuracy of any spreadsheet calculations should be reviewed. The auditor's review should determine that the user adequately test micro application functions.

The purpose of most microcomputer applications is to provide information to management. Just like mainframe programs (see Chapters 10 and 17), the writing of micro-based programs should be approved by management, but in reality, most of these programs will not have written approval. The auditor will have to corroborate the approval by talking with the enduser's manager to determine if he or she approved it (see Figure 18–10).

FIGURE 18–10   User-Developed Micro Applications

Audit Test Objective

Determine the procedures to validate the accuracy of data processed by the application, and the adequacy of user-developed documentation

Key Controls

1. Testing
2. Validation of results
3. Documented procedures

Audit Procedures

1. Review the accuracy of the spreadsheet logic/calculations by running Spreadsheet Auditor[9] using the user spreadsheet file as input

Determine:

2. The user has tested the application program thoroughly prior to relying on the program results
3. That calculations (if applicable) are verified to ensure they produce the intended results
4. The fields used in calculations are verified to ensure they contain the desired information
5. The user-developed programs are authorized by management
6. The user has documented the functions and operating instructions for each spreadsheet, database or basic application
7. The program documentation adequately describes the application

---

Adapted from Wilmington Trust Co., Internal Audit Division

The user's documentation of application functions, and operating instructions should also be focused on. This is the area in which most weaknesses will be found. The documentation should include a program listing or template with field descriptions and formulas documented and sample output reports.

Finally, auditor judgment is called for in assessing the adequacy of documentation; the criteria are 1) whether a person not familiar with the program can successfully execute the program, and 2) whether a person not familiar with the program can make changes to the program with minimal effort?

NOTES

1. PC/AUDIT Card is a registered trademark of Bay Computer Corporation.

2. IRMA is a registered trademark of Data Communications Associates, Inc.

3. MVS/TSO (Multiple Virtual Storage) and (Time Sharing Option) are registered trademarks of International Business Machines, Inc.

4. VM/CMS (Virtual Machine) and (Conversational Monitor System) are registered trademarks of International Business Machines, Inc.

5. VTAM is a registered trademark of International Business Machines, Inc.

6. CA-Top Secret is a registered trademark of Computer Associates, Inc.

7. CA-ACF2 is a registered trademark of Computer Associates, Inc.

8. IBM-RACF is a registered trademark of International Business Machines, Inc.

9. Lotus 123 is a registered trademark of Lotus Development Corp.

19

The Microcomputer
as an Audit Tool

19.1 INTRODUCTION

Microcomputers have brought incredible productivity to the audit function. This chapter provides information about the evolution of microcomputer use for auditors.

The most productive use thus far has been using the word processor in producing audit reports, audit programs, and audit procedures manuals. These audit publications prepared for internal management and internal audit use typically require several draft stages of editing before a final product is produced. Creating these documents with a typewriter requires retyping of entire pages to correct one error. Just avoiding this justifies the cost of the word processor.

The business community is rapidly increasing its reliance on microcomputers—local area networks and electronic mail are quickly becoming the standard rather than the exception. The auditor now needs a microcomputer to access company information. As the number of financial applications increases, the auditor will need knowledge of microcomputer operations and software to audit the financial information stored on microcomputers.

The audit function of many companies has typically used on-line terminals to access information stored on the mainframe. The technology is now available to permit the auditor to replace the terminal with a microcomputer, thereby serving two functions. Mainframe information can be downloaded to the microcomputer, permitting the completion of audit procedures on the desktop. Portable computers and tcom technology provide the off-site auditor with remote access to company information at headquarters or remote locations. In addition, the auditor may communicate with other audit microcomputers at any site. This permits sharing of standard audit programs and internal control questionnaires, that is, efficient and effective customizing to satisfy the audit objectives at any field site. Furthermore, standard audit criteria used for the evaluation of financial statements, documentation, and other performance issues can be stored on disk for use by all auditors. The tcom technology permits microcomputer access to various on-line libraries of information the auditor may want to use for research. The auditor's use of microcomputers is limited only by his or her imagination and the cost justification of this approach.

19.2 IMPLEMENTATION

Microcomputer hardware and software are typically considered a capital item, depreciable over five years. Capital items typically require documented cost justification and management approval. The cost is justified by the benefit of microcomputer usage, translated into monetary terms. However, not all audit uses can be easily translated to monetary savings because it is difficult to estimate the number of hours that will be saved.

19.2.1 Justification

The first step is to identify the potential uses and tools available to accomplish the purpose. The auditor needs to identify the estimated time required to develop the targeted uses and tools. The monetary value of this time is combined with the cost of hardware and software to yield a one-time implementation cost. These costs plus ongoing maintenance costs, software and hardware maintenance agreements, and the amount of auditor time needed to maintain the audit tools is compared to the benefit derived, also translated into monetary terms. This reveals the cost benefit of the purchase. However, some uses cannot be expressed in monetary terms.

The fact that a microcomputer is needed to gain access to system information or complete an audit of a microcomputer application cannot really be expressed in monetary terms. The issue is accomplishing the audit objectives and servicing management, the audit committee, and ultimately the shareholders.

Microcomputers could be used to test all accounts instead of a sample, or to analyze a problem and quantify the total impact as opposed to identifying samples of items that only indicate a problem exists.

It is difficult to quantify increased efficiency without detailed time and motion studies, which the auditor does not have time for.

The microcomputer will make the audit function more efficient and help the auditor work "smarter." These intangible benefits are real and a legitimate part of the justification.

19.2.2 Training

Peak efficiency cannot be obtained until near the end of the learning curve. Many of the commercial software packages are user friendly, menu-driven systems. A working knowledge can be obtained in a very short time through hands-on usage combined with a review of the user's manual. However, a working knowledge of the operating system will make the auditor more effective and flexible. The extent of training needed depends upon the sophistication or complexity of the system being used.

Audit management will need to make a judgment call on the training needed, which depends upon the level of existing skill, knowledge, and the extent of urgency to obtain a working knowledge of a system. A hands-on walk-through, combined with reading of users' manuals, can be sufficient training if there is enough time available.

The EDP auditor should keep pace with the microcomputer industry in terms of developments, new technology, uses, and availability. This is best accomplished through regular review of microcomputer magazines and publications, the selection of which depends upon the auditor's needs and interests. These magazines and publications are an extremely valuable resource and are vital in keeping pace with the microcomputer industry.

19.3 AUDIT USES OF MICROCOMPUTERS

Word processing packages provide the ability to prepare and edit audit reports with minimal effort after the first draft is entered. In the past, audit report comments and recommendations were handwritten on a finding form (see in Chapter 3). These forms were used to handwrite the formal comment, which was turned over to a typist.

19.3.1   Audit Reports

An additional efficiency can be gained by having the staff auditor document the condition, cause, effect, and recommendation directly into a microcomputer or use the handwritten finding form to enter the formal comment into the micro. The objective is to replace the pencil-and-paper transcription with keyboard entry into the microcomputer. Several different auditors will enter the comments on the same audit. A typist or secretary can then merge all the comments and print the first draft of the report for review and editing.

The auditor must be cautious in judging the difference between typing from a handwritten document and transferring thoughts to print with the microcomputer.

19.3.2   Audit Programs

Audit programs and internal control questionnaires (ICQs) are used repeatedly from one audit cycle to another. Changes may be needed to the audit programs that are easily accomplished by retrieving the prior year's program from disk, entering the modification, and printing it for review by other members of the audit team. After the purchase of the initial microcomputer and word processor, the audit programs can be entered from handwritten documents by a typist at the end of each audit. Writing audit programs by hand and having them typed creates no payback or benefit during the current audit; it just looks nice. The payback comes during the next audit cycle when the audit programs must be handwritten again, repeating the same process that occurred the year before. With the audit program stored on the microcomputer, the programs can be called up, edited, printed, reviewed, and edited again, probably in less time than it took to originally handwrite the original programs.

With audit programs and ICQ's on disk, a new audit program for a new area with functions similar to other areas can be cut and pasted to generate a customized document specific to the new audit area. These same benefits accrue for audit procedures manuals, which can be readily changed to match new operating conditions as the need arises.

19.3.3 Workpapers

Some audit workpapers are conducive to automation, whereas others are not. The automation of specialized workpapers unique to each audit in each audit cycle does not provide sufficient payback for entry into the microcomputer. However, the workpapers that utilize standard formats can be stored on disk as templates, retrieved, and the data can be entered to complete the workpaper.

Workpapers illustrated in this book are conducive to automation. Microcomputer storage provides an additional benefit. These workpapers are 1) the identification of existing and nonexisting controls, and 2) the scope summary. The identification of control workpapers can be used to facilitate compliance with SAS No. 44 when generating a report on internal control by the company's external auditors. The SAS No. 44 report requires, among other things, a description of operations and internal controls; documentation of existing controls stored on the microcomputer can be used as the foundation for creating that formal document.

The scope summary for the individual audit remains more or less the same from year to year with minor additions and deletions of the transactions. The preliminary survey and compliance testing transaction schedules change the most from year to year. Automation of this document saves complete rewriting by hand on each audit. Furthermore, the key controls, control objectives, and risks and exposures could be used to enhance the content of audit reports.

19.3.4 Workpaper File Storage

Image technology has reached the marketplace that permits copies of documents to be stored on floppy or cadmium disk (CD). Technology is also emerging that would permit the manipulation of these photographs, or images, making way for the storage of massive volumes of data on a five-inch disk. Retrieval systems are in the market for micro film. These image technologies can permit the storage of all pages of the workpaper file on magnetic or film media. As these image technologies evolve and become more affordable, auditors will be able to prepare and store workpapers on them.

19.3.5 Generalized Audit Software

A few packages exist that come close to the definition of generalized audit software (see Chapter 5), but the best so far are CA-EDP Auditor or Pansophic's PANAUDIT. As financial processing applications migrate to the microcomputer, audit demand for a microcomputer-based generalized audit software product will increase.

19.3.6 Analytical Review

The spreadsheet packages have made the auditor's analytical review work simple. The financial balances of accounts for each year can be stored along with the formulas in the spreadsheets. The current year's information can be inserted by copy, macro, or input commands. The task of manually recording numbers on a columnar pad and running a calculator tape for each line item has been eliminated.

The auditor must exercise caution and implement procedures to ensure the accuracy and integrity of the formulas used in the analytical review, for if the formulas in the spreadsheet are inadvertently changed, the calculations will yield erroneous results.

19.3.7 Audit Management

Spreadsheet, or specific software packages, can be used for audit job scheduling and monitoring, salary and expense budgeting, and risk analysis. The spreadsheet packages can be adapted for use in each of these three areas. Some commercial software development companies have marketed packages to perform these specific functions. The spreadsheet packages have also opened the door to fast and efficient compilation of financial statement information. A major part of an external auditor's analytical review process is to compare the current year's financial information to that of prior years, through the use of ratios and other formulas. The spreadsheet eliminates the need for transcribing numerous lines of financial data for various years, and also eliminates the "number crunching" associated with ratio analysis.

19.3.7.1   JOB SCHEDULING AND MONITORING

This involves recording and tracking the time spent on audit engagements by using start, target completion dates, and budget hours. The package tracks the actual start and actual completion date, and actual hours charged to events as they occur. The input data is entered from time sheets and other special forms. An application can be developed that would track budget and actual hours by audit task, budget and actual hours spent by week, hours spent in each audit phase, and elapsed time spent in field work. The reports produced by the system would aid audit management in controlling actual hours spent, compliance with target dates, and elapsed time parameters.

19.3.7.2   SALARY AND EXPENSE BUDGETING

The spreadsheet packages are easily adaptable to this function permitting audit management to track budget and actual salary information on a yearly and monthly basis. Formulas can be designed to project actual versus budget performance based on simulated salary increases. Salary expense and budget pool dollars can be calculated by the formulas. With proper design, the key numbers of total actual versus budgeted expense can be re-calculated each time a change to an individual salary is made. Furthermore, the information provided by this tool can facilitate reconciliation to a general ledger or other management accounting reports.

19.3.7.3 RISK ANALYSIS

This is another beneficial use of the spreadsheet package. This tool permits audit management to assign weights and scores to various risk factors present throughout the company. The total calculated score is translated to an audit priority that establishes the frequency and necessity of an individual audit. The formulas are not complex, but in an example with five scoring categorizes, the number of manual calculations could increase the error rate of the risk analysis exercise. With a spreadsheet, the weights and scores for individual risk factors in individual audit areas can be changed to experiment or simulate the effect of various levels of risk.

19.3.7.4 SYSTEMS ACCESS

Microcomputers can be linked to mainframe systems by dial-up technology to retrieve and analyze information. Even though generalized audit software packages are the primary tool, there may be some instances in which a microcomputer may be more appropriate.

Simulations and audit data collection could be adapted to the micro environment (see Chapter 2). The auditor would need to write the programs in either a basic programming language or high-level language. The data needed could be extracted from the mainframe and saved on disk, which the audit software programs could be executed against. These areas of microcomputer development are the current leading edge. Their usage and development is limited only by the auditor's imagination.

19.4   EVALUATION OF PACKAGES

It is easier to explain how to evaluate a package than to complete the research and evaluation process. The objective is to purchase a package that exactly fits the needs.

The first step is to define the objectives that need to be accomplished by the software package. The more specifically defined these needs, the more comprehensive the evaluation will be. The objectives are translated to package functions. Because the auditor may not know what package functions are available, or how the packages operate, he or she must research them and their capabilities. As each function or capability is identified and understood, the auditor can decide on its value in accomplishing the audit objective. When all capabilities are decided upon, these can be scheduled in a matrix format with the capabilities on one axis and the individual package names on the other axis. Completing the evaluation is a matter of checking off the desired capabilities present in each package. This matrix will provide a means quickly to identify the package that best suits the auditor's needs. However, cost is always a factor; some capabilities may be sacrificed for reduced cost.

19.5   PRODUCT INFORMATION

The following section describes some of the microcomputer software packages available for use by auditors. This information was taken from the vendor's product brochures or documentation. This section is neither an endorsement nor criticism of the quality, usefulness, or functionality of the systems.

Word processing, spreadsheet, and data base packages are not mentioned because they have other uses. Software packages mentioned are those which the vendor promotes as having some audit or security application.

THE SPREADSHEET AUDITOR™

This package consists of three separate programs: audit, sideprint, and cell noter. The audit program contains documentation and debugging utilities that are fully interactive, to simplify error location and correction of useful worksheet documentation. The audit program contains 20 tests that point out anomalies and potential errors. For example, ranges outside worksheet boundaries, formulas referencing empty cells, and cells that have error messages. The test results appear on screen. They provide user-defined tests that trace the relationships of worksheet cells to each other, and an index function locates copies of original formulas. The reporting function lists the worksheet's vital statistics and the contents of each cell, including results of different range, formula, and cell tests and cell interrelationships.

The sideprint function permits printing of worksheets, reports, and files sideways for creating unbroken printouts. The cell noter function permits the auditor to create memos on screen while in the worksheet program and append the notes to specific cells for later research.

The package provides an interactive tutorial, on-line help, and permits the creation of back-up disks. A product upgrade plan is available. The system requires an IBM PC, XT, AT[1] running MS-DOS[2] V2.0 or later with at least 192K of RAM. It will run on totally IBM-compatible computers. This package is marketed by Consumers Software, Inc., 73 Water Street, Vancouver, B.C.

Expert Auditor™

The Expert Auditor™ is a PC-based analysis and reporting system consisting of a series of menu-driven programs that lead the auditor through step-by-step analysis of hardware systems. It provides detailed audit plans that tell the auditor what questions to ask, analyzes the results, identifies areas of risk, displays findings on the screen, suggests recommended controls, and produces an audit report.

The package consists of seven products; CICS, IMS, System/36, System/38, data center, disaster recovery, and microcomputers. The system requires an IBM PC or compatible with 256K of RAM, 2-360K disk drives, or hard disk and will operate under MS-DOS or PC-DOS. This product is marketed by MIS Training Institute, 4 Brewster Road, Framingham, MA.

PC Auditor™

This package performs automated procedures, examines disks, locates and displays files, tests for deleted data and change control, produces exception tickets, summarizes the analysis and findings of system control memorandums, and provides a complete auditing methodology. An optional maintenance program is available. This system runs on an IBM PC and compatibles, PS/2, with 156K of RAM. Disk requirements were not available. This package is marketed by TACT Specialist, Inc., P.O. Box 4691, Lynchburg, VA.

Audit Master Plan®

This is a menu-driven system with seven modules in the main menu: system management, risk factors management, audit portfolio management, personnel skills management, long-term planning and budgeting, short-term planning and scheduling, and time reporting and activity monitoring. This system is a scientifically designed computer-based planning system with user-defined risk categories that can customize the plan to individual corporate needs. The system offers six months of free customer support and operates under MS-DOS or PC-DOS on IBM PC's or compatibles. This system can be made LOTUS[3]-compatible. Disk and memory requirements were not available. This package is marketed by the Institute of Internal Auditors, P.O. Box 140099, Orlando, FL.

MAP (MODULAR AUDIT PROGRAM)

This package is endorsed by the Bank Administration Institute. Training is provided by Arthur Young (now Ernst & Young). This system is a total audit program that allows development of audit plans, performance of the audit, and recording and reporting of results, using either a personal computer or a hardcopy system. It covers areas of regulations compliance management; a set of tests and procedures to determine whether the internal control system is in place and the area is in compliance; and management reporting, including summaries and audit progress, results of tests, findings and recommendations.

MAP is a self-help program with builtin formatted worksheets, procedures, and tests. This system is geared to an audit of the banking industry. The system operates on IBM PC's and compatibles or MacIntosh. System specifications were not available. This package is marketed by MicroAnalysis Products Industries, Inc., 1113 Spruce Street, Boulder, CO.

FOCAUDIT and PC/FOCUS

FOCAUDIT is a menu-driven system that includes interactive procedures that perform a full range of audit functions: field analysis, sampling routines, validating data, testing and converting dates, statistical summaries, exception reports, and match file routines. PC/FOCUS provides an English nonprocedural language, formal reporting, on-line help facilities, TableTalk Natural language windows, financial modeling language, a dialogue manager to build menu-driven procedures and applications, database manager, full-screen database editor, full-screen text editor, graphics, and statistics. The system is compatible with asynchronous and synchronous PC/mainframe file transfer and communications programs and has the ability to process FOCUS sequential, and DIF format files. It can operate in distributed processing and PC networks. Operating requirements include IBM, Wang,[4] or Texas Instruments[5] PC with minimum 512K RAM and operates under PC/DOS and requires 1-360K floppy disk and a 5MB hard disk. This package is marketed by Information Builders, Inc., 1250 Broadway, New York, NY.

AUDISTAT™

This system is an auditor's statistical financial tool for generating random number tables, projecting the audited value of a sample with accuracy and reliability measurements, integrity checking of selected samples, sample size calculations to achieve a certain degree of accuracy, and a more efficient stratified sampling technique to reduce sample size. The program can be used for estimating interim gross profit, effects of price and cost changes, labor costs and other cost components, LIFO inventory calculations, estimating allowance for obsolescence, and uncollectible accounts. This product is marketed by DKB, Inc., 425 Farnsworth Drive, Broomall, PA.

FAST!C™

This system is a microcomputer software tool for corporate controllers, financial analysts and internal auditors. It automates labor-intensive clerical and mathematical procedures producing automated financial, tax, and analytical review workpapers and reports. It interfaces with popular spreadsheet and database packages. It is expandable to include statistical sampling, time control, confirmation, and consolidation. This package is marketed by Financial Audit Systems, 3801 Wake Forest Road, Raleigh, NC.

focus:ABC™

This system is a LOTUS-based audit and tax workpaper program. It is designed to produce accountants' workpapers; trial balances, adjusting journal entries, financial statements, consolidations, and various tax forms summarizations. This package is marketed by Hemming Morris, Inc., 1700 S. El Camino Real, San Mateo, CA.

Organization Chart Maker

This system is an organizational chartmaker that permits control of chart structure and style with 430 characters across and 150 lines down. Boxes can be drawn of any size or mixed sizes, and explanatory text can be placed anywhere. It operates on IBM PC, XT, AT, PS/2, or compatibles, under MS-DOS with 256K RAM and 2 floppy disk drives or hard disk. This package is marketed by KD Systems, Inc., P.O. Box 97024, Raleigh, NC.

Flow Charting II+™

This system is a flowcharting preparation package with 10 font styles, a variety of shapes, and the ability to print multiple files without interruption. The flowcharts can be printed in presentation quality or laser quality. It offers a shrink-screen capability for examining the entire organization chart of 200 columns by 120 lines on-screen. It was created specifically for flowcharts. It will run on IBM PC, XT, AT, or PS/2, and compatibles, and the HP Portable Plus.[6] It requires 256K RAM with 1-5 1/4 inch or 3 1/2 inch disk drive and screen graphics capabilities. The company's promotional literature identifies a number of printers supported by the package. This package is marketed by Patton and Patton Software Corp., 81 Great Oaks Blvd., San Jose, CA.

PC DRAW™

This system is a flowchart generation package permitting production of drawings up to 99 pages long. Templates come with the package including flowcharting, office layout, and alternate text. The user can create and store an unlimited number of user defined samples. The package includes an interactive tutorial and operates on IBM PC, XT, AT or compatibles. It requires IBM hardware or compatible graphics adapter and graphics monitor. It also has a light pin capability, available from Micrografx. This package is marketed by Micrografx, Inc., 1701 North Greenville Ave., Richardson, TX.

Electronic Index to Technical Pronouncements

This is a product of the AICPA and includes a recorded question-and-answer phone hotline. The electronic index permits microcomputer dial-up connection for research of technical pronouncements issued by the FASB, Emerging Issues Task Force, U.S. Securities and Exchange Commission groups and other publications of the AICPA.

AY/ASQ™

The acronym stands for Arthur Young/"Audit Smarter, Quicker." The system was marketed by Arthur Young Co. (now Ernst & Young). This MACINTOSH-based system was geared to an external audit approach, permitting micro-based evaluation of internal control procedures whose end product is a suggested audit approach and audit program that can be customized through the use of a supplied text editor. In December 1987, the system was advertised as the first "expert system" for auditing. Inasmuch as Arthur Young and Ernst & Whinney merged into one firm, this package is currently being evaluated to identify enhancements to meet the needs of the combined audit firm.

Z Math®

This system is a complete time value and money calculator that operates on IBM PC, XT, AT or compatibles with LOTUS 1-2-3 or Symphony. It performs all loan and savings calculations, amortizations, and "what if" comparisons. It is designed for compliance officers, auditors, loan review officers, and controllers. The package will produce a printed proof of every APR calculation for permanent record. This package is marketed by the Bank Administration Institute, 60 Gould Center, Rolling Meadows, IL.

ACCESS SECURITY PRODUCTS

PC Audit Card™

This package consists of a circuit board, "card" insertable in one of the microcomputer expansion slots, and software loadable from a floppy diskette. This system is designed to automatically create an audit trail of all computer usage. It is an independent hardware device that has its own battery-powered clock. This system records operator usage using the time and date of its own independent clock based on the user's password. Users can be classified by privilege levels of general user, reader, and system manager. The system permits addition, changing, and deletion of users and privileges. It can control read access by time-of-day and day-of-week for each person. This system permits formatting of the audit trail reports of user access, with ten filters to format and convert information in the audit trail. The system operates on IBM PC, XT, AT, PC portables and IBM compatibles, operating under MS-DOS or PC-DOS. Disk space requirements for general purposes are 64K, for the system manager—128K, and for the filter programs—224K. This product is marketed by Bay Computer Corporation, York and Haverhill Streets, Andover, MA.

TRAQNET 2000™

This is an access control system for dial-up networks. This product contains a series B version for stand-alone systems and a series N version for network systems. The network system is accompanied by a TRAQSTAT™, an audit trail statistical analysis package. This system provides disconnect and dial-back capability for dial-up networks and has optional features for controlling access, answer modes, and routing modes. This package is marketed by Comprehensive Communication Systems, Inc., 86 East Illinois, Pallatine, IL.

KINETIC ACCESS™

This is an access control system to provide data security. The system includes a hardware device to control the booting process and a resident control program that requires 45K of RAM. The hardware device can be either an EPROM for insertion into an available RAM socket, or a circuit board for insertion into an expansion slot. The functions of the system include procedures for log-on and log-off, restricted access through the simple menu, limited DOS access, assignment of DOS commands to individuals, automatic log-off after a period of inactivity, and write protection. It operates on an IBM PC, XT, AT, and IBM compatibles with 256K RAM. This package is marketed by Kinetic Corporation, 240 Distillery Commons, Lexington Road, Louisville, KY.

StopLock IV™

It is a menu-driven computer information security system, with its security features in a printed circuit board. It provides system access control for up to 32 users by time of day and day of week. Access is denied until a valid ID and password are entered. File access control is provided for each user, who can be granted different levels of access. Protection can be expanded to encompass ports, printers, and other peripherals. The system utilizes DES encryption for specified files and a SuperErase function that deletes all data from a disk. The screen and keyboard can be locked with a software command. Audit trail reports are provided, detailing authorized system usage and unauthorized access attempts to permit detection of security violations. The audit trail reports can be printed or displayed on the screen. All functions are incorporated in the printed circuit board and provides its own realtime clock with power backup. The system operates on an IBM PC, XT, AT, or IBM compatibles with an internal hard disk, and a full expansion slot. It operates under DOS 2.1 or higher. This package is marketed by Century Systems, Inc., 1044 Main, Kansas City, MO.

Gordian System Access Key™

This is an access control device. The access device is the user's requiring possession of a "key" and a password to gain access to the system. The user holds the access key up to the screen and data contained in the pattern is read (similar to light-pen technology). The access code is entered and, if correct, access is granted. The system is accompanied by all equipment needed to program the keys. This package is marketed by Gordian Systems, Inc., 3512 West Bayshore Road, Palo Alto, CA.

ThumbScan™

This is a fingerprint identification device to control access to microcomputers. It is compatible with numerous microcomputer and mainframe systems. This package is marketed by Thumb-Scan, Inc., 2 Mid-America Plaza, Oakbrook Terrace, IL.

Defender IID™

This is an access control and security hardware system for placement between microcomputers and host computers. The dial-up lines are connected to the Defender, which is connected to the host. This system is physically independent because the hardware is in a self-contained metal enclosure designed for mounting in a standard communication cabinet. Protection is accomplished through the use of a user access code and an optional code referred to as "SNK key." An audit trail of all access activity is maintained whether access was successful or not. It utilizes RS-232 communication ports with a CMOS RAM memory board with battery-back protection. This system requires a user ID, password, and/or an SNK. Security can be defined for each person by time and date and is available in three different models, which handle various number of telephone lines in a network. The system is marketed by Digital Pathways, Inc., 201 Ravendale Drive, Mountainview, CA.

NOTES

1. IBM, IBM-PC, XT, AT, PC-DOS, PS/2, CICS, IMS, System/36, and System/38 are products and registered trademarks of International Business Machines, Inc.

2. MS-DOS is a registered trademark of Microsoft Corporation.

3. LOTUS, LOTUS 1-2-3, and SYMPHONY are registered trademarks of Lotus Development Corp.

4. Wang is a registered trademark of Wang Computer Corporation.

5. Texas Instruments is a registered trademark of Texas Instruments, Inc.

6. HP and HP Portable Plus are registered trademarks of Hewlett Packard, Inc.

20

Integrated Audit Approach

20.1   INTRODUCTION[1]

Systems are designed as integrated units, but the traditional audit approach treats systems as two parts that are audited separately. The traditional audit approach places the focal point of environment control at the general-auditor-level, but the control analysis is performed by staff-level auditors. As a result, serious control weaknesses may be overlooked. Compounding this problem is the delivery of fragmented information delivered by separate audit reports.

The term "financial audit" refers to the audit of the application users and their interface with the system to complete their business function. This audit includes analytical review, compliance, and substantive testing of the financial transactions within the operations area of a company.

20.2   OVERVIEW OF AUDIT APPROACHES

During the late 1970s, the integrated audit approach emerged; its objective was to achieve productivity improvements by auditing both the EDP and the financial portions of systems with one auditor.

20.2.1   Separate Audits

Internal control systems have traditionally been reviewed by separate EDP and financial staffs, which implies the overhead cost of two separate management teams and the production of separate audit reports. Salary levels, training costs, and management needs, however, are forcing auditors to reevaluate the use of separate audits.

Separate audits, which have one budget for the review of the application user department and another for the EDP application, consist of separate audit programs, (ICQs), audit management teams, time schedules, testing, and audit reports.

The organizational structure of the two separate audit teams ideally includes a manager, a supervisor, an in-charge, and staff auditors for each audit. This organizational structure and the lack of coordinated timing forces the general auditor to become the focal point of detailed information about computer applications and operations control systems. In addition, fragmented information and the delivery of separate audit reports can produce substandard results for senior management. Figure 20–1 illustrates this organizational structure and the information flow problem.

FIGURE 20–1   Separate Audit Approach Job Organization Structure

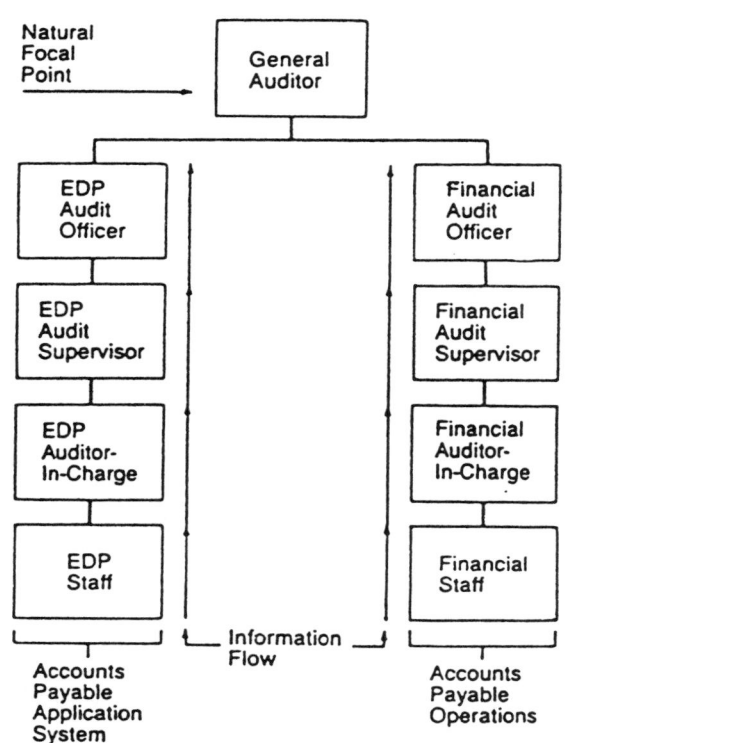

20.2.2 Coordinated Planning

The second attempt to improve audit productivity involved coordinating the planning of the EDP and financial audits as well as the time it took to complete the different types of field work involved. Unfortunately, coordinating field work completion time is burdensome because the time it takes to complete testing varies between financial and EDP audits. In addition, two separate management teams maintain the overhead.

20.2.3 Concurrent Audits

Expanding the concept of coordinated planning, the concurrent audit approach was implemented. This still involved using the separate staffs, but using a methodical management interface to coordinate the audit approach. In addition, all audit work was to be completed simultaneously, using the same testing samples. Significant coordination and consulting among management team members was necessary to complete the audit. This concurrent audit phase was similar to the separate approach except that:

- Field work was timed to coincide,
- Testing samples were identical,
- One report was issued,
- Functional audit work was coordinated, and
- Methodical audit management team cooperation was required.

A certain amount of the redundancy in the preliminary survey, ICQ, and compliance testing steps was eliminated through concurrent audits. Nevertheless, the concurrent approach required extensive coordination between the management teams of the separate audit staffs. The decrease in functional audit time was, therefore, offset by an increase in administrative time. The concurrent approach still kept staff auditors divided into separate sections, which prevented them from gaining the total-system exposure that is vital to the development of systems auditors.

Knowledge and experience requirements were basically the same as those for the separate approach except for the need to learn administrative coordination techniques at the in-charge, supervisory, and managerial levels. Adequate coordination shifted the focal point of the audit from the general auditor to the supervisor and in-charge, who had to constantly communicate audit results up the management chain.

The concurrent audit organization structure was similar to the separate audit structure, except formalized information flow procedures were required at the in-charge, supervisory, and managerial levels. This increased the scope of knowledge at the staff levels, but the interface procedures were still cumbersome and inefficient.

20.2.4 One-Team Approach

Once coordinated planning was established, there was a push to share resources and to use one management team with a mix of both EDP and financial auditors to audit the complete system. Financial and EDP auditors were assigned to the audit under the supervision of one manager, one supervisor, and one in-charge that planned the audit and designed the testing for both sides of the audit. However, a single audit program was not always developed, and the management teams did not usually have sufficient training to prepare proper testing or to review workpapers.

20.2.4.1 TECHNICAL SUPPORT

An additional change involved the development of a technical support group consisting of high-level EDP audit specialists skilled in advanced EDP topics to handle database systems, on-line systems and systems software audits, among others. They provided technical consulting to the audit staff and conducted system development reviews.

20.2.5   Integrated Audits

The final evolutionary phase[2], which has not been widely achieved, is total integration. The internal audit industry is currently moving toward this goal. In this phase, all management team members are trained in EDP and financial audit disciplines, with little crossover consulting. Staff auditors are trained in both audit disciplines and use a single audit program. An EDP audit technical support group handles the hi-tech EDP audits, and a single audit report is issued that covers the whole system, including compensating controls and problems. Audit efficiency is at its peak with this approach.

The integrated audit approach combines audit staff resources to analyze the complete control environment. EDP and non-EDP auditors are combined into one team with one scope and one audit program to review the total system, evaluate results, and present an audit report covering the total control environment. This approach permits evaluation and testing of the manual and automated systems from the perspective of how the data flows from transaction origination to output.

The audit methodology discussed in Chapter 3 is conducive for use in the integrated approach.

20.2.6   Organizational Considerations

Because technical expertise is required to understand special business activities, audit departments are often organized around an organization's major business units. Data processing supports all company activities; therefore, it does not qualify as a separate line of business; but the audit organization typically separates the EDP audit and financial groups because of the technical expertise required to perform EDP audits. This approach requires both the financial and EDP audit staffs to be aware of the results of both audit efforts.

This structure produces specialists, thus limiting career paths and exposure to the total organization. People entering the internal audit profession view it as a springboard to other areas, because management looks to the audit department as a training ground. Many auditors do not want to specialize early in their careers, because it is to their advantage to gain a total view of the organization. Therefore, the internal audit group creates specialists of people who want to gain general exposure.

A long-range solution is to train all auditors in both audit disciplines and develop an approach that permits total system review. As non-EDP auditors review the total system, they gain experience in dealing with the interface between EDP and the manual environment and, in turn, evolve into more experienced systems auditors.

After several years of experience with integrated audits, EDP auditors begin specializing in environmental and developmental audits. Environmental auditors are technical specialists who concentrate on audits of on-line systems, systems software, and database administration, and other highly technical areas. They are also best suited to perform system development reviews. Training costs are minimized because expensive technical training is limited to a small group of people.

20.3 THE INTEGRATED AUDIT APPROACH

There are two methods to accomplish integration.

The first is one-team audit, which merges the audits of EDP and non-EDP systems into one total review, eliminating the redundancies in completing the preliminary survey, internal control questionnaire, compliance testing, and administrative duties. The objective of integrated staffing is to produce a balance of EDP and financial audit expertise that matches the system's sophistication and to eliminate redundant management, specifically the in-charge, the supervisor, and the manager. As the auditors gain experience, the audit department evolves toward total integration.

The second is total integration. With staff auditors trained in both disciplines, there is no distinction between EDP and financial auditors, and only one audit program is used. Total integration is the next logical step after the successful use of the one-team approach. By either means, the integrated audit approach:

- Produces an opinion of the total control environment,
- Reduces job staffing requirements,
- Reduces the time needed to audit a system,
- Evaluates the manual system flow as it relates to computer processing,
- Reduces scheduling and interface problems of two separate approaches,
- Lowers the recognition and resolution focal point of weaknesses in the total system,
- Simplifies supervision,
- Increases education of the user and programming personnel regarding the total system, and
- Improves career path options for auditors.

Either approach requires one manager, one supervisor, and one in-charge. The one-team audit uses an appropriate mix of EDP and financial auditors to review a given area. The disadvantage of the one-team audit is staff supervision and review of workpapers by supervisors and managers without EDP audit experience.

20.3.1 Focal Point

The focal point of the audit work under the integrated organizational structure is the staff auditor, because both the automated and manual portions of the system are observed by one single auditor. The knowledge gained from preliminary survey and testing is passed up from the staff level. All audit team members, therefore, have more knowledge of the total system.

The focal point of the audit work under the one-team structure is the in-charge auditor, because both the automated and manual portions of the system are observed by separate auditors and passed to the in-charge auditor. The knowledge gained from preliminary survey and testing is passed up from the in-charge level to audit management.

20.3.2 Training

The manager, supervisor, and in-charge must eventually gain sufficient experience to manage, design, and control the technical EDP audit aspects of the audit; these management techniques can be learned. During this learning period, design, implementation, and control of the technical aspects can be achieved through use of the EDP auditors on a direct assignment or consultant basis until sufficient experience is gained.

Training, knowledge, and experience are critical to total integration, but they can be difficult and expensive to obtain at the audit management level.

20.3.3 Audit Testing

The compliance test program is designed by a single team on the basis of a preliminary survey of the entire system. The transactions subject to review are completely flowcharted, from transaction origination to report output. The testing of a transaction flow is designed to include the effects of the entire system. Therefore, all input, processing, and output controls (manual or automated) are reviewed for each selected transaction to prevent inconclusive testing. This allows for continuity of testing and documentation of the control weaknesses and permits the issuance of a single report.

20.4 COMPARISON OF APPROACHES

20.4.1 Separate Audits

The EDP application audit analyzes computer processing controls. To adequately accomplish this, the auditors must consider transaction origination, input, processing, and output controls performed in the manual environment. However, some of these controls are also examined during the financial audit, resulting in redundancy. Data integrity controls are the user's responsibility during input and output phases, which require coverage in both audits.

The separate audit approach does not address the timing of the two audits, often resulting in inconclusive testing or redundancy. Input, processing, and output control reviews are performed by separate staffs during different periods. Procedural changes in user operations implemented after the first (usually financial) audit but before the application audit may either correct or exacerbate control weaknesses previously detected. This requires repeating certain audit steps.

If compensating controls in the manual or automated portions of the system are not reviewed, audit findings may be invalid. A simplistic example is the omission of vendor number verification during input by an accounts payable clerk, permitting generation of checks to fictitious vendors. Verification, however, could be performed by the accounts payable system posting program, which checks vendor numbers against an authorized list on a disk file and rejects transactions for vendors not included. Testing during the separate financial audit may not uncover this control, but the EDP application audit probably would. The financial team would report a weakness that does not exist, wasting valuable time in research, documentation, comment preparation, and review.

The separate approach creates an environment in which the EDP auditor's knowledge and experience become one-sided from concentrating on the EDP aspects, and although some review of the manual system is required, the EDP auditor is often unfamiliar with the manual operation, accounting framework, or business activities within which computer systems must operate.

Supervision of the separate audits requires more time and duplicates effort, because both audits require separate management teams. The specialized scope of the separate audits and the experience of staff auditors dictate the extent of supervision needed. The non-EDP audit requires knowledge of the technical aspects of user operations and business activities. For example, an audit of installment lending requires knowledge of acceptable interest rate practices, loan documentation requirements, loan approval limits, credit scoring requirements, loan proceeds distribution, and charge-offs. Staff auditors may not have this knowledge, but the respective EDP and financial audit managements should. Separate audits also produce redundancies in preliminary surveys, internal control questionnaires, compliance testing, and administration.

20.4.2 Concurrent Audits

An audit department desiring to use state-of-the-art techniques will evolve to a point at which separate audits create frustration with the quality of service provided to senior management and the audit committee. Trial and error leads to the next logical step—the concurrent audit approach.

Timing: The functional audit work of the separate teams does not permit exact coincident timing. The time-intensive tasks of EDP documentation research, computer program analysis, and programming for automated testing typically extend the EDP audit staff completion date beyond that of the financial staff. The EDP audit staff often needs additional time to competently design, code, debug, and follow-up on automated testing. Timing rarely permits issuance of only one report within acceptable time-frames, resulting in disjointed report comments, which does little to correct deficiencies from a total system perspective.

Inconclusive Testing: Tests are established by both teams to determine whether the control points isolated in the transaction review are working properly. For example, in testing a control point that requires review of critical data before input, the control objective is to isolate erroneous data, and the control technique could be manual data review by a clerk. Financial team testing might also reveal that the clerical review is not being consistently performed and recommend that the required data review be conducted before input. The EDP audit testing of the application edit programs could find that particular date is validated by programmatic edits, preventing the posting of transactions with erroneous data. No weakness actually exists, because the control objective is satisfied by a programmatic edit; the purpose of the comment is thus eliminated. If the information focal point is at the general auditor level and separate untimed reports are used, the control may be missed and erroneously reported as a weakness.

Time Budget: The concurrent audit approach requires two audit teams, and the organizational focal point usually remains at the general auditor level. Limited time savings are produced by distribution of functional audit work, but dual management allows no administrative time savings; therefore, significant budget reductions are not produced by the concurrent audit approach.

Concurrent audit of the manual and automated portions of the system are completed in the same time interval. This duplicates staffing but is still more efficient than separate audits, because it is possible to issue one report given the proper time constraints of testing. The true problem occurs when the EDP audit team must program the automated testing, which requires more time than non-EDP testing. Testing performed by the financial staff is generally manual and can be prepared and completed more quickly than EDP audit testing. EDP auditors must program audit software after performing extensive research into file definitions and processing. With a new audit, file definitions must be coded and programs must be developed and tested. Although these programs save time in subsequent audits, their initial development is more time consuming than manual testing.

20.4.3   Integrated Audits

The one-team audit still uses EDP and financial auditors. Total integration refers to an audit staff composed of auditors trained in both disciplines, but it still does not suggest total elimination of EDP audit specialists. There will always be the need for EDP audit technicians to review the highly technical areas of EDP, because the entire audit staff cannot be cost-effectively trained to keep up with the rapid technological changes of on-line, operating, and database management systems. The high-level technical EDP audit specialist, however, is only a small part of what is needed; therefore, integration can reduce overall audit staff requirements and costs. The integrated approach provides auditors with experience in system controls and permits their participation (after sufficient exposure) in systems development projects, which reduces a large personnel resource drain.

Familiarity with system details decreases in higher levels of the audit management organization, regardless of the audit approach. The separate and concurrent approaches position the general auditor as the focal point. The integrated audit approach, however, lowers the focal point of the details of the total system to the in-charge or staff auditor level. Therefore, although the level of this detailed knowledge continues to decrease at higher audit management levels, a more extensive knowledge now exists within the audit department. Figure 20–2 depicts the integrated organizational structure and the lowering of the focal point (in contrast to Figure 20–1).

Testing: Compliance testing is designed to test the controls throughout transaction processing instead of in separate segments that require separate tests. The auditor observes the entire flow and all control points associated with that transaction in place of two separate auditors with two objectives observing two distinct and separate portions of the system that actually relate to each other. The testing is more efficient, takes less time, and is accompanied with a greater probability of isolating all true errors in control techniques. This testing design permits formation of an opinion of the total environment, reduction in time to perform the audit evaluation of the manual operations flow as it relates to computer processing, and reduced scheduling and interface problems.

Most programming of automated testing should be left to experienced technicians to permit its timely completion. Simple audit software programming, if closely supervised, can be performed by the inexperienced as a training exercise.

FIGURE 20–2   Integrated Audit Approach Job Organization Structure

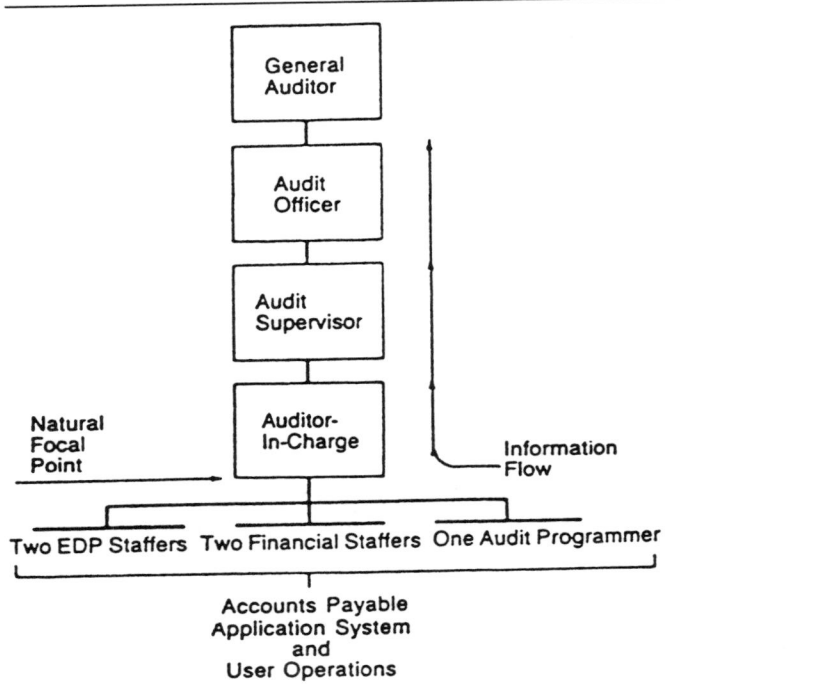

Timing: The timing of audit work is totally controlled by one management group and is increasingly manageable as staff become available. As information gathering phases give way to testing phases, staff size can be altered without regard to coordinating test results with a separate team. The auditors leaving one audit must advise the rest of the team of any testing results, perceptions, and opinions that they have accumulated during their work. The type of supervision differs with type of the audit functions. EDP and financial matters require different planning disciplines in terms of time and technical expertise required.

Budget Considerations: Initially, the budget remains close to the subtotal of the two audits. As experience increases, however, the hours to complete the integrated audit decrease, becoming less than the sum of the two parts.

Productivity: In today's business environment, productivity management constantly searches for methods to reduce cost without reducing quality. The separate and concurrent audit approaches, although necessary in some circumstances, require more time to cover the extra administrative and functional audit activities.

Through persistent effort in implementing the approach, reductions in hours will be gained slowly in the evolutionary process from separate to integrated audits. The exact reduction is difficult to determine, because it is highly dependent on the organization's requirements. But, generally speaking, a 20% decrease in chargeable time is reasonable. Administrative time reductions are the most obvious; however, other time improvements can be gained by more efficient test design and work assignment.

User and EDP Exposure: The separate and concurrent approaches induce the auditor to hold post-audit conferences with the user for the manual portion and EDP personnel for the EDP portion. Although EDP personnel share certain insights into manual operations, they do not always completely understand the effect of internal control weaknesses on the total system. With the integrated approach, user and EDP representatives are usually invited to post-audit conferences, exposing both parties to the audit results. This technique gradually increases total system control understanding of EDP and user personnel.

Career Paths: Traditional audit approaches require a certain degree of specialization for each business unit and EDP situation. College graduates entering the internal audit profession view it as a stepping stone, because of the wide exposure obtained. These people are very willing to work for overall EDP and business unit exposure, but few are willing to commit to specialization early in their careers. Integration, system flow evaluation, and staff pooling permits broad exposure, providing more auditors with details of the total system.

Training: The training necessary depends on the overall job mix, job assignment in the management team, and existing level of experience. For example, an EDP audit manager responsible for certain financial areas may need accounting or technical training concerning that area's operation. The financial audit manager assigned to EDP areas will need EDP audit exposure or consulting assistance. Most important, the manager should possess strong management skills.

Figure 20–3 provides a matrix of the exposure level typically required by the management team. These levels indicate a goal that can be obtained over a two-year period, but by no means indicate a prerequisite to begin the integrated approach. The EDP expertise can be supplanted by using existing EDP technicians as consultants on an as-needed basis.

Staff auditors should receive the regular basic audit and industry training. EDP concepts must also be included in the training. This facilitates effective communications with EDP auditors and helps staff auditors understand the EDP functions they encounter. Basic EDP concepts can be learned through training and through use of an audit software package that provides exposure to the rudiments of EDP application concepts, file structures, job control language, documentation, programming department procedures, and data center procedures. This exposure answers such questions as how the EDP departments fit into the overall organizational structure, and it begins to remove the mystique of the computer.

In-house classroom training of EDP concepts not covered by audit software exposure can be taught by experienced EDP auditors. Textbook reading can be assigned for employees to

FIGURE 20–3   Management Exposure-Level Matrix

Area	In-Charge	Supervisor	Officer
EDP Concepts	Basic	Intermediate	Inter.—advan.
EDP Audit Concepts	Basic	Intermediate	Advanced
EDP Audit Techniques	Basic	Intermediate	Advanced
Industry Concepts	Intermediate	Advanced	Advanced
User Operations	Intermediate	Advanced	Advanced
Audit Concepts	Intermediate	Advanced	Advanced

complete on their own time. Initial training should be limited to basic concepts relating to applications and functional EDP areas.

The next logical step exposes trainees to application audit concepts by walking them through the standard control questionnaire and audit program that explains transaction origination, input, processing, and output. It is impossible in a short time to explain all controls; covering basic control techniques and objectives should suffice.

The senior staff assuming in-charge responsibilities have undergone basic training but need experience with the integrated approach as well as additional exposure to EDP. The objective is to provide the senior-level person with sufficient knowledge to understand total system processing, analyze all control techniques and objectives, and design the necessary manual and automated testing of control techniques.

Training needs depend on these environmental factors:

- Extent of EDP sophistication,
- Experience and education of existing audit staff,
- Speed of training needed, and
- Available training sources (*e.g.,* the EDP department, audit, external seminars, external auditors, and professional associations).

EDP exposure provided by the integrated audit approach can produce auditors skilled in both EDP and financial audit disciplines. Figure 20–4 shows the typical exposures of the financial, EDP, and integrated auditors.

20.5 IMPLEMENTATION

As with any change, the implementation of the integrated approach requires a plan that depends on the exiting audit philosophy and approach.

FIGURE 20–4   Integrated Audit Approach—Typical Training and Experience

Financial Auditor		EDP Auditor
Financial ◀------	Business Unit Operations* ---------▶	EDP
Auditor ◀------	Financial Audit Concepts	Auditor
◀------	Accounting	
◀------	Audit Planning Concepts ---------▶	
◀------	Input Handling --------------▶	
	Input Processing ---------------▶	
	Application System ------------▶	
	Output Generation ------------▶	
◀------	Output Handling ---------------▶	
	Data Processing Concepts ---------▶	
	Application Audit Concepts -------▶	
	Audit Software ---------------▶	
	Advanced Systems ------------▶	

Systems Auditor

* EDP auditor exposure to business unit operations is limited compared with that of the financial auditor.

20.5.1 Overnight Change

Implementation can be accomplished through an evolutionary process or an overnight change (*i.e.*, all audits after today will be accomplished through the integrated approach). The overnight change assumes that:

- Audit management possess sufficient administrative skills,
- Audit management possess sufficient EDP and EDP audit skills,
- The staff is adequately trained,
- An effective standardized planning technique exists, and
- Organizational changes are accepted by the staff.

A suggested implementation plan is listed below. The point at which a particular audit staff begins depends on its overall approach. The suggested steps are:

1. Adopt a system flow audit methodology,

2. Adopt a detailed planning technique, including:

   —Task hours, monitoring budgeted versus actual performance,

   —Task start and target dates,

3. Adopt appropriate audit management approval for, and a methodology to, identify:

   —Audit objectives,

   —Audit scope exclusions,

   —All transactions that exist and those to be reviewed,

   —Control objectives by transaction,

   —Key controls by transaction,

   —Risks and exposures and their priority by transaction,

   —Budget hours by task for each major phase,

   —Staffing, assignments, and time frames,

4. Run EDP and financial audits of the same area concurrently using standardized communication procedures for the management team, issuing one report if time permits,

5. Integrate audit procedures for integrated system evaluation and issuing one report,

6. Assign one team to the audit with dual in-charges, supervisors, and managers when necessary to achieve an appropriate technical and management skill mix, and

7. Adopt the integrated approach with one management team.

20.5.2 Evolution

The evolutionary process permits:

- All audit personnel to learn new techniques on the job over a period of time, eliminating intense classroom training in all topics,

- Audit management to learn new administrative and planning techniques through experience instead of in the classroom,
- Implementation of a new planning technique, if needed, and
- A series of gradual minor organization changes, if needed, instead of major changes all at once.

This gives people time to adjust and increases the chance of staffwide acceptance. Simultaneous major organizational changes may cause dissension, which could undermine the team spirit needed for this approach.

20.5.3   Phased Implementation

Experience has proven to be another effective means of implementation. If the integrated audit approach is to be beneficial to the organization, it should be phased in one audit at a time until all the "bugs" are worked out. The phased implementation approach[2] should include the following procedures:

Selection of a simple automated area that is appropriate for the integrated approach,

Preparation of a single audit program covering financial and EDP functions,

Selection of a pilot management team and staff to conduct the audit,

Extensive review of the audit program with the pilot team to ensure it is efficient and effective,

Training of the pilot team in EDP and financial audit disciplines as needed,

Training of the management team in review techniques,

Conducting the audit and closely monitoring progress of all members of the audit team,

Documentation of the complete flow of transactions, including the manual and automated interfaces, during the audit,

A review of all workpapers, including the EDP tasks, by the pilot management team—If the EDP audit manager and supervisor are not part of the pilot team, one of them should review the EDP transactions,

Preparation and issuance of a single audit report, including comments on EDP and the operations area,

Conducting a post-audit review to isolate problem areas and fine tune the audit program and planning techniques, and

Fixing any problem areas and selecting another area for the pilot team to conduct an integrated audit.

This process can be repeated until all problems are resolved. This phased implementation approach is more manageable and less expensive from a training standpoint because any problems are isolated to one audit instead of several. The usual audit coverage is therefore not disrupted, and the training needs are more readily identifiable.

20.6   CASE STUDY

Experience has shown that approximately two years are required for an efficient integrated audit approach to evolve from inception to completion. In one case, system flow evaluation was implemented to permit comprehensive evaluation of the manual systems. The checklist technique missed many weaknesses because comprehensive audit programs tailored to the environment did not exist.

As a by-product of these shortcomings, system evaluation techniques for user operations now more closely follow EDP audit techniques. Detailed planning techniques have been implemented to permit proper tracking of job performance and isolation of the many variables that accompany an audit.

The formal scope summary concept was not implemented until late in the evolutionary process. It was later realized that the scope summary and the detailed planning techniques could have been merged and implemented simultaneously, reducing overhead. In actuality, the planning occurred at the beginning of the audit. Time was allocated for scope development as the audit progressed, creating time variables difficult to manage when preliminary review results proved the anticipated audit scope inadequate.

The first positive step toward integration was the implementation of concurrent audits. It quickly became apparent that evaluation of the manual system finished before that of EDP because of the time-intensive nature of programming automated testing. Management team coordination became very cumbersome because of the staggered completion of the preliminary survey and testing. Timely report turnaround time dictated the issuance of separate reports, but complete results were not available until both teams were finished. Complete reports were difficult to achieve, and the service quality desired by management was not being satisfied.

Adopting the integrated approach seemed the best solution. Senior level personnel, however, were not adequately trained in all technical areas to permit a single management team. Audits were, therefore, planned and conducted with one staff and two management teams. Three audits provided time to expose the senior and supervisory levels to the integrated approach. The quality of the reports indicated that it was now appropriate to phase out two management teams, and the true one-team audit became a reality.

Eight years' experience with integration has shown that the benefits of the approach still hold true. Audit personnel gain extensive exposure to the total system, increasing the quality of their credentials. One difficulty, however, has been hiring new auditors who have the skills of current employees.

20.7   MANAGEMENT ROLE

The audit management team must be staffed with appropriately experienced personnel, well organized, and able to work as a team. The audit manager provides an overview, keeping the audit on track with major objectives and within acceptable time frames. The supervisor concentrates on the details of the survey, testing, and technical advice within the scope of the audit.

The in-charge is responsible for the detailed day-to-day task completion by the staff, isolating problems with the system or the staff, and reporting them to the supervisor for resolution.

The integrated approach is conducive to small audit staffs because these audit departments cannot afford to have extensive numbers of specialists for business activities. In addition, new audit standards and regulations, particularly in the banking industry, will pressure small audit staffs to conduct more frequent and more comprehensive audits. Therefore, the integrated audit approach is becoming a necessity.

NOTES

1. See Mullen, Jack B. "The Integrated Audit Approach." Reprinted from *EDP Auditing* (New York: Auerbach Publishers). © 1990, Warren, Gorham & Lamont, Inc. Used with permission.

2. Adapted from training material presented by Fred Palmer, Palmer Associates, 1988, Boca Raton, FL.

Epilogue

Each organization must evaluate the integrated approach to determine whether it is functional and beneficial. The key measurements are reduced costs, increased productivity, and more comprehensive audit coverage. Before implementation, it is necessary to develop techniques that can measure these benefits during a series of pilot audits.

The implementation costs of the integrated approach include training, development of an audit program, management and planning techniques, and intensive monitoring during the pilot, and then in final implementation. Maintenance costs include training of new staff and higher salary levels because of the EDP audit training. Although progress may be slow at first, the ultimate benefits can be rewarding.

This book was designed to permit internal and external auditors, or people aspiring to be, to learn EDP audit techniques at their own pace. This book provides one major piece of the integrated audit training puzzle. The future of the internal audit industry is integration of the audit approach and development of the systems auditor, because company managements' will demand increased productivity. Academia will address these needs and create curricula to comprehensively educate people as systems auditors.

Glossary

Abend   An abnormal ending to a computer program because of a processing error.

ACBGEN   A computer program that generates the application control blocks which define the database and programs for use by an on-line system.

Access control   Procedures used to either prevent or detect access to a device or area.

Access rules   Refers to the access definitions of an on-line access control system.

Access security package   *See* "On-line access control system."

Administrative project controls   Procedures to be completed by system development project team members in order to ensure that all required activities are completed.

Administrative reporting   The superior–subordinate relationship that includes only personnel and expense matters.

Advanced environmental audits   EDP audits of highly technical data processing areas. They are referred to as such because of the technical complexity of the function.

AICPA   American Institute of Certified Public Accountants.

Analytical review   An audit procedure that compares current activities to previous activities in order to identify the significant variances. It usually applies to financial statement balances.

Application change control   Procedures executed to ensure the accuracy of maintenance of computer application programs.

Application controls   The programmatic and manual procedures used to verify the completeness and accuracy of application processing.

Application program   An individual, but separately identified, set of program code written in a high-level language such as COBOL.

Application programming   The writing of computer code specific to application programs.

Application system   A group of programs which process data related to a business function.

Archiving   Maintaining multiple generations of computer files or records.

Assembler load-and-go   A computer technique used to create computer program code from specified input parameters for execution.

Asynchronous   A telecommunications protocol that transmits data one byte at a time.

Audit committee   A group of company directors that oversee the audit function.

Audit confirmations   A formal letter sent to a customer asking them to verify the accuracy of information regarding their account or business relationship with the company.

Audit cycle   The frequency of conducted audits.

Auditee   The management responsible for the area being audited.

Auditee activities and functions   The daily work that must be completed by the auditee.

Audit findings   Internal control, operational, or management weaknesses identified by audit procedures.

Audit independence Autonomy of the audit function from the area being reviewed.

Audit management team The general auditor, audit managers, and audit supervisors.

Audit objectives The ultimate purpose of the audit, in general or specific terms.

Audit planning phase The first phase of the audit designed to collect information about the auditee's activities and functions.

Audit priority rating A ranking of the importance of an audit as it relates to other audits.

Audit programmer An auditor whose primary responsibility is to write computer programs for audit purposes.

Audit report The final written report containing the scope, opinion, and a description of the procedures performed as well as comments and recommendations.

Audit software Computer programs used by auditors to collect data from computer system files in order to accomplish audit objectives.

Audit standards Guidelines to control the quality of an audit.

Audit test objectives The purpose of specific audit procedures in order to validate financial transactions or to determine the extent of procedural compliance.

Audit testing tasks The individual activities needed to accomplish an audit test.

Audit time budget The estimated hours it will take to complete an audit.

Audit trails A set of records providing a list of the processing tasks performed.

Audit transactions The major tasks that will be completed during the audit that specifically relate to the auditee functions.

Authorization Obtaining the right to perform some action (typically access to assets) such as accounting or application system entries.

Automated suspense error file   A computer file used to record transactions which contain errors.

Automated terminal signoff   A programmatic procedure that disconnects the terminal from the mainframe after some pre-established criteria has been met.

Automation steering committee   A group of company senior managers who prepare a data processing plan and oversee its execution.

Auxiliary storage   A place for a computer to hold data other than in main memory such as a tape or disk file.

Available hours   The amount of time a person or group can spend.

Balancing   A comparison of two numbers from independent sources to determine that the numbers match.

Base Case System Evaluation (BCSE)   A testing technique most easily described as a comprehensive test deck which evaluates all processing aspects of the application system.

BASIC (Beginner's All-purpose Symbolic Instruction Code)   A computer programming language most common to micro-computers.

Batch dollar totals   A dollar total of all items in a batch of transactions.

Batch processing   Entering all transactions from a specific time period, at one time, into a computer application for processing.

Batch system   A group of computer programs that perform batch processing.

Benchmarks   Standards used as a basis for comparison to actual results.

Budgets   Estimates of the amount of time or money expected to be spent during a particular time period, project, or event.

Budget variance analysis   Documented comparison of actual hours charged versus the budget for each individual audit transaction with explanations of significant variances.

Business expense insurance Insurance covering the cost of using outside facilities for computer processing when the data center is unusable.

Business interruption insurance Insurance covering a portion of income lost due to data center destruction.

Business interruptions Discontinuance of business and the inability to service the customer.

Business unit operations The area in a company that focuses on common objectives or activities.

Bypass label processing Skipping over the internal file label forcing the application to accept the file as input.

Camera surveillance Observation of an area with closed circuit tv cameras.

Cancellation of documents Marking a document in such a way as to prevent its reuse (such as marking an invoice "paid").

Capability The measurement of the maximum ability of a system to process data and the point at which the system can no longer accept any more data.

Capacity levels The amount of work which the system and its components can handle.

Card access system Electronic locks activated by running a plastic card with a magnetic strip through a card reader.

Change control system The procedures used to accomplish authorization of changes to computer programs.

Change request A documented order to change a computer program.

Checkpoint restart techniques Special function computer programs that can determine the transactions which have been processed and recover partially completed computer files in order to start processing from the point of failure.

Checkpoints for management review Points during the system development life cycle phases that permit management to evaluate progress and any significant changes that may require the development to be discontinued or modified.

Child segment   A subordinate part of a parent segment in a database management system.

Closing conference   A review of the audit report by auditors and auditees in order to determine that the audit report is accurate.

COBOL   COmmon Business Oriented Language. A high-level programming language.

Coding errors   Errors in computer program code.

Collusion   The participation by two or more people to commit a fraud.

Communication lines   Coaxial cable or telephone lines used to connect computers in order to pass data between them.

Compile   A computer program procedure that translates English-type statements into a machine-readable form.

Compensating control   A procedure performed to take the place of another control function.

Compliance testing   Audit review of actual transactions to verify compliance with identified control procedures.

Compliance testing–scope summary   Identification of estimated hours, during the preliminary phase, needed for compliance testing.

Computer abuse   The unauthorized use of a computer to accomplish theft, sabotage, or other malicious mischief.

Computer aided instructions   Information provided by the computer to lead a user through to the completion of his work.

Computer Aided Software Engineering (CASE)   A generic label referring to a group of fourth generation software packages which assist in computer program design, programming, and ongoing maintenance.

Computer application   A collection of computer programs designed to process data and update master files on a periodic basis.

Computer-assisted audit techniques (CAAT) Computer programs used by auditors to accomplish audit objectives.

Computer configuration The description of the components of a computer system.

Computer crime policy An insurance policy that can cover a loss from computer frauds committed by persons outside the company.

Computer files Magnetic tape or disk containing data in machine-readable form.

Computer program A set of procedures that can be executed by a computer.

Computer program listing A line-by-line printout of the coding statements of a computer program.

Computer resources The hardware and software components of a computer system.

Computer system elapsed time The amount of time that passes while a computer accomplishes a specific task including wait time.

Conflicting duties Activities or functions which when performed together provide a person with the opportunity to divert resources to personal use.

Contingency planning A documented set of instructions used to provide data processing resources after a disaster.

Contract programmers Individuals outside of the company who write computer programs and work as an independent contractor.

Control objective The purpose of procedures designed to promote the accuracy and completeness of processing.

Control techniques Specific procedures used to accomplish a control objective.

Conversion The transfer of data from the old system files to the new system.

Core The computer's internal memory.

Corrective control   An activity that fixes an error or omission.

Cost benefit   The analysis and evaluation of the cost to implement a new system as compared to the income increase or expense reduction derived from that system.

CO_2   Carbon dioxide as used to extinguish a fire.

CPA   Certified public accountant.

CPU   Central processing unit. The brain of the computer.

CPU time   The amount of processing time used by the computer excluding wait time.

CPU wait time   The time the CPU spends waiting for work.

CRT   Cathode ray tube, a computer terminal screen.

Customer privacy   Laws and regulations protecting the company records containing information about consumers.

Customized audit program   Audit procedures tailored to a specific function within a specific company.

DASD   Direct access storage device, a disk file.

Database administrator (DBA)   The DBA's major objective is to define the control elements of the DBMS. The DBA is responsible for defining the segments of the database which is a collection of data sharing some common attribute.

Database administration   The group of people working for the database administrator.

Database control libraries   A term used uniquely in this book to refer to the program libraries that contain the database definitions, the PSBs, PCBs, and other database control information.

Database definition   Identifies the segment's name, size, and key-field for each segment.

Database segment after-images   Pictures of database records after they have been updated by a transaction.

Data center   The area of the company that houses the computer equipment.

Data description language (DDL) A separate software package used to define the elements of the database.

Data dictionary (DD) A software package used to document the characteristics of all the fields in a database including data types, permitted values, and relationships to other fields.

Data edit program A computer program whose purpose is to validate the accuracy of data based on some preset criteria.

Data edits Field and record checks used to validate entered data in order to determine that the data conforms to pre-established criteria.

Data manipulation language (DML) Computer language providing the interface between an application program and the DBMS. An application program uses the DML to execute program instructions against a database.

Data processing environment controls Procedures executed within the computer operating environment in order to promote processing accuracy and completeness.

Data security Procedures used to protect computer data.

Data security administration function The computer security policeman who utilizes a security software package or other logical access control mechanism to enforce data security policies and procedures.

Data set characteristics The specifications for computer files including block size, record size, expansion constraints, and labels.

Data set definitions 1. Program coding which defines the data set to the operating system. 2. Written specifications of the characteristics of files including the standard name, file size, block size, record size, and expansion constraints.

Data set directory listing A printout of the attributes of data sets.

Data set name The identifier used to refer to a data set.

DBDGEN A computer program that defines a database to the operating system.

DBMS   Database management system.

Debug   The process of locating and correcting processing errors in a computer program.

Decentralized processing   Splitting up the processing among various company areas.

Defalcation   Fraud, theft, or embezzlement.

Deliverable   The final required product.

Detailed Design   The first major step in defining the processing aspects of the system. It is used to write functional specifications for use by programmers in writing the program code.

Detective control   An activity that finds any error, omission, unauthorized use, or fraud which has occurred.

Dial-back   Programmatic call to the originating computer by the receiving computer or peripheral equipment.

Dial-up networks   The use of phone lines to permit computers to communicate with one another.

Directory listing   The printout of the file names on a disk.

Disaster contingency plan   Documented procedures used to recover processing that has been stopped by a disaster. See "Contingency Planning."

Disaster recovery plan   *See* "Disaster contingency plan."

Documentation   Written or typed explanations of actions taken on specific transactions. It also refers to written or typed instructions which explain the performance of tasks.

Documentation revision record   A log of all changes to documentation in chronological order providing a capsulated trail of changes.

Documentation standards   Management requirements for the contents of documentation.

Dollar materiality   Dollar limit or threshold used to measure the significance of a financial event expressed in relation to the percentage of assets, liabilities, equity, or income.

Downline load Transfer of data from the host computer to a remote computer.

DP audit manager The person responsible for overseeing the completion of the DP audit plan.

DP audit plan The DP audit coverage scheduled for a future period including audit software, financial audit staff support, environmental audits, application systems audits, and system development reviews.

DP audit supervisor The person responsible for seeing that the DP auditors properly accomplish the DP audit plan.

DP environment assessment An evaluation of the sophistication of the DP operating environment. The higher the sophistication, the greater the technical DP audit skill needed.

DP resources Personnel, hardware, and software used to support data processing activities.

Dual access Separates the access function among two people, until access is achieved then, only one person handles the asset.

Dual control Two people performing the same duty simultaneously.

Dumb on-line terminals On-line input devices referred to as such because they do not contain a microprocessor.

Edit override Bypassing a data validation procedure.

Edit routines Programmatic procedures that validate entered data.

EDPAA EDP Auditors Association.

Embezzlement Internal fraud or theft.

Emergency access levels The extent of computer access needed by DP personnel to fix a processing problem when a program or system has failed.

Emergency access profiles The definitions of the emergency access levels to security software.

Emulate   To act or perform alike. Refers to a computer system that uses special software to act like another system.

Encryption   Scrambling data on computer files through the use of algorithms and a special cipher key.

End-user   The user of a computer system.

English parameters   Refers to software packages that accept instructions in English statements for translation into computer program code.

Environmental audit   Internal control review and compliance testing of an area within the DP operating environment.

Environmental protection   The temperature, humidity, and power constraints on the computer equipment which are required in order to protect the equipment.

Error messages   English statements generated by a system to notify the user or operator of a processing problem.

Errors and omissions   An exposure dealing with inaccurate or missing data.

Evaluation of results   Analysis of the outcome of a test.

Evidence   Documentation which supports a finding or conclusion.

Exception items reports   A printout of data which the program or system could not process.

Extended Records   A CAAT used to collect all data used by an on-line or batch program to bring a transaction or account to its finished end product.

Feasibility Study   The analysis and evaluation of the potential cost benefit of a new system.

Fee charging methodology   The formula used to calculate the amount to be billed for a service.

Fictitious transactions   Fake data used for testing or illegitimate data used in a fraud.

File back-up   A copy of a computer file.

File completion check　A programmatic procedure used to determine that all records from the file have been processed.

File definition　A description of a computer file. *See* "File layout."

File foot　Accumulated dollar control total of the primary control field for each record in a computer file.

File handling error correction　Procedures executed to correct file errors. These are interactive corrections between the application system and the computer operator.

File labels　Internal and external file identifiers.

File layout　Written explanation of each field including the field name, data type or format, character size, and its starting and ending displacement position in the file.

File library　The repository responsible for safekeeping and control of the computer files.

File name　The file identifier used by the system to access a file.

File retention　Standards and procedures for keeping files.

File retention schedules　Written explanations that specify the files generated, when they are generated, the programs used to generate them, and how long they should be kept.

File rotation　Moving files to and from an off-site storage location.

File transfer　Transmission of data files between computers.

Financial audit　Internal control review, compliance, and substantive testing in order to render an opinion on financial statements or individual balances.

Financial audit concepts　The body of knowledge relating to financial auditing.

Financial controls　The procedures used by the business unit and accounting department to promote the accuracy and completeness of financial information.

Financial staff support　Training, consulting, and programming provided by the DP audit staff to the financial auditors.

Financial statements   The balance sheet, the income statement, the statement of stockholders' equity, and the statement of cash flow and footnotes.

Financial transactions   Events or activities having a financial effect on a business.

Firmware   A computer component using both hardware and software to accomplish its function.

Fixed length record   A computer file record whose size is constant.

Flagging   Marking a report and record with a special character so that data stands out.

Flowchart   A graphical picture using specialized symbols to describe an activity or function.

Floppy disk   A removable magnetic disk used in microcomputers.

Follow-up phase   Audit procedures used to ensure that the auditee management responds to the audit report and that the response adequately addresses all audit comments and recommendations.

Front-end development cost   Money spent for hardware, software, and programming to initially create a program or system.

Functional reporting   The superior–subordinate relationship covering functional duties alone and excluding administrative duties.

General audit objectives   The purpose of the audit in broad terms.

General auditor   The person responsible for managing the complete audit function.

General control evaluation (GCE)   An evaluation performed annually by external auditors to determine the adequacy of the company's data processing environment internal control structure.

General Design The definition of a proposed program or system, in broad terms, which is used later to complete the detailed design or functional specifications.

Generalized audit software A pre-packaged set of programs which accepts user-coded instructions in English-type instruction form.

Generally accepted accounting principles (GAAP) A set of guidelines designed to promote the quality, consistency, accuracy, and fairness of accounting procedures.

Generally accepted auditing standards (GAAS) A set of guidelines designed to promote the quality, consistency, and accuracy of external auditing.

Grandfather–father–son A method of generation data set creation. Each day's newly created master file is the son file, yesterday's master is the father, while the prior day's file is the grandfather.

Guidelines Suggested rules to follow with some latitude for individual judgment.

Hacker A person who attempts unauthorized access to, commits sabotage of, does malicious damage to, or obtains data from a computer system usually through the use of a microcomputer.

Halon gas A chemical, in a gaseous form, used to extinguish fire.

Hardcopy report Computer output printed on paper.

Hard disk A fixed non-removable disk drive used in a microcomputer.

Hardwired lines Direct connection of a terminal or microcomputer to a computer with coaxial cable.

Hardwired tap Direct connection into an existing communication line.

Hierarchical database A DBMS structure that looks similar to a corporate organization chart using a search technique of left to right and top to bottom.

Identification of existing controls Auditor explanation and documentation of control procedures that do exist.

Identification of non-existing controls Auditor explanation and documentation of controls that should exist but do not.

Identification of transactions Determining the activities and functions for which the auditee is responsible.

Ignore label No programmatic reading of the internal file label forcing the program to accept the file whether it is the correct one or not.

IIA Institute of Internal Auditors.

IIA standards A set of guidelines issued by the IIA and designed to promote the accuracy, consistency, and quality of internal audit procedures.

Illegitimate code Program code which does not belong in a computer program.

Implementation To bring a new or changed program or system into production.

Implementation costs The money spent for hardware, software development, programming, and testing of a computer system.

Inbound message to host A string of data sent from a remote computer or terminal to the host computer.

Incompatible duties Activities or functions performed by the same person providing the opportunity for erroneous or fraudulent activity.

Independence Autonomy and separation of a person or function.

Inherent control Procedures that exist within computer software to promote data security and the accuracy and completeness of processing.

Inherent technical security limitation The inability of a computer system to accomplish specific control procedures requiring compensating controls.

In-house design Development of a computer system or program by company employees.

In-house support The maintenance of systems or programs by company employees.

Input Data to be entered into a computer system for processing.

Input control totals Summation of a dollar field of all transactions entered into a system for processing.

Input file Data stored on a tape or disk file to be entered into a computer program for processing.

Input/output verification Comparing the information generated by a computer system to the input documents.

Installation dependent Specifications unique to the company.

Installation standards Operating procedures and guidelines specified by data processing management that are needed to maintain control, efficiency, and effectiveness.

Integrated Test Facility (ITF) A CAAT used to enter test data into the live production system without affecting live accounts or transactions. It utilizes the creation of fictitious accounts, companies, or other entity on production files.

Interactive programming system An on-line programming system that permits on-line usage of mainframe computer resources.

Internal audit objectives The purpose of the internal control review and compliance testing performed by internal auditors.

Internal control Any policy, procedure, or activity which promotes the protection of assets, the accuracy of financial data, operational efficiency, and enforces compliance with company policies and procedures.[1]

Internal control evaluation Audit analysis of auditee activities and functions to determine the quality of control.

Internal control questionnaires Questions used by auditors to evaluate the effectiveness of internal controls and collect information about auditee activities and functions.

Internal control system   The set of procedures and practices used to accomplish internal control. *See* "Internal control."

Internal file label   Information magnetically recorded at the beginning of a file to identify the file name, creation date, and other critical information in order to permit specific identification of the file by a computer program.

Internally generated transactions   Data generated by the computer program based on some pre-established criteria.

IPL   Initial Program Load. A cold start of a computer system usually in reference to a mainframe.

Item count   A count of items in a batch.

JCL   Job Control Language. The means by which a computer program tells the operating system how to process the program.

Job accounting utility   A computer program used to collect and record data about a system and job-related activities.

Job descriptions   Documented definitions of the duties of a job.

Job execution categories   Processing priority assigned to a specific program by the operating system supervisor program.

Job performance evaluation   Communicating to an employee his or her strengths and weaknesses.

Job scheduling   Definition of when computer jobs should be executed on a computer.

Job setup instructions   Documented instructions for the computer operator and tape librarian to follow in order to accomplish program execution.

Job status reporting   Summary of the extent of completion of a project, computer program, or an audit job.

Job summary listings   A printout of all the tasks performed by the operating system in executing a computer program.

Justification proposal   An information document for senior management to use in deciding whether or not to proceed with purchasing or designing a new system. May be part of the feasibility study.

Kybtes   1,000 bytes or characters.

Keycard access   *See* "Card access system."

Key controls   The primary procedures used to promote processing accuracy and completeness upon which audit efforts are focused.

Key-field   A field within each database segment that is used as the means to locate the needed data in that segment.

Key-to-disk   A minicomputer with a terminal and software connected to a disk drive for transcribing data to machine-readable form directly onto a disk file.

Key-to-tape   Same as key-to-disk except the data is transcribed to a tape file.

Label checking   Programmatic reading of the internal file label located at the beginning of a tape file or in the directory of a disk file.

Lapping   Payment of one account with funds intended for another account.

Learning curve   The time needed to become acquainted with how to perform an activity or function.

Library level security   The ability of a security software system to control access to specific libraries.

License agreement   The formal contract between a software vendor and the purchaser specifying the uses of the software package.

Line function   A group that supports only one group or activity.

Line protocol   The means of on-line communication, usually asynchronous or synchronous.

Link-edit   The creation of a linking map that tells the operating system where to find the resources needed by a program.

List of programs   An inventory log of all programs in an application providing a quick reference for the programmer so as to find a program by name.

Log files   Files used to capture before and after images of master record updates and transactions entered.

Logical access control   (On-line access control.) Involves the use of the on-line security software system in order to establish access profiles for each user.

Long-range plan   Documented explanation of the activities which a company plans to engage in over an extended period of time, usually, at least, five years.

Loss potential   The amount of money or other commodity (goodwill, reputation) that could most likely be lost.

Machine language   Computer program instructions in machine-readable form.

Magnetic media   Tape or disk files.

Mainframe hardware   The CPU, tape and disk drives, controllers, concentrators, multiplexors, printers, and other hardware components attached to the mainframe.

Maintenance request   *See* "Change request."

Major new release   A major enhancement to an existing product or a complete replacement of all program code.

Make it fail approach   A testing philosophy referring to the design of test data that will cause the system to fail so the failures will not occur during production.

Management controls   Policies and procedures concerned with the planning, legal compliance, and use of company resources.

Manual system flow   The sequential activities that occur in transaction processing by business unit personnel which are not computerized.

Master file   The tape or disk file which contains the primary records of the company.

Master file control records   Special records that do not contain account data but contain dollar control totals, item counts, or other control information used to promote processing accuracy and completeness.

Master file posting acceptance   A phrase indicating that a transaction was accepted and the master file information was updated to reflect the new information.

Master record   The individual records within the master file.

Master security terminal   Computer terminals that have access to the security control system.

Matching   The comparison of key fields between two files for equality.

Media insurance coverage   Covers replacement costs of physical disks and tape files plus the cost of reproducing the data recorded on them.

Media-in-transit insurance   Covers theft or losses of tape and disk files being transported.

Memo post file   A computer file that holds transactions which do not have an immediate direct effect on the master but need to be considered during on-line processing in order to prevent financial loss.

Message control system   A system where all data transmitted between terminals and mainframes are carried by control information in order to permit tracking of all messages.

Microprocessor   The CPU or brain of a microcomputer.

Middle management   The group responsible for developing the tactical plans, activities, and functions necessary to accomplish strategic objectives.

Modem   MOdulator-DEModulator. A device which translates telecommunication signals from analog to digital or vice versa.

Module level security   The ability of a system to control the access of individual modules or files within a library.

Naming conventions   Each character in the name for data files, program libraries, individual program names, application identifiers, and reports having a specific meaning for identification.

Narrative description A documented explanation of an activity or function in prose form.

Negative opinion An auditor's statement indicating that internal controls were inadequate or were not functioning as intended.

Negotiable items Documents which can be converted to cash.

Network controller A hardware component which controls the routing of telecommunication messages between terminals and mainframes.

Network structure A DBMS structure which permits access to data elements by connection with any other member.

Off-site processing Computer processing at a different location.

Off-site storage Retention and safekeeping of files or records at a different location from where they are processed.

One-team audit The merging of the audits of DP and non-DP systems into one review under the supervision of one audit management team.

On-line access control mechanism The computer programming procedures used to identify, verify, and authorize a person attempting on-line access.

On-line access control system Computer software that performs the functions of an on-line access control mechanism in order to prevent or detect unauthorized activity.

On-line application programs The computer programs which process data or transactions passed from the on-line communication programs.

On-line batch proof Dollar amount of each entered transaction is accumulated and compared to the batch total at the end of the batch.

On-line capture The use of an on-line system in order to record transactions to a disk file for later processing by a batch system.

On-line communication system The use of computer terminals connected to a mainframe via a telecommunications monitor for the processing or passing of data.

On-line data entry function The use of on-line terminals to enter input transactions.

On-line inquiry terminal Computer terminal used solely for data retrieval with no ability to update files.

On-line memo posting Using on-line capture with accumulation of key-fields in order to provide ongoing status.

On-line programming system (OPS) An on-line computer system that permits programmers to write program code.

On-line programs Refers to the telecommunications monitor programs.

On-line real-time The process of posting transactions to a master file as they are received in real-time.

On-line security *See* "On-line access control system."

On-line security package Computer software that performs on-line access control functions. *See also* "On-line access control system."

On-line system change control The procedures used to accomplish maintenance of the programs that make up the on-line telecommunications monitor.

On-line systems The use of terminals to communicate with applications on the mainframe while updating tape and disk files as the work day progresses.

On-line terminal input The use of a computer terminal to enter transactions for mainframe processing.

On-line transaction capture *See* "On-line capture."

Operating environment The data processing functions such as the data center, file library, on-line system, database administration, program change control, and system software.

Operating system A set of highly complex computer programs that control and supervise CPU and mainframe resources and programs.

Operational procedures Step-by-step instructions of how to perform an activity or function.

Operator ID A set of characters that uniquely identifies a terminal operator.

Operator procedures Instructions to the mainframe operator on how to operate the system or application.

Organization chart A graphical picture of the relationships of the various areas of a company.

Organization controls Policies and procedures concerned with the management decision process that leads to management's authorization of transactions.

Organization structure The reporting relationships of the areas of a company.

Outbound message from host A string of data sent to a terminal from a host computer.

Out-of-balance conditions Non-match of key financial balances.

Output analysis Evaluating test results and researching any exceptions.

Output categories Instructions to the operating system whether the computer output is printed to an on-line terminal, hard copy report, or both.

Output control totals Summation of a key-dollar field by a program in order to control processing accuracy and completeness.

Output distribution Procedures used to ensure that all required output is generated and that only the authorized user receives the output.

Output layouts Description of the fields and their position on computer-printed reports or terminal screens.

Out-sourcing Using an outside service bureau for computer processing or programming.

Package Acceptance Testing An SDLC phase. The processing of test transactions to determine if a software package(s) being considered for purchase meets the company's requirements.

Package Evaluation   An SDLC phase. The process used to determine if the software package(s) under consideration for purchase will meet the organization's needs.

Package Modifications   An SDLC phase. Changes required to a software package being purchased so it will meet a company requirements.

Parallel simulation   A CAAT involving the re-creation of an application process or function using the same input and creating comparable output.

Parent segment   Can be a subordinate segment of the root segment in a DBMS that must have dependent segments.

Password   A string of characters or symbols entered into a computer system in combination with the operator ID permits the access control mechanism to identify the operator.

Password file   A computer file containing operator passwords.

Password protected library   A program library requiring the input of a specific password to gain access to the programs in the library.

PCB   Program control block. A control which defines the program functions allowed within a certain view of a database.

Pending file   Accumulated memoranda and other documents obtained at times other than when the audit is running which may prove relevant in future audits.

Performance benchmarks   Processing capabilities that the system should or can achieve.

Peripherals   Hardware components attached to a computer.

Permanent files   Evidential matter obtained or prepared during completion of the planning and preliminary review phases relevant to more than one year.

Personnel costs   Dollars spent on salary and benefits.

Pervasive weakness A malfunctioning or nonexisting control that effects more than one area.

Physical security Control over physical access to computer equipment or other asset.

Planning phase Accumulation of information needed to define the audit work to be performed.

Policies Similar to standards. The key difference from standards is that policies are generally approved by a senior management committee or board of directors.

Polling A method of system checking in order to determine if a terminal is still connected to the network or mainframe.

Port An outlet on a computer for connection of a peripheral computer device or terminal.

Post audit conference A face-to-face conference with representatives from the auditee's area and the appropriate members of the audit team in order to discuss the final audit report.

Posting program The computer program that updates transactions to the master file.

Posting totals report Identifies dollar totals and item counts processed by the system for each transaction code or processing category.

Pre-Audit conference A discussion between the auditors and auditee to review the audit scope, objectives, and any control concerns.

Pre-authorized Advance approval to carry out some responsibility.

Preliminary review An audit phase including information gathering, documentation of auditees activities and functions, and evaluation of the internal control system.

Preliminary review–scope summary Documentation in the scope summary of the transactions that will be reviewed during the preliminary review phase and the estimated hours to be spent.

Prepackaged audit programs Audit procedures prepared by a group or person outside of the company that are not customized for the specific company environment.

Preventive control An activity that stops an error, omission, unauthorized use, or fraud from occurring.

Procedures Step-by-step instructions to follow in the completion of a task or activity.

Processing limit parameters A means of controlling the amount of computer processing performed such as CPU-time and print-line limits.

Processing logic Computer program code defined to manipulate data records and fields, perform arithmetic calculations, and compare data fields.

Production data files Computer files containing live data.

Production library The program library that contains the source or object version of the program used in production.

Production object The machine-readable version of the source program for production only.

Production programs Computer programs executed to process "live" input data.

Production source The English version of the program code used in production.

Productivity tools Programming aids which increase the amount of work that personnel can perform, for example, prototyping, computer aided system engineering, and program code generators.

Program change reporting system The means for an independent control group to keep track of program changes updated to the computer system.

Program code A set of computer instructions designed to perform a specific task.

Program code comparison Comparison of two versions of a program in order to isolate the different lines of code in each program.

Program code review A manual review of changed computer program code to detect erroneous changes.

Program deletion Purging programs from libraries.

Program documentation Written explanations of computer program functions.

Program errors Mistakes in computer programs that cause erroneous processing or program failure.

Program execution The act of running the computer program on the computer.

Program flowchart A graphical picture using specialized symbols to describe computer program functions.

Programmatic edits Computer executed validation of input data.

Programmatic procedures Procedures completed by a computer program.

Programming The translation of specifications into instructions that a computer will understand.

Programming costs The money spent for personnel who write computer programs.

Program module A set of computer code within a program that accomplishes a specific purpose.

Program narratives Detailed explanations of each program's functions describing input, processing, and output functions.

Program specifications (1) A detailed description of what the programmer should code the computer program to do. (2) An SDLC phase. The systems analyst's instructions to the programmer that adequately documents and explains all necessary elements of the programs.

Program testing The processing of fictitious transactions by a program to detect processing errors.

Proprietary information Information or data owned by the company.

Protocol converter   A software program or firmware that translates asynchronous transmission to synchronous and vice versa.

Prototyping   A fourth generation system development technique that uses special computer software to create examples (prototypes) of proposed computer processing.

PSB   Program specification block. Defines the logical picture or view of a database.

PSBGEN   A computer program that defines the program specification blocks to the DBMS.

Purchased package   Computer software programs bought from a vendor.

RAM   Random access memory.

Read-only access   An on-line programming access level that lets the user of the access level only read the program or data.

Reasonable assurance   The impression, feeling, level of conviction, or the extent of proof that the auditor has or obtains about the quality of internal control in the function or activity being reviewed.

Reciprocal backup agreements   Mutual consent between two companies to use each others computer equipment in the event of a disaster.

Reconcilement   The comparison of two independently generated dollar totals to identify the causes and amounts of any differences, in order to prove the processing accuracy of the application or on-line system.

Record length   The length of a file record in bytes.

Record type   Designation of whether the record is of fixed or variable length.

Recurring costs   Money that must be spent repeatedly to maintain an activity.

Rejects   Transactions which are kicked-out by an application program, usually the update program, because data in the fields failed an edit check or matching check; the program could not figure out what to do with the data.

Relational database   A DBMS structure that uses a table-type format similar in appearance to a microcomputer spreadsheet containing columns and rows.

Report files   All audit reports issued during a year retained in a separated binder or file for easy reference.

Report generation   Production of computer reports by a program.

Report preparation phase   The audit phase where the audit report is being prepared.

Resident operating system   The operating system that is currently being used by the CPU.

Resident software   The computer programs to which the operating system has access.

Resource crisis   Having insufficient computer resources to accomplish needed processing.

Response time   The elapsed time from entry of an on-line transaction to delivery of the response screen.

Restart/recovery procedures   Written explanations of how to recover partially processed files and restart application processing.

Restricted use programs   *See* "Sensitive utilities."

Resubmitted transaction   A transaction that was in error and was rejected by the application that has been corrected and reentered.

Right-to-audit clause   A service bureau contract provision that gives the servicee the opportunity to send their own audit team into the servicer's installation and conduct reviews as they see fit.

Risk evaluation   Determination of the exposure that each area imposes upon the company.

ROM   Read Only Memory.

Root segment   The highest level segment within a database.

Run frequency   The frequency of program or application execution, for example daily, weekly, monthly and so on.

Run schedule   Documented listing of the time of day when programs or applications are executed.

Run-to-run control totals   The control record containing a summation of a dollar field, passed to each successive program in a jobstream in order to permit the programs to validate that all data was processed.

Safekeeping   Securing assets under lock and key, in a desk drawer, file cabinet, storeroom, or vault.

Schema   A term used with network databases to refer to the database definition. A map of the logical structure of a network database.

Scope summary   A documented schedule prepared during the audit planning phase to identify audit scope and objective, the transactions that will be reviewed, and the time estimated to be spent in the preliminary review and testing phases.

Securities and Exchange Commission (SEC)   A federal agency that oversees the activities of all publicly traded companies. The SEC has a significant effect on accounting principles and auditing standards.

Security software system   A computer system that controls logical access (on-line) to computer resources through the use of access profile definitions.

SDLC project manager   The leader, coordinator, or manager of the development project.

Security software access profiles   Definitions of the computer resources that can be used by each person including terminals, programs, files, libraries, and others.

Security software deactivation   Turning off the security software system so that there is no access control.

Segment definition   Defines the field names, data type, start position, and field size of a database segment.

Segregation of duties   Assigning incompatible duties or functions to separate people to provide reasonable assurance against fraud and provide an accuracy check of the other person's work.

Senior DP auditor   An intermediate level DP audit staff position.

Senior management   The level of management reporting to the company CEO or president.

Sensitive utilities   General-use computer programs that can perform system functions with simple commands in order to modify data files, program libraries, or operating system program code. They may or may not create an audit trail.

Sequence checking   The programmatic accounting for the numerical sequence of each input item.

Sequential file   A computer file that has all of its records in order one after the other (in sequence).

Sequentially numbered documents   Working documents with preprinted sequential numbers to permit detection of missing items.

Service bureau   Companies who provide data processing services on a contract basis. Services can vary from servicing one application to providing all data processing services.

Servicee   The company using a service bureau or out-sourcing firm.

Servicer   The provider of outside data processing services.

Settlement   Reconciliation of the application system dollar totals to the entries made to the general ledger for that day.

Set-up sheets   Documentation of the input files that will be read and the output files that will be created by the application system during its execution.

Shared resources   Computer hardware and software components used by multiple users.

Short-range planning The process of establishing and documenting the goals, objectives, functions, and activities needed to meet all of the elements of the long-range plan.

Simulated results Output from a program that processes data like the real program to test the logic and accuracy of the real programs.

Snap Shot A daily technique used by systems and application programmers to assist in debugging computer processing problems. The technique is called snap shot because a utility program is used to take a picture of the memory at a specific point. It is also considered a computer-assisted audit technique.

Software package Any vendor-packaged computer program such as utilities, programming aids, and application programs which can be purchased and implemented.

Sort program A computer program that reads the edited data and creates a transaction file in another specified order.

Source code Computer code written in the readable statements of the programming language.

Source documents The piece of paper that begins a transaction.

Source program listings A printout of the program language statements in readable form.

Spreadsheet package A microcomputer program designed to perform mathematical calculations organizing the data in rows and columns.

Staff function Organizing a group or function to service multiple areas that perform different activities and functions.

Standards The required rules to follow. Omission or deviation requires pre-approval by a manager or supervisor.

Statistical sampling The use of mathematical analysis techniques to perform compliance and substantive testing, for example attribute, stop and go, discovery, and dollar-value sampling.

Subject-to opinion   Auditor statement that internal controls were adequate except for those areas discussed in the comments and recommendations section of the report.

Sub-schema   A subset of a network database definition. *See also* "Schema."

Substantive testing   An audit review of financial transactions to validate the accuracy of financial transactions and balances.

Supervisor state   A component of the operating system software that controls and directs the usage of the CPU. A program cannot gain access to the CPU without direction of the supervisor program.

Synchronous   An on-line communications protocol that transmits a string of characters instead of handling a byte at a time.

System analyst   The person responsible for designing application systems and programs.

System configuration   A description of the network hardware components, software, and type.

System data sets   The computer files containing the operating system program code.

System development   Shorthand term for system development life cycle.

System development audit approach   The methodology associated with audit review and testing of the SDLC process.

System development contractor   A person or group outside the company that designs and programs computer systems.

System development control review   The audit evaluation of the controls designed into a computer system which is being designed for implementation.

System development controls   The administrative procedures which ensure that all tasks of development are performed.

System development guidelines   Definition of the administrative tasks that must be performed during the development of a computer system.

System development life cycle (SDLC) The administrative process consisting of phases used to develop and implement computer systems.

System effectiveness When the computer system accomplishes the users objective.

System efficiency When the computer system processes data at the least possible cost.

System flow evaluation An audit methodology including seven phases: planning; preliminary review; compliance testing; substantive testing; reporting; wrap-up; and follow-up.

System messages Statements displayed on terminals or printed on reports to warn the user or operator of an error or other condition.

System narrative A brief written description of the application's functions describing input methods and files, processing techniques, the form of the output produced, and the purpose of the application.

System performance evaluation Measuring and comparing the capabilities versus actual work processed by a computer system such as CPU usage and capacity, disk usage and capacity, on-line terminal transaction volumes and capacity, and on-line terminal response.

System shutdown procedures A structured approach to turning off a computer system in order to prevent damage to the equipment.

System status reporting Printouts of performance attributes. *See also* "System performance evaluation."

System Testing Validation processing accuracy and completeness through the processing of fictitious transactions.

Systems programmer Responsibilities include writing and maintaining systems programs, resolving hardware and software problems, and providing technical support for data processing activities.

Systems programming group   Data processing personnel responsible for maintaining the operating environment software.

Systems software   *See* "Systems programming group."

Tactical goals and objectives   The daily activities and functions that must be performed to accomplish the long-range plan.

Tagging   A CAAT involving the identification of a transaction or account with a one-byte flag in order to distinguish it from other accounts and to identify a transaction, account, or record for later review by an auditor.

Tape library   The safekeeping function responsible for all tape and disk files.

Tapping the network   Unauthorized break-in into the communications network.

Tcom monitor   *See* "Telecommunications monitor."

Telecommunications monitor   Computer programs that support online interaction between the mainframe and terminals or microcomputers.

Telecommunications software   *See* "Telecommunications monitor."

Temporary disk file   A computer file used as a work disk whose use discontinues when the program finishes.

Terminal backup assignments   Specifications of the on-line terminals that will be used when the primary terminals are inoperable.

Terminal operator expertise   The training and experience of a computer terminal operator.

Terminal operators manual   Documented procedures that explain seven groups of activities: terminal usage; password maintenance; transaction usage; monetary balancing; output handling; error processing; and restart recovery.

Test data method   Also referred to as *test deck.* A CAAT used to test program edits and application functions. It uses transaction data created by the auditor that is entered into the application for processing.

Test environment The files and programs set up separately from the production environment for testing of programs.

Test Object Version The machine-readable version of the source program for test purposes only.

Test plan Definition of the program or system aspects that will be tested and to what extent.

Test program libraries The on-line data sets or files that hold the source and object program code as well as the JCL parameters to be used for testing in order to keep the development environment from adversely affecting production.

Test results The computer output generated by a test execution of a program.

Test Source Version The English version of the program code on a file utilized for test purposes only.

Test specifications Documented requirements of system functions and activities that should be tested.

Testing workpapers Evidential matter arranged in files generated as a result of compliance and substantive testing relevant mainly to the current year.

Third party internal control opinion An external auditor's letter stating their opinion of the internal control system.

Throughput The measurement of the total data processing work successfully completed during an hour, a shift, a day, or other time period.

Tickler activities A system or method of keeping track of upcoming critical dates or activities that must be performed.

Time variances The difference between actual hours and budget hours.

Total integration The act of performing the DP and non-DP audits with staff auditors trained in financial and DP disciplines. One audit program is used. There is no distinction between DP and financial auditors.

Tracing Validating transactions at various points during processing in order to determine that activities and functions were performed properly.

Training needs assessment An evaluation of the skill level of existing staff in order to determine the extent of training needed.

Training velocity The speed at which expertise is needed.

Transaction assignment Definition of on-line transactions to be used on specific terminals.

Transaction authorization A broad control objective. Approval to process or complete a transaction.

Transaction code A shorthand identifier to direct the system to process the associated input data in a specific way.

Transaction code explanations A written explanation of the function and use of the application's transaction codes.

Transaction file A list of all the transactions that were entered during a certain time period stored on a tape or disk.

Transaction flow The sequential activities or functions needed to process a transaction.

Transaction journal A listing of all processed input transactions.

Transaction password control A condition requiring the operator to enter a password in order to use a specific transaction.

Transaction recording A broad control objective. The record-keeping of transactions.

Transaction source data The originating information of a financial event.

Transaction volume The number of transaction processed in a given time period.

Transmittal documents A cover sheet describing the contents of the items attached to it. It can also be sent separately and usually includes dollar totals and an item count of all items in the group.

Trial balance   A list of all accounts or master records from the master file which lists critical data including the updated balanced.

Turnaround time   The elapsed time from the start of input to delivery of final output.

Unauthorized transactions   Erroneous or fraudulent financial events.

Unposted items   Transactions which the application could not process.

Unqualified opinion   An auditor statement that internal controls were adequate in all material respects or that financial statements were fairly stated.

Unrestricted programmer access   When programmers have access to all program libraries.

Up-line load   The transfer of information from a remote computer to a host computer.

User/application operating procedures   Detailed written explanations for the user to follow to properly operate the application.

User friendly   Program or computer functions that are understandable to a person who is unfamiliar with data processing.

User liaison   A person responsible for understanding application processing aspects of the applications that support the business unit to which they are assigned.

User requirements   An SDLC phase. The shopping list of everything the user wants the system to do.

Utility programs   General-use computer programs used to perform common data processing tasks such as structure and also to modify data used in the system and in data sets, prepare peripheral equipment for interface with the system, list system control data, copy data sets, change access methods, and dump and restore data files.

Variable length record   A file record whose size varies.

Vendor support   Advice, consultation, and programming assistance provide by the seller of a software package.

Volume serial number   A unique number assigned to tape and disk files in order to identify them to the system.

Volume table of contents   The directory listing of all files on a DASD.

Volume testing   Testing which simulates the actual number of transactions that will be processed by the application during production.

Word processing package   Microcomputer software that provides the ability to prepare and edit text with minimal effort.

Work order   A request to make a change to a computer program, (see "change request").

Workpapers   Audit documentation that provides evidence of audit work performed.

Wrap-up phase   Final assembly of all workpaper and permanent files, completion of performance evaluations, and preparation of the budget variance analysis.

Zap program   A computer program that can change data or program code on a file to anything the user wishes without creating an audit trail, (see "sensitive utility").

NOTES

1. American Institute of Certified Public Accountants AICPA Professional Standards, New York, 1989.

Index